YUIKO-SAN'S LATEST OBSESSIONS: A DIGEST♥

IN THE WORLD OF SHOUNEN MANGA CURRENTLY BEING SERIALIZED IN *WEEKLY SHOUNEN STEP*. GLOOMY AND WITHDRAWN MIDDLE SCHOOLER TAKURO SEBA IS POSSESSED BY THE MYSTERIOUS SEPA SPIRIT. WITH HIS CAPTAIN AND TEAMMATES OF THE MAREI MIDDLE SCHOOL SEPAK TAKRAW TEAM, HE SETS HIS SIGHTS ON THE NATIONAL TOURNAMENT. IT'S A PERFECTLY NORMAL AND TRADITIONAL SHOUNEN MANGA, BUT FOR SOME REASON, TAIGA IS BEING FORCED TO WRITE A CAPTAIN x TAKURO B.L. NOVEL.

DREAMING NOUVELLE MARIE

AN INSTALLMENT OF THE ETERNAL SWEET ROMANCE SERIES ("ESROMA" AMONG FANS), A WILDLY POPULAR LINE OF GAMES FOR GIRLS. THE HEROINE, MARIE HANABISHI, IS A POTENTIAL BRIDE FOR A LIST OF HANDSOME PRINCES FROM ANOTHER WORLD. YUIKO-SAN'S FAVORITE IS PRINCE MAXIMILLIAN. BUT HER TOP COUPLING IS ANSELM (THE SMART ONE WITH GLASSES) x HEROLD (THE DARK AND HANDSOME ONE).

THESE ARE BOTH ORIGINAL TO THE MANGA VERSION OF "MY GIRLFRIEND'S A GEEK"! YOU WON'T FIND THEM ANYWHERE ELSE! ♡

HERE'S THE **ORIGINAL★**

My Girlfriend's a
GEEK
Pentabu

Volumes 1 and 2 available now!

MY GIRLFRIEND'S A GEEK

WRITTEN BY PENTABU

A love diary about a *fujoshi* and a normal man? The infamous blog has made the transition to paperback! Pentabu lovingly dishes out withering smackdowns to every nerdy *fujoshi* comment his girlfriend makes. Feel the sympathy course through your veins as you witness his daily struggles!
If you haven't checked out the inspiration for this manga, what are you waiting for?♥

It's the final volume! ☆

My Girlfriend's a GEEK

*This manga is a work of fiction based upon "My Girlfriend's a Geek" Volumes 1 and 2, by Pentabu.

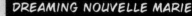

CONTENTS ♥

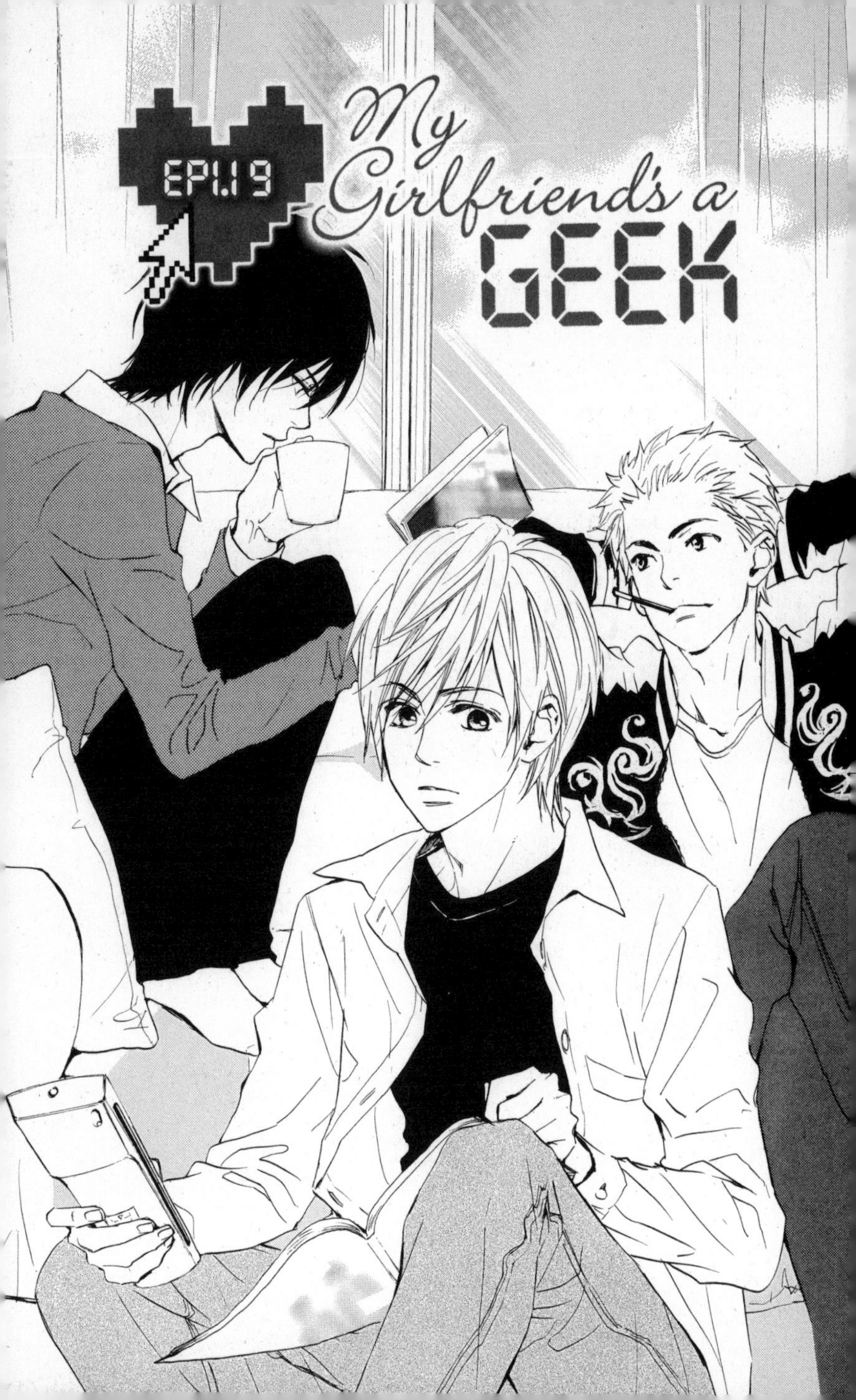
EPI.1 9
My Girlfriend's a GEEK

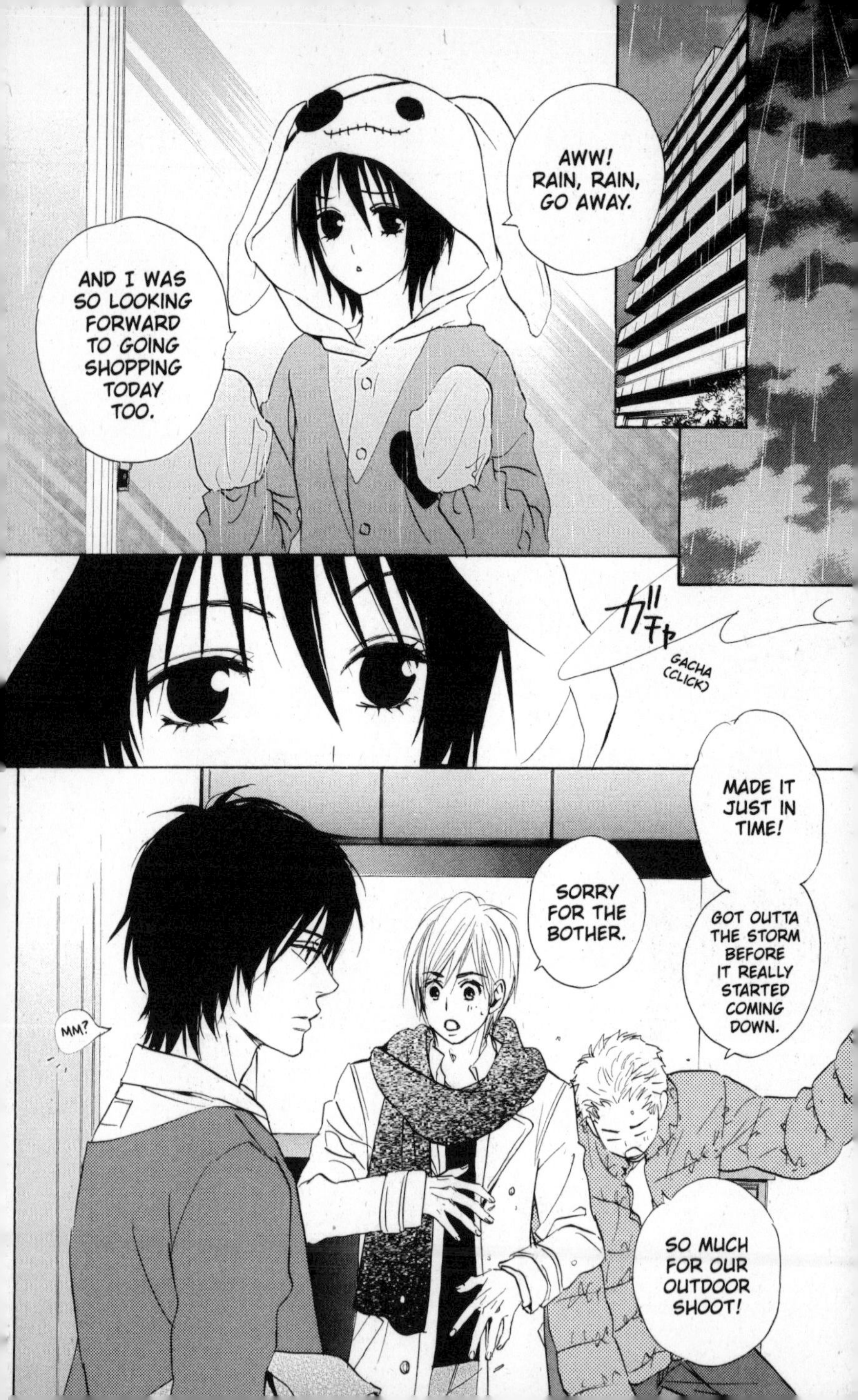
AWW! RAIN, RAIN, GO AWAY.
AND I WAS SO LOOKING FORWARD TO GOING SHOPPING TODAY TOO.
ガチャ
GACHA (CLICK)
MADE IT JUST IN TIME!
GOT OUTTA THE STORM BEFORE IT REALLY STARTED COMING DOWN.
SORRY FOR THE BOTHER.
MM?
SO MUCH FOR OUR OUTDOOR SHOOT!

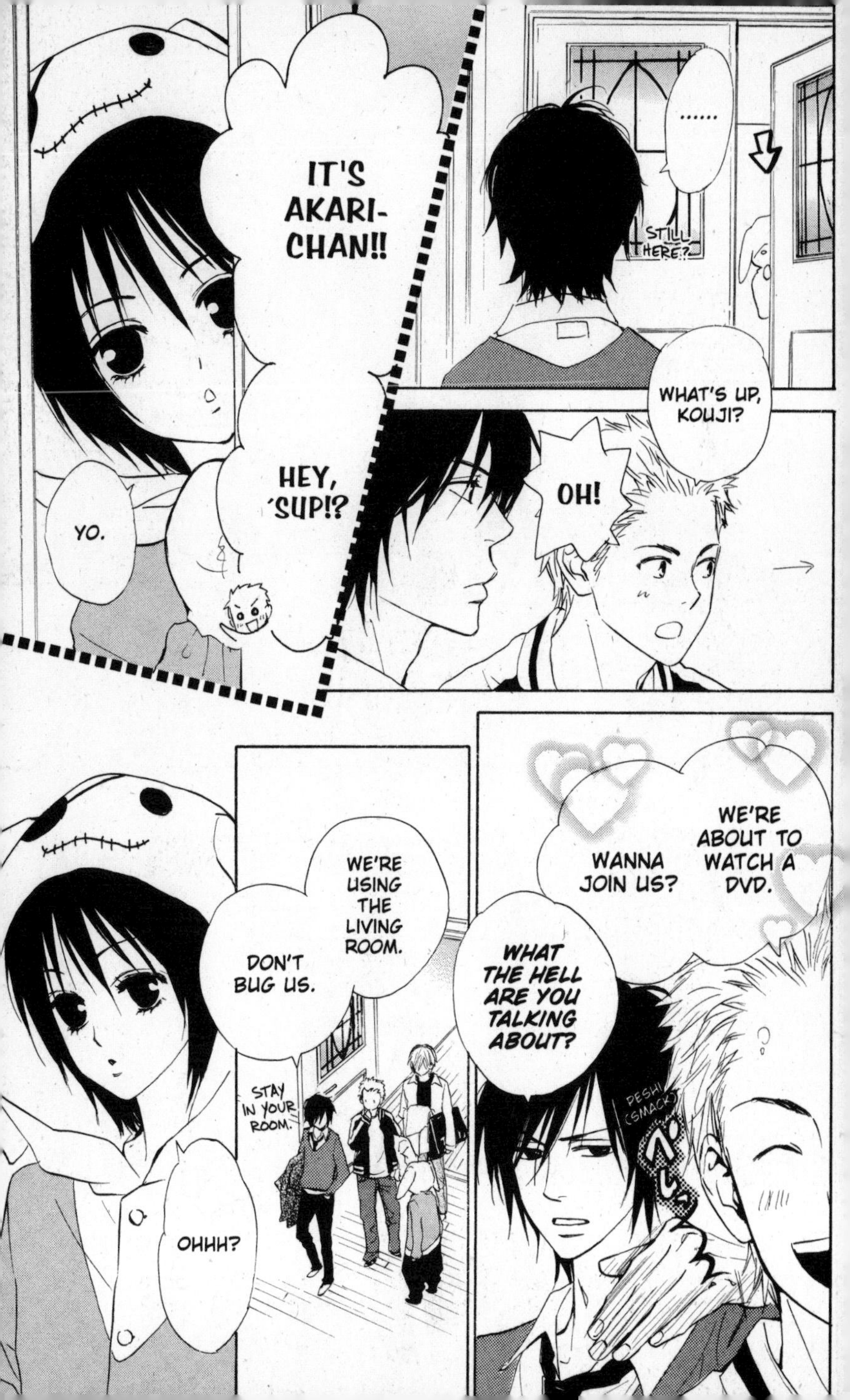
......
STILL HERE?
WHAT'S UP, KOUJI?
OH!
IT'S AKARI-CHAN!!
HEY, 'SUP!?
YO.
WE'RE ABOUT TO WATCH A DVD.
WANNA JOIN US?
WHAT THE HELL ARE YOU TALKING ABOUT?
PESHI (SMACK)
WE'RE USING THE LIVING ROOM.
DON'T BUG US.
STAY IN YOUR ROOM.
OHHH?

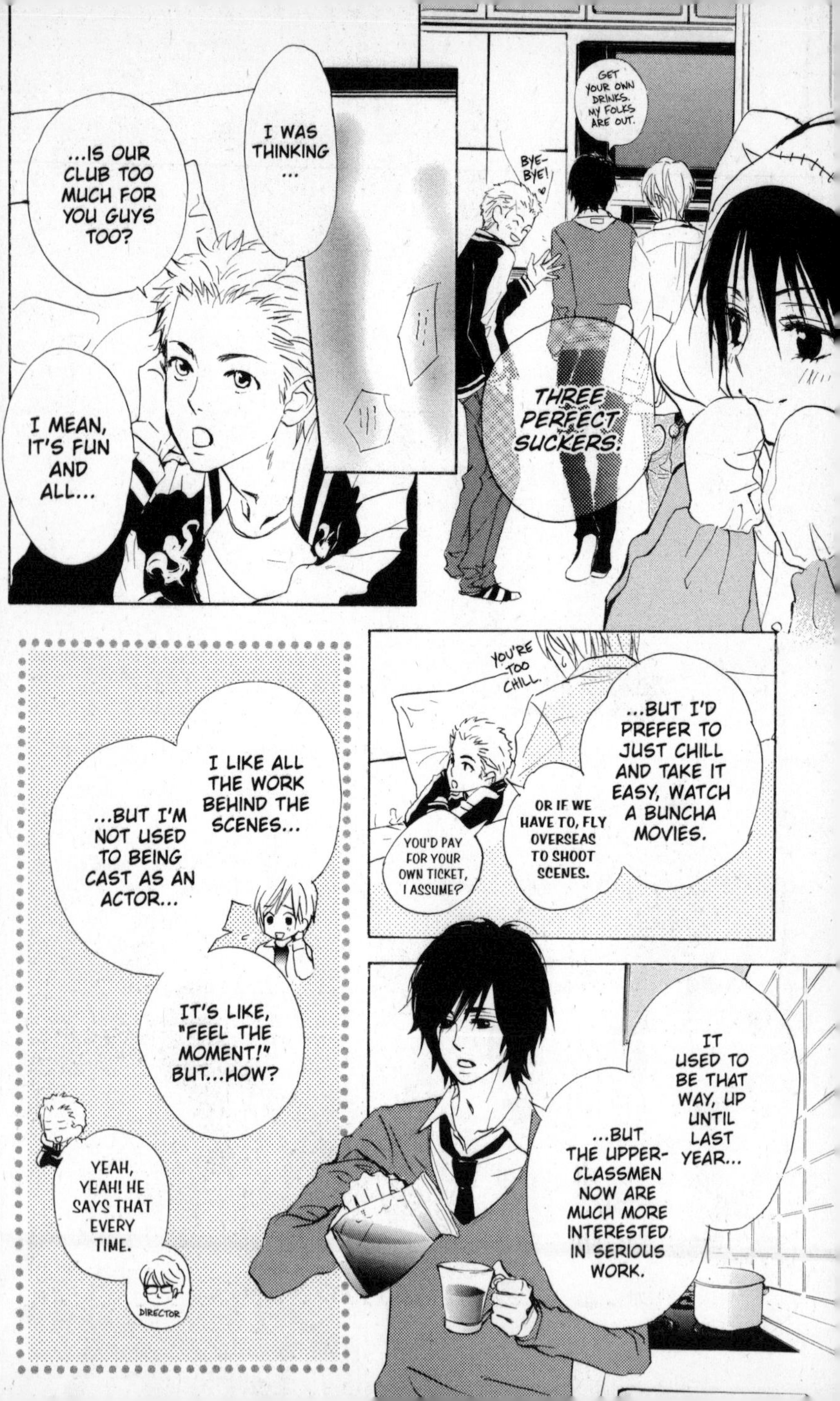
GET YOUR OWN DRINKS. MY FOLKS ARE OUT.
BYE-BYE!
THREE PERFECT SUCKERS.
I WAS THINKING...
...IS OUR CLUB TOO MUCH FOR YOU GUYS TOO?
I MEAN, IT'S FUN AND ALL...
YOU'RE TOO CHILL.
...BUT I'D PREFER TO JUST CHILL AND TAKE IT EASY, WATCH A BUNCHA MOVIES.
OR IF WE HAVE TO, FLY OVERSEAS TO SHOOT SCENES.
YOU'D PAY FOR YOUR OWN TICKET, I ASSUME?
IT USED TO BE THAT WAY, UP UNTIL LAST YEAR...
...BUT THE UPPER-CLASSMEN NOW ARE MUCH MORE INTERESTED IN SERIOUS WORK.
I LIKE ALL THE WORK BEHIND THE SCENES...
...BUT I'M NOT USED TO BEING CAST AS AN ACTOR...
IT'S LIKE, "FEEL THE MOMENT!" BUT...HOW?
YEAH, YEAH! HE SAYS THAT EVERY TIME.
DIRECTOR

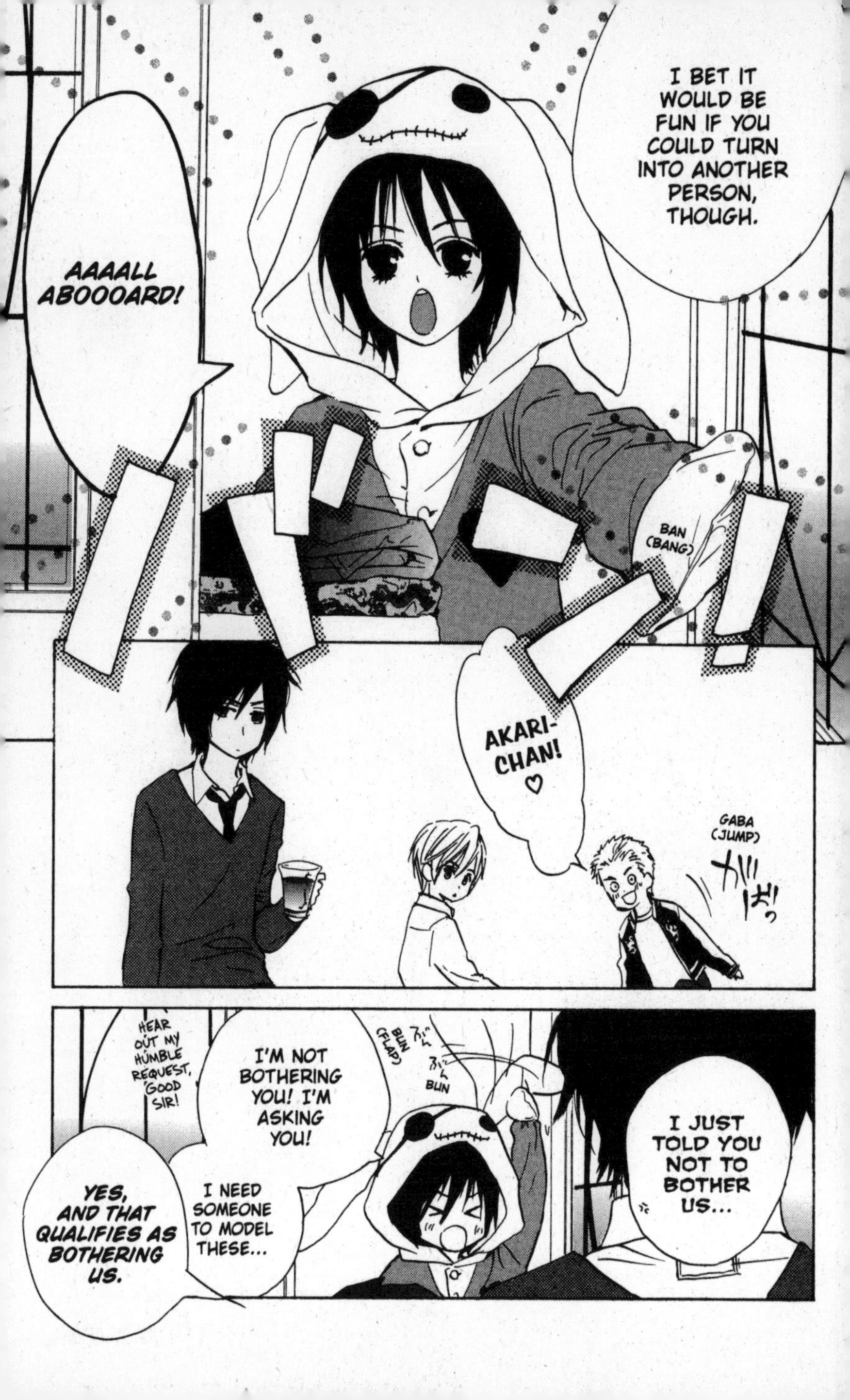
I BET IT WOULD BE FUN IF YOU COULD TURN INTO ANOTHER PERSON, THOUGH.
AAAALL ABOOOARD!
BAN (BANG)
GABA (JUMP)
AKARI-CHAN! ♡
I JUST TOLD YOU NOT TO BOTHER US...
BUN (FLAP) BUN
I'M NOT BOTHERING YOU! I'M ASKING YOU!
HEAR OUT MY HUMBLE REQUEST, GOOD SIR!
I NEED SOMEONE TO MODEL THESE...
YES, AND THAT QUALIFIES AS BOTHERING US.

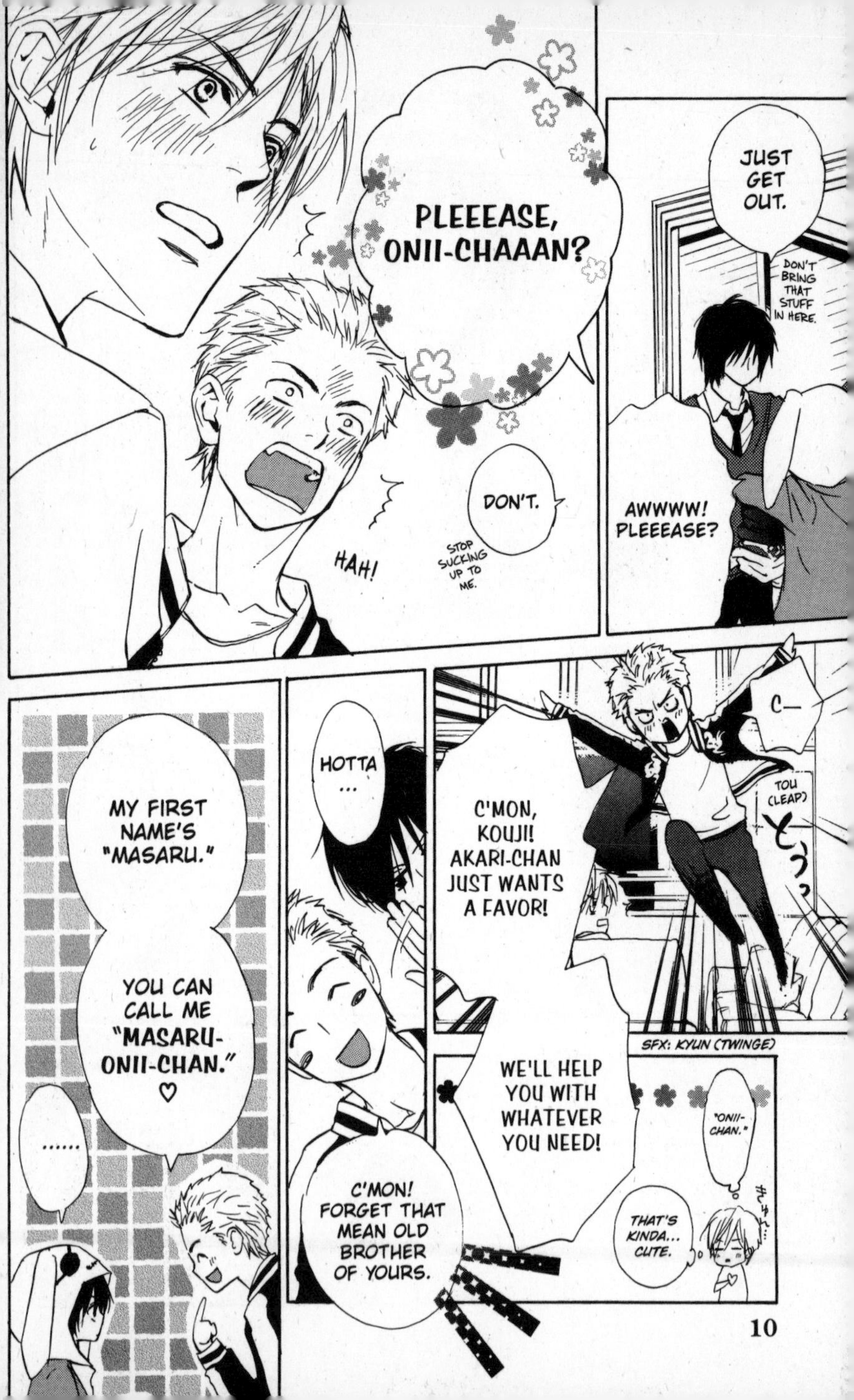
JUST GET OUT.
DON'T BRING THAT STUFF IN HERE.
AWWWW! PLEEEASE?
PLEEEASE, ONII-CHAAAN?
DON'T.
STOP SUCKING UP TO ME.
HAH!
C—
TOU (LEAP)
C'MON, KOUJI! AKARI-CHAN JUST WANTS A FAVOR!
SFX: KYUN (TWINGE)
WE'LL HELP YOU WITH WHATEVER YOU NEED!
"ONII-CHAN."
THAT'S KINDA... CUTE.
HOTTA...
C'MON! FORGET THAT MEAN OLD BROTHER OF YOURS.
MY FIRST NAME'S "MASARU."
YOU CAN CALL ME "MASARU-ONII-CHAN." ♡
......

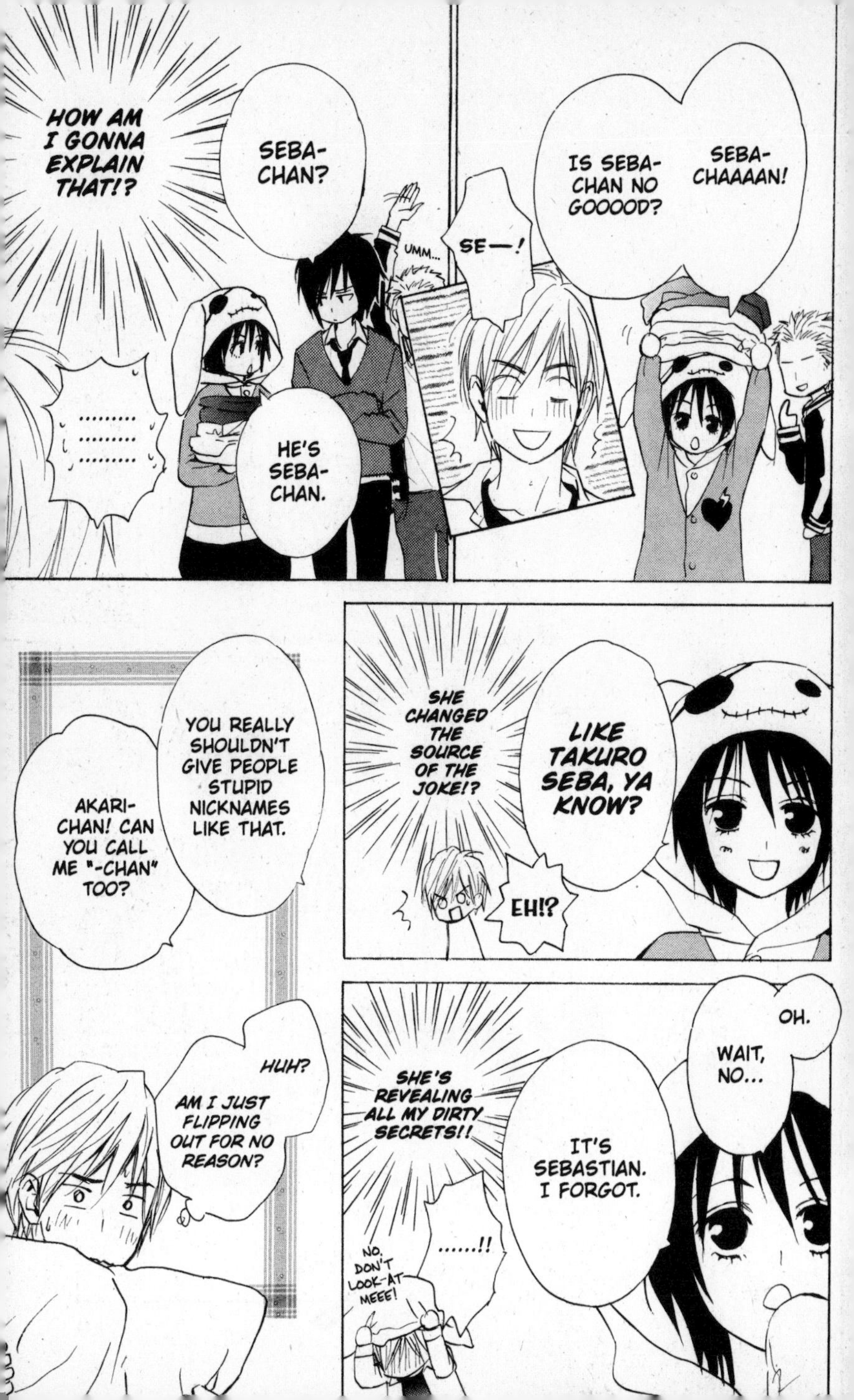
SEBA-CHAAAAN!
IS SEBA-CHAN NO GOOOOD?
SE—!
SEBA-CHAN?
UMM...
HOW AM I GONNA EXPLAIN THAT!?
....
....
....
HE'S SEBA-CHAN.
LIKE TAKURO SEBA, YA KNOW?
SHE CHANGED THE SOURCE OF THE JOKE!?
EH!?
OH.
WAIT, NO...
IT'S SEBASTIAN. I FORGOT.
SHE'S REVEALING ALL MY DIRTY SECRETS!!
......!!
NO. DON'T LOOK AT MEEE!
YOU REALLY SHOULDN'T GIVE PEOPLE STUPID NICKNAMES LIKE THAT.
AKARI-CHAN! CAN YOU CALL ME "-CHAN" TOO?
HUH?
AM I JUST FLIPPING OUT FOR NO REASON?

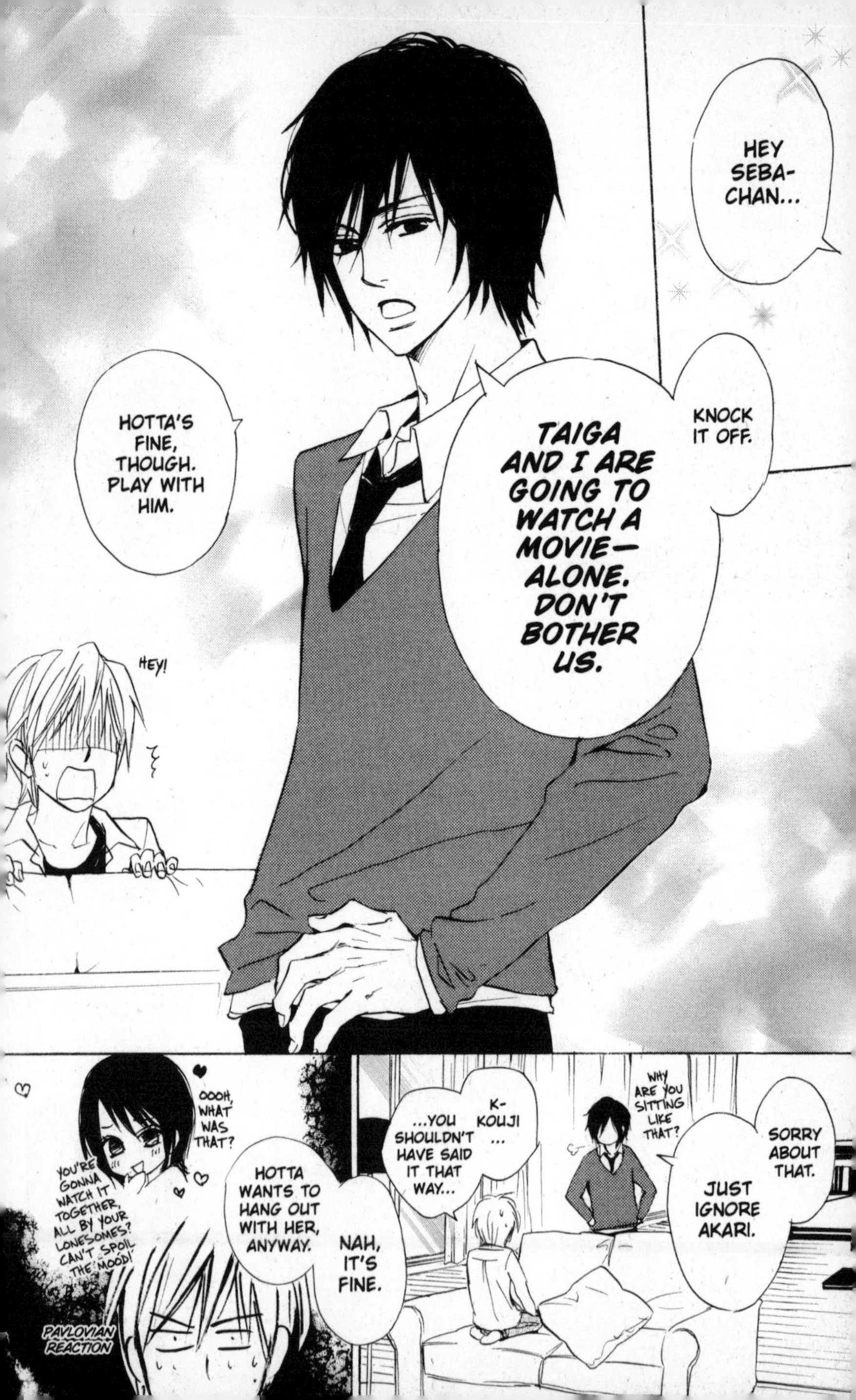
HEY SEBA-CHAN...
KNOCK IT OFF.
TAIGA AND I ARE GOING TO WATCH A MOVIE—ALONE. DON'T BOTHER US.
HOTTA'S FINE, THOUGH. PLAY WITH HIM.
HEY!
SORRY ABOUT THAT.
JUST IGNORE AKARI.
WHY ARE YOU SITTING LIKE THAT?
K-KOUJI...
...YOU SHOULDN'T HAVE SAID IT THAT WAY...
NAH, IT'S FINE.
HOTTA WANTS TO HANG OUT WITH HER, ANYWAY.
OOOH, WHAT WAS THAT?
YOU'RE GONNA WATCH IT TOGETHER, ALL BY YOUR LONESOMES? CAN'T SPOIL THE MOOD!
PAVLOVIAN REACTION

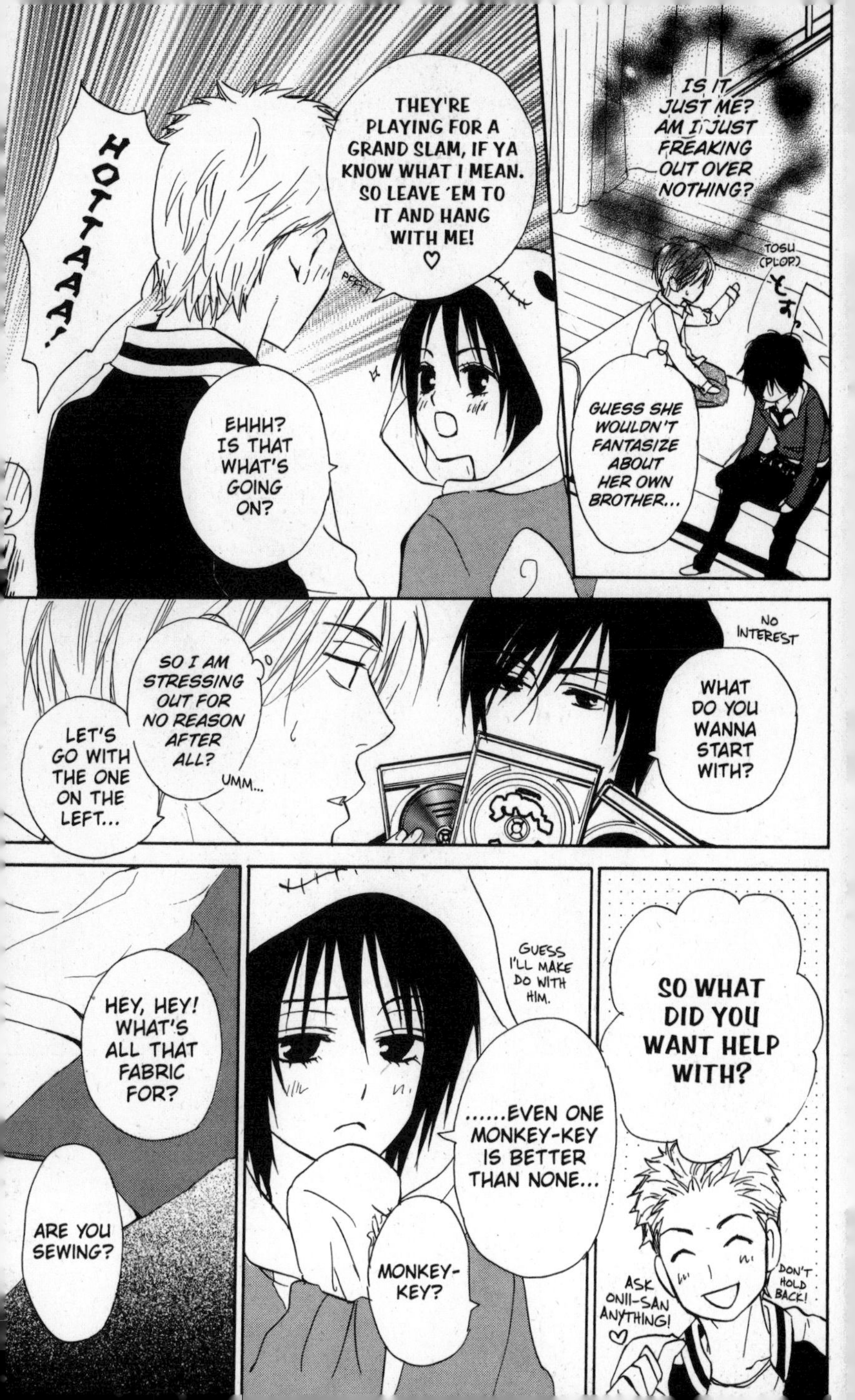
IS IT JUST ME? AM I JUST FREAKING OUT OVER NOTHING?
TOSU (PLOP)
GUESS SHE WOULDN'T FANTASIZE ABOUT HER OWN BROTHER...
THEY'RE PLAYING FOR A GRAND SLAM, IF YA KNOW WHAT I MEAN. SO LEAVE 'EM TO IT AND HANG WITH ME! ♡
HOTTAAA!
PFFT
EHHH? IS THAT WHAT'S GOING ON?
NO INTEREST
WHAT DO YOU WANNA START WITH?
SO I AM STRESSING OUT FOR NO REASON AFTER ALL?
UMM...
LET'S GO WITH THE ONE ON THE LEFT...
SO WHAT DID YOU WANT HELP WITH?
DON'T HOLD BACK!
ASK ONII-SAN ANYTHING! ♡
GUESS I'LL MAKE DO WITH HIM.
......EVEN ONE MONKEY-KEY IS BETTER THAN NONE...
MONKEY-KEY?
HEY, HEY! WHAT'S ALL THAT FABRIC FOR?
ARE YOU SEWING?

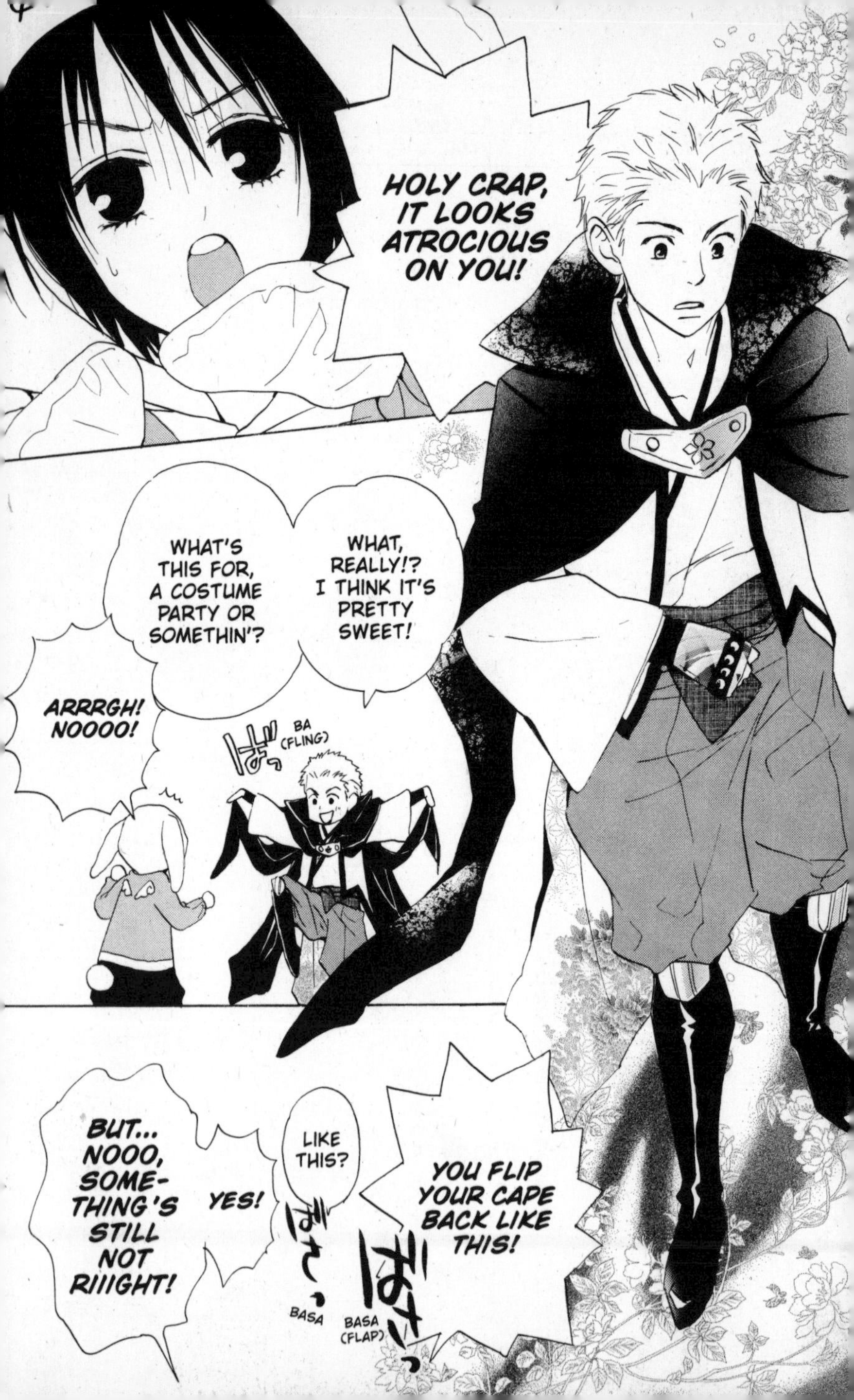
HOLY CRAP, IT LOOKS ATROCIOUS ON YOU!
WHAT, REALLY!? I THINK IT'S PRETTY SWEET!
WHAT'S THIS FOR, A COSTUME PARTY OR SOMETHIN'?
BA (FLING)
ARRRGH! NOOOO!
YOU FLIP YOUR CAPE BACK LIKE THIS!
BASA (FLAP)
LIKE THIS?
BASA
YES!
BUT... NOOO, SOME-THING'S STILL NOT RIIIGHT!

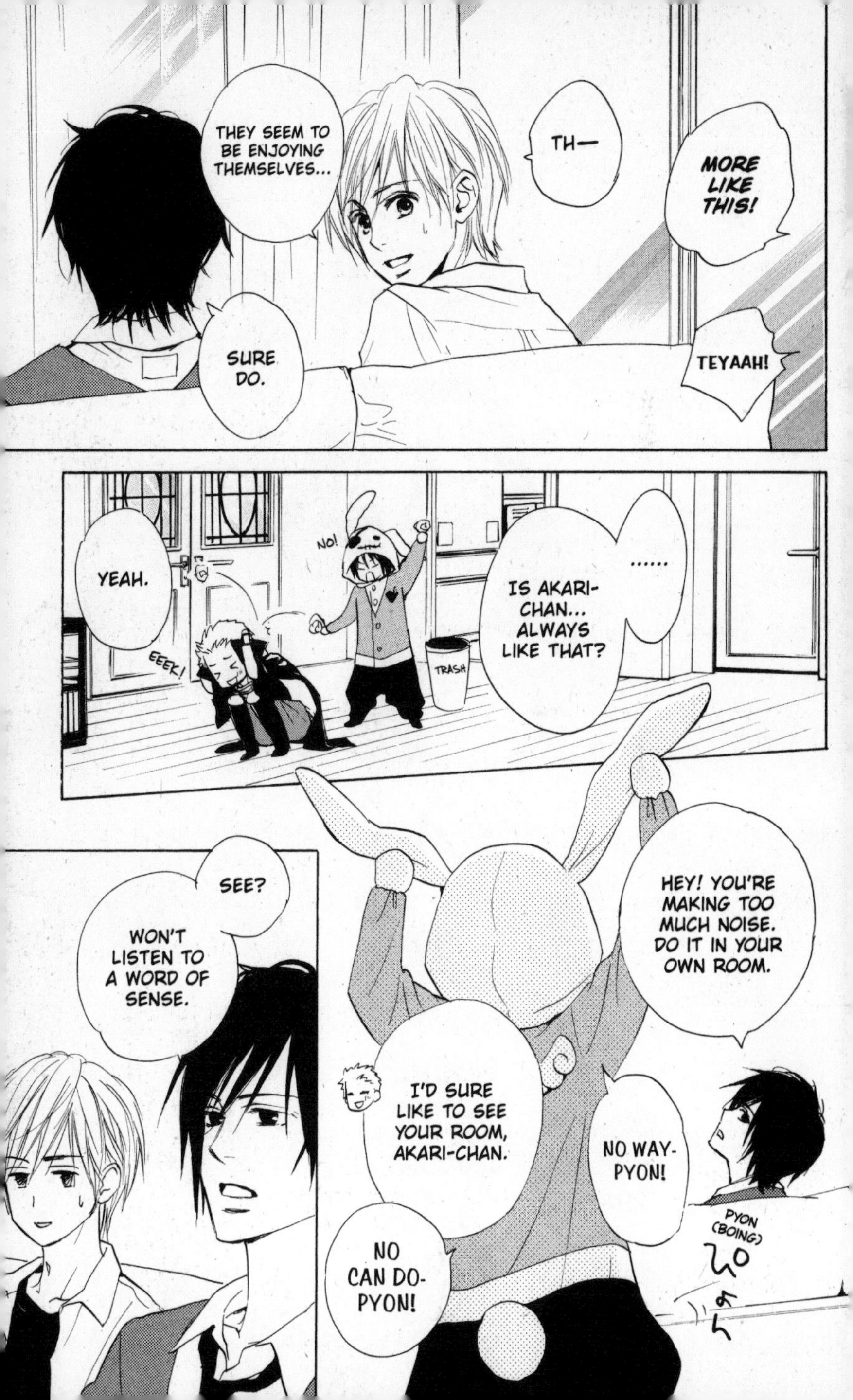
MORE LIKE THIS!
TEYAAH!
TH—
THEY SEEM TO BE ENJOYING THEMSELVES...
SURE DO.
......
IS AKARI-CHAN... ALWAYS LIKE THAT?
NO!
EEEK!
YEAH.
TRASH
HEY! YOU'RE MAKING TOO MUCH NOISE. DO IT IN YOUR OWN ROOM.
NO WAY-PYON!
PYON (BOING)
I'D SURE LIKE TO SEE YOUR ROOM, AKARI-CHAN.
NO CAN DO-PYON!
SEE?
WON'T LISTEN TO A WORD OF SENSE.

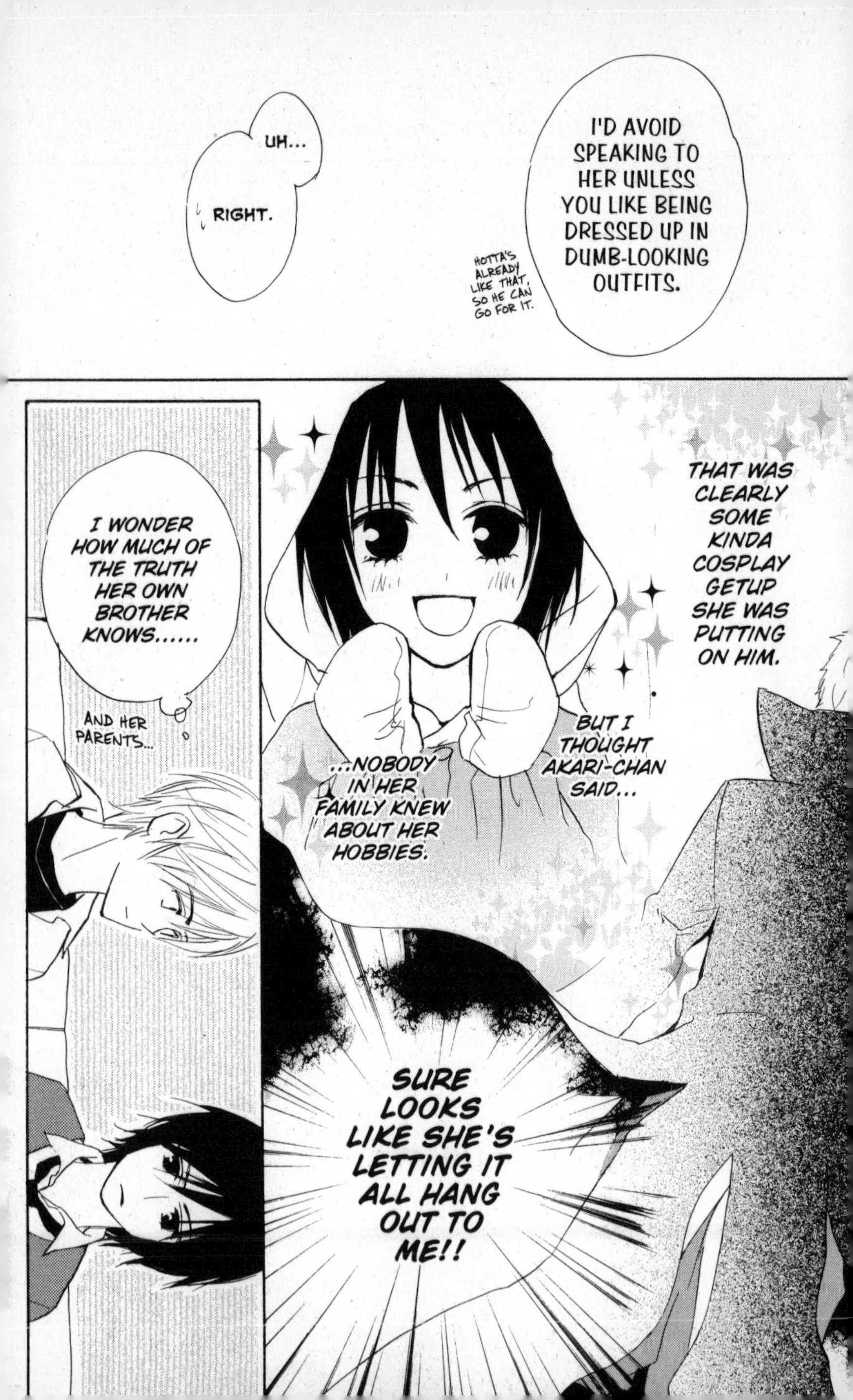

I'D AVOID SPEAKING TO HER UNLESS YOU LIKE BEING DRESSED UP IN DUMB-LOOKING OUTFITS.
HOTTA'S ALREADY LIKE THAT, SO HE CAN GO FOR IT.
UH...
RIGHT.
THAT WAS CLEARLY SOME KINDA COSPLAY GETUP SHE WAS PUTTING ON HIM.
BUT I THOUGHT AKARI-CHAN SAID...
...NOBODY IN HER FAMILY KNEW ABOUT HER HOBBIES.
SURE LOOKS LIKE SHE'S LETTING IT ALL HANG OUT TO ME!!
I WONDER HOW MUCH OF THE TRUTH HER OWN BROTHER KNOWS......
AND HER PARENTS...

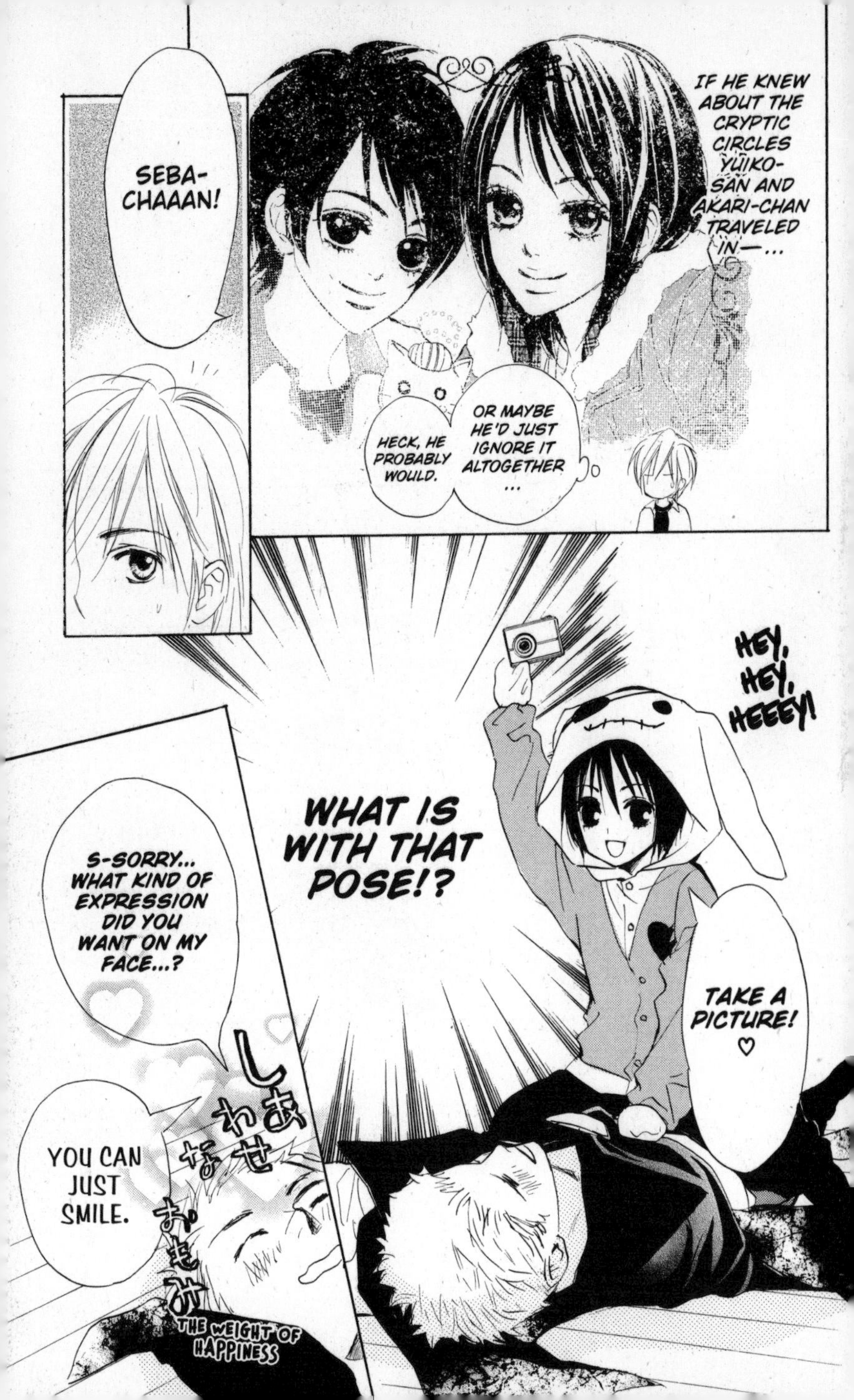
IF HE KNEW ABOUT THE CRYPTIC CIRCLES YUIKO-SAN AND AKARI-CHAN TRAVELED IN—...
OR MAYBE HE'D JUST IGNORE IT ALTOGETHER ...
HECK, HE PROBABLY WOULD.
SEBA-CHAAAN!
HEY, HEY, HEEEY!
TAKE A PICTURE! ♡
WHAT IS WITH THAT POSE!?
S-SORRY... WHAT KIND OF EXPRESSION DID YOU WANT ON MY FACE...?
YOU CAN JUST SMILE.
しあわせなおもみ
THE WEIGHT OF HAPPINESS

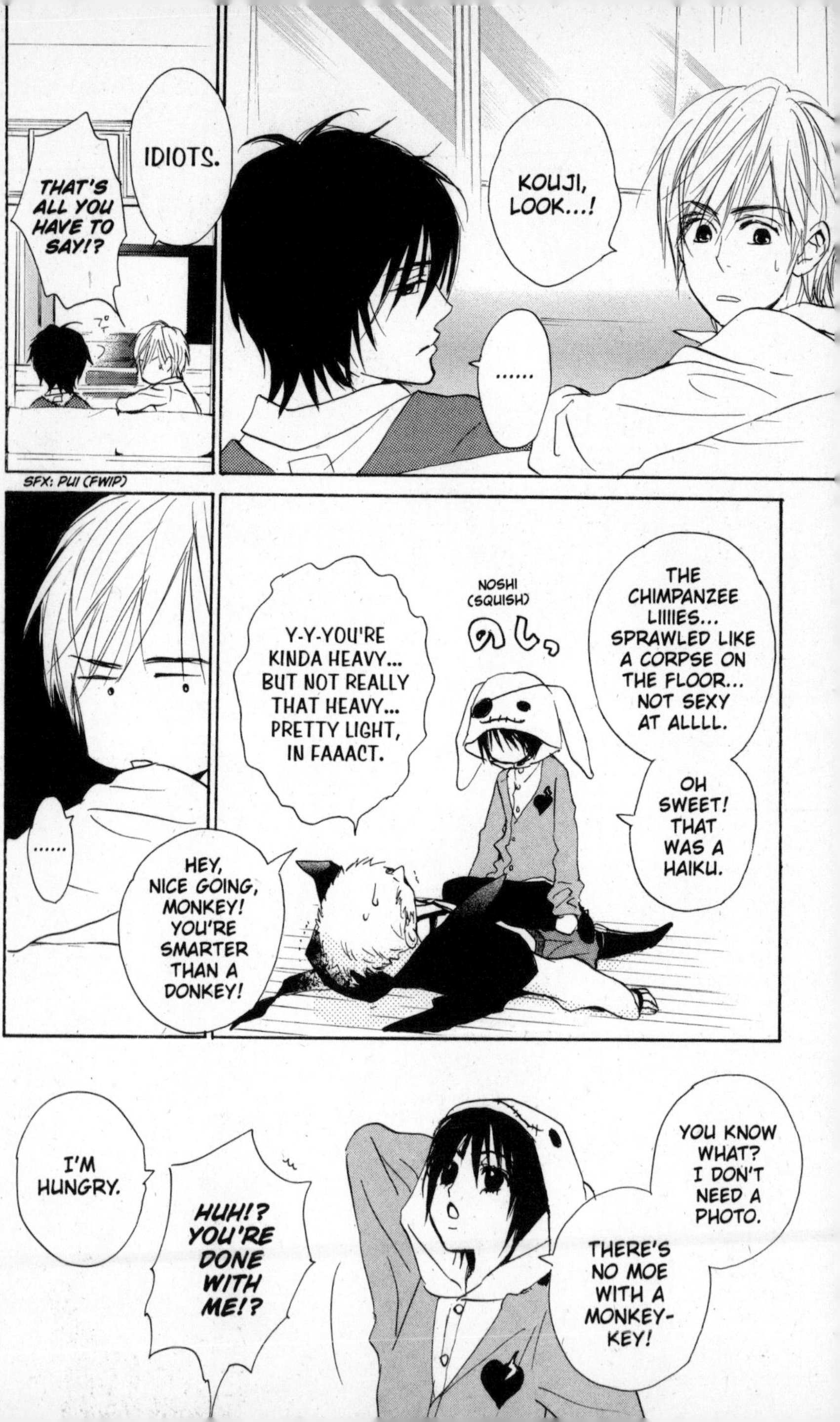
KOUJI, LOOK...!
......
IDIOTS.
THAT'S ALL YOU HAVE TO SAY!?
SFX: PUI (FWIP)
THE CHIMPANZEE LIIIIES... SPRAWLED LIKE A CORPSE ON THE FLOOR... NOT SEXY AT ALLLL.
NOSHI (SQUISH)
のし
Y-Y-YOU'RE KINDA HEAVY... BUT NOT REALLY THAT HEAVY... PRETTY LIGHT, IN FAAACT.
OH SWEET! THAT WAS A HAIKU.
HEY, NICE GOING, MONKEY! YOU'RE SMARTER THAN A DONKEY!
......
YOU KNOW WHAT? I DON'T NEED A PHOTO.
THERE'S NO MOE WITH A MONKEY-KEY!
HUH!? YOU'RE DONE WITH ME!?
I'M HUNGRY.

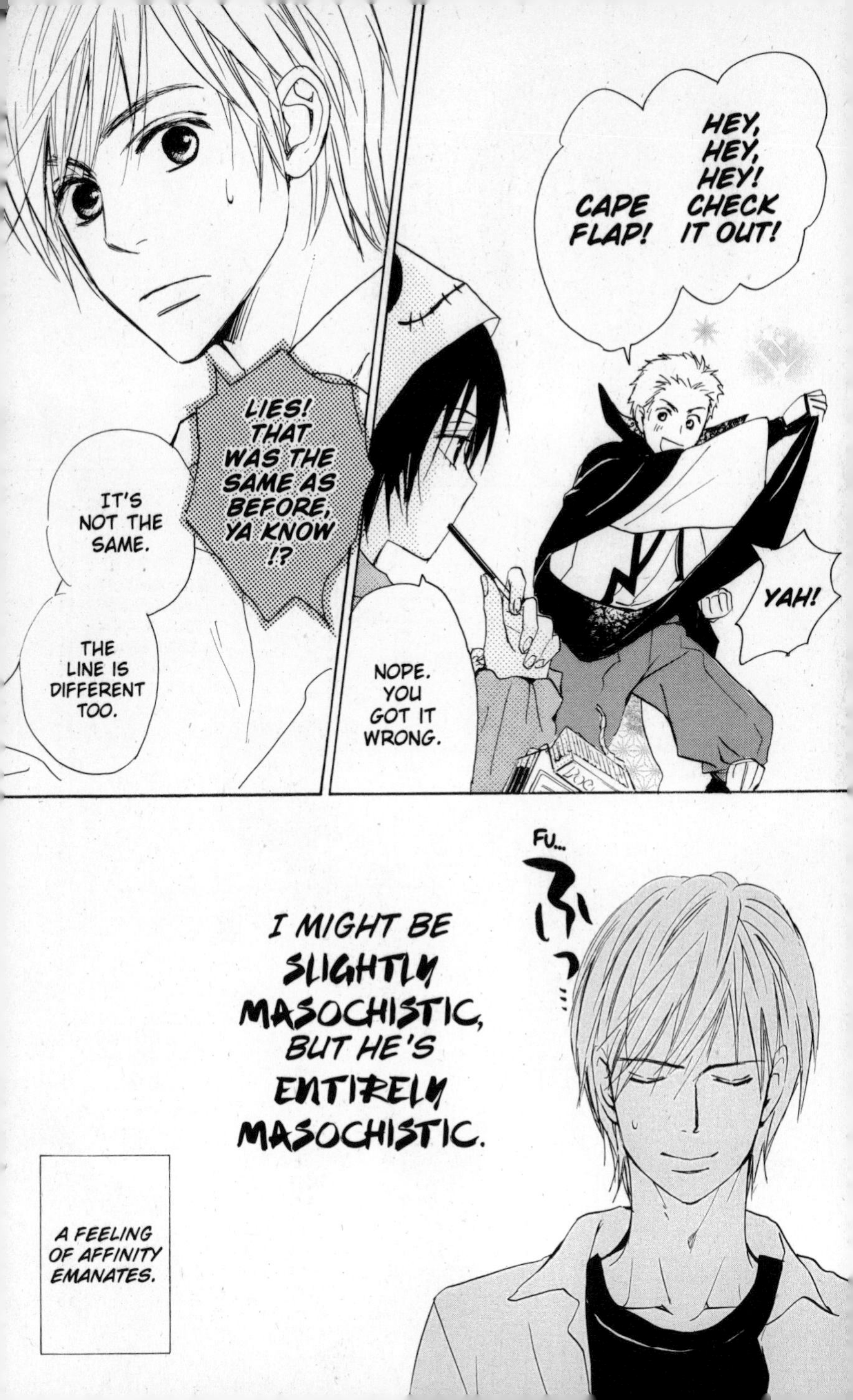
HEY, HEY, HEY! CHECK IT OUT!
CAPE FLAP!
YAH!
NOPE. YOU GOT IT WRONG.
LIES! THAT WAS THE SAME AS BEFORE, YA KNOW!?
IT'S NOT THE SAME.
THE LINE IS DIFFERENT TOO.
FU...
I MIGHT BE SLIGHTLY MASOCHISTIC, BUT HE'S ENTIRELY MASOCHISTIC.
A FEELING OF AFFINITY EMANATES.

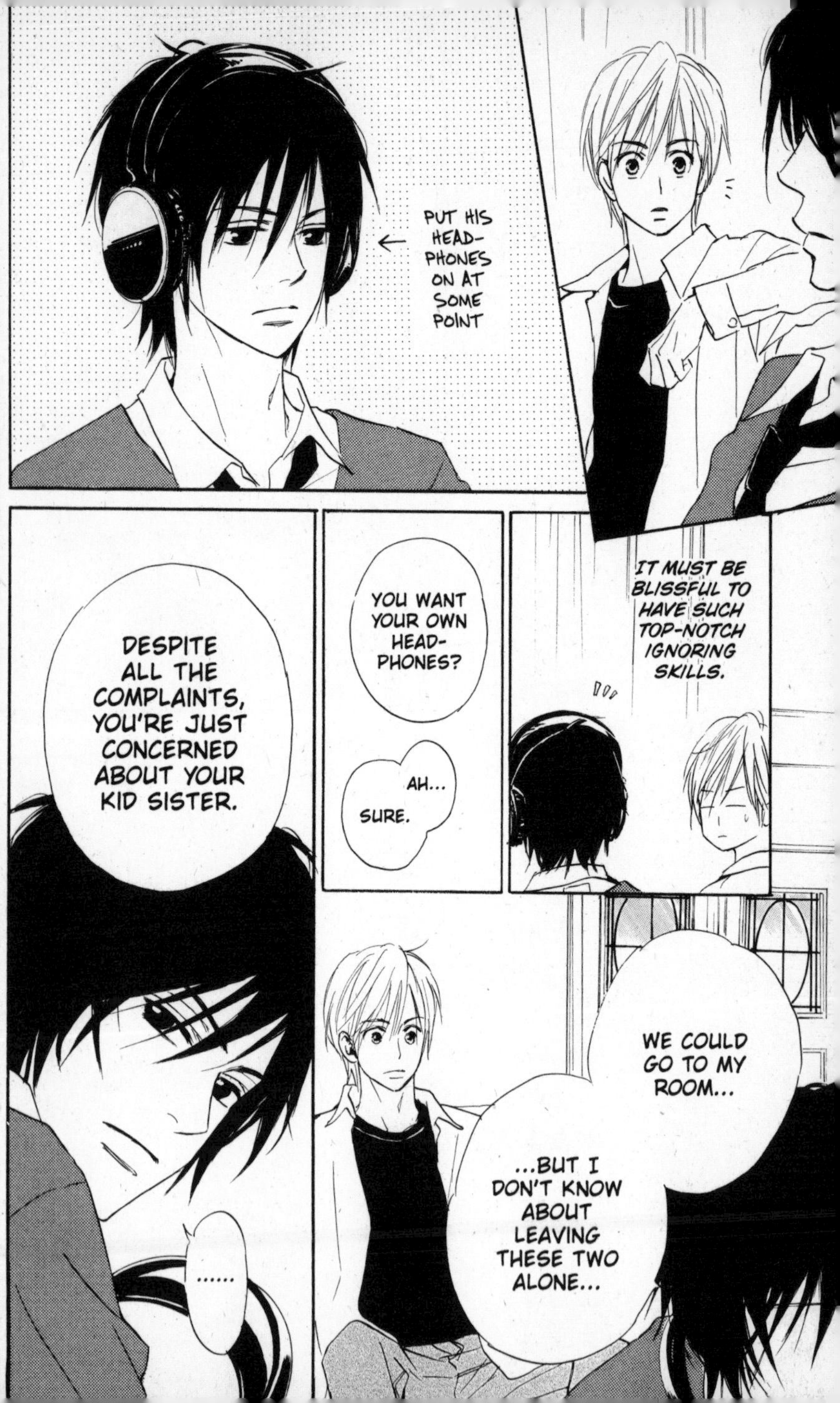
PUT HIS HEAD-PHONES ON AT SOME POINT
IT MUST BE BLISSFUL TO HAVE SUCH TOP-NOTCH IGNORING SKILLS.
YOU WANT YOUR OWN HEAD-PHONES?
AH... SURE.
WE COULD GO TO MY ROOM...
...BUT I DON'T KNOW ABOUT LEAVING THESE TWO ALONE...
DESPITE ALL THE COMPLAINTS, YOU'RE JUST CONCERNED ABOUT YOUR KID SISTER.
......

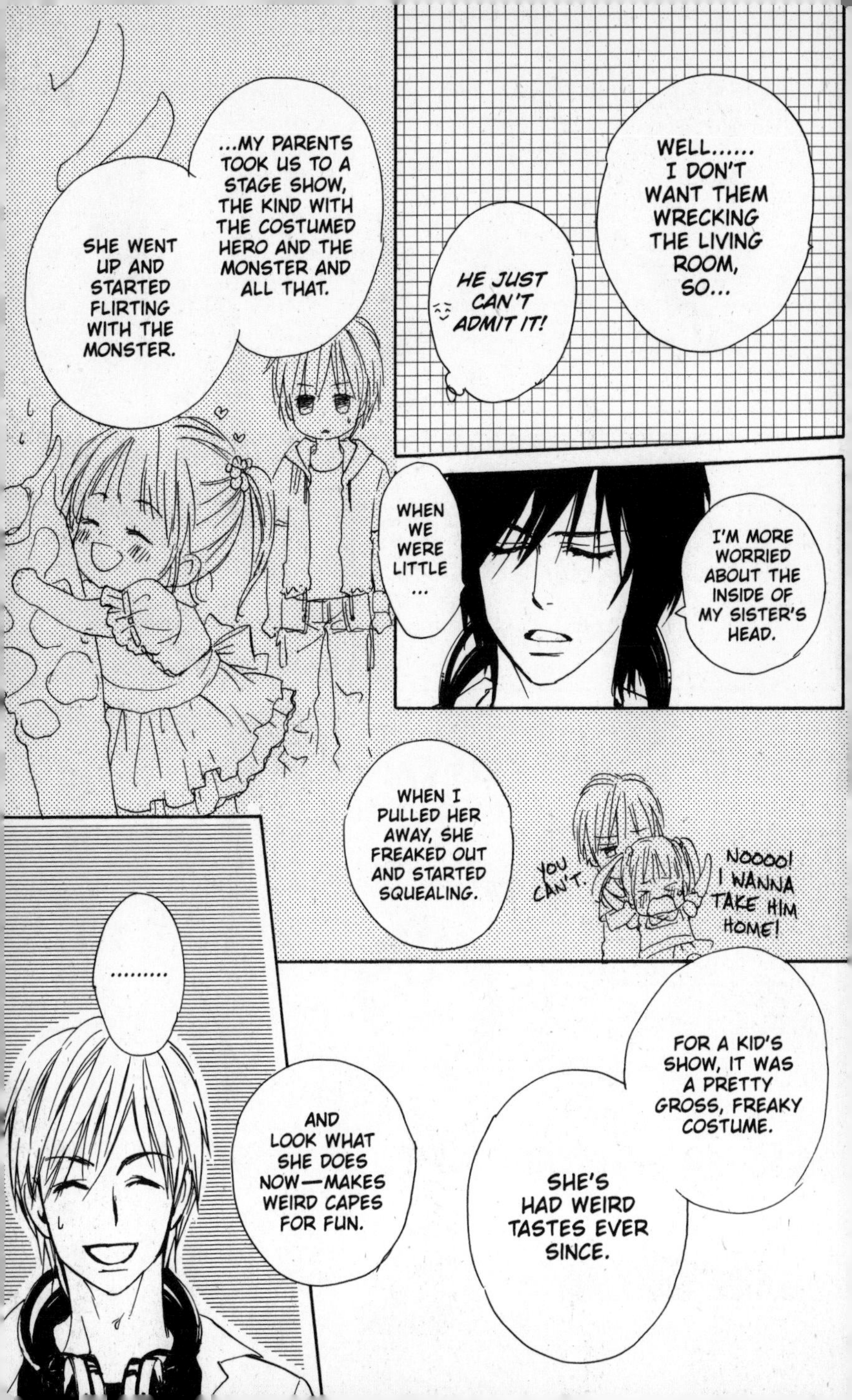
WELL...... I DON'T WANT THEM WRECKING THE LIVING ROOM, SO...
HE JUST CAN'T ADMIT IT!
I'M MORE WORRIED ABOUT THE INSIDE OF MY SISTER'S HEAD.
WHEN WE WERE LITTLE...
...MY PARENTS TOOK US TO A STAGE SHOW, THE KIND WITH THE COSTUMED HERO AND THE MONSTER AND ALL THAT.
SHE WENT UP AND STARTED FLIRTING WITH THE MONSTER.
WHEN I PULLED HER AWAY, SHE FREAKED OUT AND STARTED SQUEALING.
NOOOO! I WANNA TAKE HIM HOME!
YOU CAN'T.
FOR A KID'S SHOW, IT WAS A PRETTY GROSS, FREAKY COSTUME.
SHE'S HAD WEIRD TASTES EVER SINCE.
....
AND LOOK WHAT SHE DOES NOW—MAKES WEIRD CAPES FOR FUN.

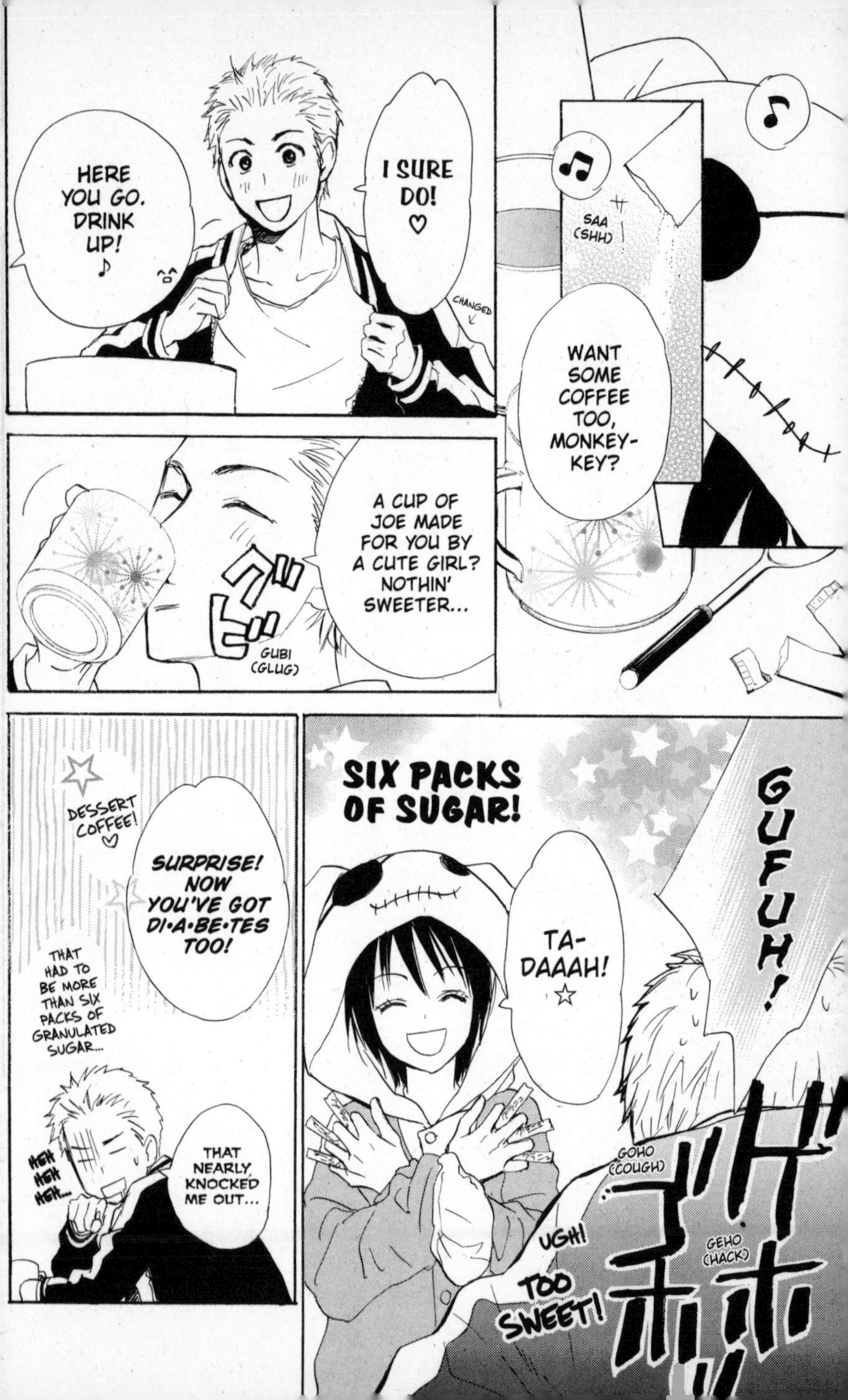
SAA (SHH)
WANT SOME COFFEE TOO, MONKEY-KEY?
I SURE DO! ♡
CHANGED
HERE YOU GO. DRINK UP! ♪
A CUP OF JOE MADE FOR YOU BY A CUTE GIRL? NOTHIN' SWEETER...
GUBI (GLUG)
GUFUH!
SIX PACKS OF SUGAR!
TA-DAAAH! ☆
GOHO (COUGH)
GEHO (HACK)
UGH!
TOO SWEET!
DESSERT COFFEE! ♡
SURPRISE! NOW YOU'VE GOT DI·A·BE·TES TOO!
THAT HAD TO BE MORE THAN SIX PACKS OF GRANULATED SUGAR...
THAT NEARLY KNOCKED ME OUT...
HEH HEH HEH...

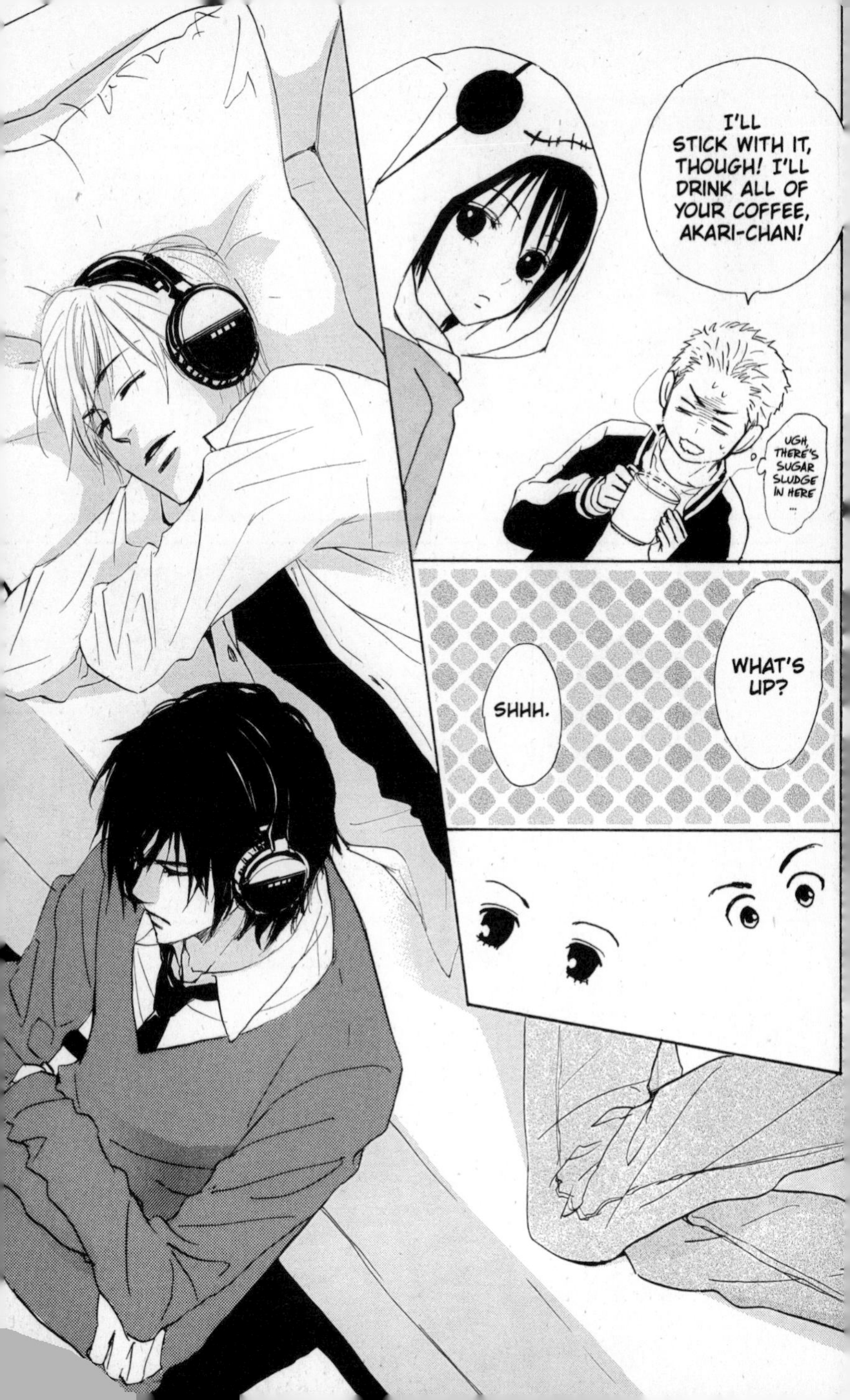
I'LL STICK WITH IT, THOUGH! I'LL DRINK ALL OF YOUR COFFEE, AKARI-CHAN!
UGH, THERE'S SUGAR SLUDGE IN HERE ...
WHAT'S UP?
SHHH.

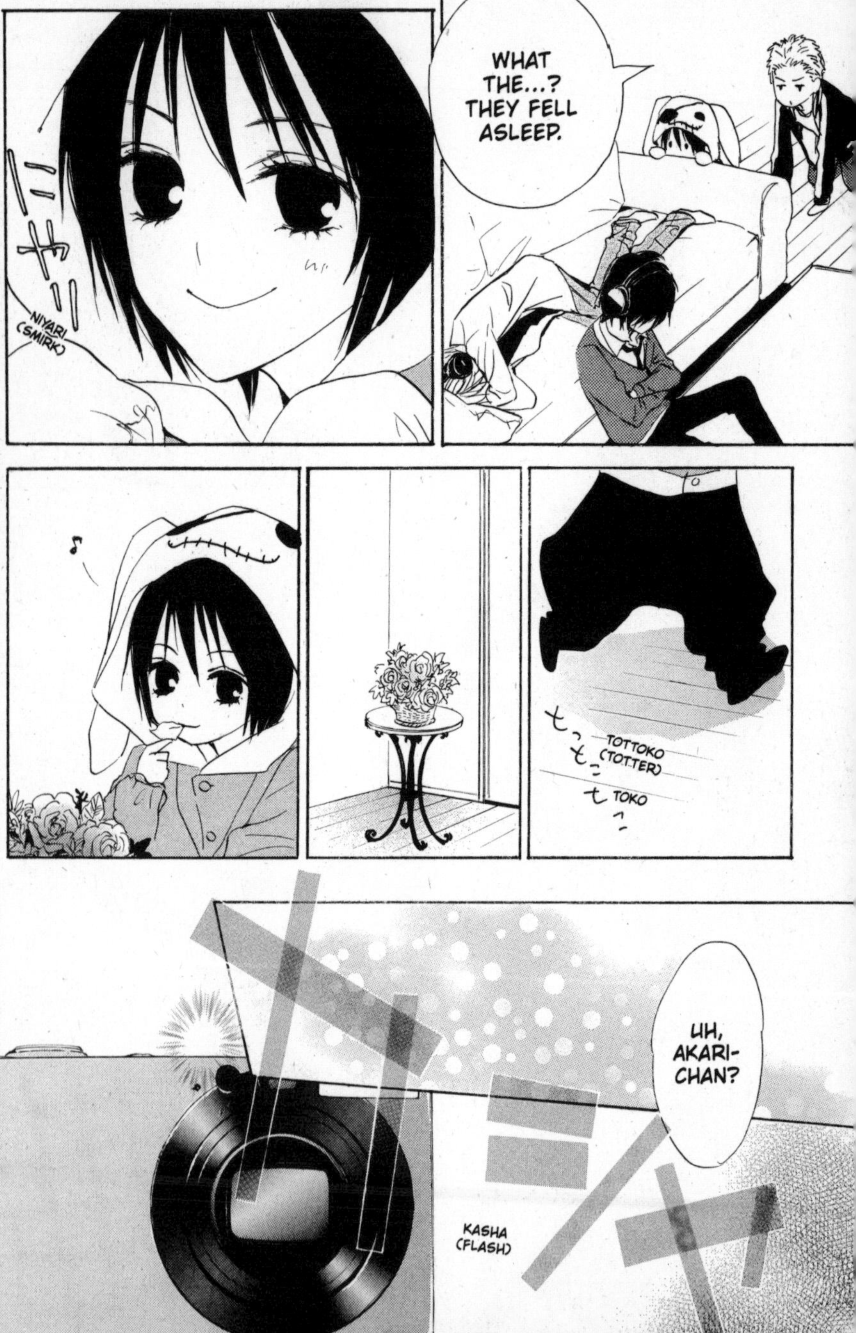
WHAT THE...? THEY FELL ASLEEP.
NIYARI (SMIRK)
TOTTOKO (TOTTER)
TOKO
UH, AKARI-CHAN?
KASHA (FLASH)

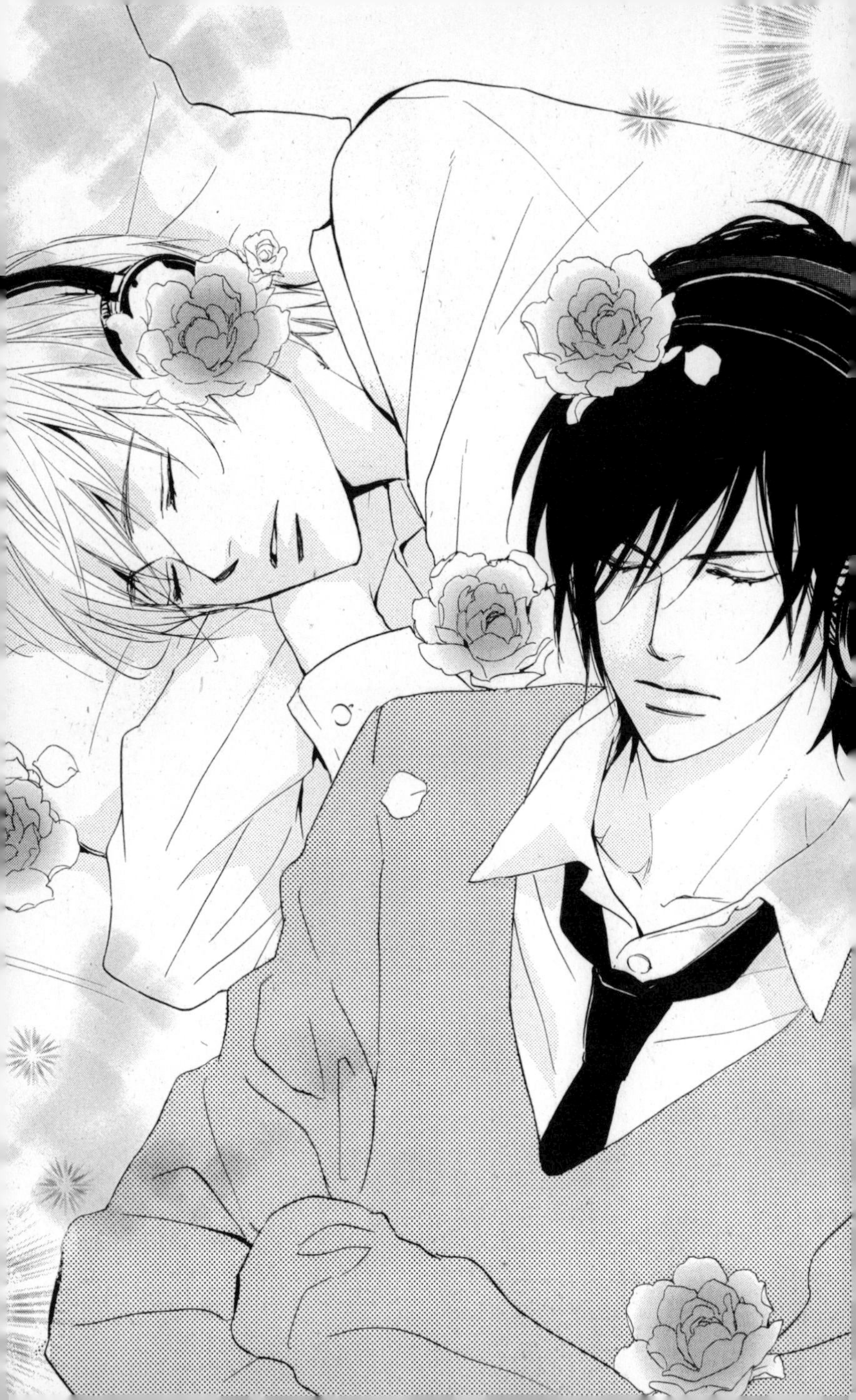

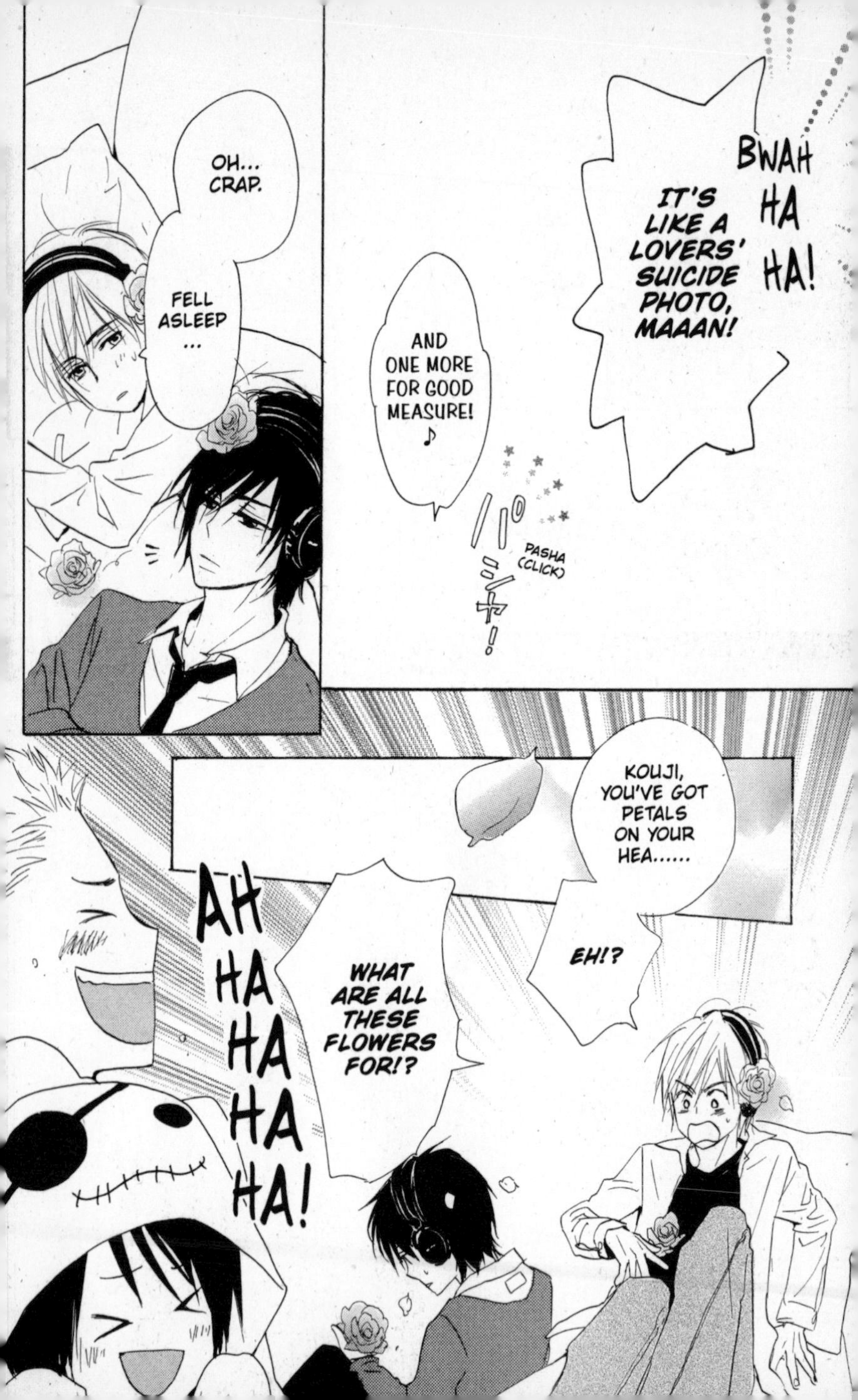
BWAH HA HA!
IT'S LIKE A LOVERS' SUICIDE PHOTO, MAAAN!
AND ONE MORE FOR GOOD MEASURE! ♪
PASHA (CLICK)
OH... CRAP.
FELL ASLEEP ...
KOUJI, YOU'VE GOT PETALS ON YOUR HEA......
EH!?
WHAT ARE ALL THESE FLOWERS FOR!?
AH HA HA HA HA HA!

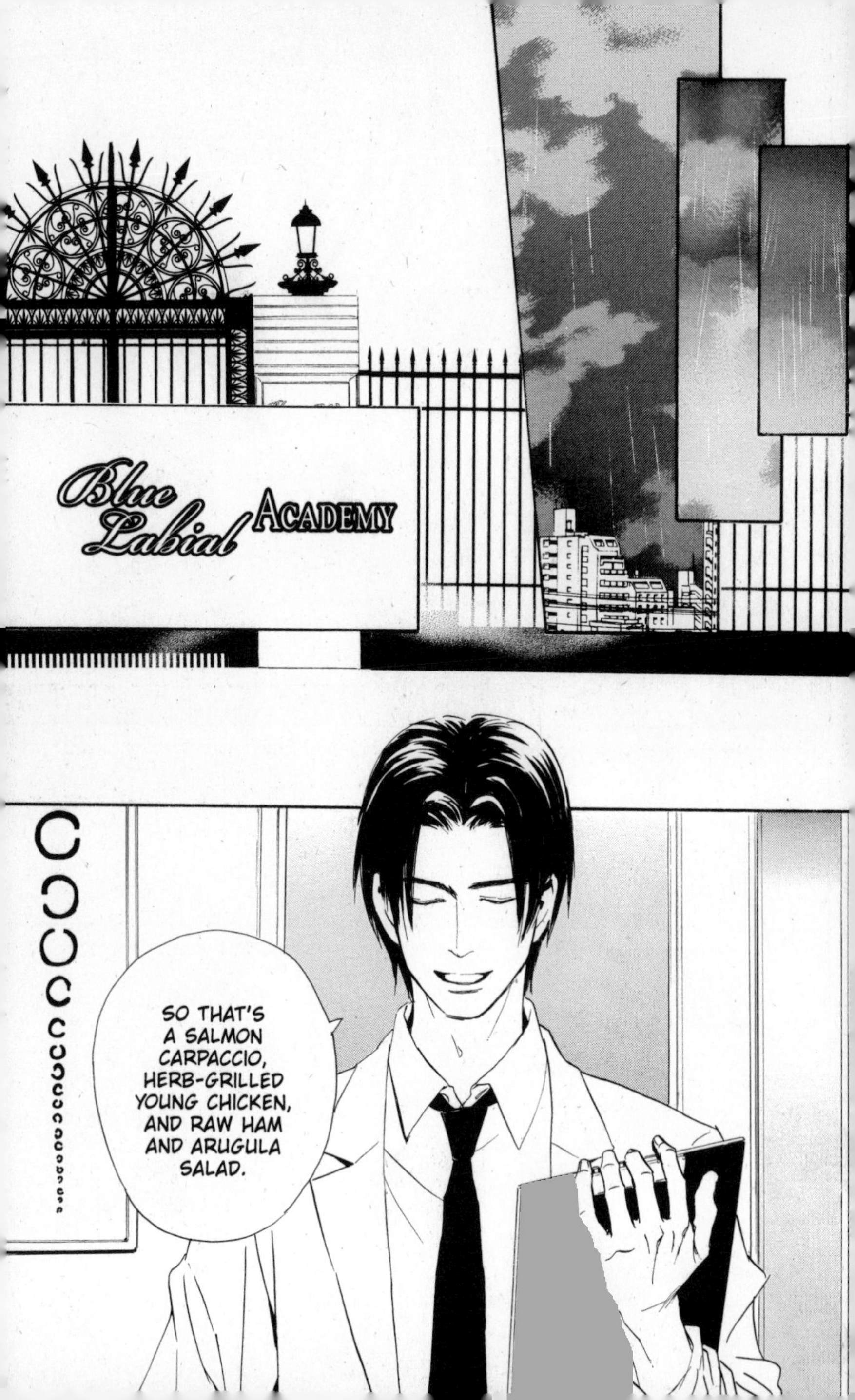
Blue Labial ACADEMY
SO THAT'S A SALMON CARPACCIO, HERB-GRILLED YOUNG CHICKEN, AND RAW HAM AND ARUGULA SALAD.

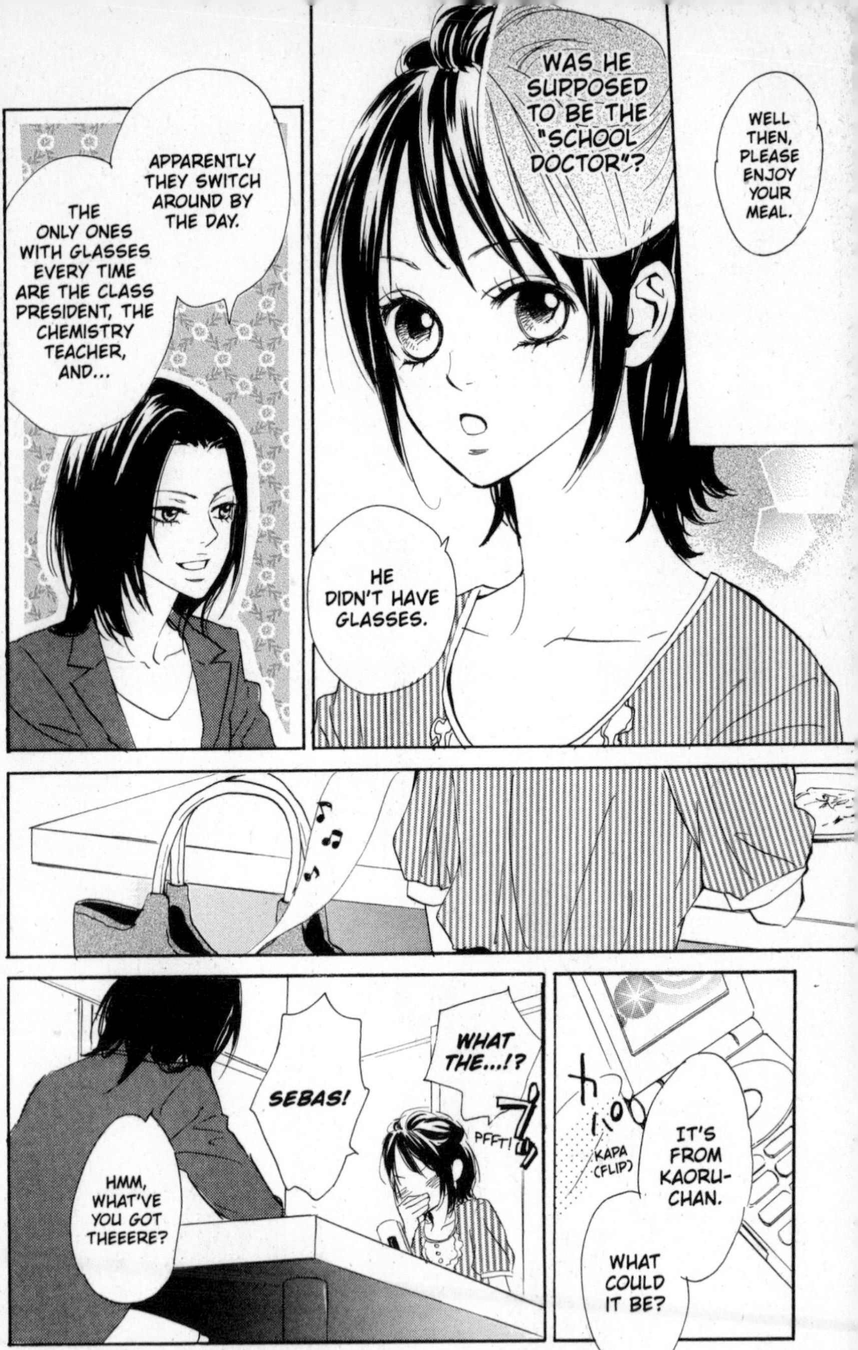
WELL THEN, PLEASE ENJOY YOUR MEAL.
WAS HE SUPPOSED TO BE THE "SCHOOL DOCTOR"?
HE DIDN'T HAVE GLASSES.
APPARENTLY THEY SWITCH AROUND BY THE DAY.
THE ONLY ONES WITH GLASSES EVERY TIME ARE THE CLASS PRESIDENT, THE CHEMISTRY TEACHER, AND...
KAPA (FLIP)
IT'S FROM KAORU-CHAN.
WHAT COULD IT BE?
WHAT THE...!?
PFFT!
SEBAS!
HMM, WHAT'VE YOU GOT THEEERE?

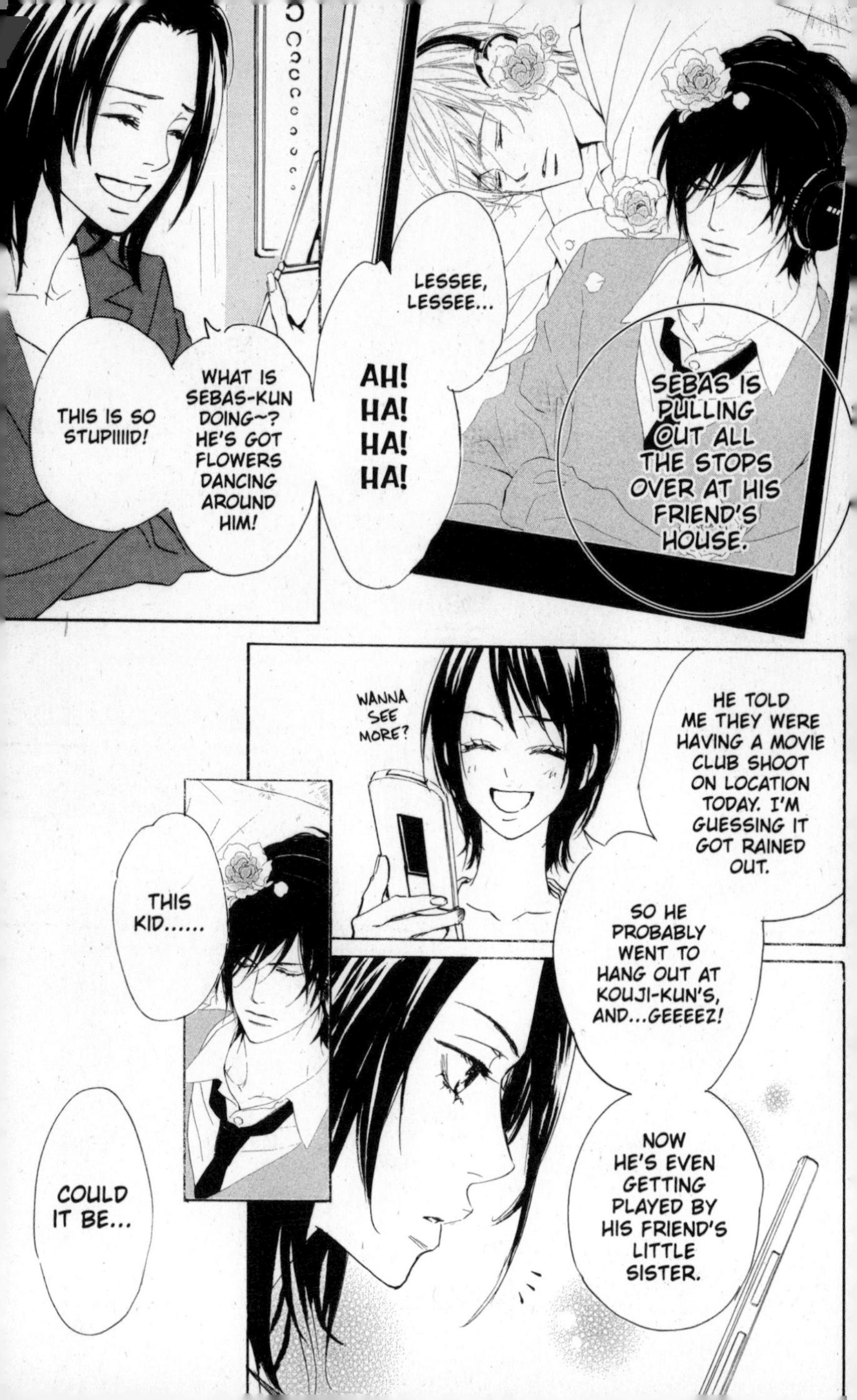
SEBAS IS PULLING OUT ALL THE STOPS OVER AT HIS FRIEND'S HOUSE.
LESSEE, LESSEE...
AH! HA! HA! HA!
WHAT IS SEBAS-KUN DOING~? HE'S GOT FLOWERS DANCING AROUND HIM!
THIS IS SO STUPIIIIID!
HE TOLD ME THEY WERE HAVING A MOVIE CLUB SHOOT ON LOCATION TODAY. I'M GUESSING IT GOT RAINED OUT.
WANNA SEE MORE?
SO HE PROBABLY WENT TO HANG OUT AT KOUJI-KUN'S, AND...GEEEEZ!
NOW HE'S EVEN GETTING PLAYED BY HIS FRIEND'S LITTLE SISTER.
THIS KID......
COULD IT BE...

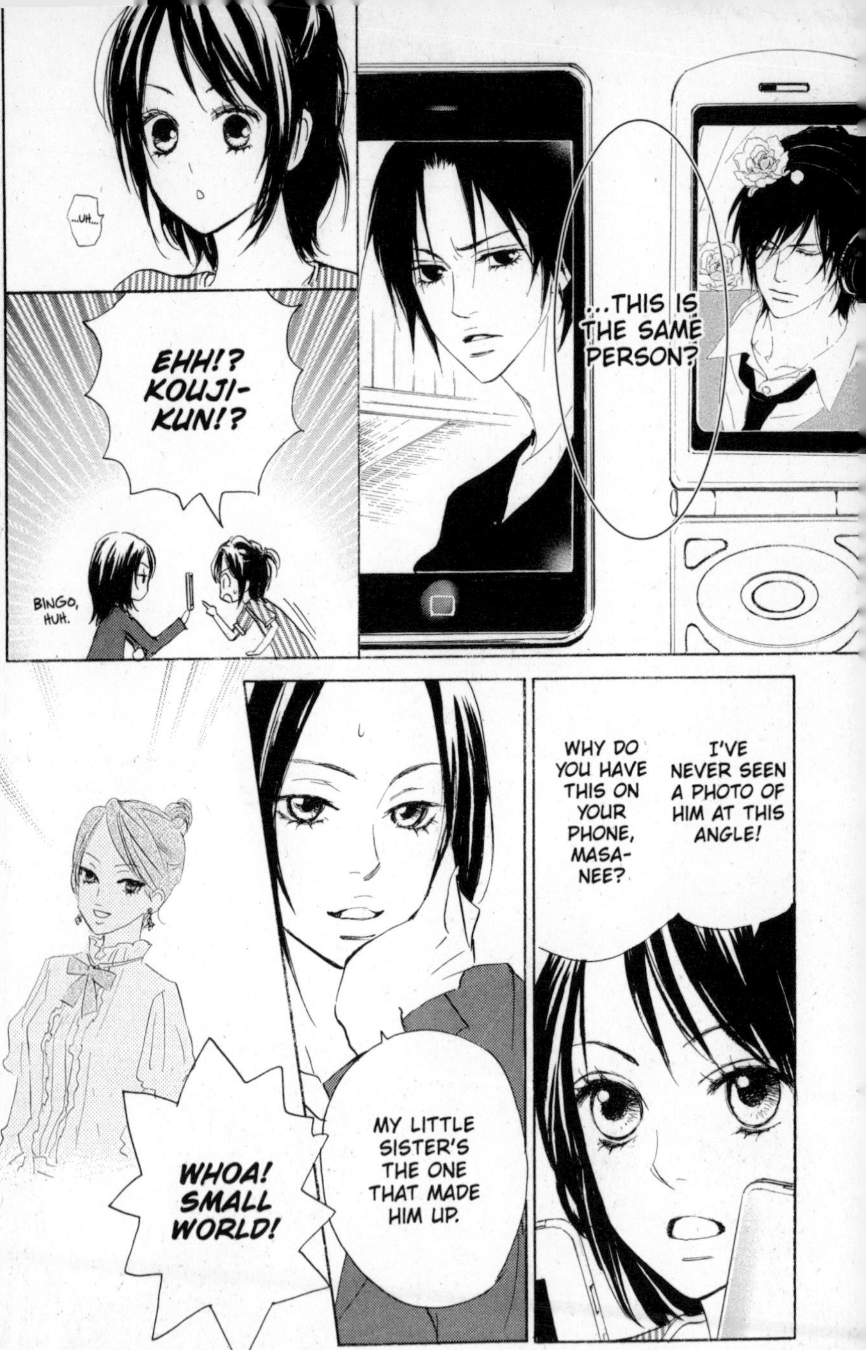
...THIS IS THE SAME PERSON?
...UH...
EHH!? KOUJI-KUN!?
BINGO, HUH.
I'VE NEVER SEEN A PHOTO OF HIM AT THIS ANGLE!
WHY DO YOU HAVE THIS ON YOUR PHONE, MASA-NEE?
MY LITTLE SISTER'S THE ONE THAT MADE HIM UP.
WHOA! SMALL WORLD!

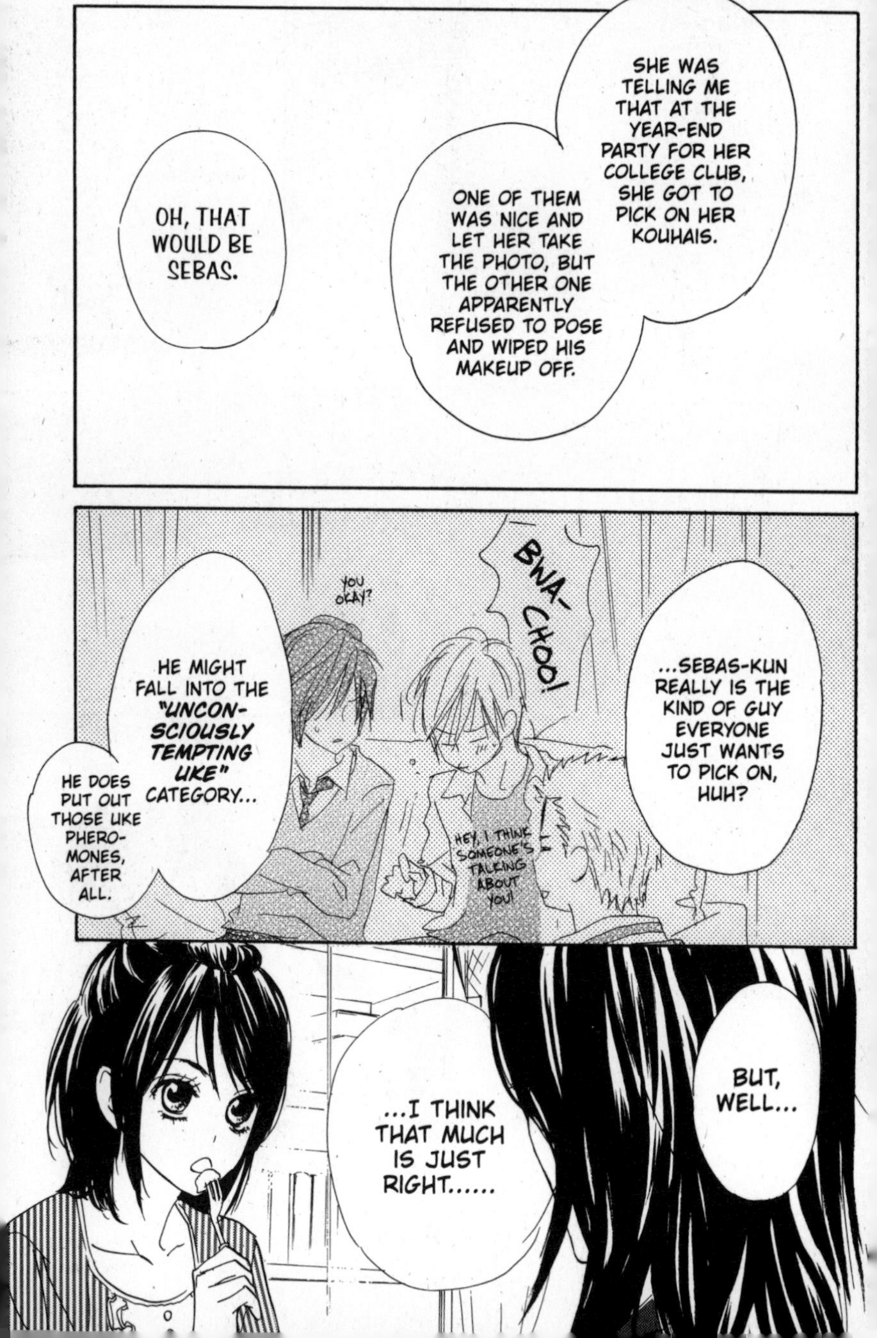
SHE WAS TELLING ME THAT AT THE YEAR-END PARTY FOR HER COLLEGE CLUB, SHE GOT TO PICK ON HER KOUHAIS.
ONE OF THEM WAS NICE AND LET HER TAKE THE PHOTO, BUT THE OTHER ONE APPARENTLY REFUSED TO POSE AND WIPED HIS MAKEUP OFF.
OH, THAT WOULD BE SEBAS.
...SEBAS-KUN REALLY IS THE KIND OF GUY EVERYONE JUST WANTS TO PICK ON, HUH?
BWA-CHOO!
YOU OKAY?
HEY, I THINK SOMEONE'S TALKING ABOUT YOU!
HE MIGHT FALL INTO THE *"UNCONSCIOUSLY TEMPTING UKE"* CATEGORY...
HE DOES PUT OUT THOSE UKE PHEROMONES, AFTER ALL.
BUT, WELL...
...I THINK THAT MUCH IS JUST RIGHT......

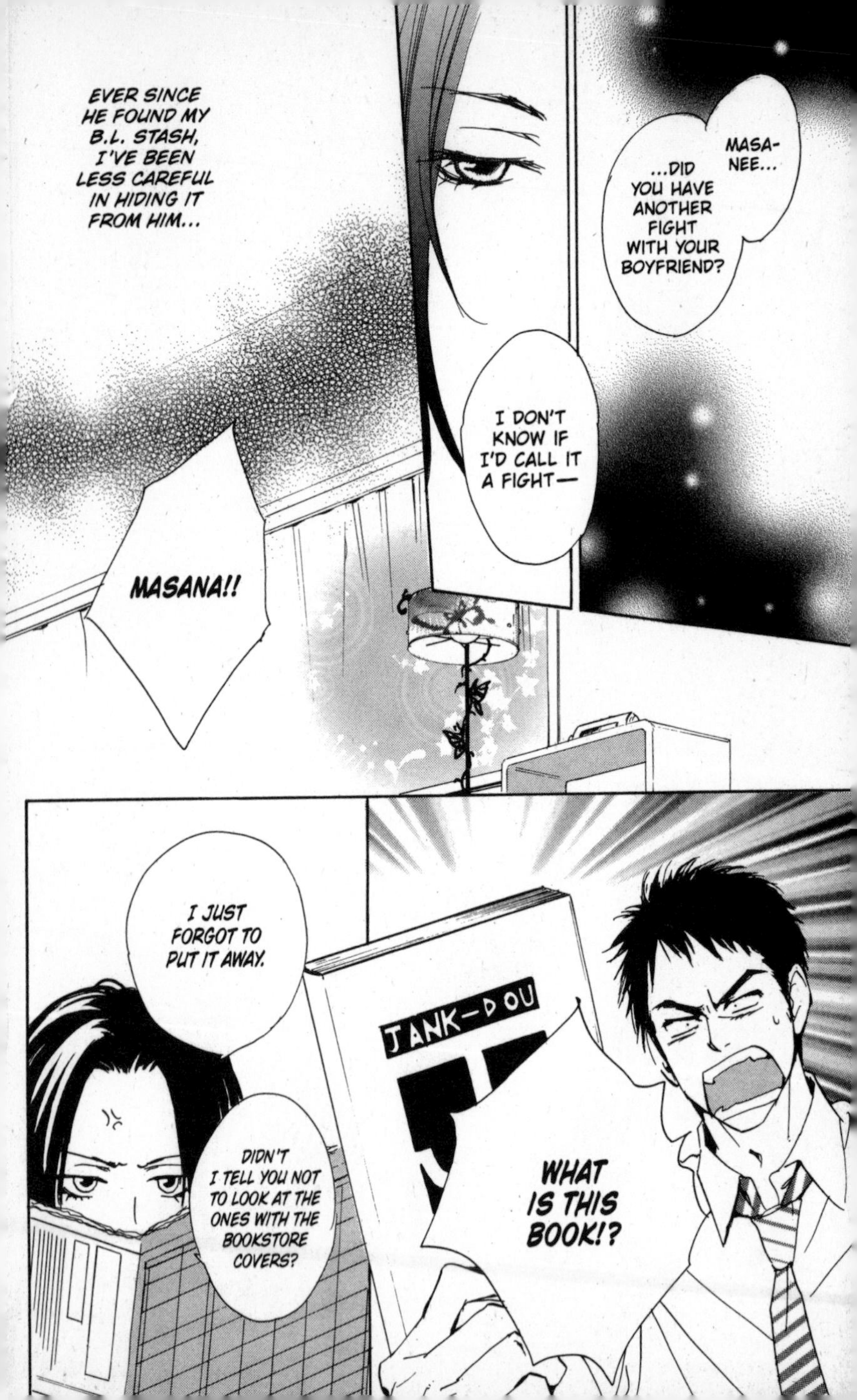
MASA-NEE...
...DID YOU HAVE ANOTHER FIGHT WITH YOUR BOYFRIEND?
I DON'T KNOW IF I'D CALL IT A FIGHT—
EVER SINCE HE FOUND MY B.L. STASH, I'VE BEEN LESS CAREFUL IN HIDING IT FROM HIM...
MASANA!!
JANK-DOU
WHAT IS THIS BOOK!?
I JUST FORGOT TO PUT IT AWAY.
DIDN'T I TELL YOU NOT TO LOOK AT THE ONES WITH THE BOOKSTORE COVERS?

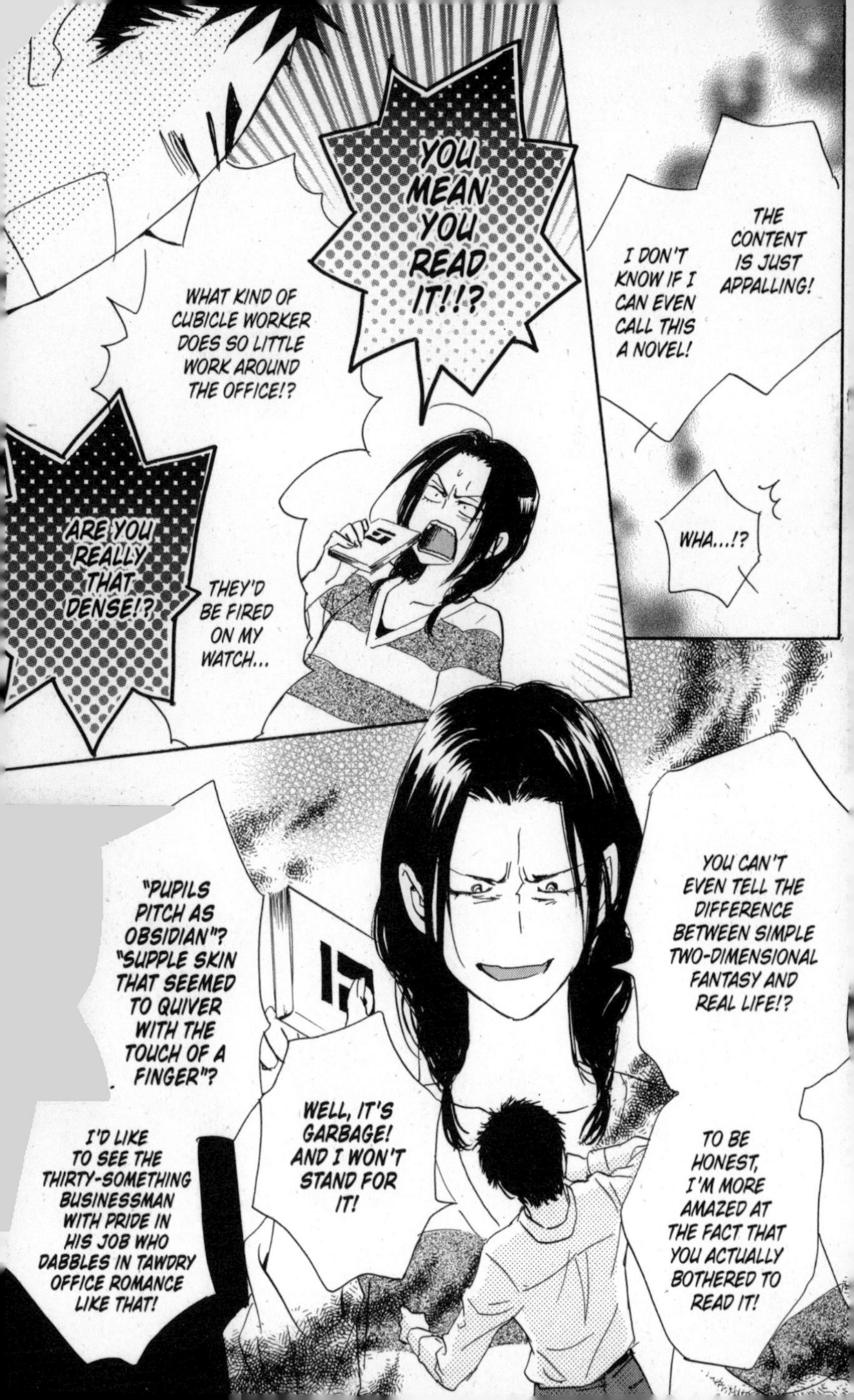
THE CONTENT IS JUST APPALLING!
I DON'T KNOW IF I CAN EVEN CALL THIS A NOVEL!
WHA...!?
YOU MEAN YOU READ IT!!?
WHAT KIND OF CUBICLE WORKER DOES SO LITTLE WORK AROUND THE OFFICE!?
THEY'D BE FIRED ON MY WATCH...
ARE YOU REALLY THAT DENSE!?
YOU CAN'T EVEN TELL THE DIFFERENCE BETWEEN SIMPLE TWO-DIMENSIONAL FANTASY AND REAL LIFE!?
"PUPILS PITCH AS OBSIDIAN"? "SUPPLE SKIN THAT SEEMED TO QUIVER WITH THE TOUCH OF A FINGER"?
TO BE HONEST, I'M MORE AMAZED AT THE FACT THAT YOU ACTUALLY BOTHERED TO READ IT!
WELL, IT'S GARBAGE! AND I WON'T STAND FOR IT!
I'D LIKE TO SEE THE THIRTY-SOMETHING BUSINESSMAN WITH PRIDE IN HIS JOB WHO DABBLES IN TAWDRY OFFICE ROMANCE LIKE THAT!

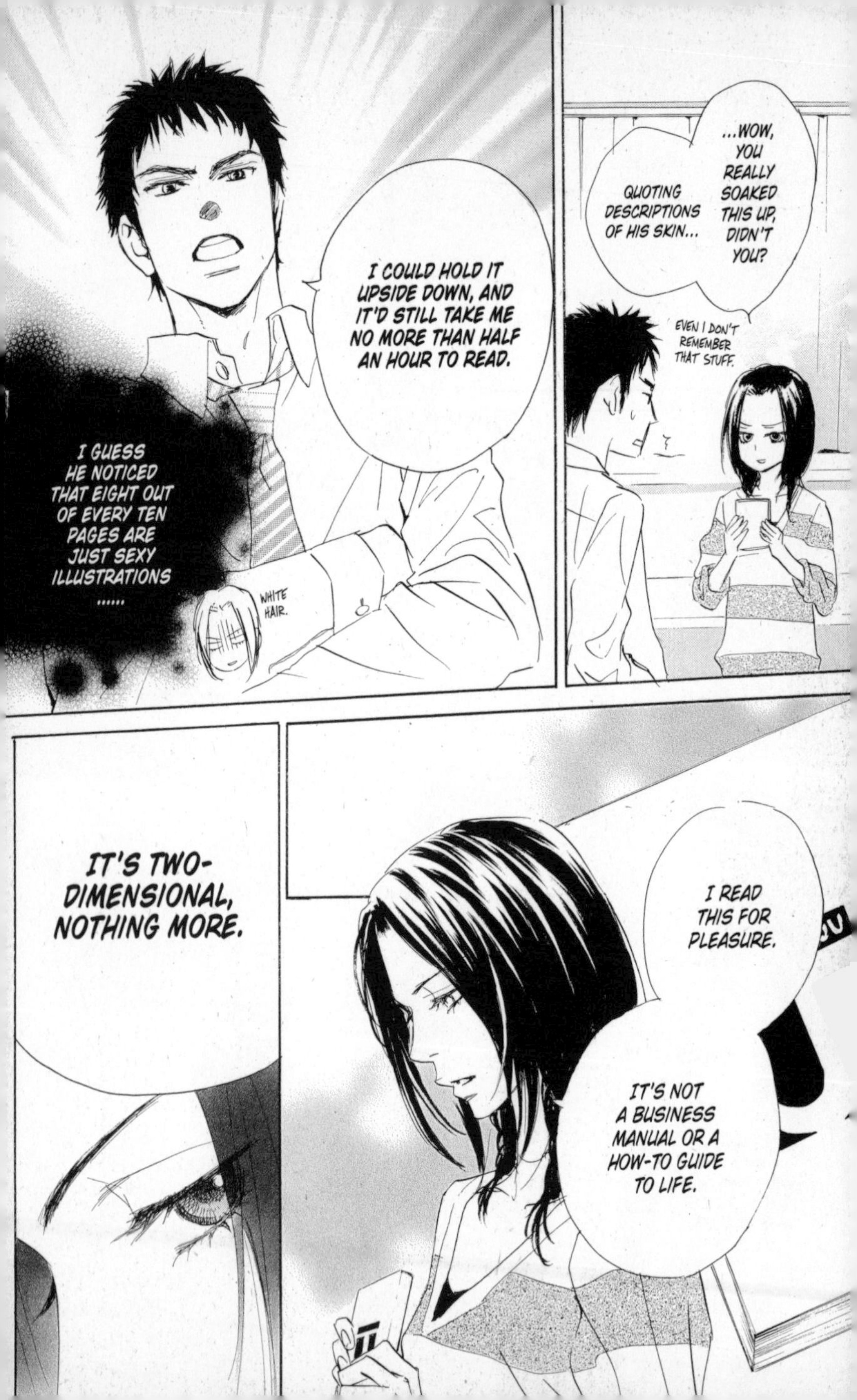
...WOW, YOU REALLY SOAKED THIS UP, DIDN'T YOU?
QUOTING DESCRIPTIONS OF HIS SKIN...
EVEN I DON'T REMEMBER THAT STUFF.
I COULD HOLD IT UPSIDE DOWN, AND IT'D STILL TAKE ME NO MORE THAN HALF AN HOUR TO READ.
I GUESS HE NOTICED THAT EIGHT OUT OF EVERY TEN PAGES ARE JUST SEXY ILLUSTRATIONS ......
WHITE HAIR.
I READ THIS FOR PLEASURE.
IT'S NOT A BUSINESS MANUAL OR A HOW-TO GUIDE TO LIFE.
IT'S TWO-DIMENSIONAL, NOTHING MORE.

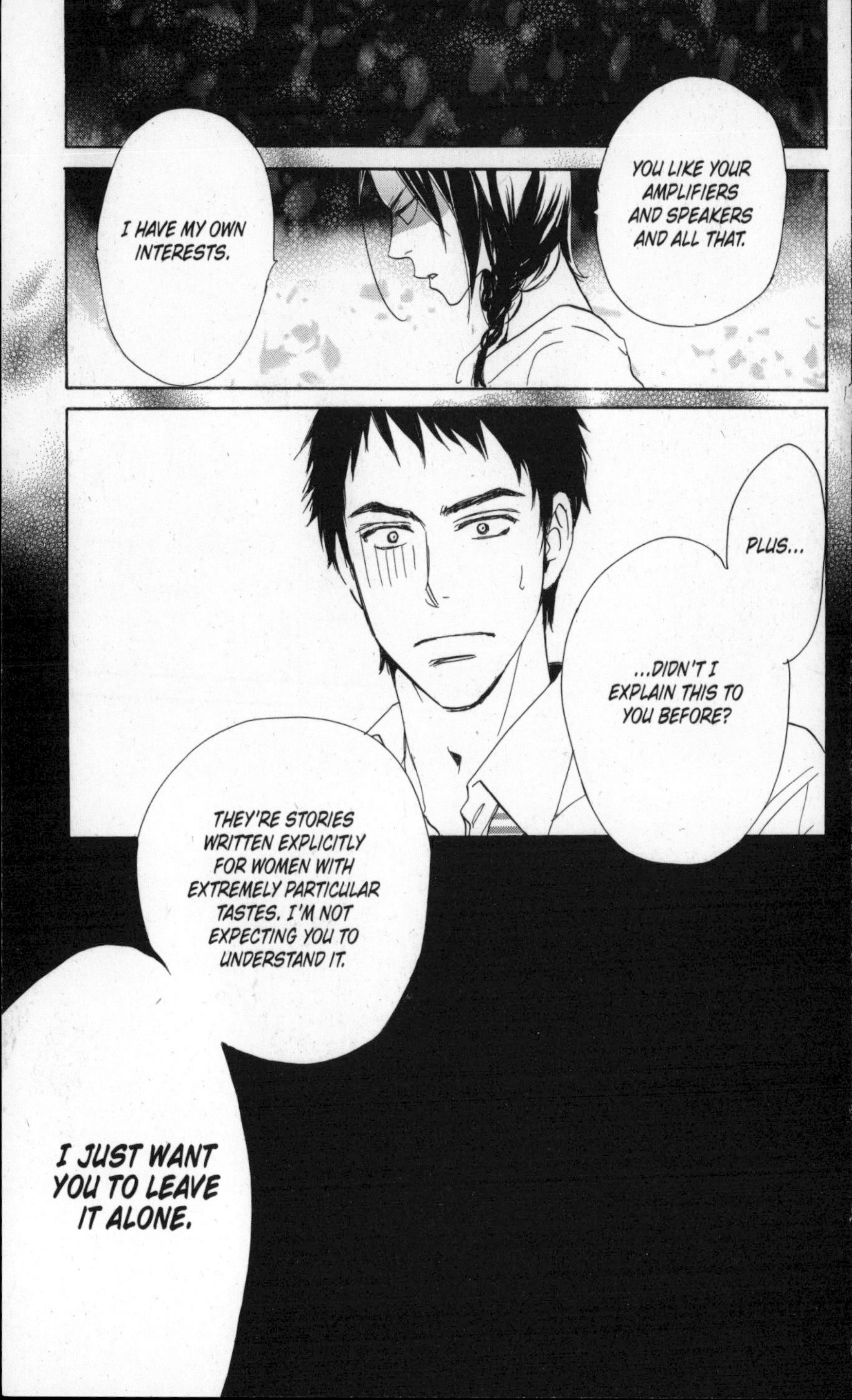
YOU LIKE YOUR AMPLIFIERS AND SPEAKERS AND ALL THAT.
I HAVE MY OWN INTERESTS.
PLUS...
...DIDN'T I EXPLAIN THIS TO YOU BEFORE?
THEY'RE STORIES WRITTEN EXPLICITLY FOR WOMEN WITH EXTREMELY PARTICULAR TASTES. I'M NOT EXPECTING YOU TO UNDERSTAND IT.
I JUST WANT YOU TO LEAVE IT ALONE.

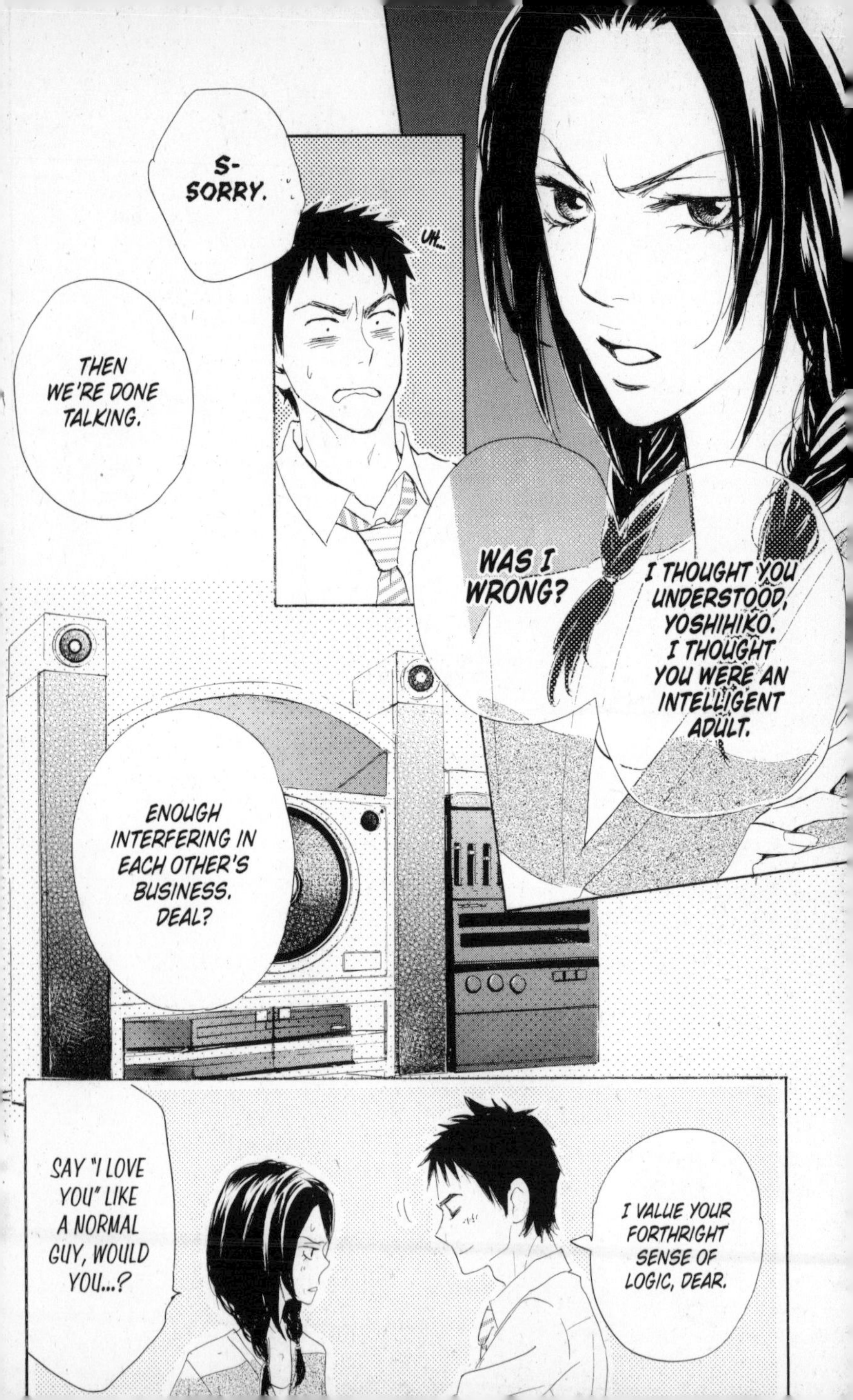
I THOUGHT YOU UNDERSTOOD, YOSHIHIKO. I THOUGHT YOU WERE AN INTELLIGENT ADULT.
WAS I WRONG?
UH...
S-SORRY.
THEN WE'RE DONE TALKING.
ENOUGH INTERFERING IN EACH OTHER'S BUSINESS. DEAL?
I VALUE YOUR FORTHRIGHT SENSE OF LOGIC, DEAR.
SAY "I LOVE YOU" LIKE A NORMAL GUY, WOULD YOU...?

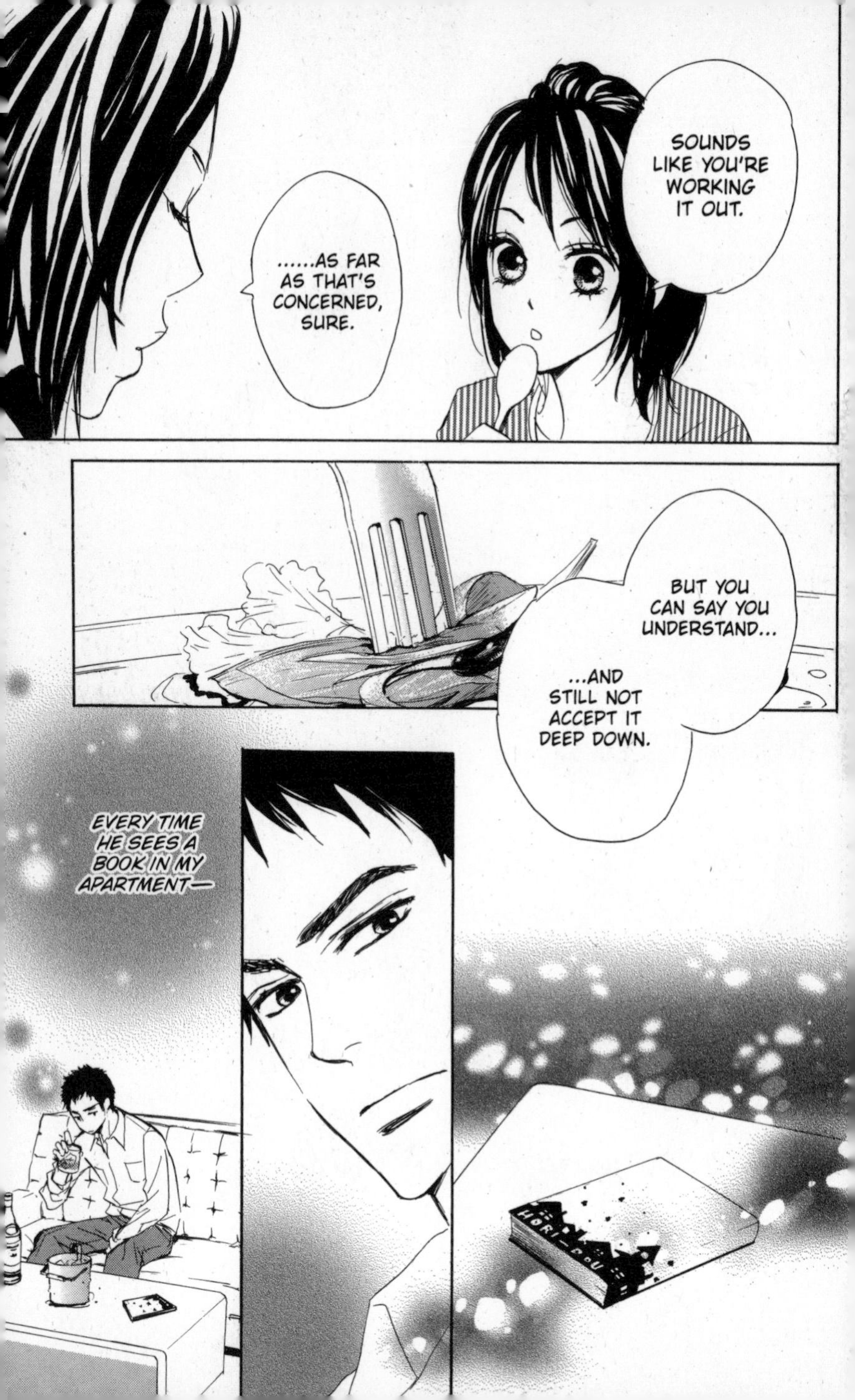
SOUNDS LIKE YOU'RE WORKING IT OUT.
......AS FAR AS THAT'S CONCERNED, SURE.
BUT YOU CAN SAY YOU UNDERSTAND...
...AND STILL NOT ACCEPT IT DEEP DOWN.
EVERY TIME HE SEES A BOOK IN MY APARTMENT—

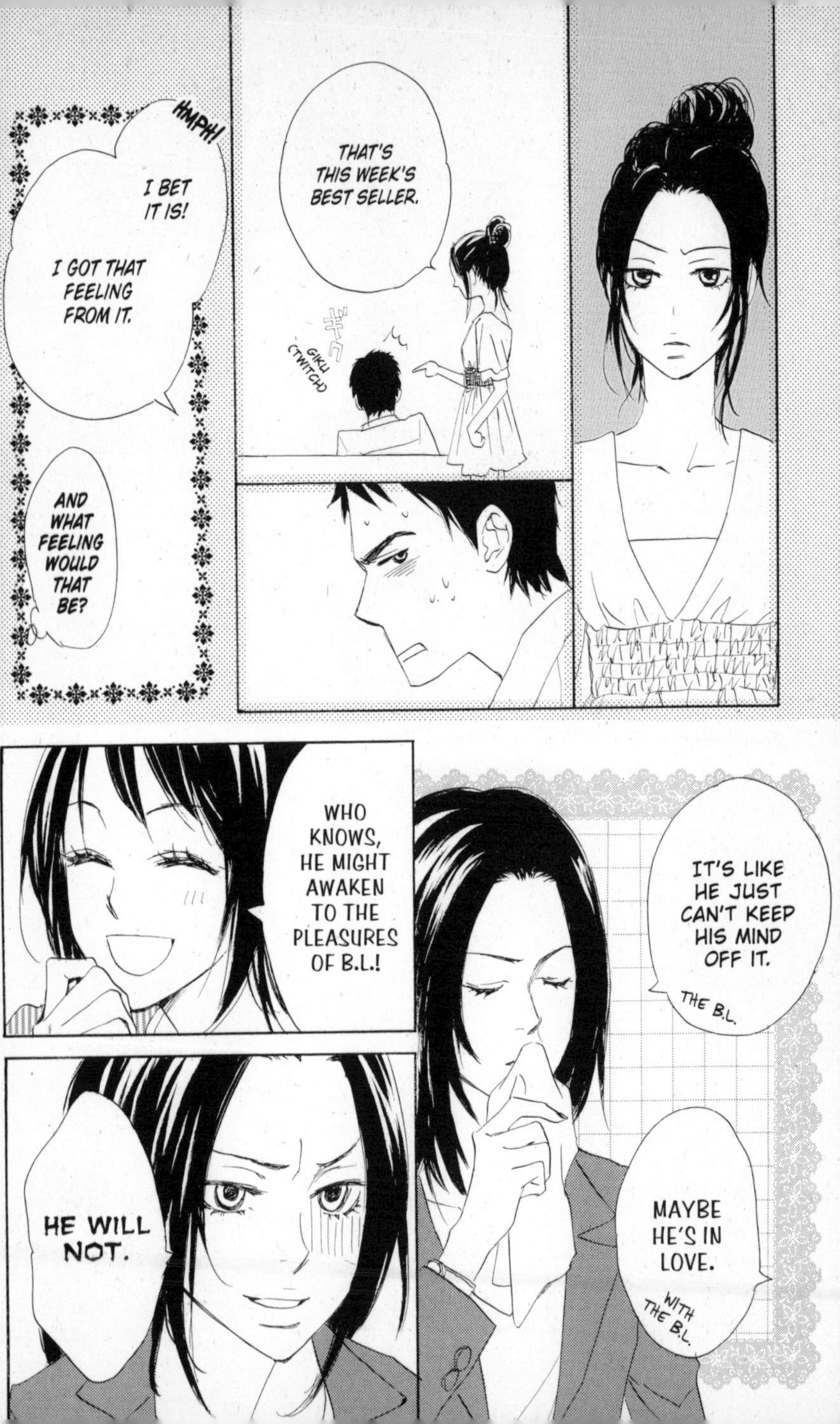
THAT'S THIS WEEK'S BEST SELLER.
ギク
GIKU (TWITCH)
HMPH!
I BET IT IS!
I GOT THAT FEELING FROM IT.
AND WHAT FEELING WOULD THAT BE?
IT'S LIKE HE JUST CAN'T KEEP HIS MIND OFF IT.
THE B.L.
MAYBE HE'S IN LOVE.
WITH THE B.L.
WHO KNOWS, HE MIGHT AWAKEN TO THE PLEASURES OF B.L.!
HE WILL NOT.

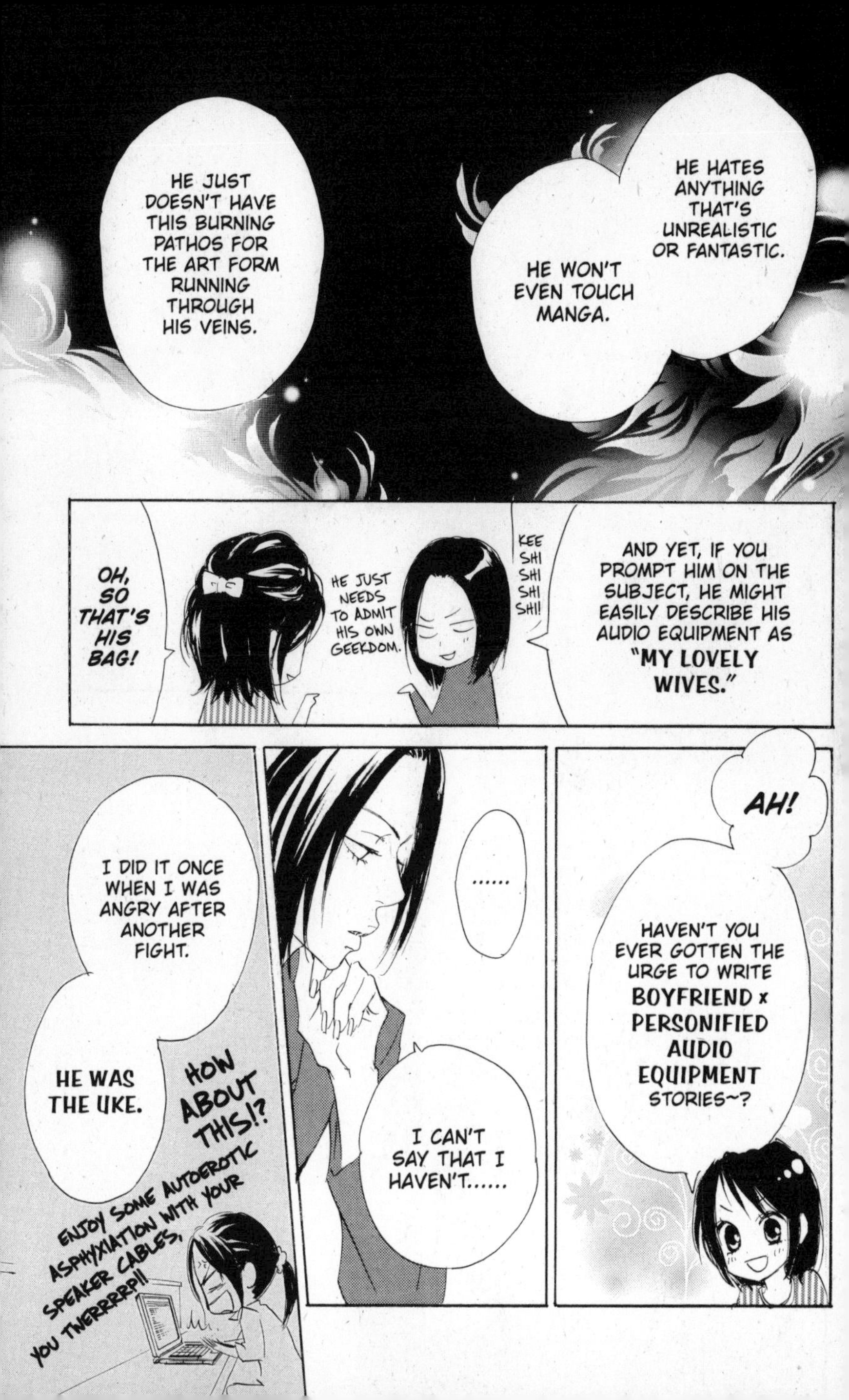
HE HATES ANYTHING THAT'S UNREALISTIC OR FANTASTIC.
HE WON'T EVEN TOUCH MANGA.
HE JUST DOESN'T HAVE THIS BURNING PATHOS FOR THE ART FORM RUNNING THROUGH HIS VEINS.
AND YET, IF YOU PROMPT HIM ON THE SUBJECT, HE MIGHT EASILY DESCRIBE HIS AUDIO EQUIPMENT AS "MY LOVELY WIVES."
KEE SHI SHI SHI SHI!
HE JUST NEEDS TO ADMIT HIS OWN GEEKDOM.
OH, SO THAT'S HIS BAG!
AH!
HAVEN'T YOU EVER GOTTEN THE URGE TO WRITE BOYFRIEND x PERSONIFIED AUDIO EQUIPMENT STORIES~?
......
I CAN'T SAY THAT I HAVEN'T......
I DID IT ONCE WHEN I WAS ANGRY AFTER ANOTHER FIGHT.
HE WAS THE UKE.
HOW ABOUT THIS!?
ENJOY SOME AUTOEROTIC ASPHYXIATION WITH YOUR SPEAKER CABLES, YOU TWERRRRP!!

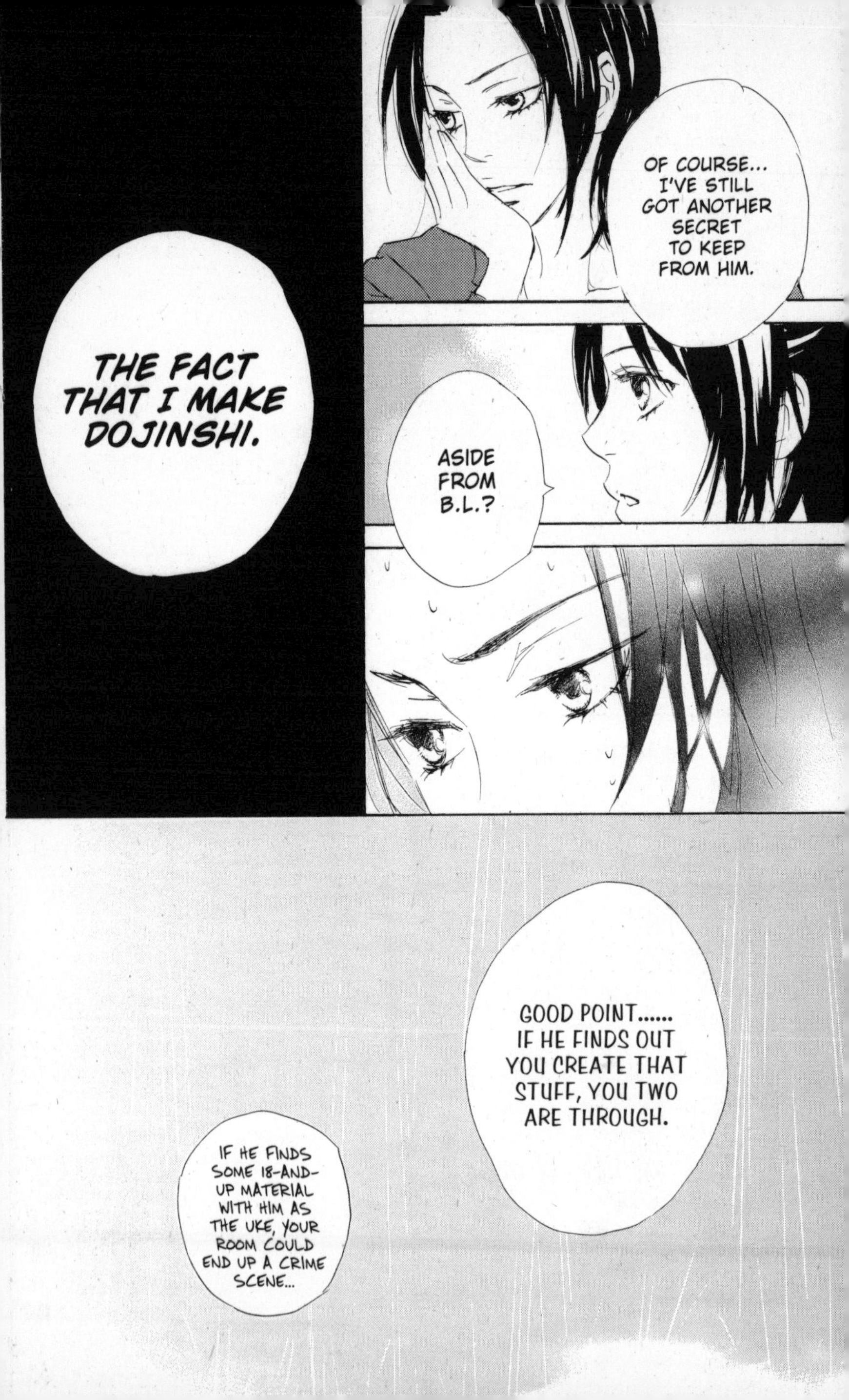
OF COURSE... I'VE STILL GOT ANOTHER SECRET TO KEEP FROM HIM.
ASIDE FROM B.L.?
THE FACT THAT I MAKE DOJINSHI.
GOOD POINT...... IF HE FINDS OUT YOU CREATE THAT STUFF, YOU TWO ARE THROUGH.
IF HE FINDS SOME 18-AND-UP MATERIAL WITH HIM AS THE UKE, YOUR ROOM COULD END UP A CRIME SCENE...

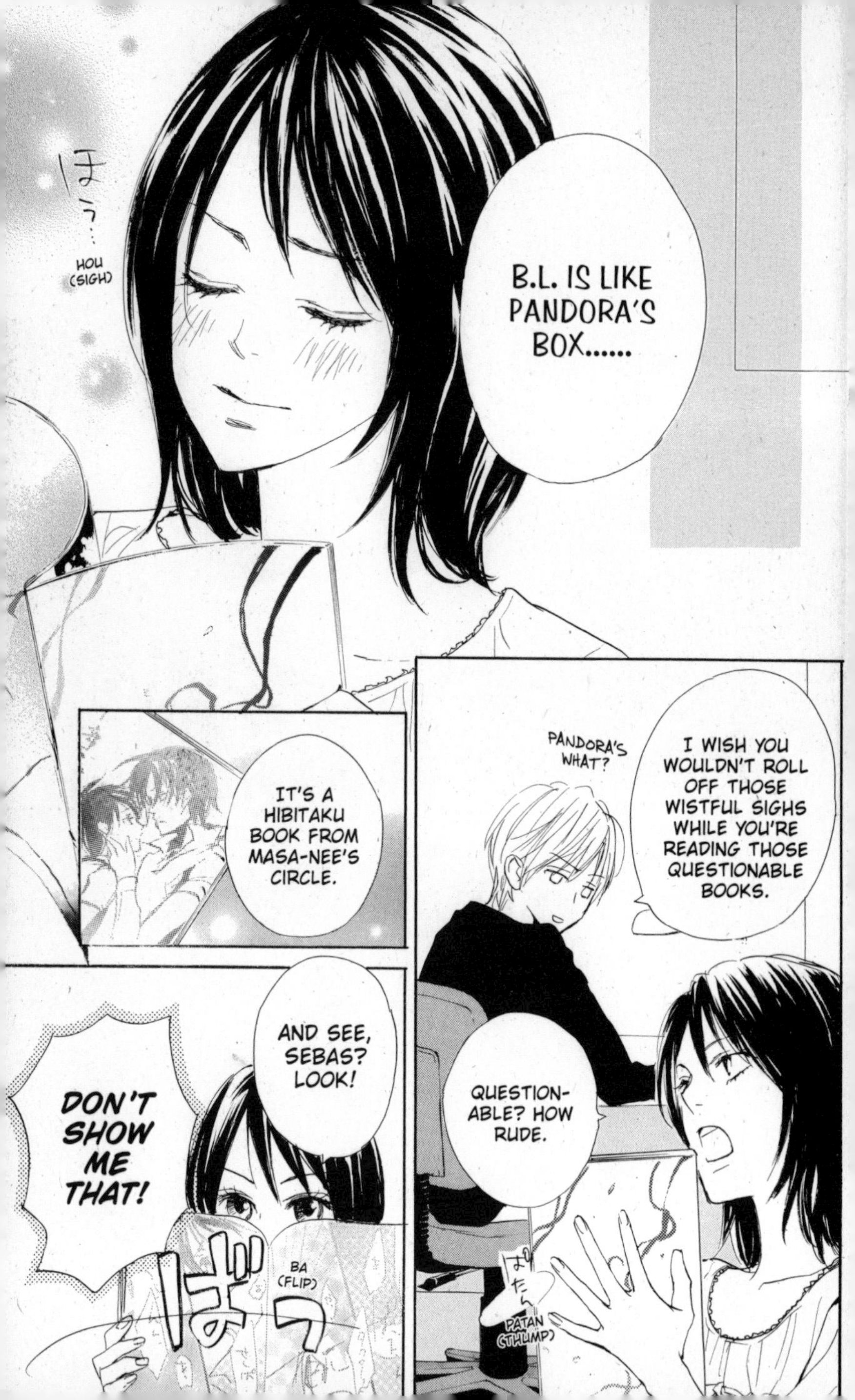
B.L. IS LIKE PANDORA'S BOX......
ほう…
HOU (SIGH)
PANDORA'S WHAT?
I WISH YOU WOULDN'T ROLL OFF THOSE WISTFUL SIGHS WHILE YOU'RE READING THOSE QUESTIONABLE BOOKS.
QUESTION-ABLE? HOW RUDE.
ぱたん
PATAN (THUMP)
IT'S A HIBITAKU BOOK FROM MASA-NEE'S CIRCLE.
AND SEE, SEBAS? LOOK!
DON'T SHOW ME THAT!
ぱっ
BA (FLIP)

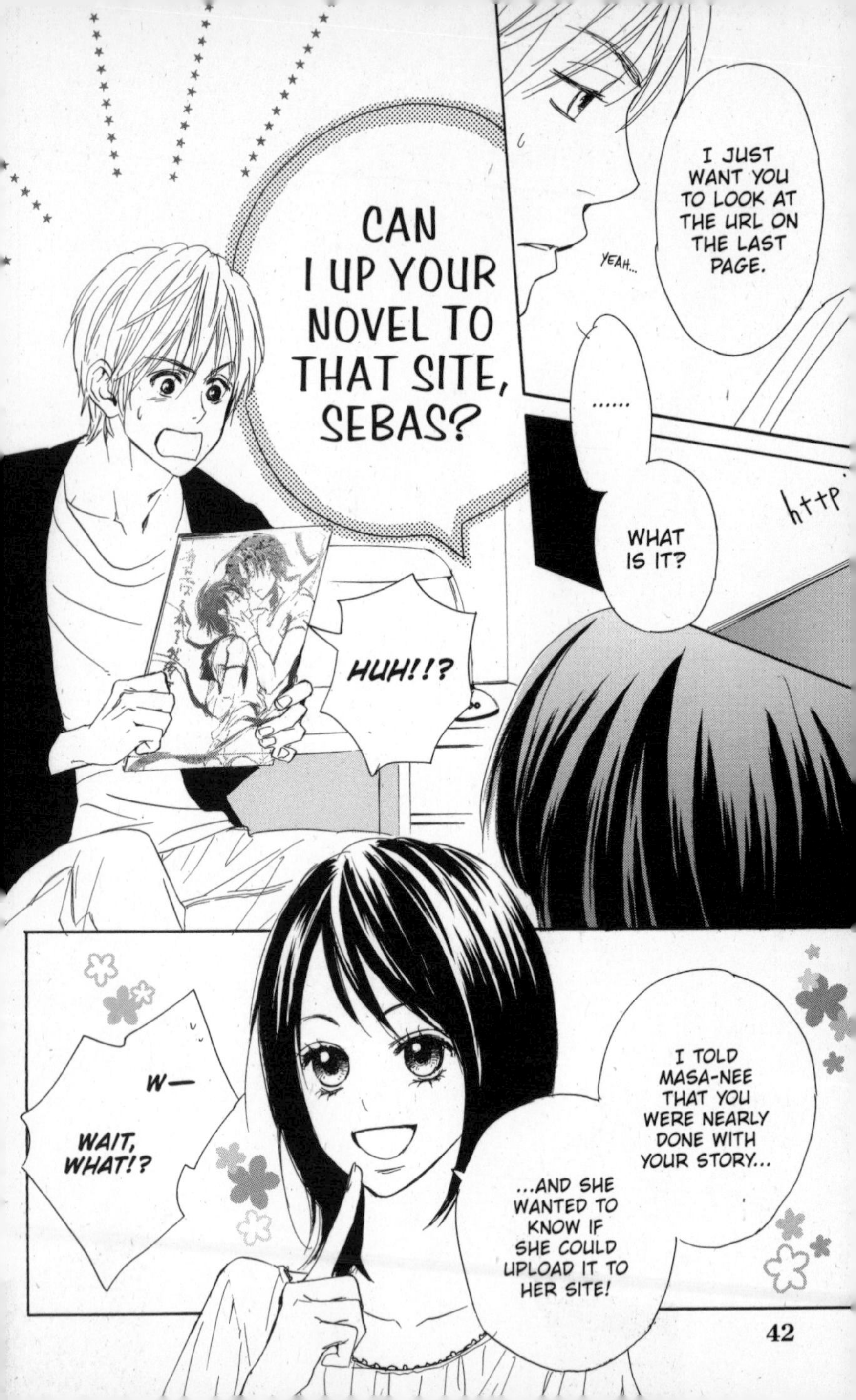
I JUST WANT YOU TO LOOK AT THE URL ON THE LAST PAGE.
YEAH...
......
WHAT IS IT?
http
CAN I UP YOUR NOVEL TO THAT SITE, SEBAS?
HUH!!?
I TOLD MASA-NEE THAT YOU WERE NEARLY DONE WITH YOUR STORY...
...AND SHE WANTED TO KNOW IF SHE COULD UPLOAD IT TO HER SITE!
W—
WAIT, WHAT!?

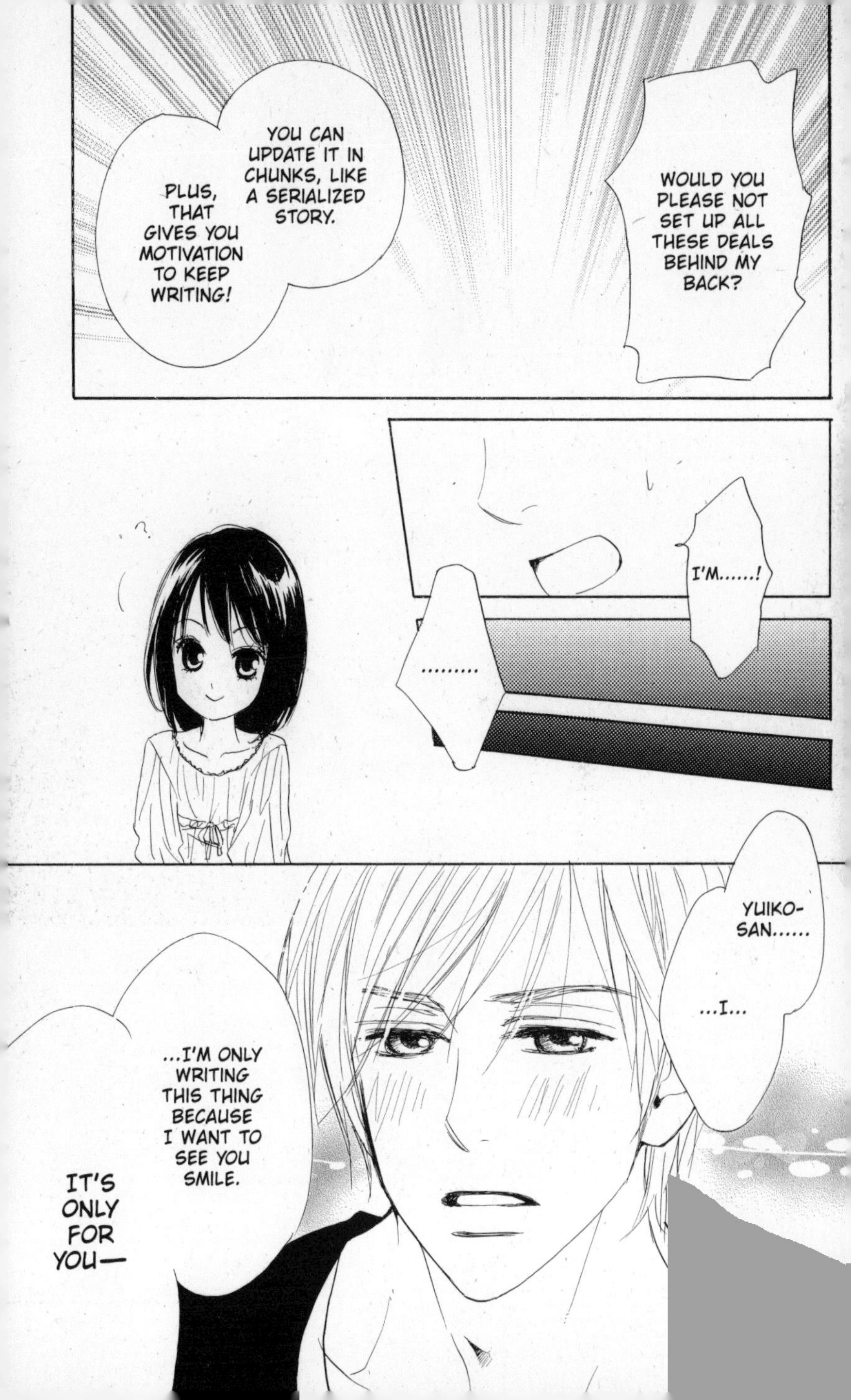
WOULD YOU PLEASE NOT SET UP ALL THESE DEALS BEHIND MY BACK?
YOU CAN UPDATE IT IN CHUNKS, LIKE A SERIALIZED STORY.
PLUS, THAT GIVES YOU MOTIVATION TO KEEP WRITING!
I'M......!
....
YUIKO-SAN......
...I...
...I'M ONLY WRITING THIS THING BECAUSE I WANT TO SEE YOU SMILE.
IT'S ONLY FOR YOU—

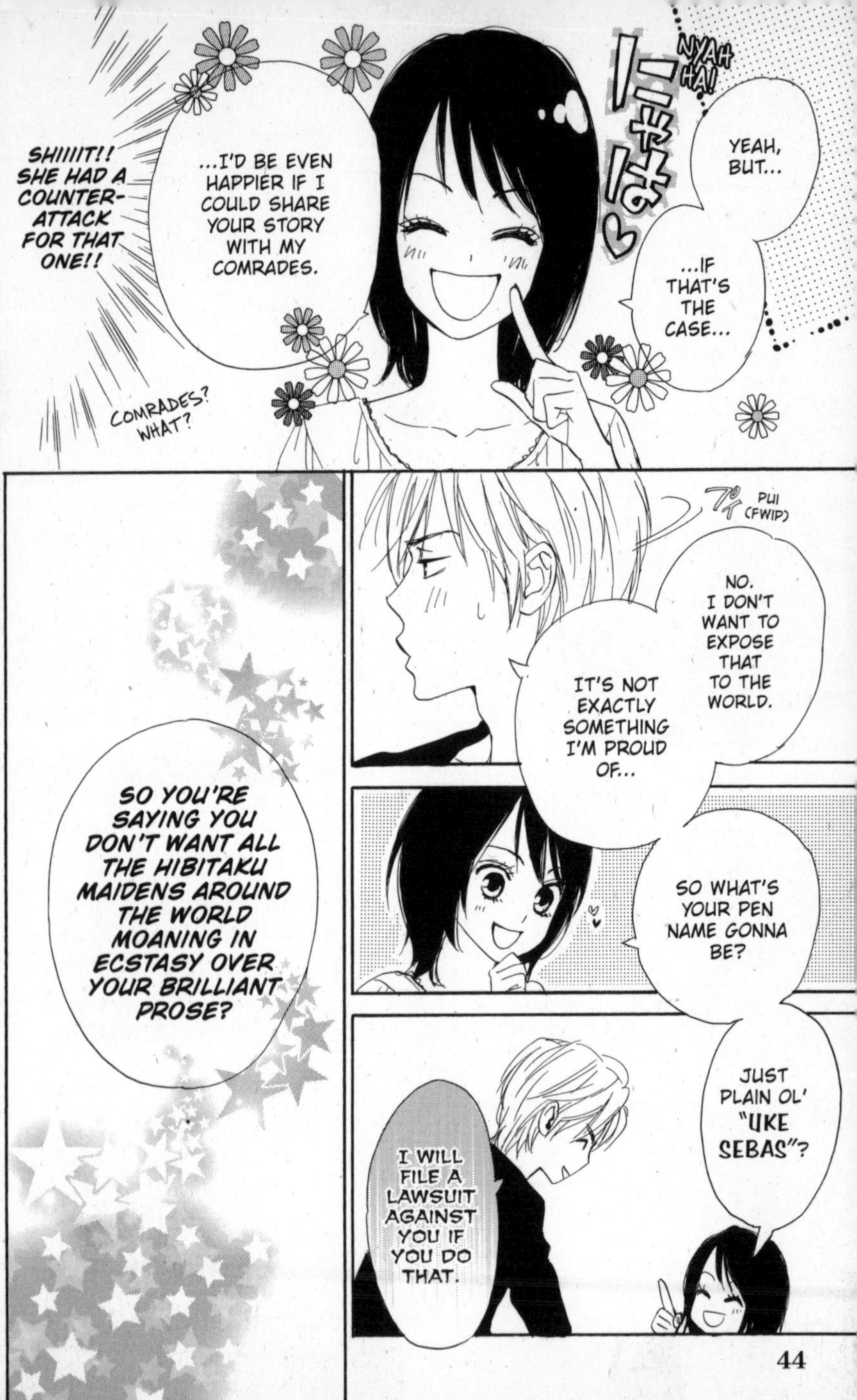
NYAH HA!
にゃは♥
YEAH, BUT...
...IF THAT'S THE CASE...
...I'D BE EVEN HAPPIER IF I COULD SHARE YOUR STORY WITH MY COMRADES.
SHIIIIT!! SHE HAD A COUNTER-ATTACK FOR THAT ONE!!
COMRADES? WHAT?
プイ
PUI (FWIP)
NO. I DON'T WANT TO EXPOSE THAT TO THE WORLD.
IT'S NOT EXACTLY SOMETHING I'M PROUD OF...
SO WHAT'S YOUR PEN NAME GONNA BE?
JUST PLAIN OL' "UKE SEBAS"?
I WILL FILE A LAWSUIT AGAINST YOU IF YOU DO THAT.
SO YOU'RE SAYING YOU DON'T WANT ALL THE HIBITAKU MAIDENS AROUND THE WORLD MOANING IN ECSTASY OVER YOUR BRILLIANT PROSE?

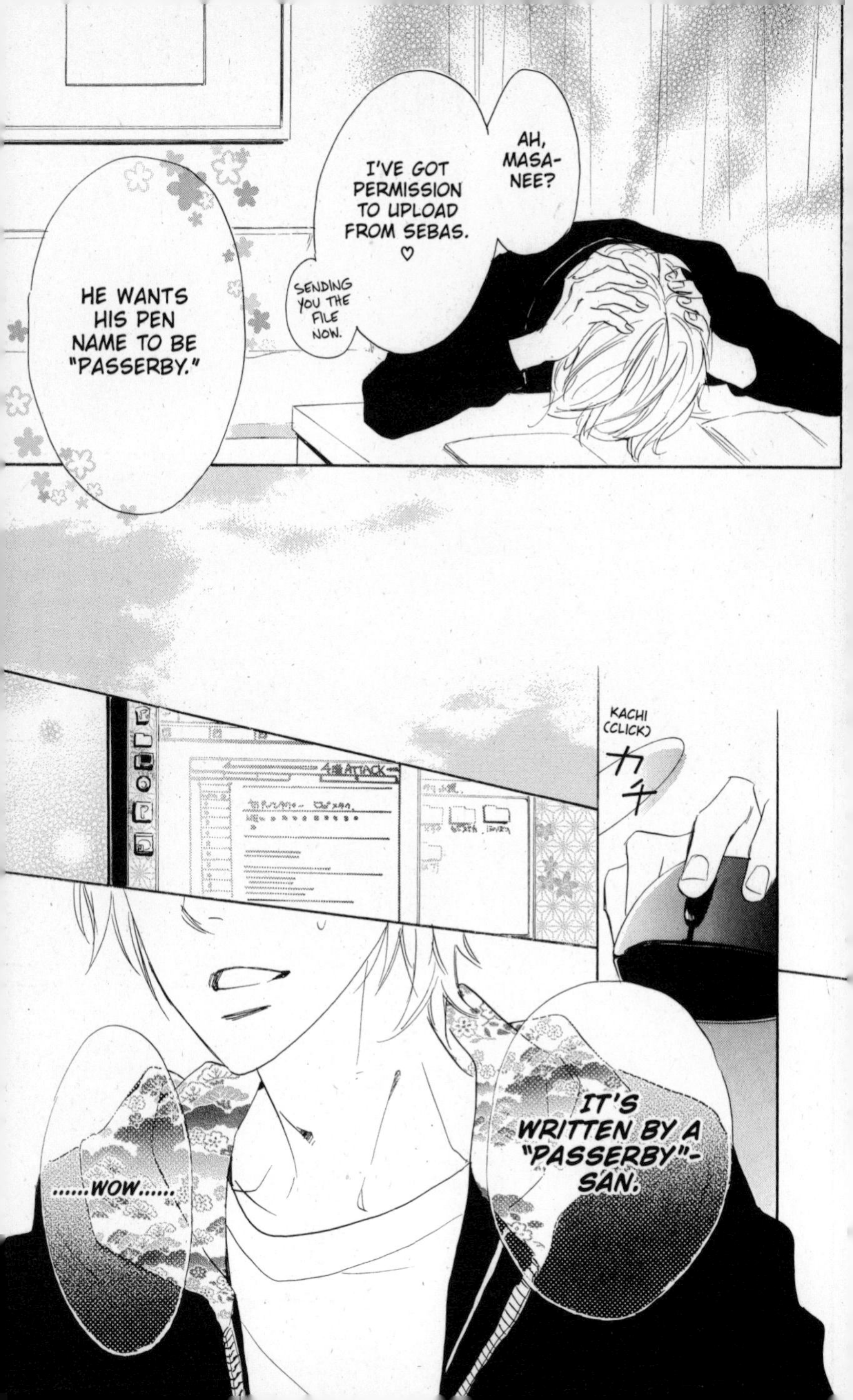
AH, MASA-NEE?
I'VE GOT PERMISSION TO UPLOAD FROM SEBAS. ♡
SENDING YOU THE FILE NOW.
HE WANTS HIS PEN NAME TO BE "PASSERBY."
KACHI (CLICK)
カチ
IT'S WRITTEN BY A "PASSERBY"-SAN.
......WOW......

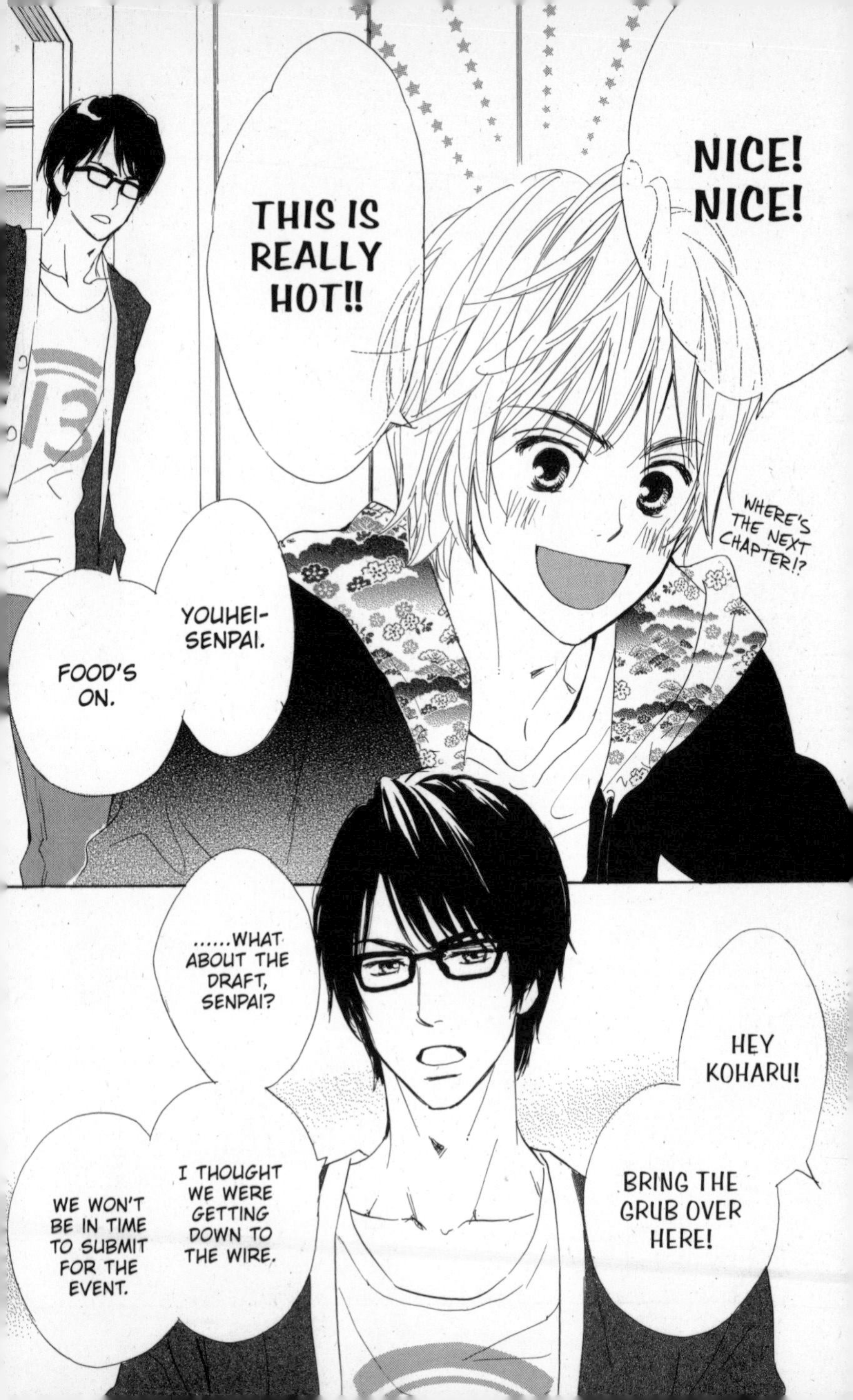
NICE! NICE!
THIS IS REALLY HOT!!
WHERE'S THE NEXT CHAPTER!?
YOUHEI-SENPAI.
FOOD'S ON.
HEY KOHARU!
BRING THE GRUB OVER HERE!
......WHAT ABOUT THE DRAFT, SENPAI?
I THOUGHT WE WERE GETTING DOWN TO THE WIRE.
WE WON'T BE IN TIME TO SUBMIT FOR THE EVENT.

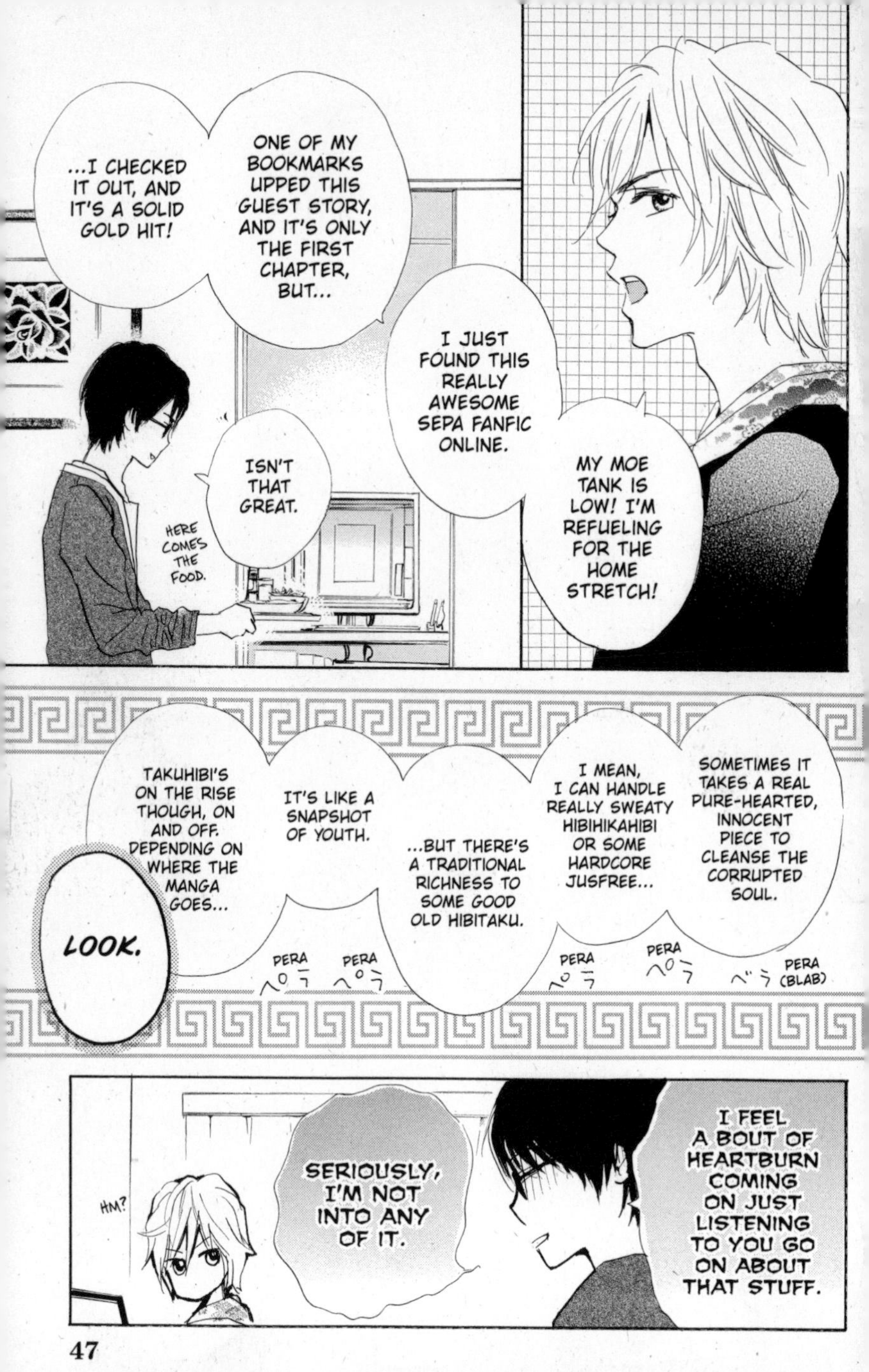

MY MOE TANK IS LOW! I'M REFUELING FOR THE HOME STRETCH!
I JUST FOUND THIS REALLY AWESOME SEPA FANFIC ONLINE.
ONE OF MY BOOKMARKS UPPED THIS GUEST STORY, AND IT'S ONLY THE FIRST CHAPTER, BUT...
...I CHECKED IT OUT, AND IT'S A SOLID GOLD HIT!
ISN'T THAT GREAT.
HERE COMES THE FOOD.
SOMETIMES IT TAKES A REAL PURE-HEARTED, INNOCENT PIECE TO CLEANSE THE CORRUPTED SOUL.
PERA (BLAB)
PERA
I MEAN, I CAN HANDLE REALLY SWEATY HIBIHIKAHIBI OR SOME HARDCORE JUSFREE...
PERA
...BUT THERE'S A TRADITIONAL RICHNESS TO SOME GOOD OLD HIBITAKU.
IT'S LIKE A SNAPSHOT OF YOUTH.
PERA
TAKUHIBI'S ON THE RISE THOUGH, ON AND OFF. DEPENDING ON WHERE THE MANGA GOES...
PERA
LOOK.
I FEEL A BOUT OF HEARTBURN COMING ON JUST LISTENING TO YOU GO ON ABOUT THAT STUFF.
SERIOUSLY, I'M NOT INTO ANY OF IT.
HM?

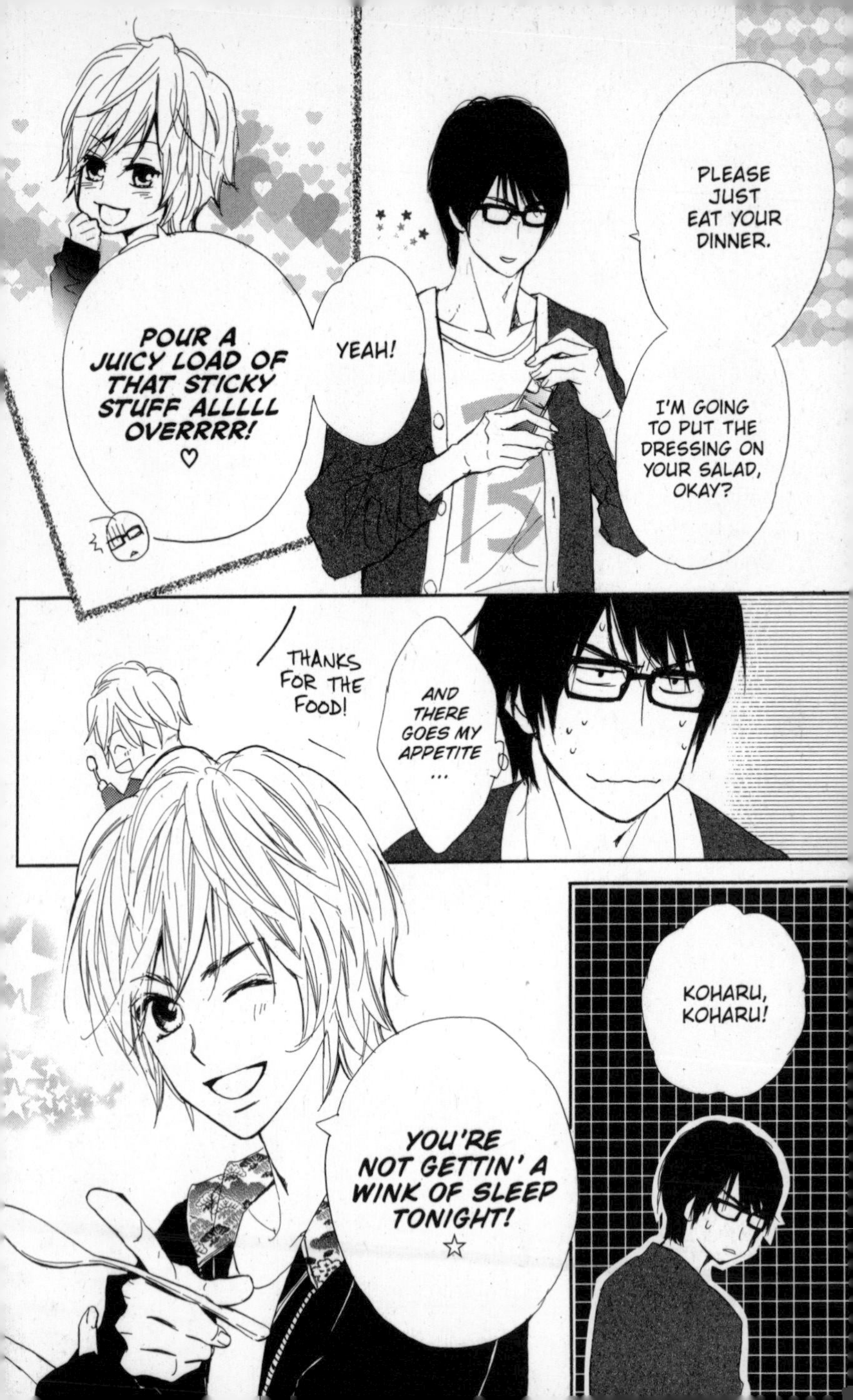
PLEASE JUST EAT YOUR DINNER.
I'M GOING TO PUT THE DRESSING ON YOUR SALAD, OKAY?
YEAH!
POUR A JUICY LOAD OF THAT STICKY STUFF ALLLLL OVERRRR! ♡
AND THERE GOES MY APPETITE ...
THANKS FOR THE FOOD!
KOHARU, KOHARU!
YOU'RE NOT GETTIN' A WINK OF SLEEP TONIGHT! ☆

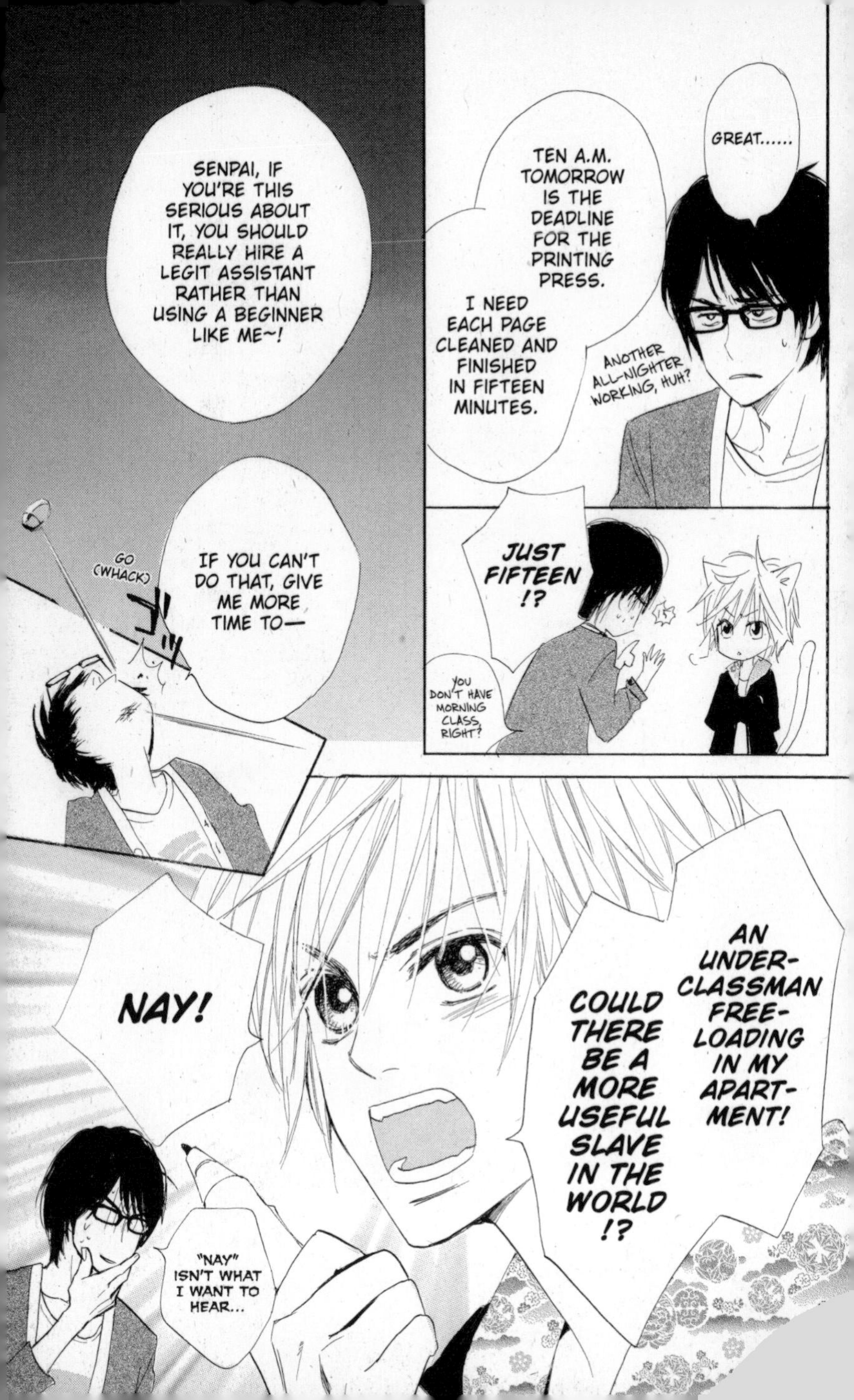
GREAT......
TEN A.M. TOMORROW IS THE DEADLINE FOR THE PRINTING PRESS.
I NEED EACH PAGE CLEANED AND FINISHED IN FIFTEEN MINUTES.
ANOTHER ALL-NIGHTER WORKING, HUH?
JUST FIFTEEN !?
YOU DON'T HAVE MORNING CLASS, RIGHT?
SENPAI, IF YOU'RE THIS SERIOUS ABOUT IT, YOU SHOULD REALLY HIRE A LEGIT ASSISTANT RATHER THAN USING A BEGINNER LIKE ME~!
IF YOU CAN'T DO THAT, GIVE ME MORE TIME TO—
GO (WHACK)
AN UNDER-CLASSMAN FREE-LOADING IN MY APART-MENT!
COULD THERE BE A MORE USEFUL SLAVE IN THE WORLD !?
NAY!
"NAY" ISN'T WHAT I WANT TO HEAR...

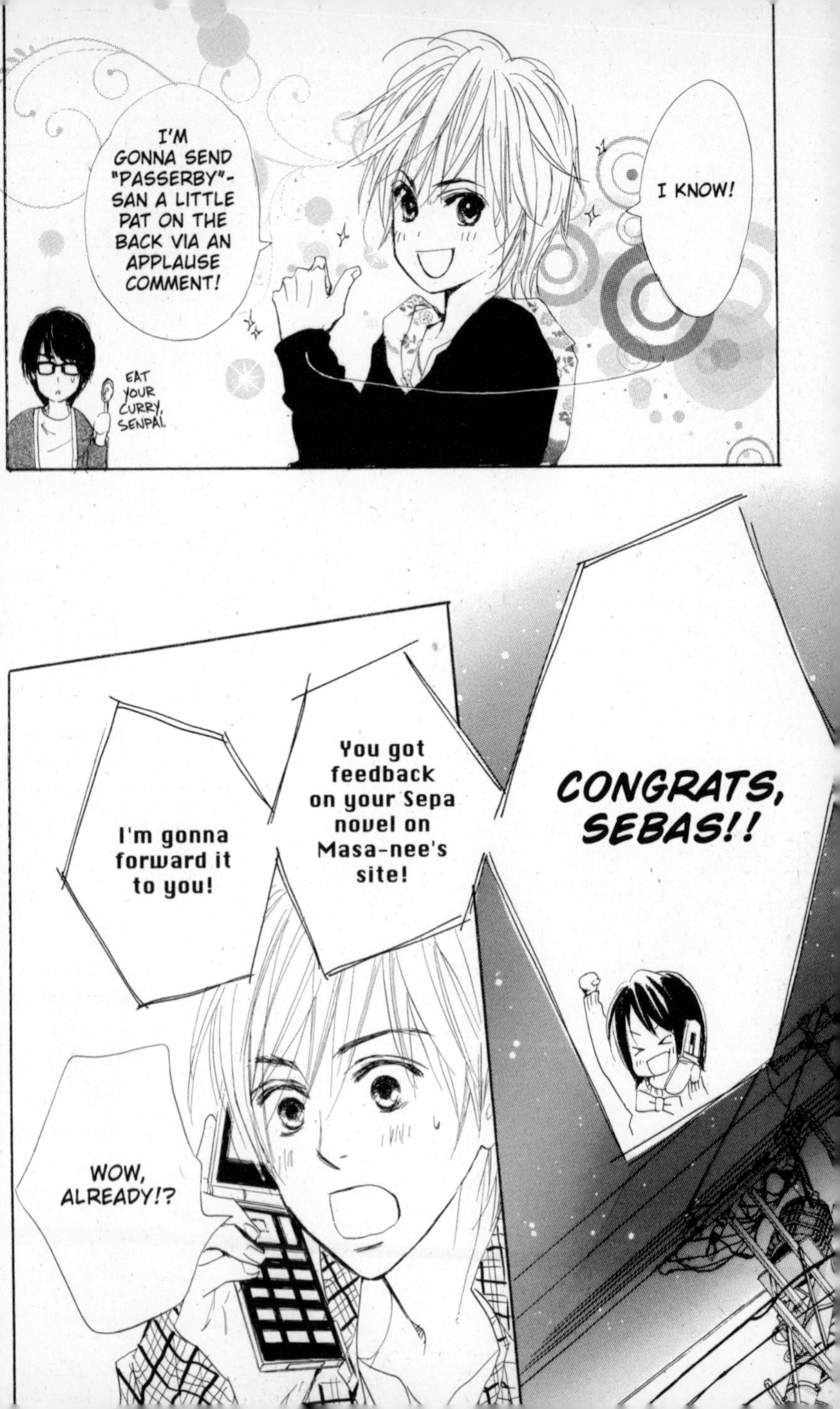
I KNOW!
I'M GONNA SEND "PASSERBY"-SAN A LITTLE PAT ON THE BACK VIA AN APPLAUSE COMMENT!
EAT YOUR CURRY, SENPAI.
CONGRATS, SEBAS!!
You got feedback on your Sepa novel on Masa-nee's site!
I'm gonna forward it to you!
WOW, ALREADY!?

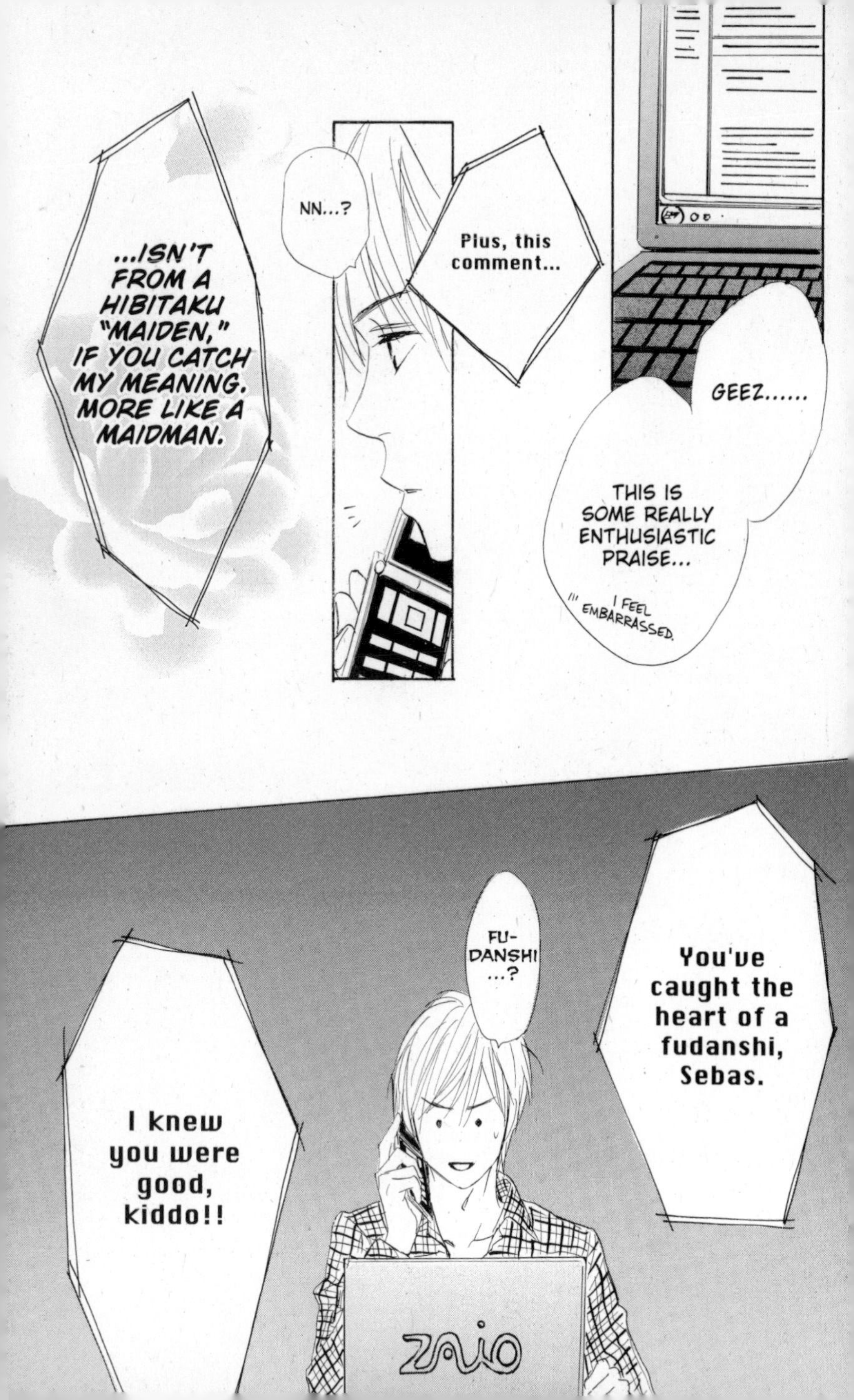
GEEZ......
THIS IS SOME REALLY ENTHUSIASTIC PRAISE...
I FEEL EMBARRASSED.
Plus, this comment...
NN...?
...ISN'T FROM A HIBITAKU "MAIDEN," IF YOU CATCH MY MEANING. MORE LIKE A MAIDMAN.
You've caught the heart of a fudanshi, Sebas.
FU-DANSHI ...?
I knew you were good, kiddo!!
ZAIO

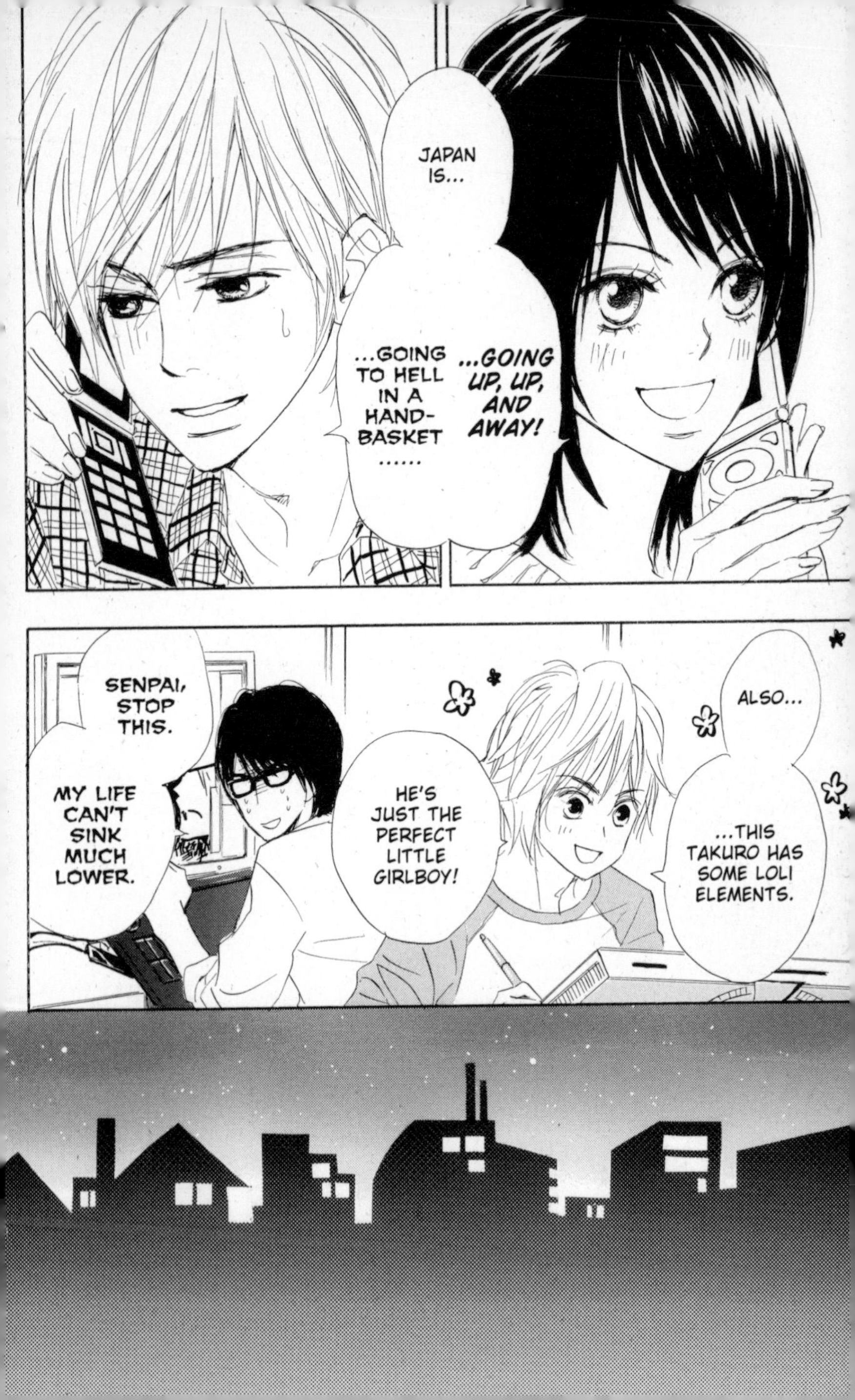
JAPAN IS...
...GOING UP, UP, AND AWAY!
...GOING TO HELL IN A HAND-BASKET ......
ALSO...
...THIS TAKURO HAS SOME LOLI ELEMENTS.
HE'S JUST THE PERFECT LITTLE GIRLBOY!
SENPAI, STOP THIS.
MY LIFE CAN'T SINK MUCH LOWER.

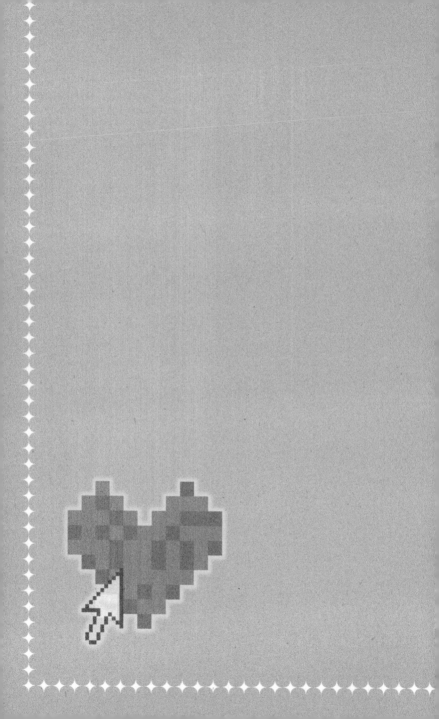

FUJOSHI NEWS vol.14

ROUGH SKETCHES & CHARACTER DESIGNS

SHINBA-SENSEI SKETCHED THESE DESIGNS BEFORE THE MANGA BEGAN. WHAT SUBTLE DIFFERENCES CAN YOU SPOT? TAKE A GOOD CLOSE LOOK!

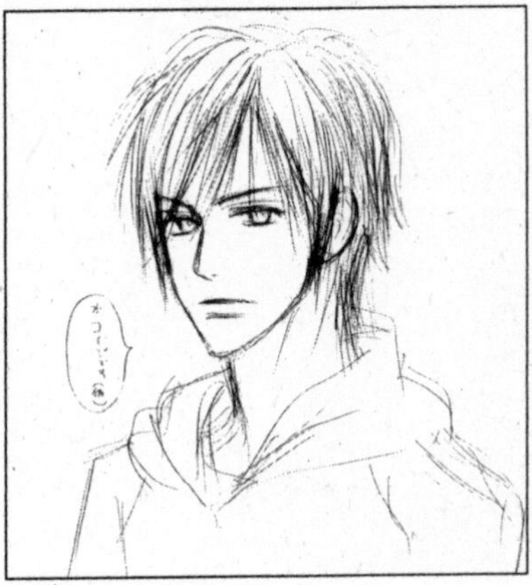

▲KOUJI'S PROTOTYPE. HE SEEMS EVEN MORE COOL AND SEVERE THAN THE KOUJI WE KNOW! AT THE TIME, "KOUJI" WAS STILL A TEMPORARY NAME.

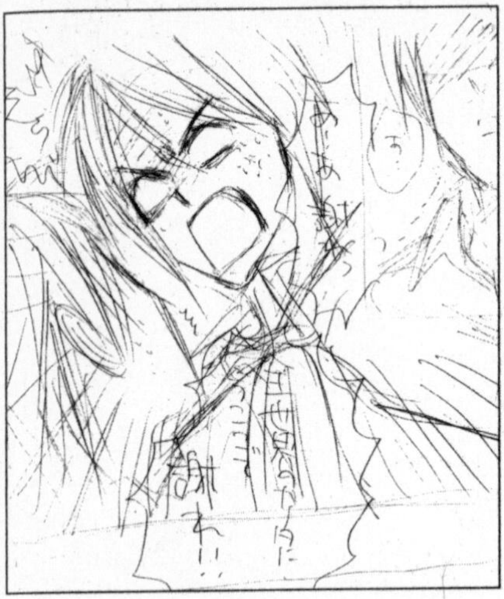

▲"APOLOGIZE TO EVERY GUNOTA (GUNDAM OTAKU) IN THE NATION!!" YUIKO-SAN SCREAMS AT TAIGA, HIS SHIRT IN HAND. IS IT ME, OR DOES SHE LOOK MORE VIOLENT THAN USUAL!?

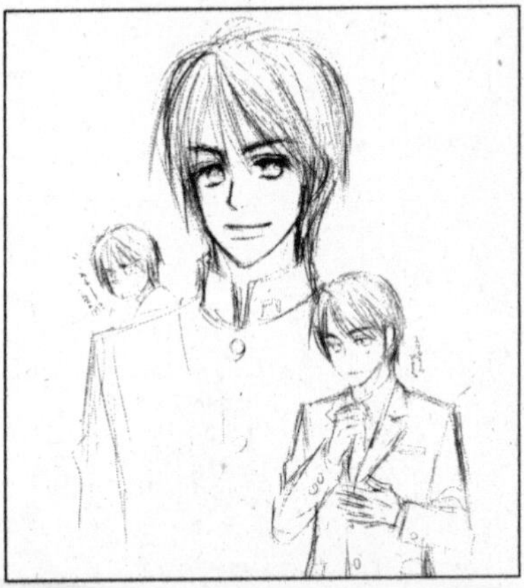

▲TAIGA COSPLAYING IN A SCHOOL UNIFORM AND IN A SUIT. HE SEEMS YOUNGER THAN HE DOES NOW. WAS THIS A DRESS REHEARSAL FOR HIS UNIFORM COSPLAY IN THE FINAL CHAPTER?

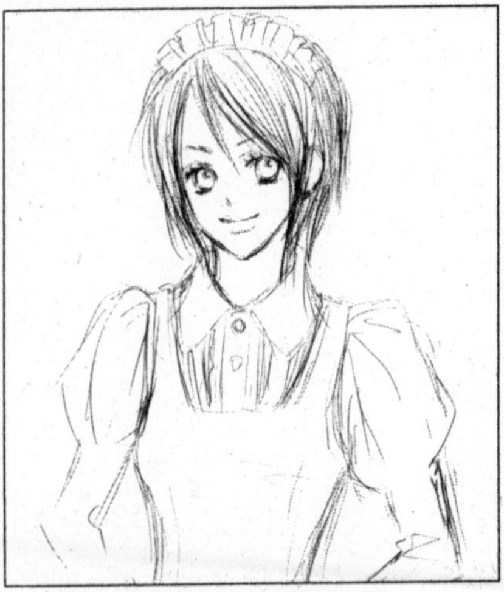

▲YUIKO-SAN IN MAID COSPLAY. HER HAIR'S A BIT LONGER, AND THERE'S SOMETHING A BIT...DEVILISH ABOUT HER! THE HEADBAND LOOKS GREAT. ♪

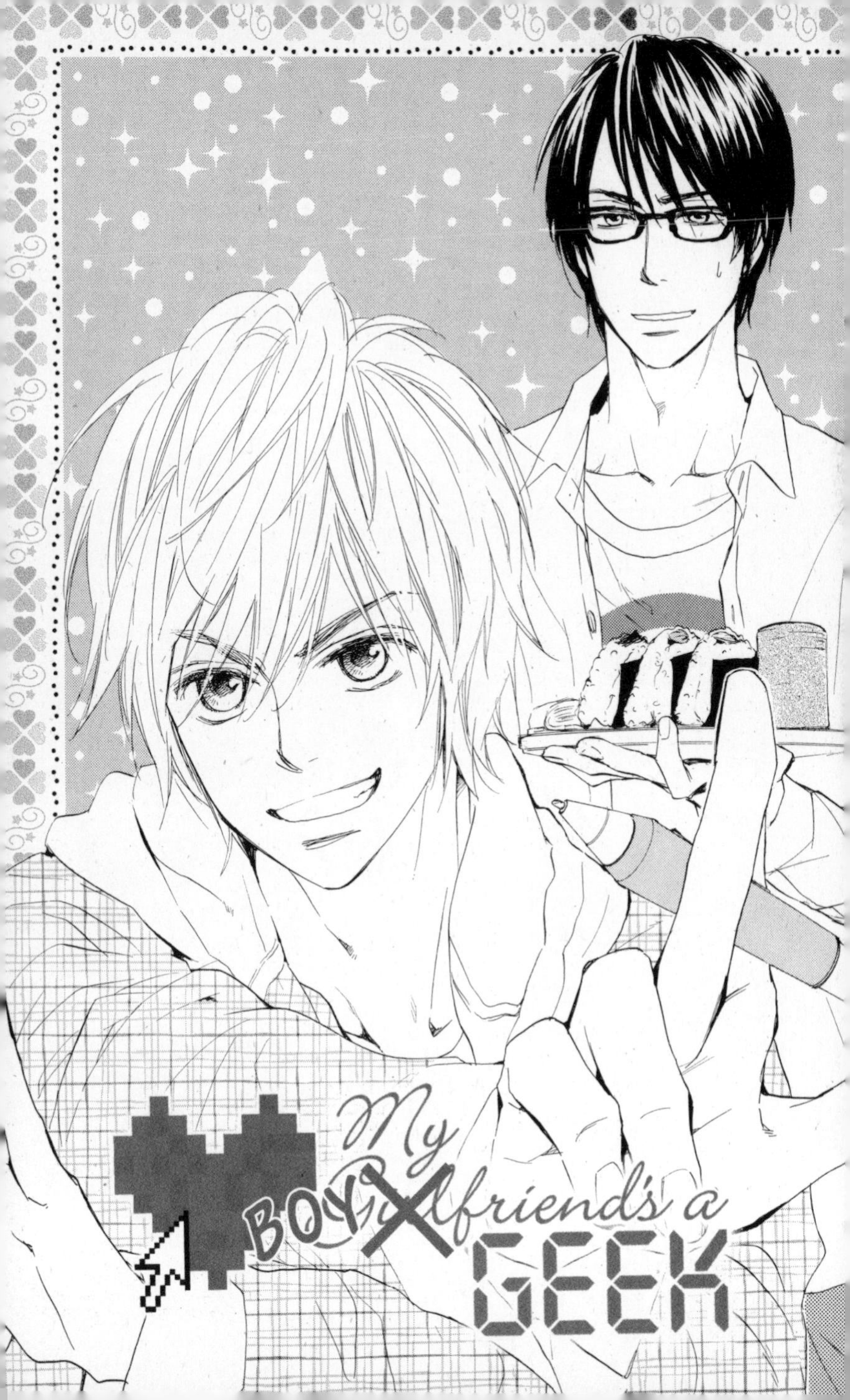
My BOYfriend's a GEEK

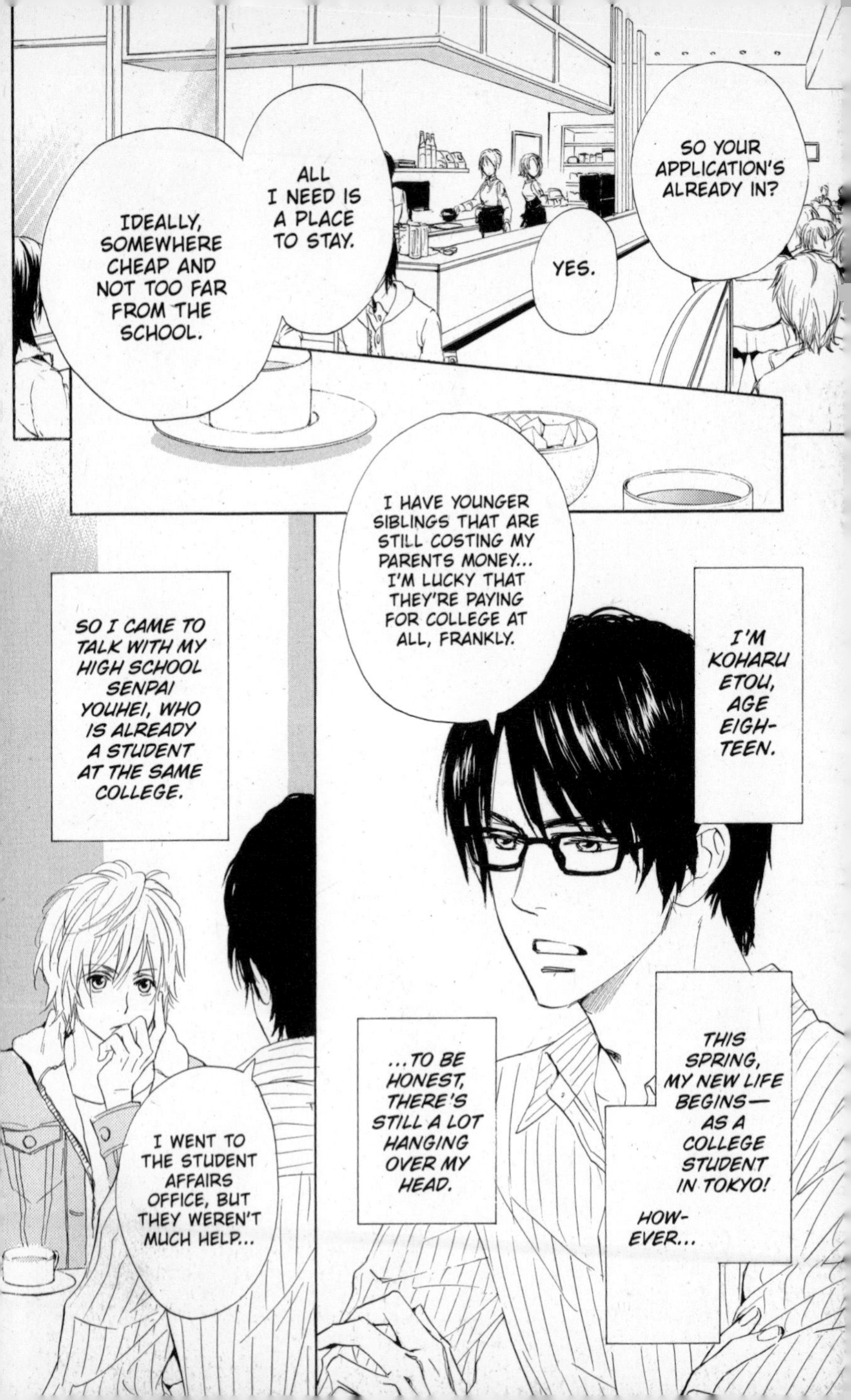
SO YOUR APPLICATION'S ALREADY IN?
YES.
ALL I NEED IS A PLACE TO STAY.
IDEALLY, SOMEWHERE CHEAP AND NOT TOO FAR FROM THE SCHOOL.
I HAVE YOUNGER SIBLINGS THAT ARE STILL COSTING MY PARENTS MONEY... I'M LUCKY THAT THEY'RE PAYING FOR COLLEGE AT ALL, FRANKLY.
I'M KOHARU ETOU, AGE EIGH-TEEN.
THIS SPRING, MY NEW LIFE BEGINS—AS A COLLEGE STUDENT IN TOKYO!
HOW-EVER...
...TO BE HONEST, THERE'S STILL A LOT HANGING OVER MY HEAD.
SO I CAME TO TALK WITH MY HIGH SCHOOL SENPAI YOUHEI, WHO IS ALREADY A STUDENT AT THE SAME COLLEGE.
I WENT TO THE STUDENT AFFAIRS OFFICE, BUT THEY WEREN'T MUCH HELP...

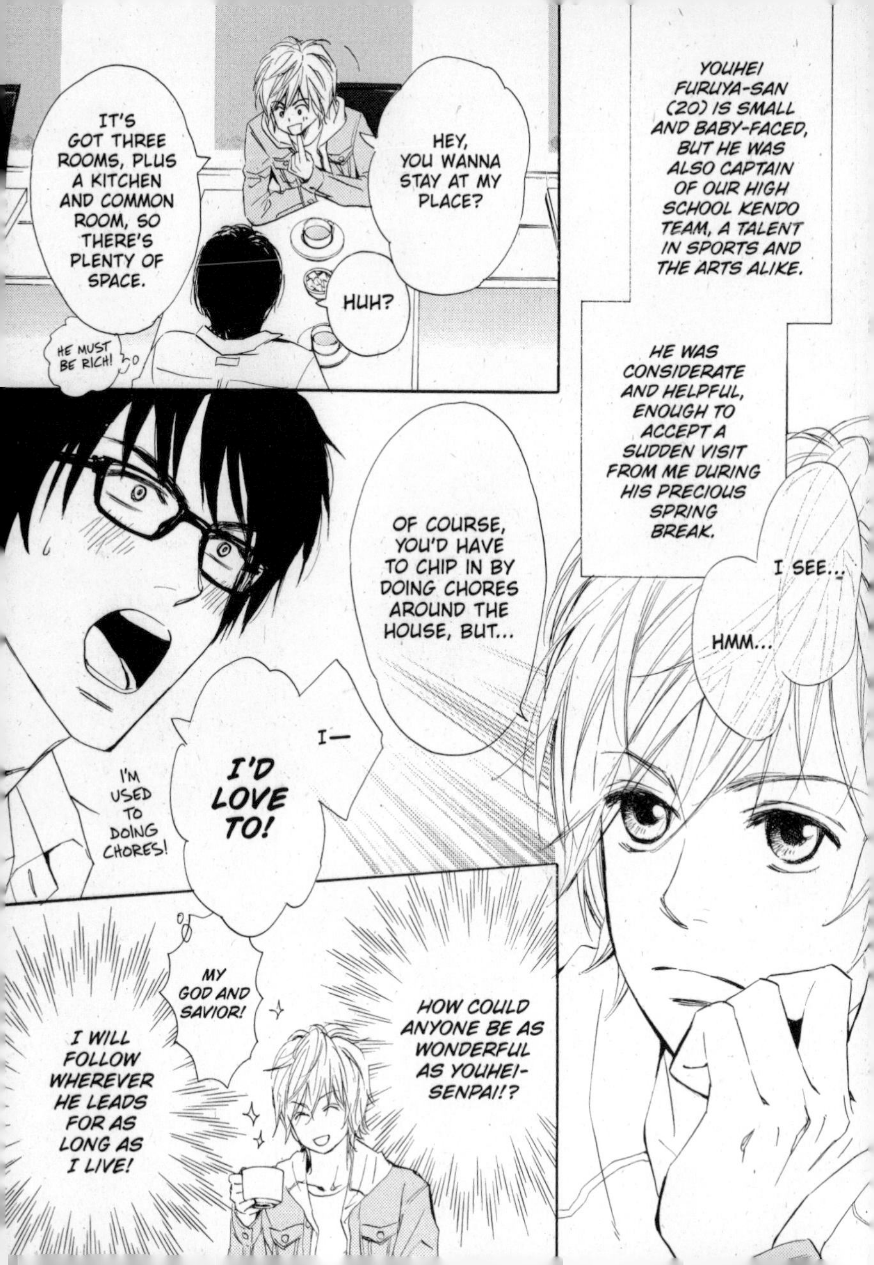
YOUHEI FURUYA-SAN (20) IS SMALL AND BABY-FACED, BUT HE WAS ALSO CAPTAIN OF OUR HIGH SCHOOL KENDO TEAM, A TALENT IN SPORTS AND THE ARTS ALIKE.
HE WAS CONSIDERATE AND HELPFUL, ENOUGH TO ACCEPT A SUDDEN VISIT FROM ME DURING HIS PRECIOUS SPRING BREAK.
I SEE...
HMM...
HEY, YOU WANNA STAY AT MY PLACE?
HUH?
IT'S GOT THREE ROOMS, PLUS A KITCHEN AND COMMON ROOM, SO THERE'S PLENTY OF SPACE.
HE MUST BE RICH!
OF COURSE, YOU'D HAVE TO CHIP IN BY DOING CHORES AROUND THE HOUSE, BUT...
I—
I'D LOVE TO!
I'M USED TO DOING CHORES!
HOW COULD ANYONE BE AS WONDERFUL AS YOUHEI-SENPAI!?
MY GOD AND SAVIOR!
I WILL FOLLOW WHEREVER HE LEADS FOR AS LONG AS I LIVE!

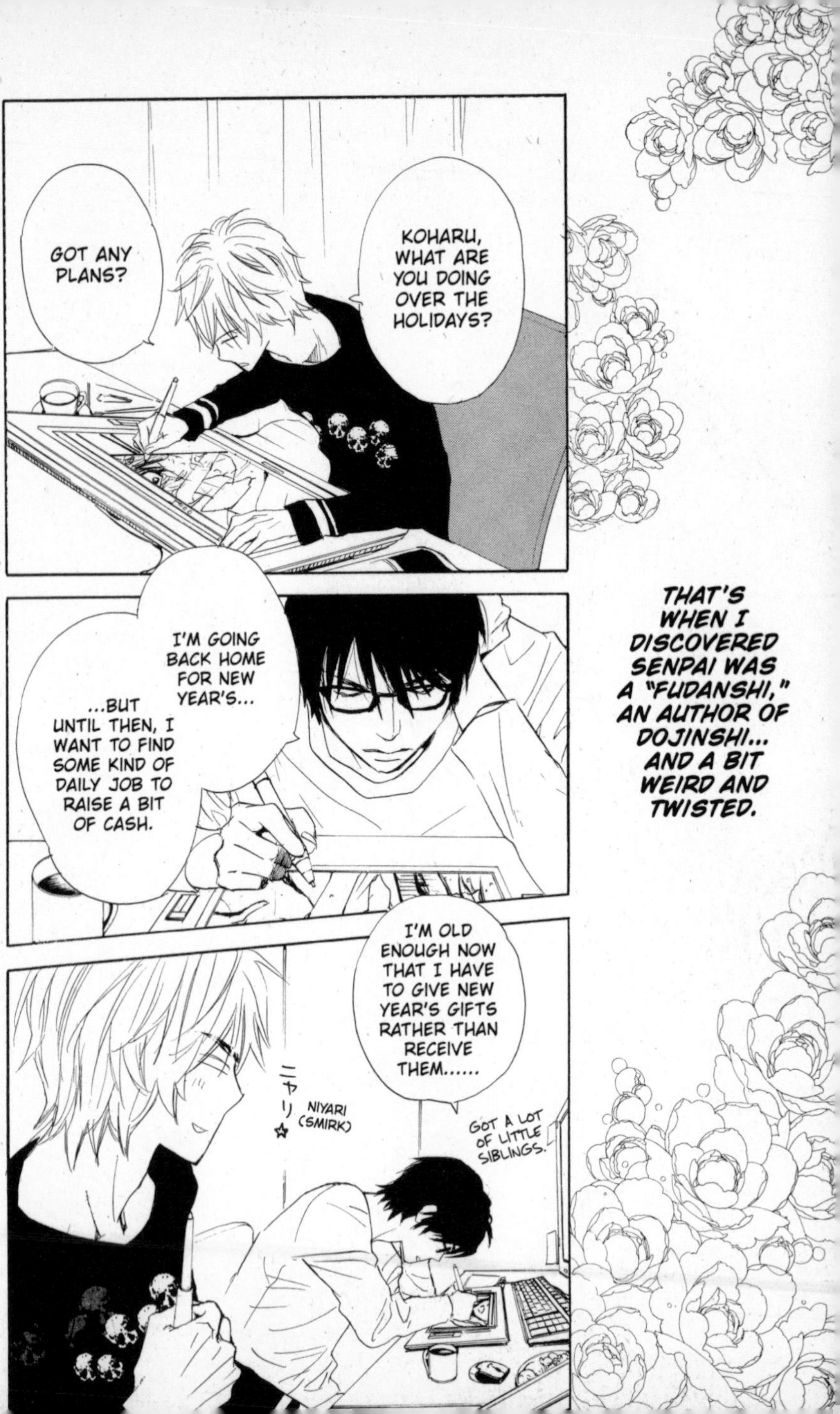
THAT'S WHEN I DISCOVERED SENPAI WAS A "FUDANSHI," AN AUTHOR OF DOJINSHI... AND A BIT WEIRD AND TWISTED.
KOHARU, WHAT ARE YOU DOING OVER THE HOLIDAYS?
GOT ANY PLANS?
I'M GOING BACK HOME FOR NEW YEAR'S...
...BUT UNTIL THEN, I WANT TO FIND SOME KIND OF DAILY JOB TO RAISE A BIT OF CASH.
I'M OLD ENOUGH NOW THAT I HAVE TO GIVE NEW YEAR'S GIFTS RATHER THAN RECEIVE THEM......
GOT A LOT OF LITTLE SIBLINGS.
ニヤリ☆
NIYARI (SMIRK)

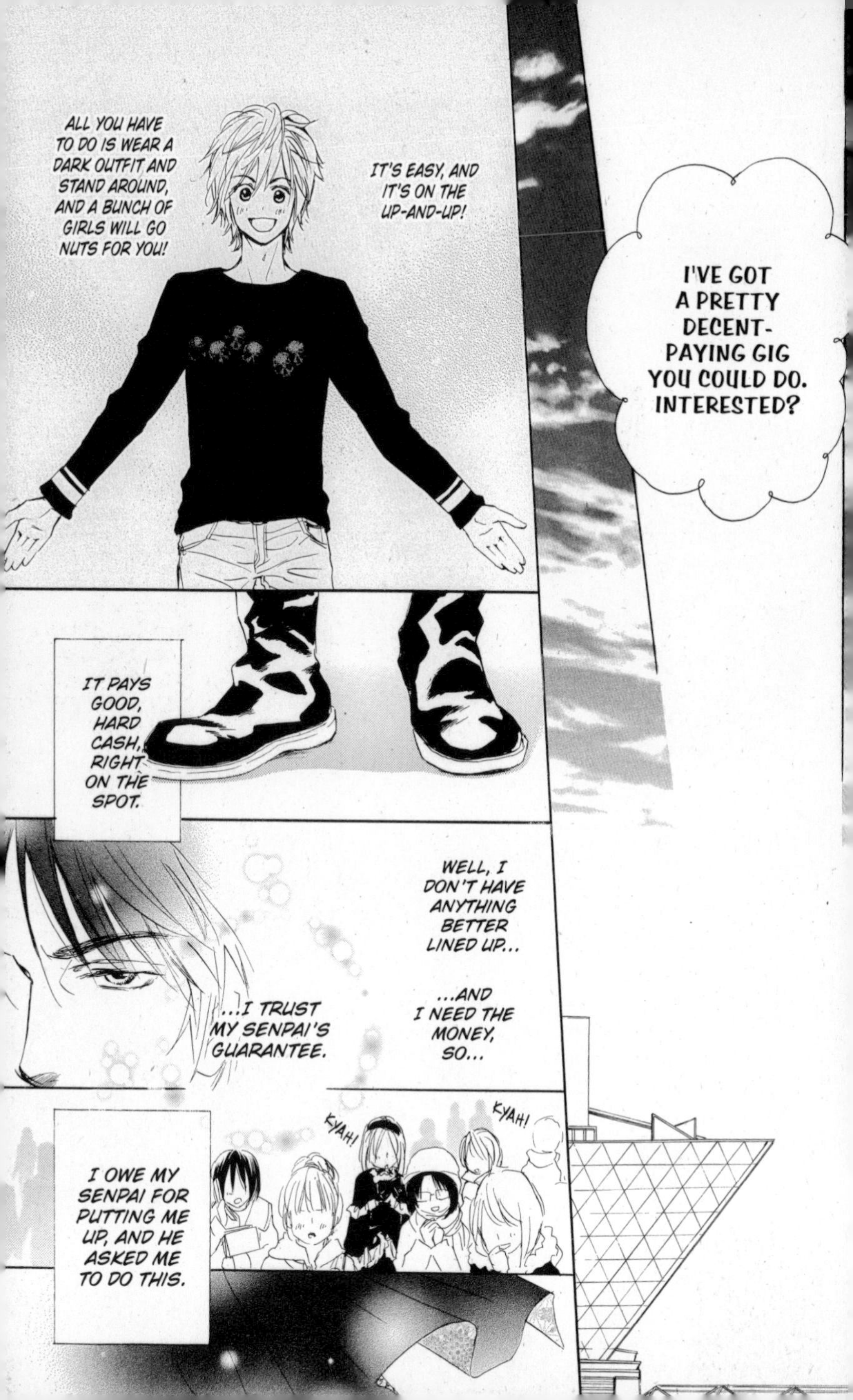
I'VE GOT A PRETTY DECENT-PAYING GIG YOU COULD DO. INTERESTED?
IT'S EASY, AND IT'S ON THE UP-AND-UP!
ALL YOU HAVE TO DO IS WEAR A DARK OUTFIT AND STAND AROUND, AND A BUNCH OF GIRLS WILL GO NUTS FOR YOU!
IT PAYS GOOD, HARD CASH, RIGHT ON THE SPOT.
WELL, I DON'T HAVE ANYTHING BETTER LINED UP...
...AND I NEED THE MONEY, SO...
...I TRUST MY SENPAI'S GUARANTEE.
KYAH!
KYAH!
I OWE MY SENPAI FOR PUTTING ME UP, AND HE ASKED ME TO DO THIS.

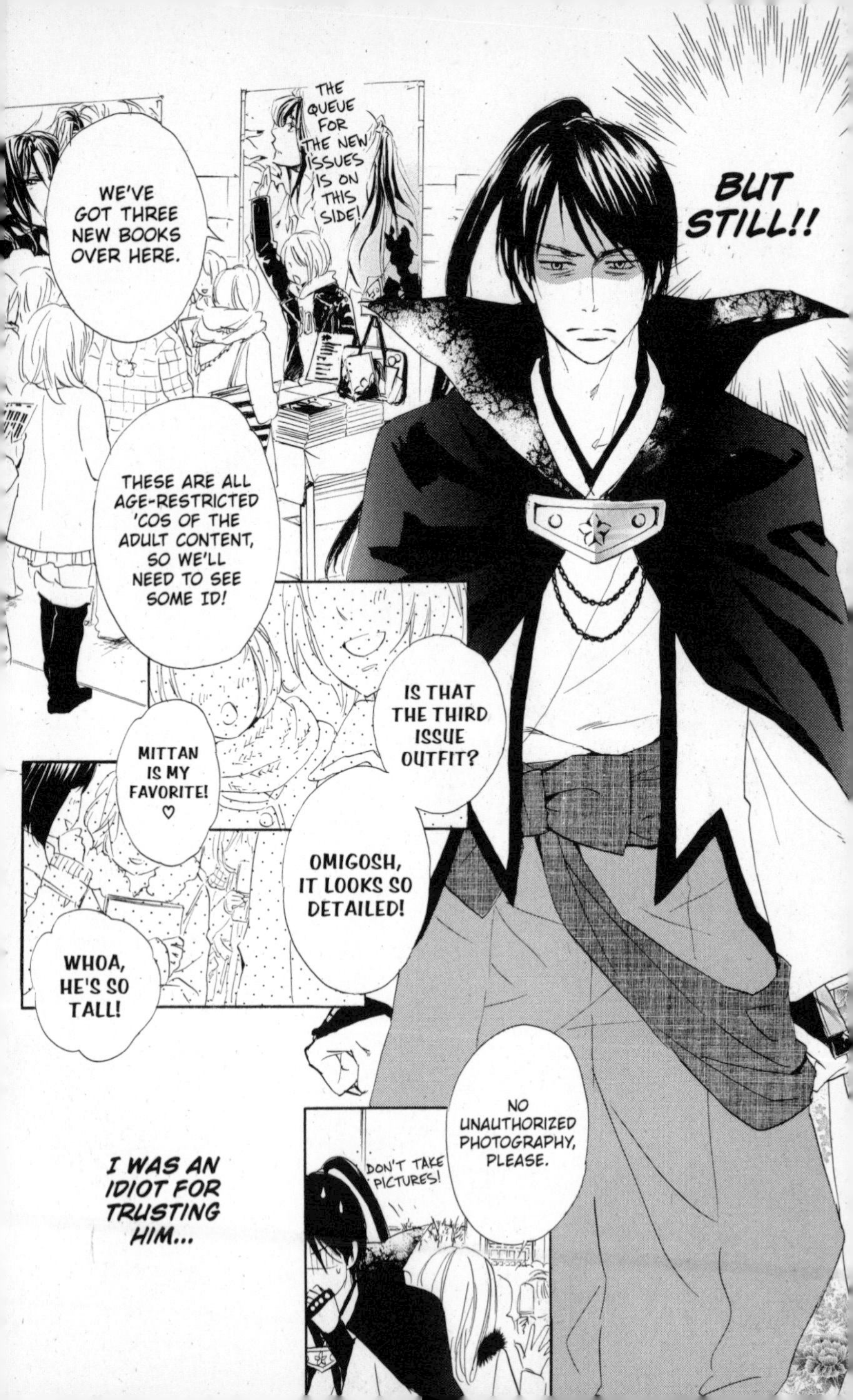
BUT STILL!!
THE QUEUE FOR THE NEW ISSUES IS ON THIS SIDE!
WE'VE GOT THREE NEW BOOKS OVER HERE.
THESE ARE ALL AGE-RESTRICTED 'COS OF THE ADULT CONTENT, SO WE'LL NEED TO SEE SOME ID!
IS THAT THE THIRD ISSUE OUTFIT?
MITTAN IS MY FAVORITE! ♡
OMIGOSH, IT LOOKS SO DETAILED!
WHOA, HE'S SO TALL!
NO UNAUTHORIZED PHOTOGRAPHY, PLEASE.
DON'T TAKE PICTURES!
I WAS AN IDIOT FOR TRUSTING HIM...

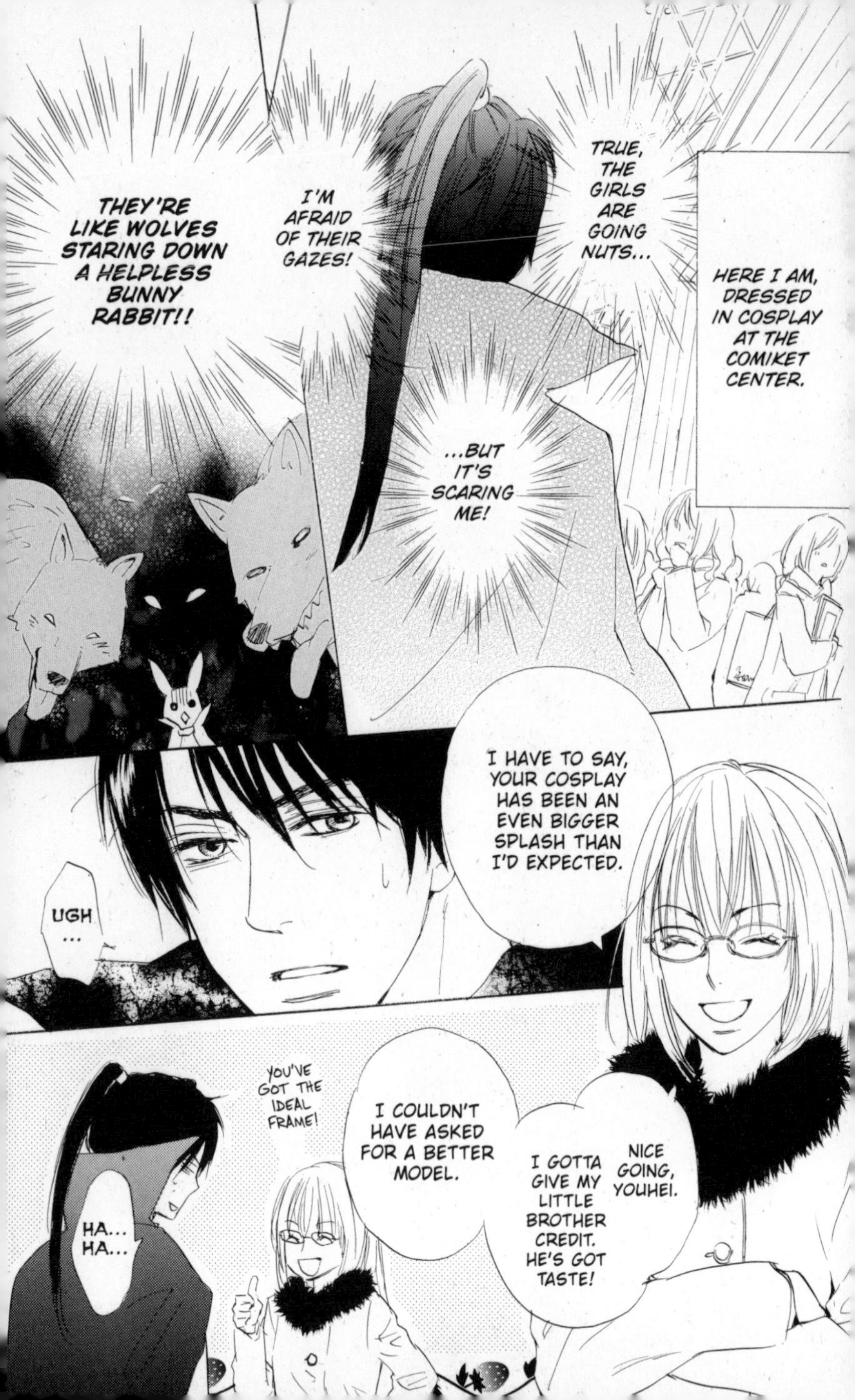
HERE I AM, DRESSED IN COSPLAY AT THE COMIKET CENTER.
TRUE, THE GIRLS ARE GOING NUTS...
...BUT IT'S SCARING ME!
I'M AFRAID OF THEIR GAZES!
THEY'RE LIKE WOLVES STARING DOWN A HELPLESS BUNNY RABBIT!!
I HAVE TO SAY, YOUR COSPLAY HAS BEEN AN EVEN BIGGER SPLASH THAN I'D EXPECTED.
UGH...
NICE GOING, YOUHEI.
I GOTTA GIVE MY LITTLE BROTHER CREDIT. HE'S GOT TASTE!
I COULDN'T HAVE ASKED FOR A BETTER MODEL.
YOU'VE GOT THE IDEAL FRAME!
HA... HA...

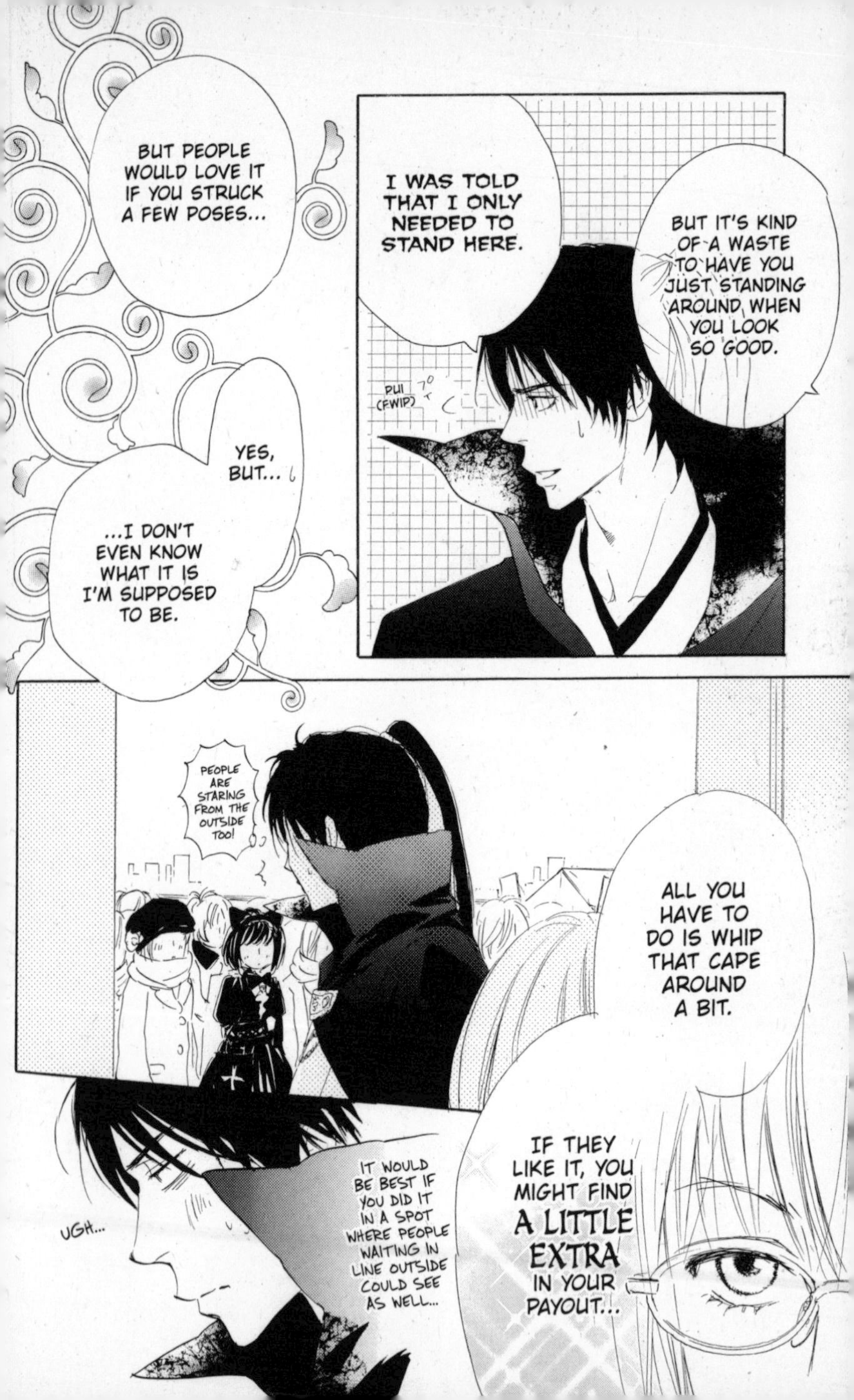
I WAS TOLD THAT I ONLY NEEDED TO STAND HERE.
BUT IT'S KIND OF A WASTE TO HAVE YOU JUST STANDING AROUND WHEN YOU LOOK SO GOOD.
PUI (FWIP)
BUT PEOPLE WOULD LOVE IT IF YOU STRUCK A FEW POSES...
YES, BUT...
...I DON'T EVEN KNOW WHAT IT IS I'M SUPPOSED TO BE.
PEOPLE ARE STARING FROM THE OUTSIDE TOO!
ALL YOU HAVE TO DO IS WHIP THAT CAPE AROUND A BIT.
IF THEY LIKE IT, YOU MIGHT FIND A LITTLE EXTRA IN YOUR PAYOUT...
IT WOULD BE BEST IF YOU DID IT IN A SPOT WHERE PEOPLE WAITING IN LINE OUTSIDE COULD SEE AS WELL...
UGH...

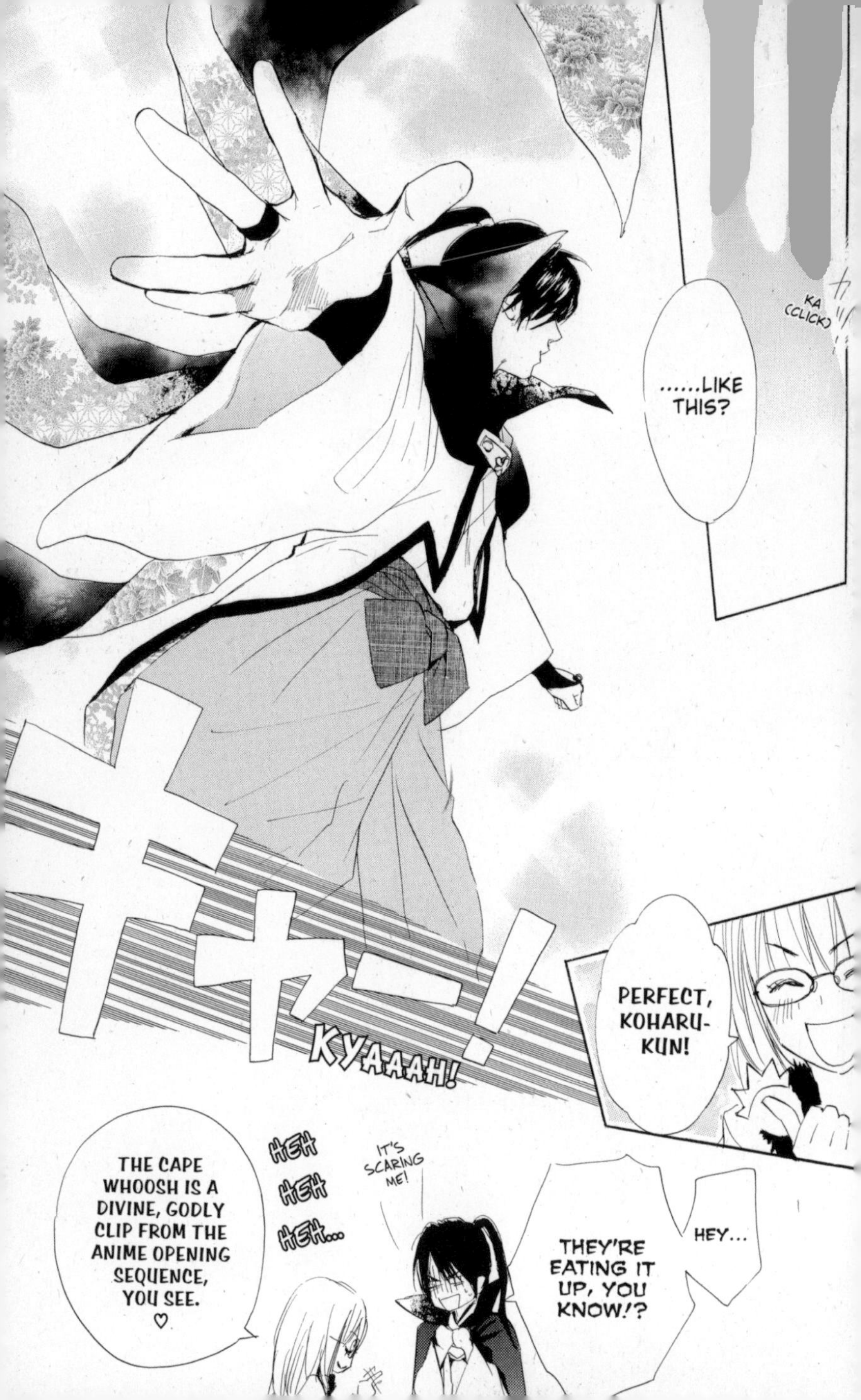

KA (CLICK)
......LIKE THIS?
キャー！
KYAAAH!
PERFECT, KOHARU-KUN!
HEY...
THEY'RE EATING IT UP, YOU KNOW!?
IT'S SCARING ME!
HEH HEH HEH...
THE CAPE WHOOSH IS A DIVINE, GODLY CLIP FROM THE ANIME OPENING SEQUENCE, YOU SEE. ♡

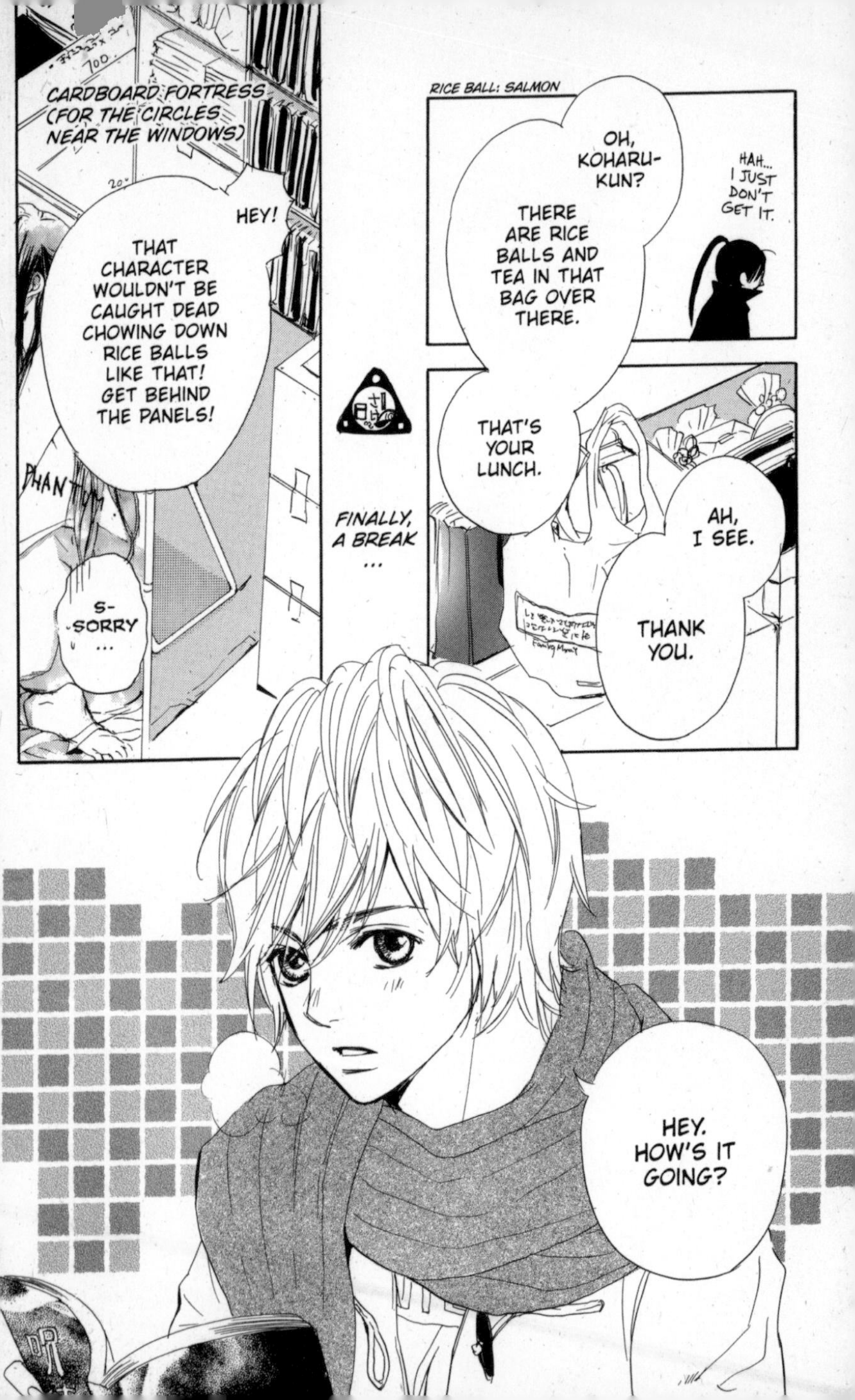
RICE BALL: SALMON
HAH... I JUST DON'T GET IT.
OH, KOHARU-KUN? THERE ARE RICE BALLS AND TEA IN THAT BAG OVER THERE.
THAT'S YOUR LUNCH.
AH, I SEE. THANK YOU.
FINALLY, A BREAK ...
CARDBOARD FORTRESS (FOR THE CIRCLES NEAR THE WINDOWS)
HEY!
THAT CHARACTER WOULDN'T BE CAUGHT DEAD CHOWING DOWN RICE BALLS LIKE THAT! GET BEHIND THE PANELS!
PHANTUM
S-SORRY ...
HEY. HOW'S IT GOING?

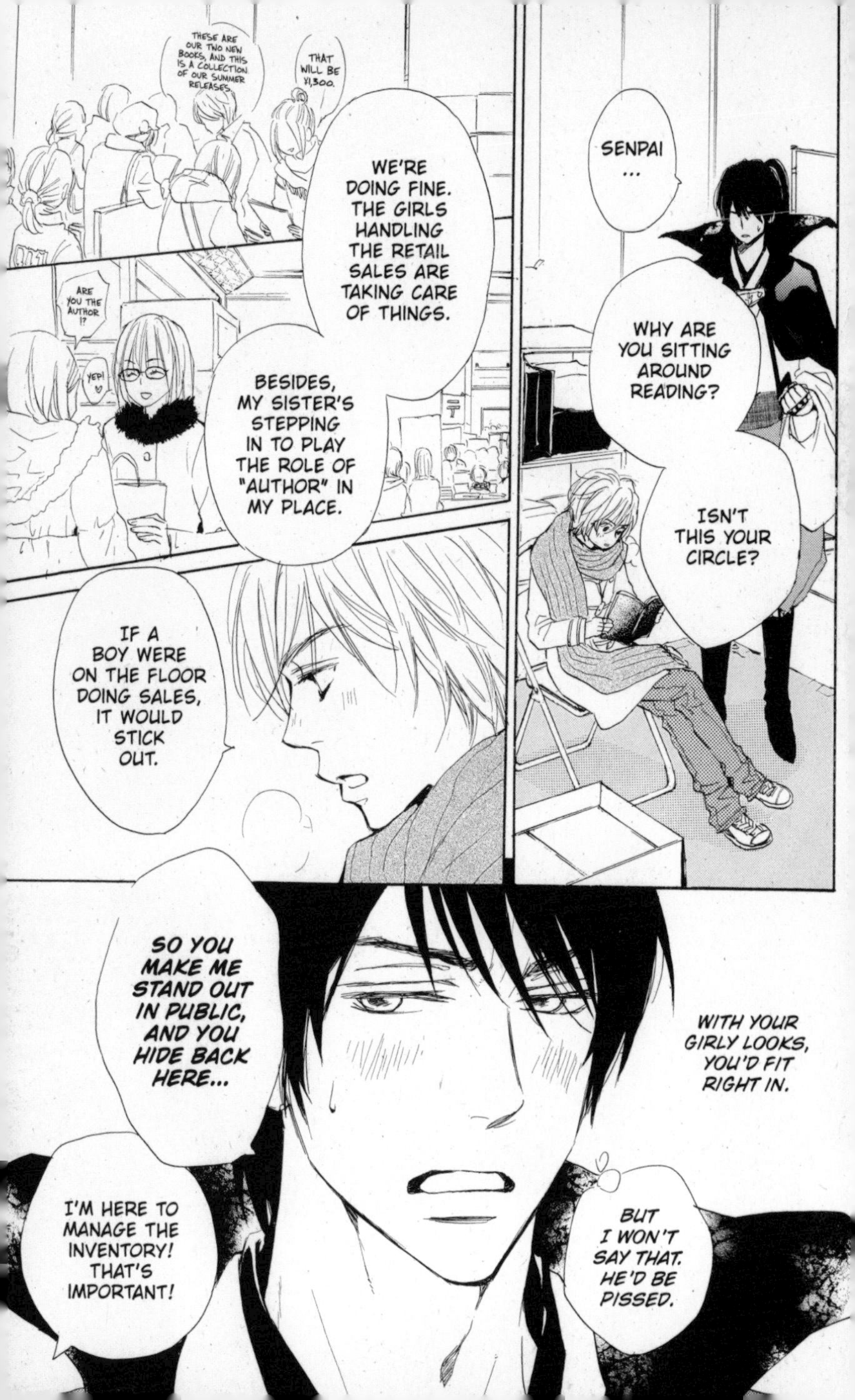

SENPAI...
WHY ARE YOU SITTING AROUND READING?
ISN'T THIS YOUR CIRCLE?
THESE ARE OUR TWO NEW BOOKS, AND THIS IS A COLLECTION OF OUR SUMMER RELEASES.
THAT WILL BE ¥1,300.
WE'RE DOING FINE. THE GIRLS HANDLING THE RETAIL SALES ARE TAKING CARE OF THINGS.
ARE YOU THE AUTHOR!?
YEP! ♡
BESIDES, MY SISTER'S STEPPING IN TO PLAY THE ROLE OF "AUTHOR" IN MY PLACE.
IF A BOY WERE ON THE FLOOR DOING SALES, IT WOULD STICK OUT.
SO YOU MAKE ME STAND OUT IN PUBLIC, AND YOU HIDE BACK HERE...
WITH YOUR GIRLY LOOKS, YOU'D FIT RIGHT IN.
I'M HERE TO MANAGE THE INVENTORY! THAT'S IMPORTANT!
BUT I WON'T SAY THAT. HE'D BE PISSED.

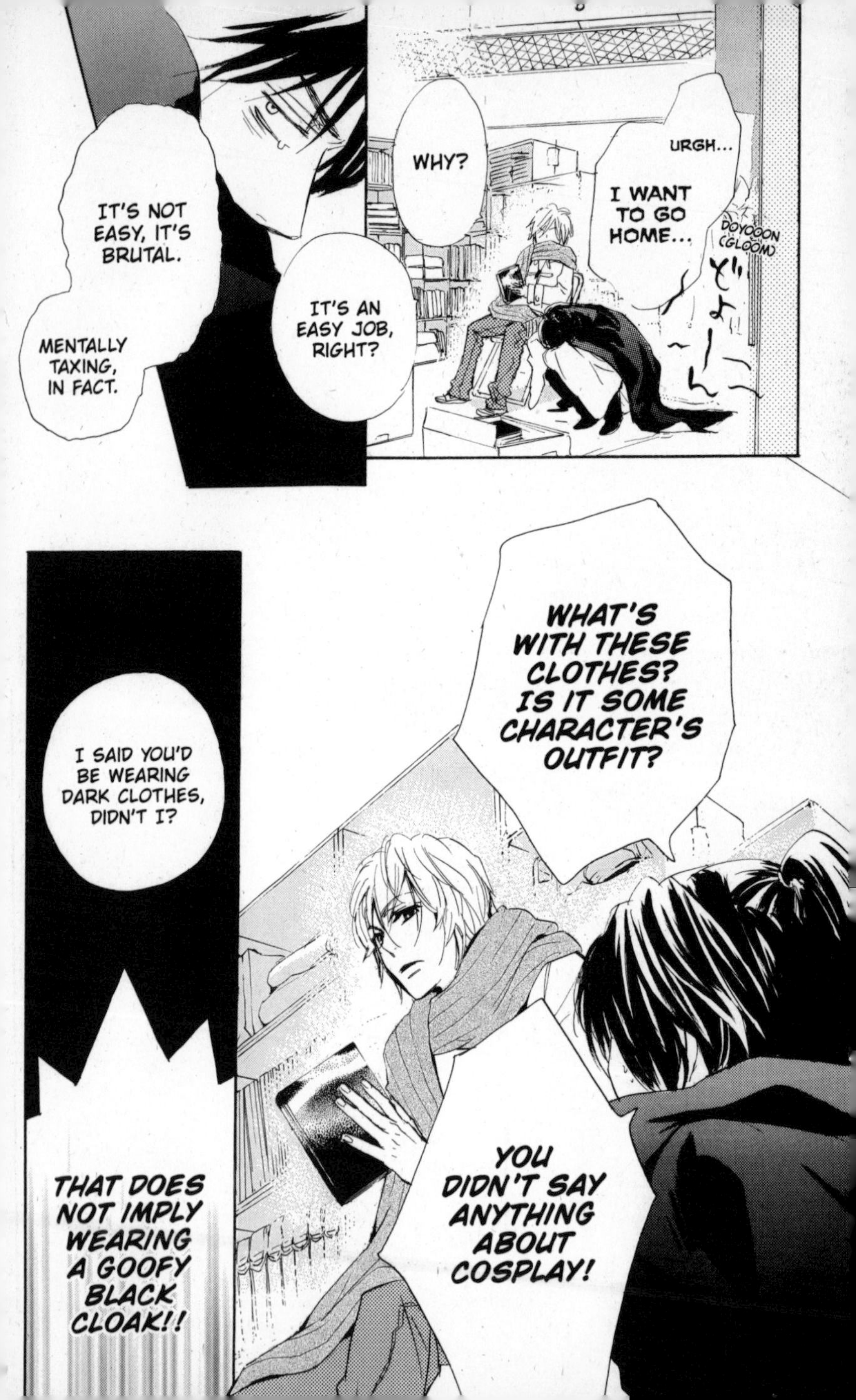
URGH...
I WANT TO GO HOME...
DOYOOON (GLOOM)
どよ～ん
WHY?
IT'S AN EASY JOB, RIGHT?
IT'S NOT EASY, IT'S BRUTAL.
MENTALLY TAXING, IN FACT.
WHAT'S WITH THESE CLOTHES? IS IT SOME CHARACTER'S OUTFIT?
I SAID YOU'D BE WEARING DARK CLOTHES, DIDN'T I?
YOU DIDN'T SAY ANYTHING ABOUT COSPLAY!
THAT DOES NOT IMPLY WEARING A GOOFY BLACK CLOAK!!

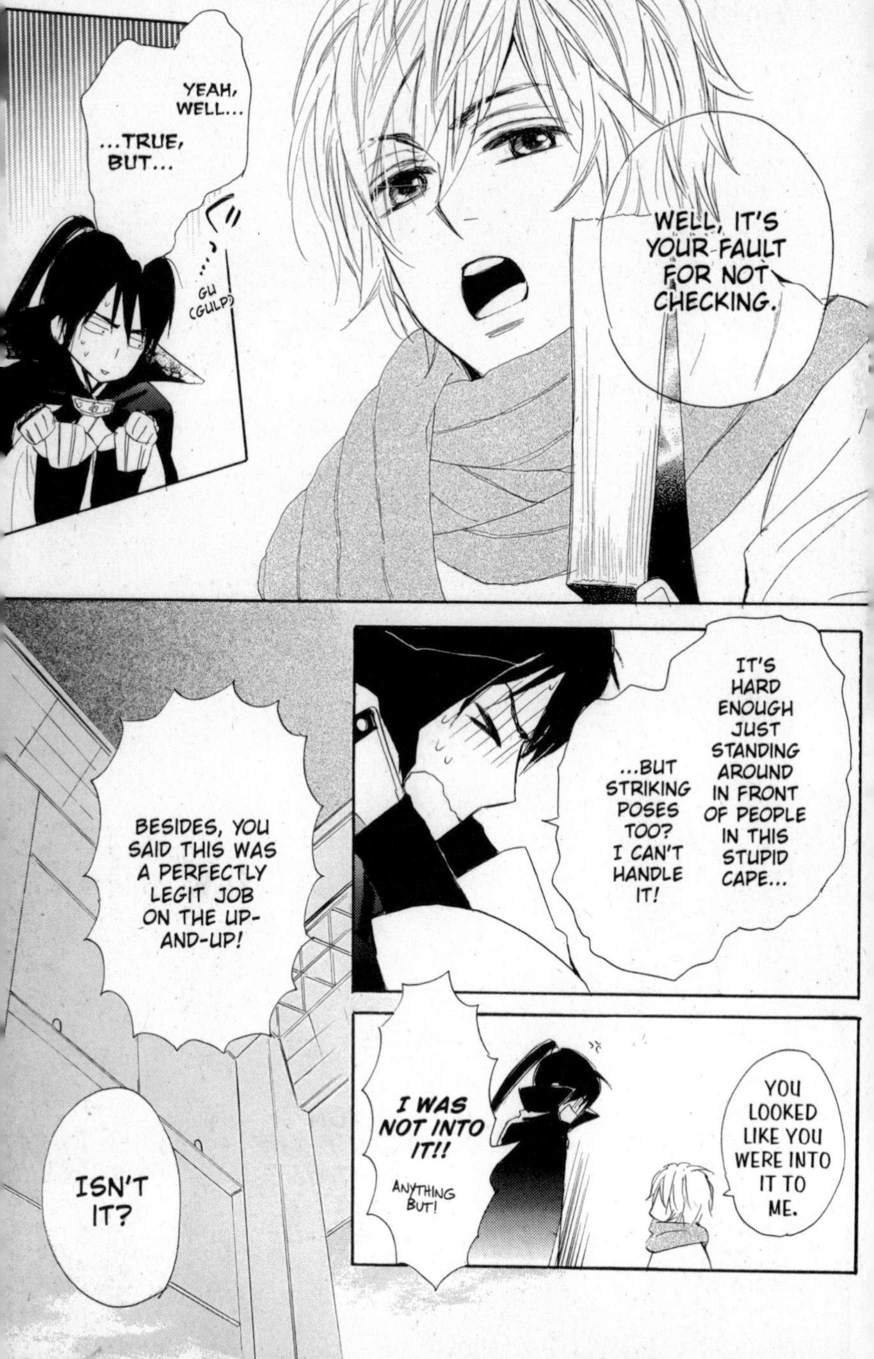
WELL, IT'S YOUR FAULT FOR NOT CHECKING.
YEAH, WELL...
...TRUE, BUT...
GU (GULP)
IT'S HARD ENOUGH JUST STANDING AROUND IN FRONT OF PEOPLE IN THIS STUPID CAPE...
...BUT STRIKING POSES TOO? I CAN'T HANDLE IT!
YOU LOOKED LIKE YOU WERE INTO IT TO ME.
I WAS NOT INTO IT!!
ANYTHING BUT!
BESIDES, YOU SAID THIS WAS A PERFECTLY LEGIT JOB ON THE UP-AND-UP!
ISN'T IT?

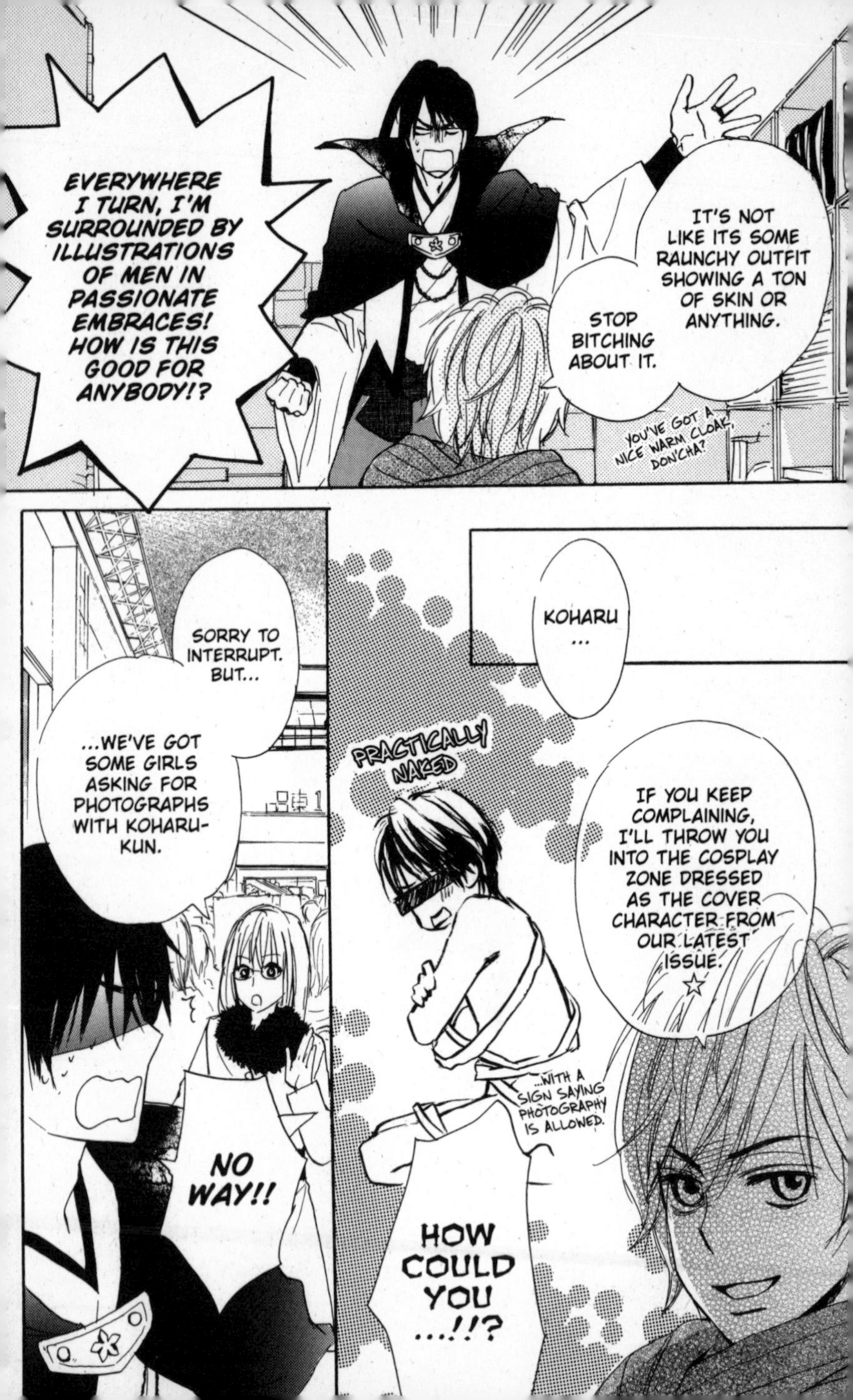
IT'S NOT LIKE ITS SOME RAUNCHY OUTFIT SHOWING A TON OF SKIN OR ANYTHING.
STOP BITCHING ABOUT IT.
YOU'VE GOT A NICE WARM CLOAK, DON'CHA?
EVERYWHERE I TURN, I'M SURROUNDED BY ILLUSTRATIONS OF MEN IN PASSIONATE EMBRACES! HOW IS THIS GOOD FOR ANYBODY!?
KOHARU ...
PRACTICALLY NAKED
IF YOU KEEP COMPLAINING, I'LL THROW YOU INTO THE COSPLAY ZONE DRESSED AS THE COVER CHARACTER FROM OUR LATEST ISSUE. ☆
...WITH A SIGN SAYING PHOTOGRAPHY IS ALLOWED.
HOW COULD YOU ...!!?
SORRY TO INTERRUPT. BUT...
...WE'VE GOT SOME GIRLS ASKING FOR PHOTOGRAPHS WITH KOHARU-KUN.
NO WAY!!

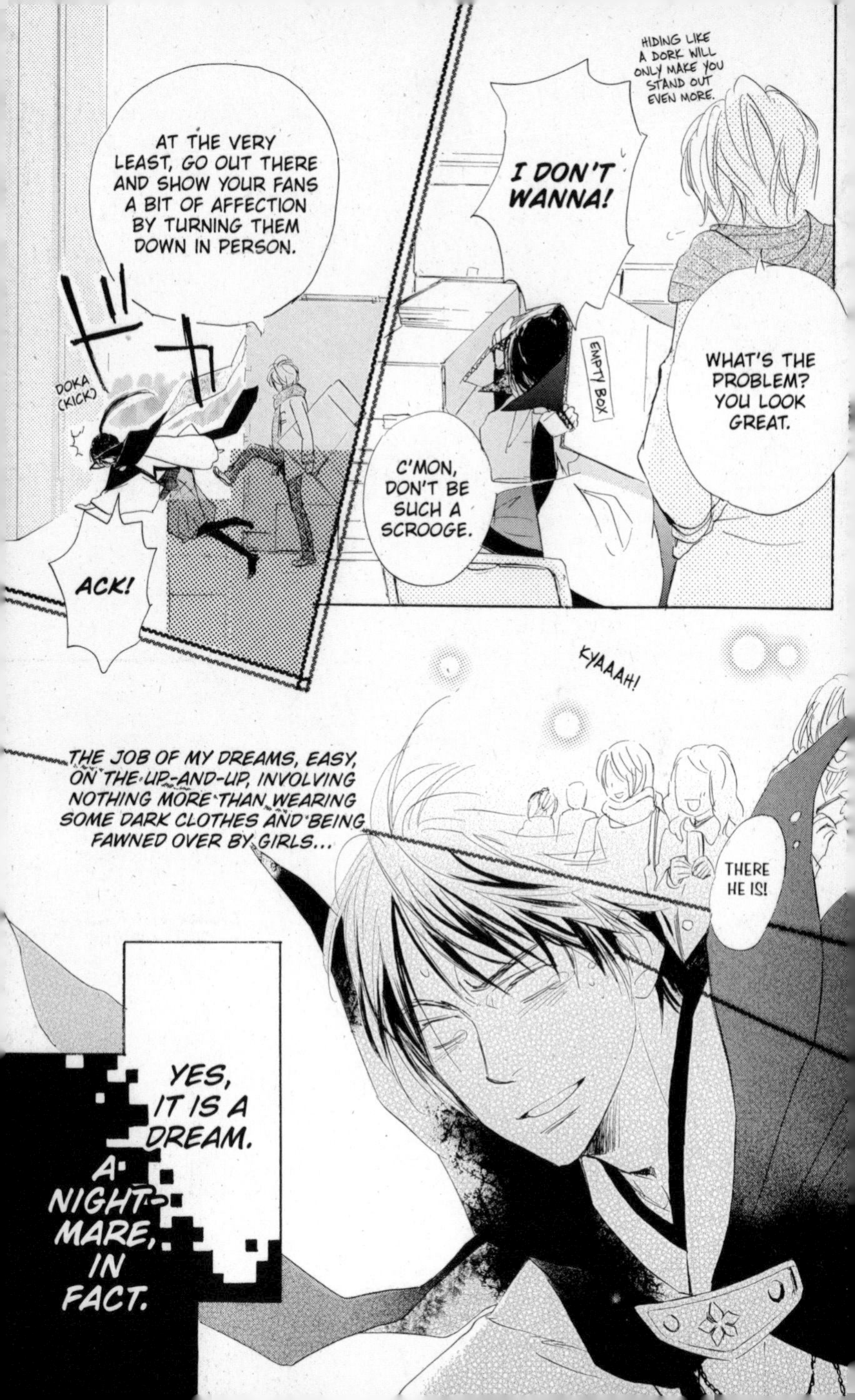
HIDING LIKE A DORK WILL ONLY MAKE YOU STAND OUT EVEN MORE.
I DON'T WANNA!
WHAT'S THE PROBLEM? YOU LOOK GREAT.
EMPTY BOX
C'MON, DON'T BE SUCH A SCROOGE.
AT THE VERY LEAST, GO OUT THERE AND SHOW YOUR FANS A BIT OF AFFECTION BY TURNING THEM DOWN IN PERSON.
DOKA (KICK)
ACK!
KYAAAH!
THERE HE IS!
THE JOB OF MY DREAMS, EASY, ON THE UP-AND-UP, INVOLVING NOTHING MORE THAN WEARING SOME DARK CLOTHES AND BEING FAWNED OVER BY GIRLS...
YES, IT IS A DREAM.
A NIGHTMARE, IN FACT.

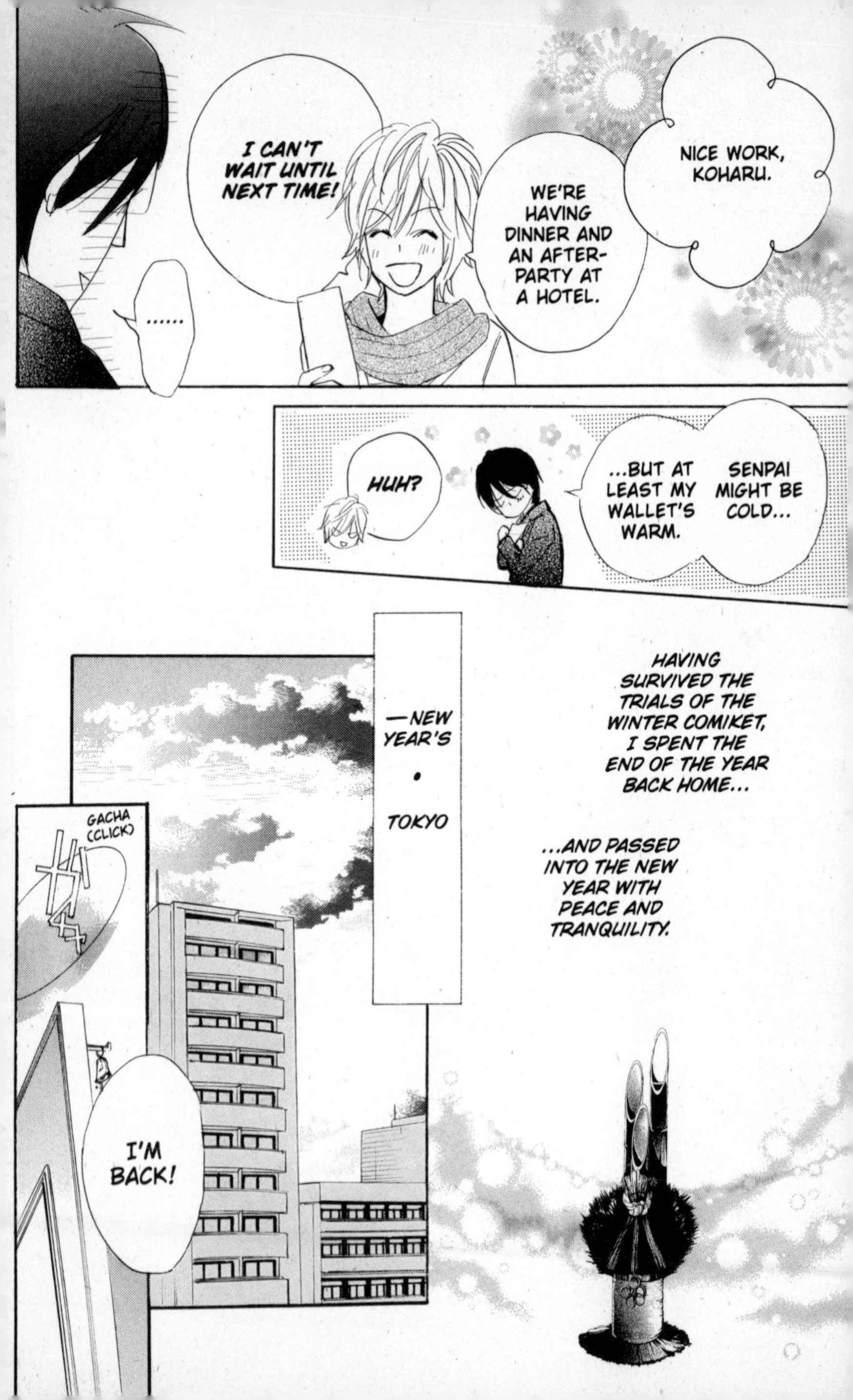
NICE WORK, KOHARU.
WE'RE HAVING DINNER AND AN AFTER-PARTY AT A HOTEL.
I CAN'T WAIT UNTIL NEXT TIME!
......
SENPAI MIGHT BE COLD...
...BUT AT LEAST MY WALLET'S WARM.
HUH?
HAVING SURVIVED THE TRIALS OF THE WINTER COMIKET, I SPENT THE END OF THE YEAR BACK HOME...
...AND PASSED INTO THE NEW YEAR WITH PEACE AND TRANQUILITY.
—NEW YEAR'S • TOKYO
GACHA (CLICK)
I'M BACK!

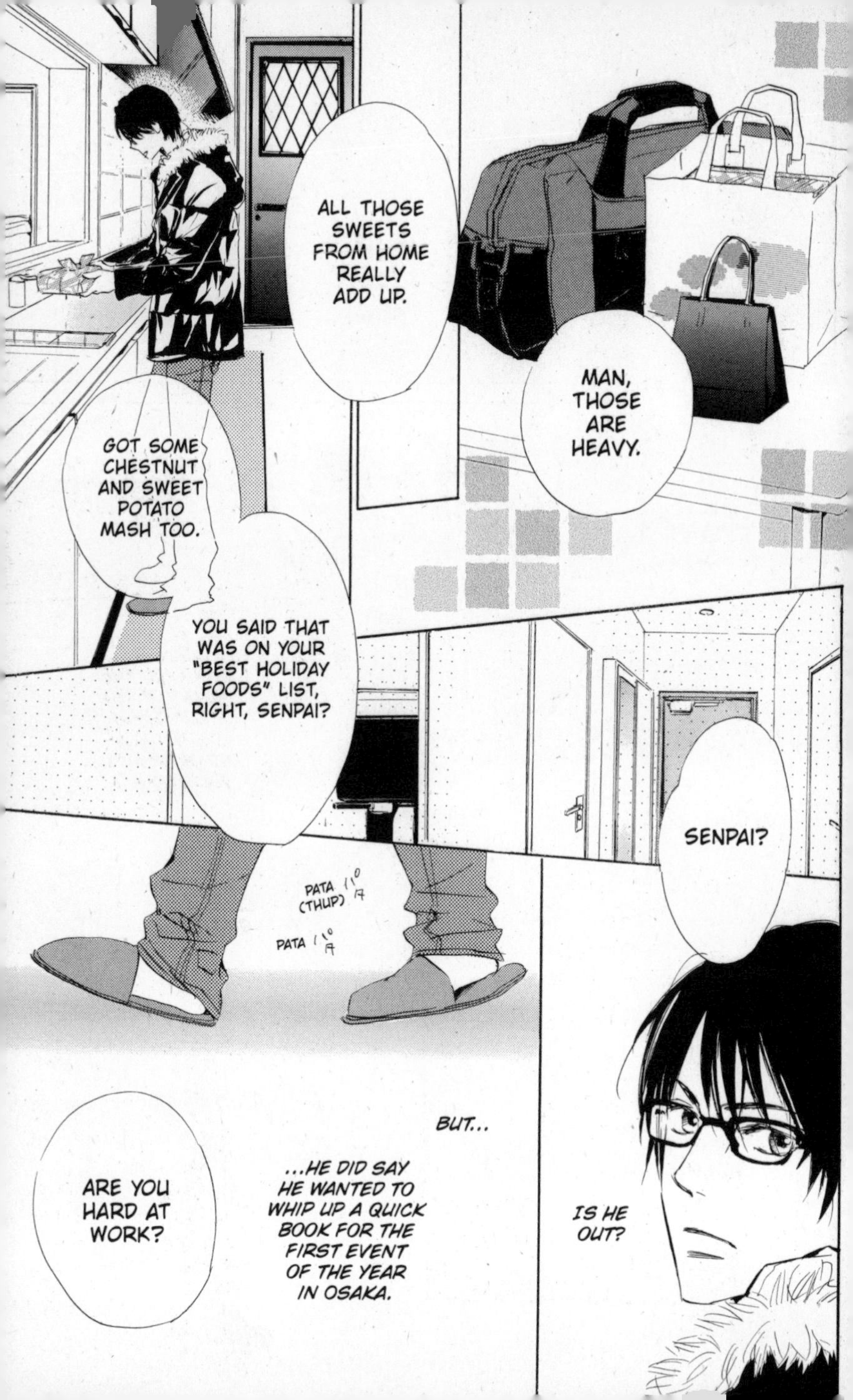

MAN, THOSE ARE HEAVY.
ALL THOSE SWEETS FROM HOME REALLY ADD UP.
GOT SOME CHESTNUT AND SWEET POTATO MASH TOO.
YOU SAID THAT WAS ON YOUR "BEST HOLIDAY FOODS" LIST, RIGHT, SENPAI?
SENPAI?
PATA (THUP)
PATA
IS HE OUT?
BUT...
...HE DID SAY HE WANTED TO WHIP UP A QUICK BOOK FOR THE FIRST EVENT OF THE YEAR IN OSAKA.
ARE YOU HARD AT WORK?

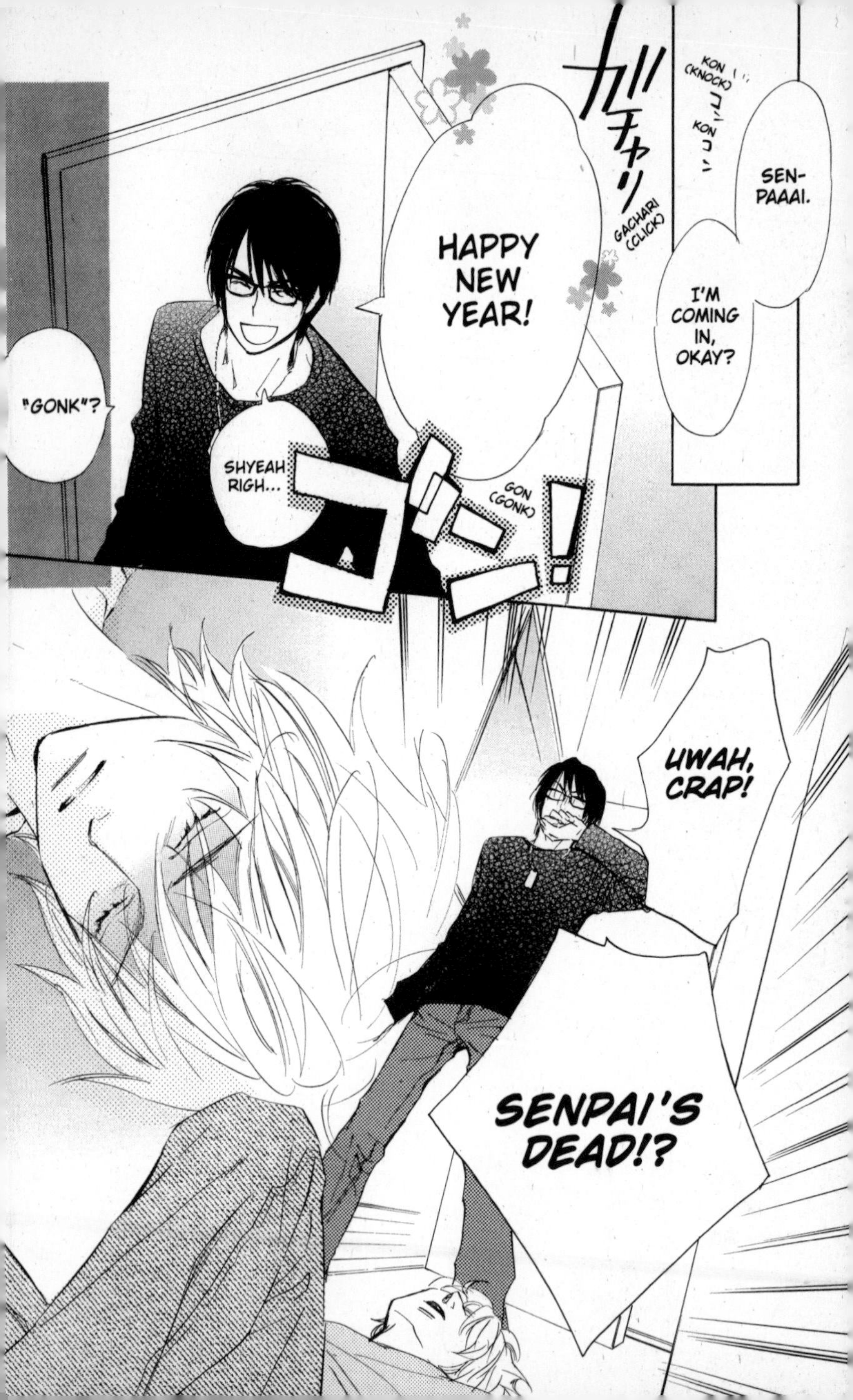
KON (KNOCK)
KON
SEN-PAAAI.
I'M COMING IN, OKAY?
GACHARI (CLICK)
HAPPY NEW YEAR!
GON (GONK)
SHYEAH RIGH...
"GONK"?
UWAH, CRAP!
SENPAI'S DEAD!?

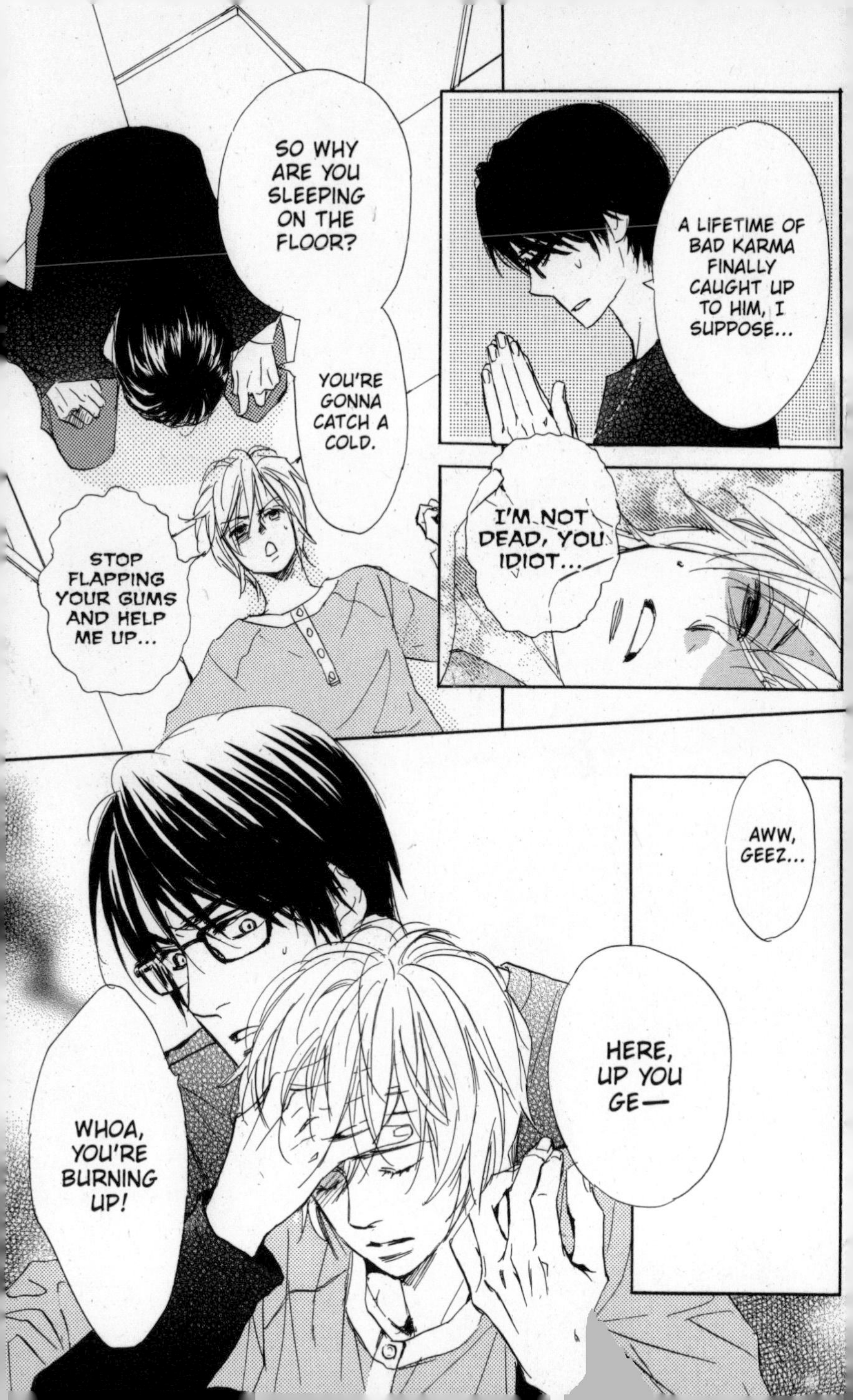

A LIFETIME OF BAD KARMA FINALLY CAUGHT UP TO HIM, I SUPPOSE...
I'M NOT DEAD, YOU IDIOT...
SO WHY ARE YOU SLEEPING ON THE FLOOR?
YOU'RE GONNA CATCH A COLD.
STOP FLAPPING YOUR GUMS AND HELP ME UP...
AWW, GEEZ...
HERE, UP YOU GE—
WHOA, YOU'RE BURNING UP!

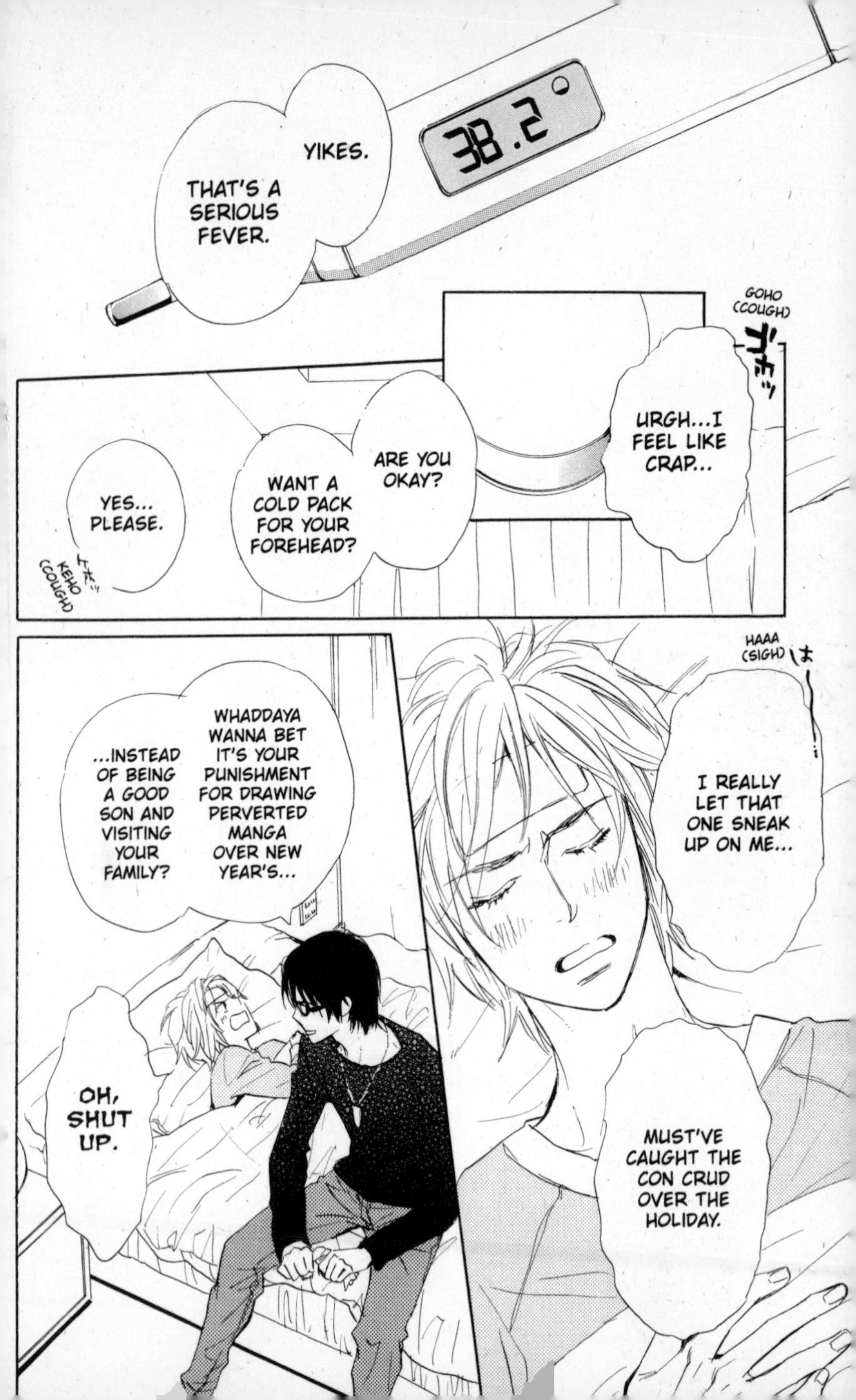
38.2
YIKES.
THAT'S A SERIOUS FEVER.
GOHO (COUGH)
ゴホッ
URGH...I FEEL LIKE CRAP...
ARE YOU OKAY?
WANT A COLD PACK FOR YOUR FOREHEAD?
YES... PLEASE.
KEHO (COUGH)
ケホッ
HAAA (SIGH)
はー…
I REALLY LET THAT ONE SNEAK UP ON ME...
MUST'VE CAUGHT THE CON CRUD OVER THE HOLIDAY.
WHADDAYA WANNA BET IT'S YOUR PUNISHMENT FOR DRAWING PERVERTED MANGA OVER NEW YEAR'S...
...INSTEAD OF BEING A GOOD SON AND VISITING YOUR FAMILY?
OH, SHUT UP.

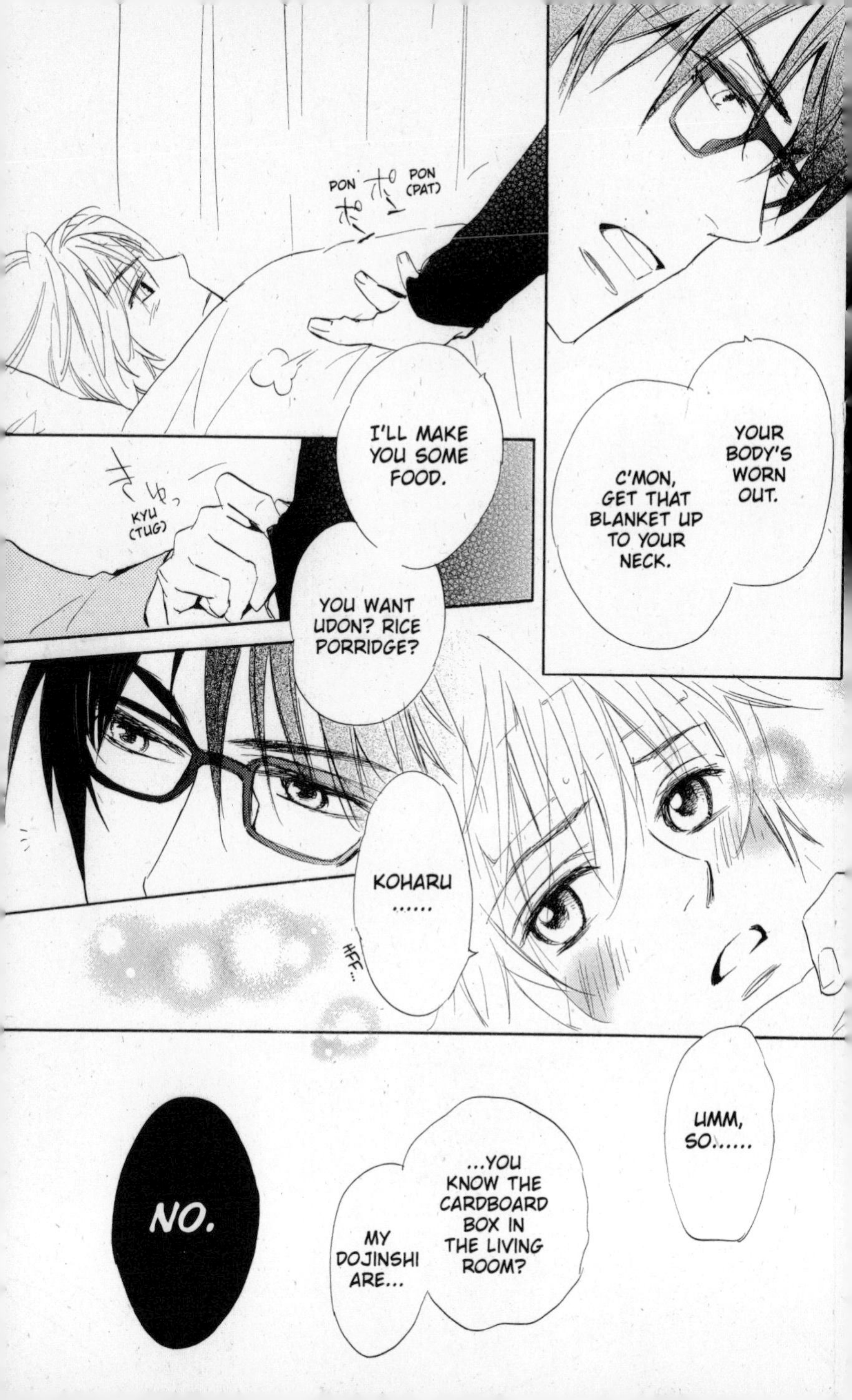
YOUR BODY'S WORN OUT.
C'MON, GET THAT BLANKET UP TO YOUR NECK.
PON PON (PAT)
I'LL MAKE YOU SOME FOOD.
KYU (TUG)
YOU WANT UDON? RICE PORRIDGE?
KOHARU ......
HFF...
UMM, SO......
...YOU KNOW THE CARDBOARD BOX IN THE LIVING ROOM?
MY DOJINSHI ARE...
NO.

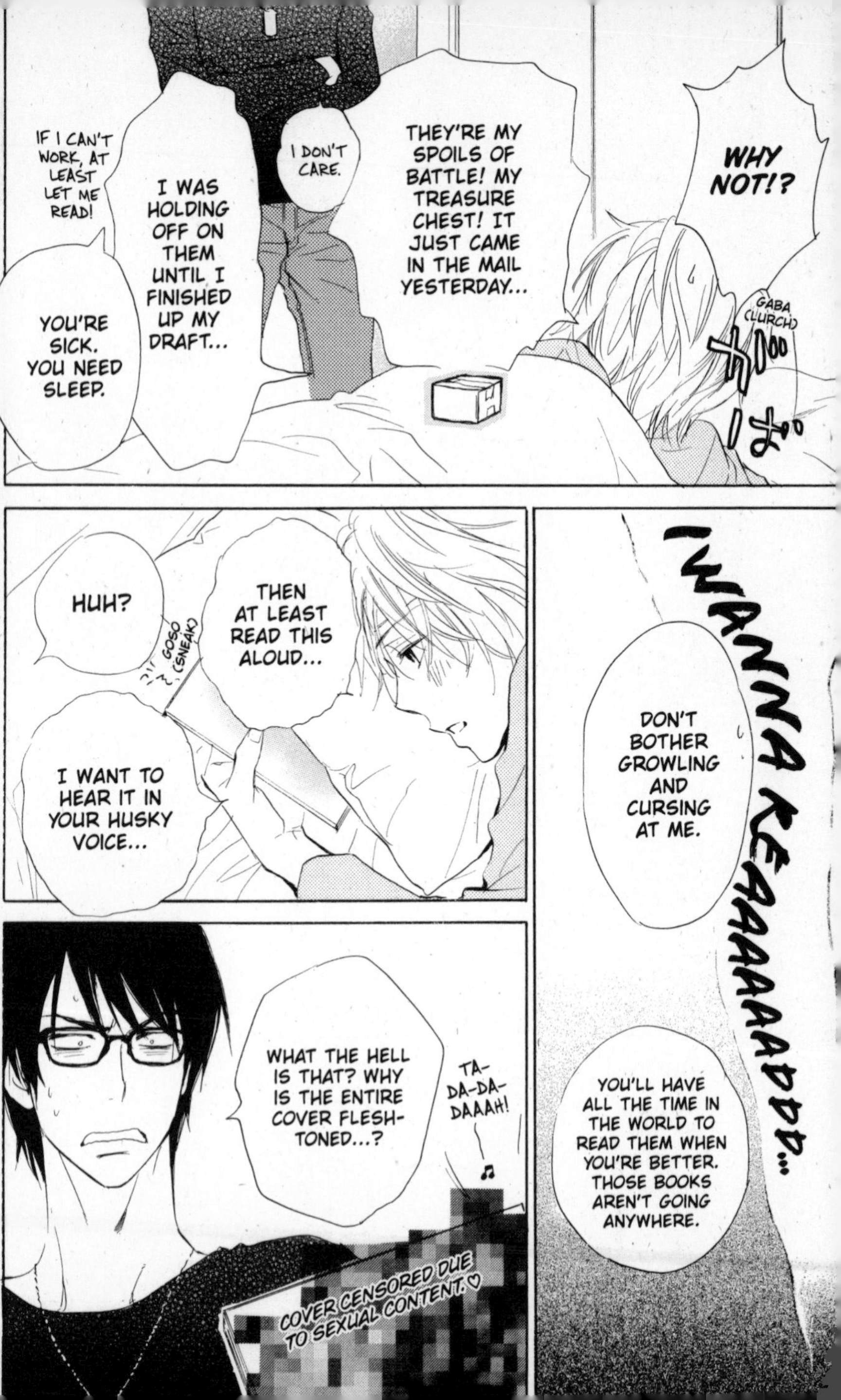
WHY NOT!?
GABA (CLURCH)
THEY'RE MY SPOILS OF BATTLE! MY TREASURE CHEST! IT JUST CAME IN THE MAIL YESTERDAY...
I DON'T CARE.
I WAS HOLDING OFF ON THEM UNTIL I FINISHED UP MY DRAFT...
IF I CAN'T WORK, AT LEAST LET ME READ!
YOU'RE SICK. YOU NEED SLEEP.
I WANNA REAAAAAADDD...
DON'T BOTHER GROWLING AND CURSING AT ME.
YOU'LL HAVE ALL THE TIME IN THE WORLD TO READ THEM WHEN YOU'RE BETTER. THOSE BOOKS AREN'T GOING ANYWHERE.
THEN AT LEAST READ THIS ALOUD...
HUH?
GOSO (SNEAK)
I WANT TO HEAR IT IN YOUR HUSKY VOICE...
TA-DA-DA-DAAAH! ♪
WHAT THE HELL IS THAT? WHY IS THE ENTIRE COVER FLESH-TONED...?
COVER CENSORED DUE TO SEXUAL CONTENT.♡

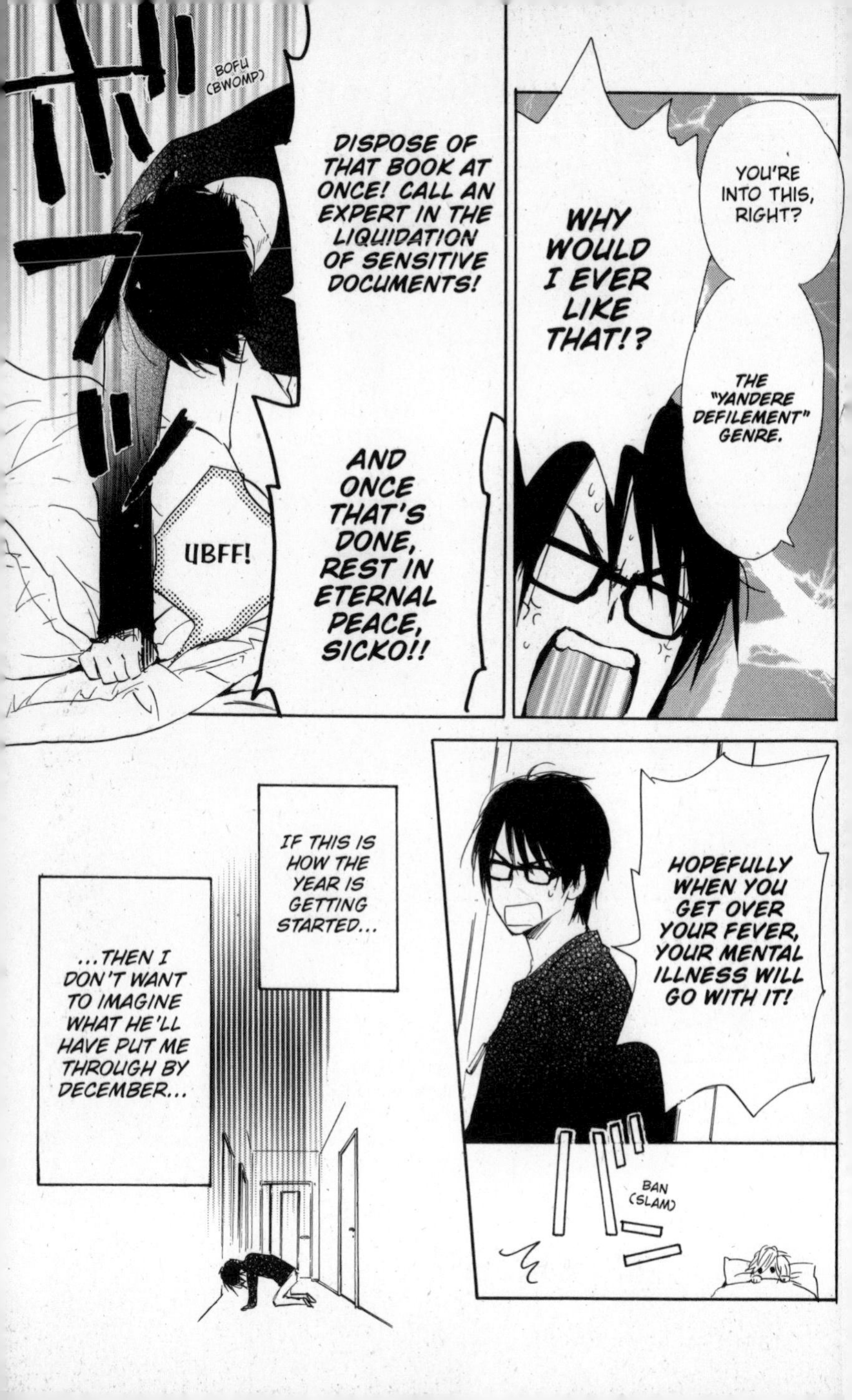
YOU'RE INTO THIS, RIGHT?
THE "YANDERE DEFILEMENT" GENRE.
WHY WOULD I EVER LIKE THAT!?
BOFU (BWOMP)
DISPOSE OF THAT BOOK AT ONCE! CALL AN EXPERT IN THE LIQUIDATION OF SENSITIVE DOCUMENTS!
AND ONCE THAT'S DONE, REST IN ETERNAL PEACE, SICKO!!
UBFF!
HOPEFULLY WHEN YOU GET OVER YOUR FEVER, YOUR MENTAL ILLNESS WILL GO WITH IT!
BAN (SLAM)
IF THIS IS HOW THE YEAR IS GETTING STARTED...
...THEN I DON'T WANT TO IMAGINE WHAT HE'LL HAVE PUT ME THROUGH BY DECEMBER...

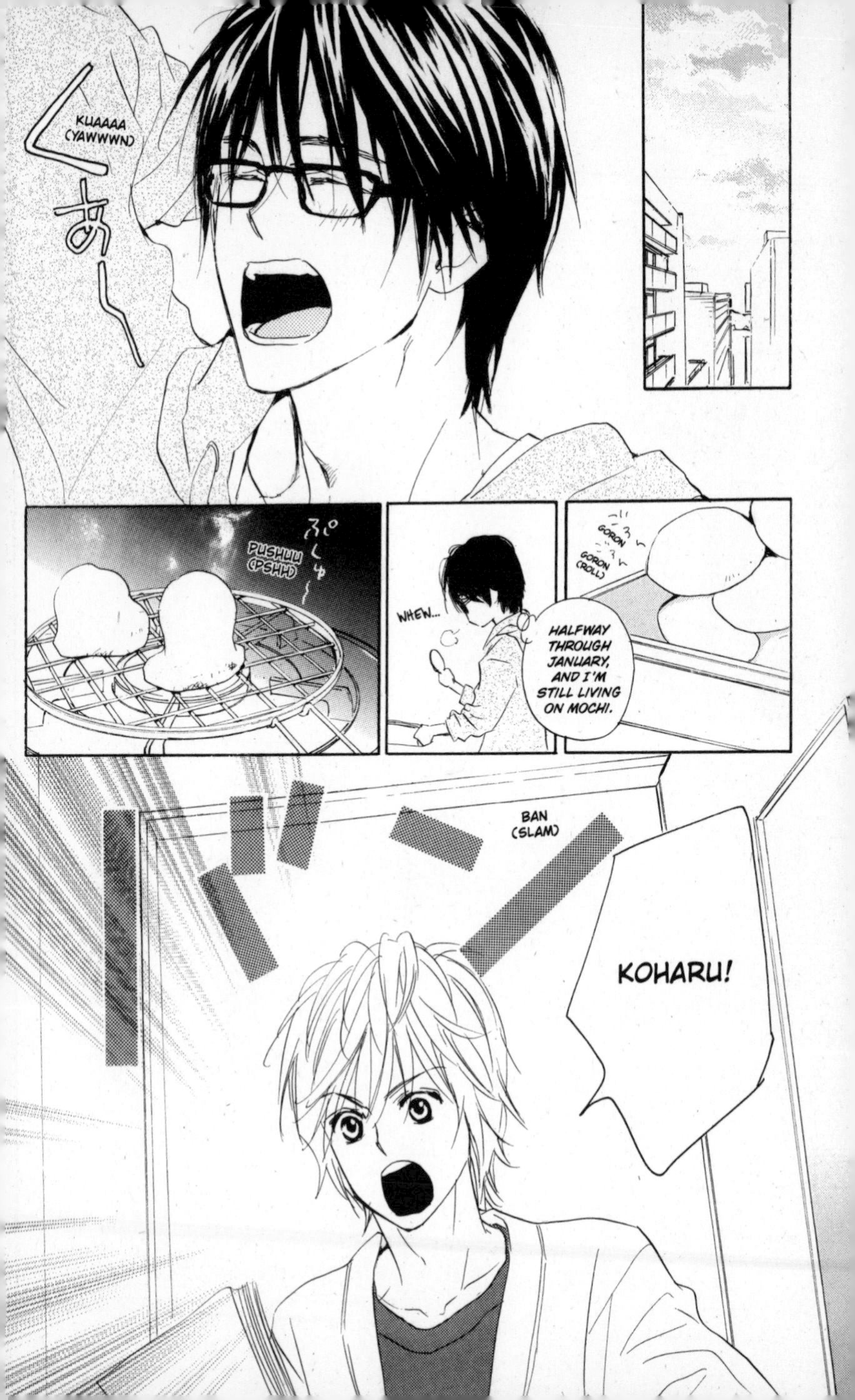

KUAAAA (YAWWWN)
くあ～
GORON GORON (ROLL)
WHEW...
HALFWAY THROUGH JANUARY, AND I'M STILL LIVING ON MOCHI.
PUSHUU (PSHH)
ぷしゅ～
BAN (SLAM)
KOHARU!

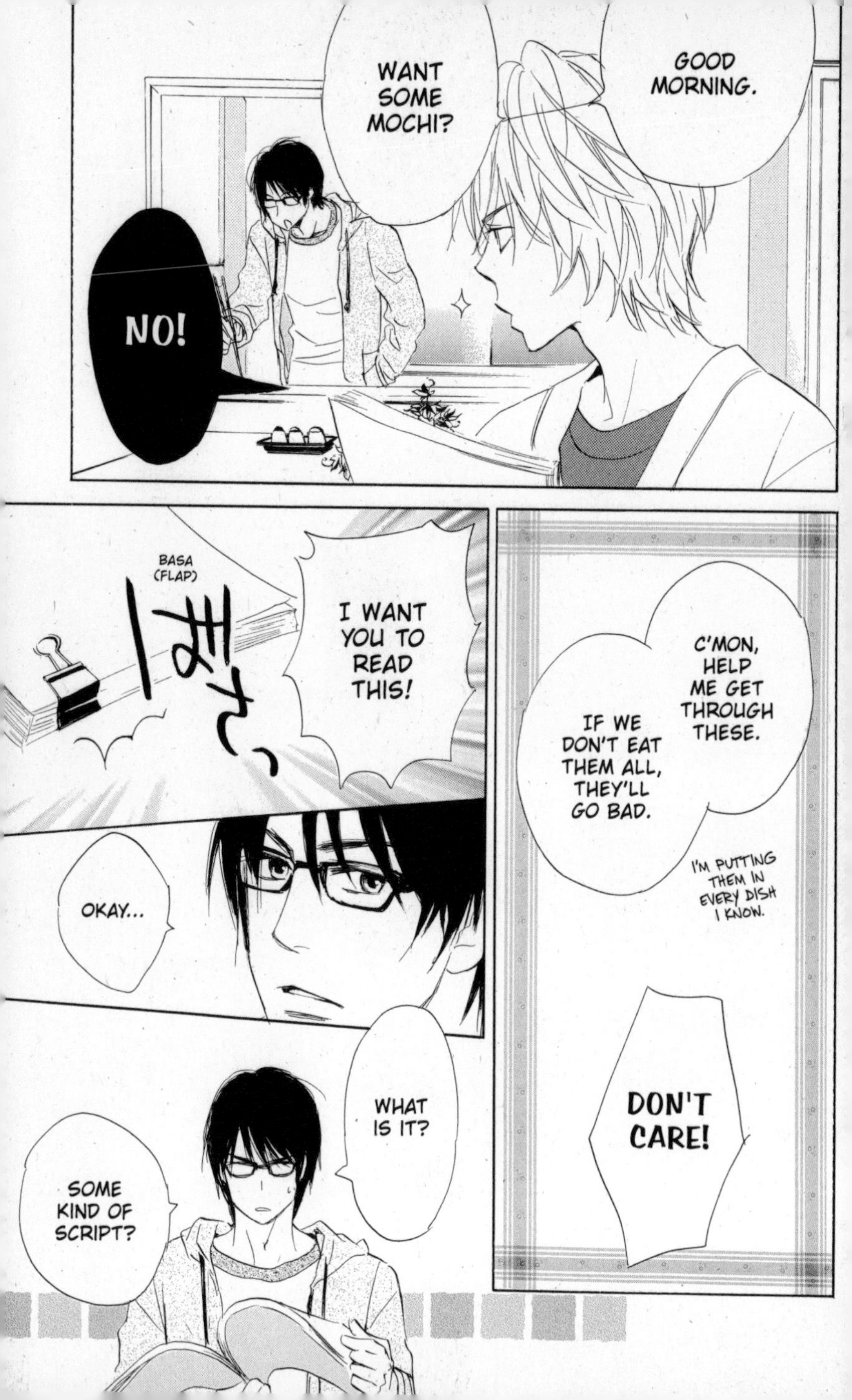
GOOD MORNING.
WANT SOME MOCHI?
NO!
C'MON, HELP ME GET THROUGH THESE.
IF WE DON'T EAT THEM ALL, THEY'LL GO BAD.
I'M PUTTING THEM IN EVERY DISH I KNOW.
DON'T CARE!
I WANT YOU TO READ THIS!
ばさっ
BASA (FLAP)
OKAY...
WHAT IS IT?
SOME KIND OF SCRIPT?

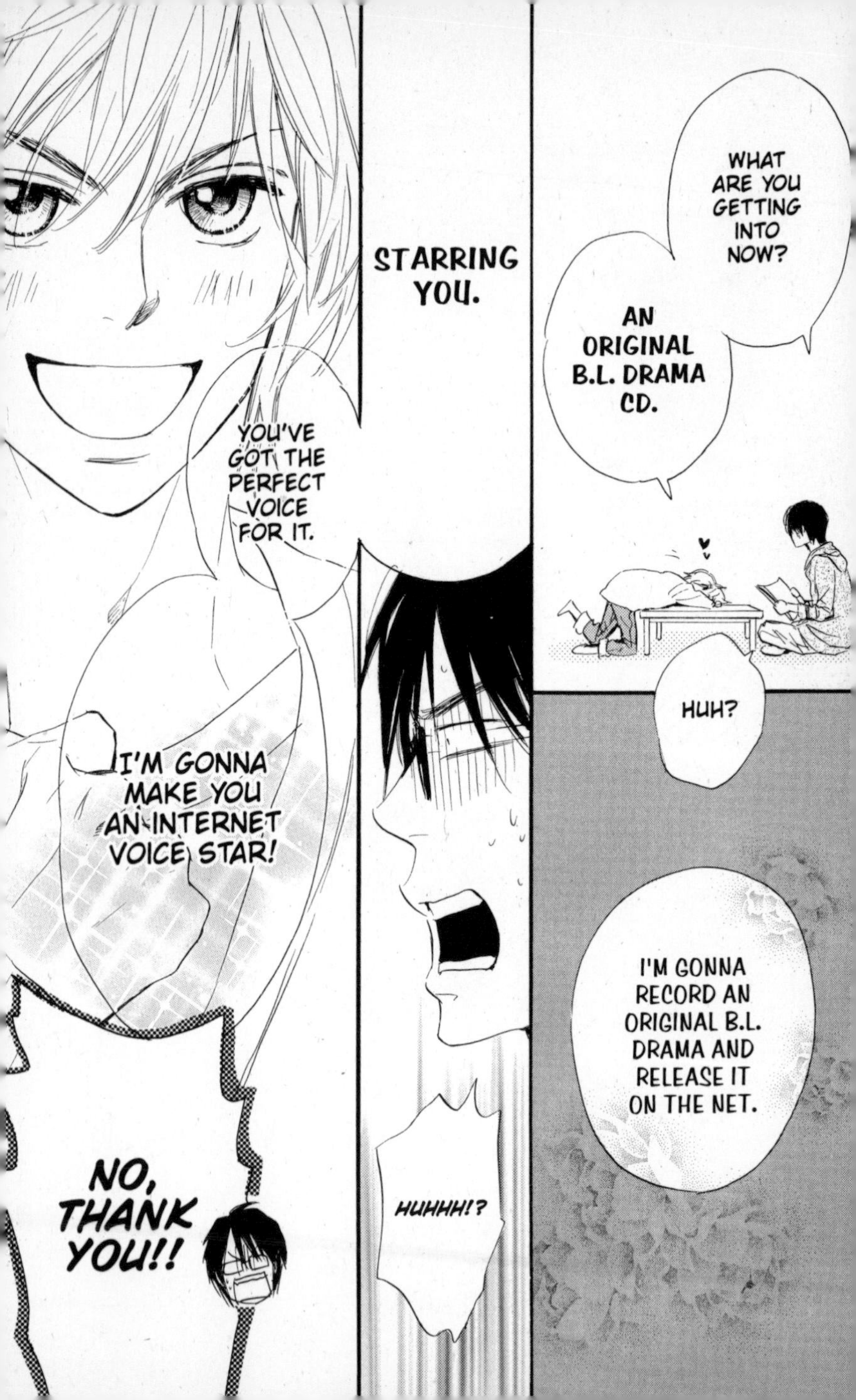
WHAT ARE YOU GETTING INTO NOW?
AN ORIGINAL B.L. DRAMA CD.
HUH?
I'M GONNA RECORD AN ORIGINAL B.L. DRAMA AND RELEASE IT ON THE NET.
STARRING YOU.
HUHHH!?
YOU'VE GOT THE PERFECT VOICE FOR IT.
I'M GONNA MAKE YOU AN INTERNET VOICE STAR!
NO, THANK YOU!!

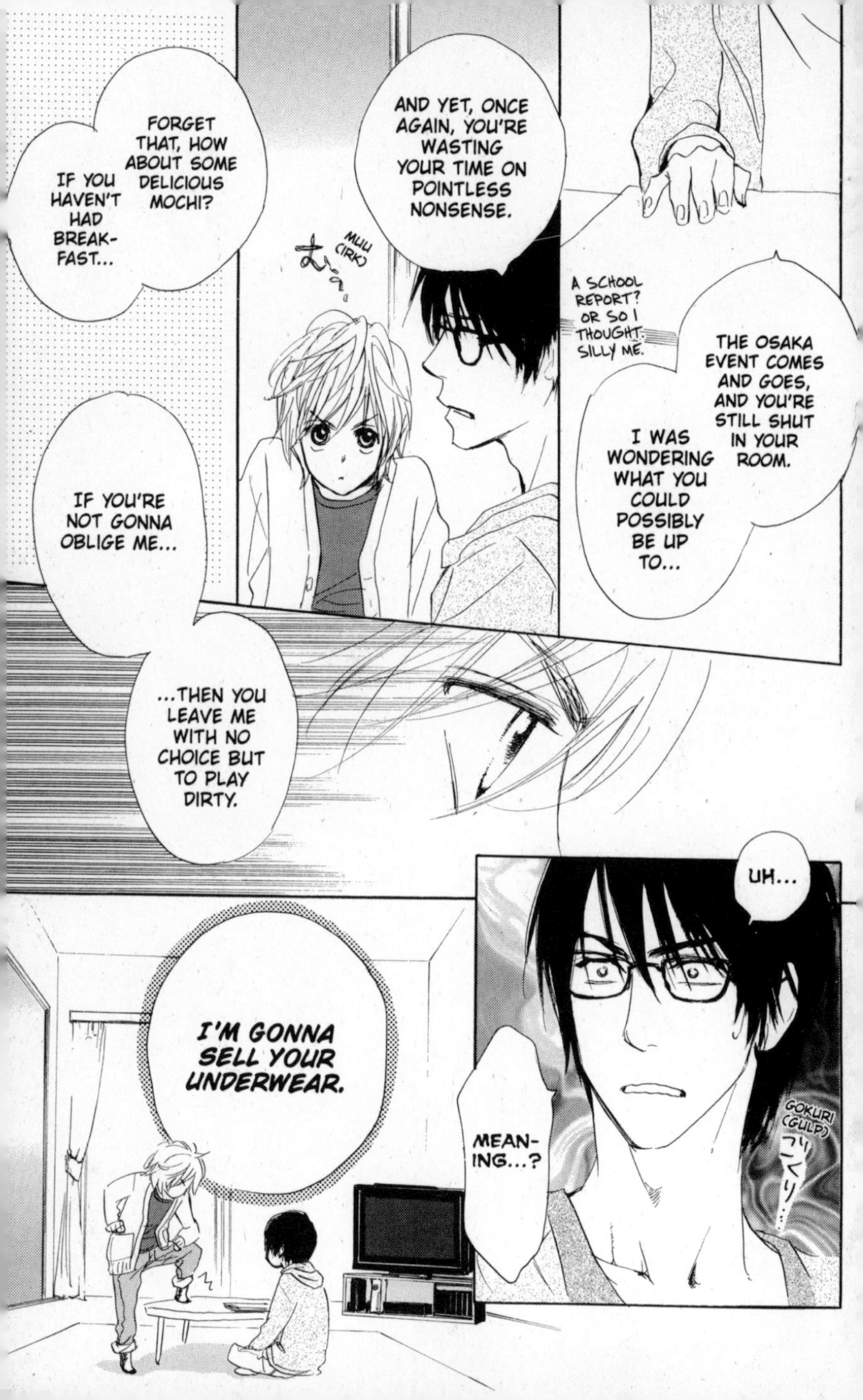

THE OSAKA EVENT COMES AND GOES, AND YOU'RE STILL SHUT IN YOUR ROOM.
I WAS WONDERING WHAT YOU COULD POSSIBLY BE UP TO...
A SCHOOL REPORT? OR SO I THOUGHT. SILLY ME.
AND YET, ONCE AGAIN, YOU'RE WASTING YOUR TIME ON POINTLESS NONSENSE.
MUU (IRK)
FORGET THAT, HOW ABOUT SOME DELICIOUS MOCHI?
IF YOU HAVEN'T HAD BREAK-FAST...
IF YOU'RE NOT GONNA OBLIGE ME...
...THEN YOU LEAVE ME WITH NO CHOICE BUT TO PLAY DIRTY.
UH...
GOKURI (GULP)
MEAN-ING...?
I'M GONNA SELL YOUR UNDERWEAR.

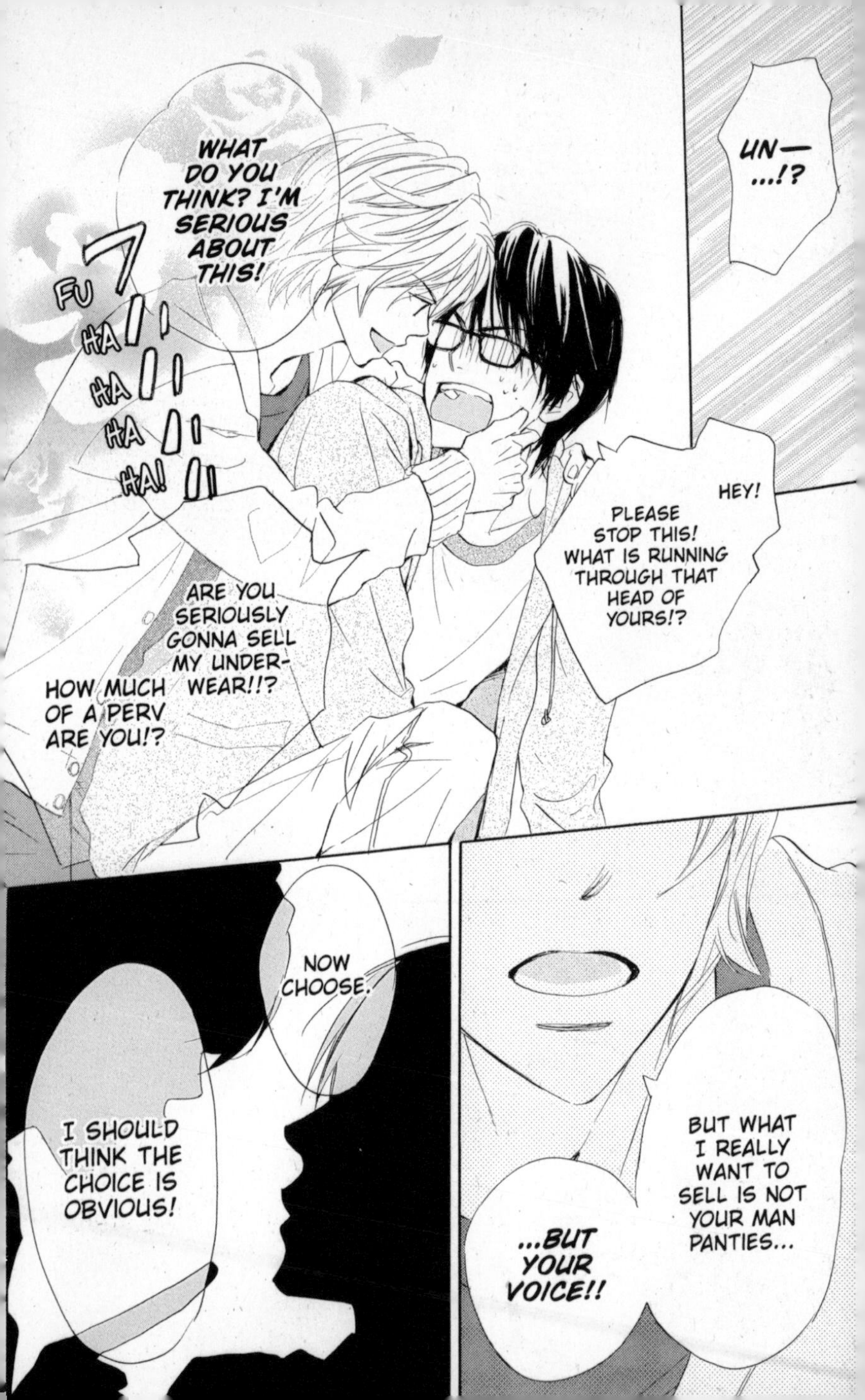
UN— ...!?
HEY!
PLEASE STOP THIS! WHAT IS RUNNING THROUGH THAT HEAD OF YOURS!?
WHAT DO YOU THINK? I'M SERIOUS ABOUT THIS!
FU HA HA HA HA!
ARE YOU SERIOUSLY GONNA SELL MY UNDER-WEAR!!?
HOW MUCH OF A PERV ARE YOU!?
BUT WHAT I REALLY WANT TO SELL IS NOT YOUR MAN PANTIES...
...BUT YOUR VOICE!!
NOW CHOOSE.
I SHOULD THINK THE CHOICE IS OBVIOUS!

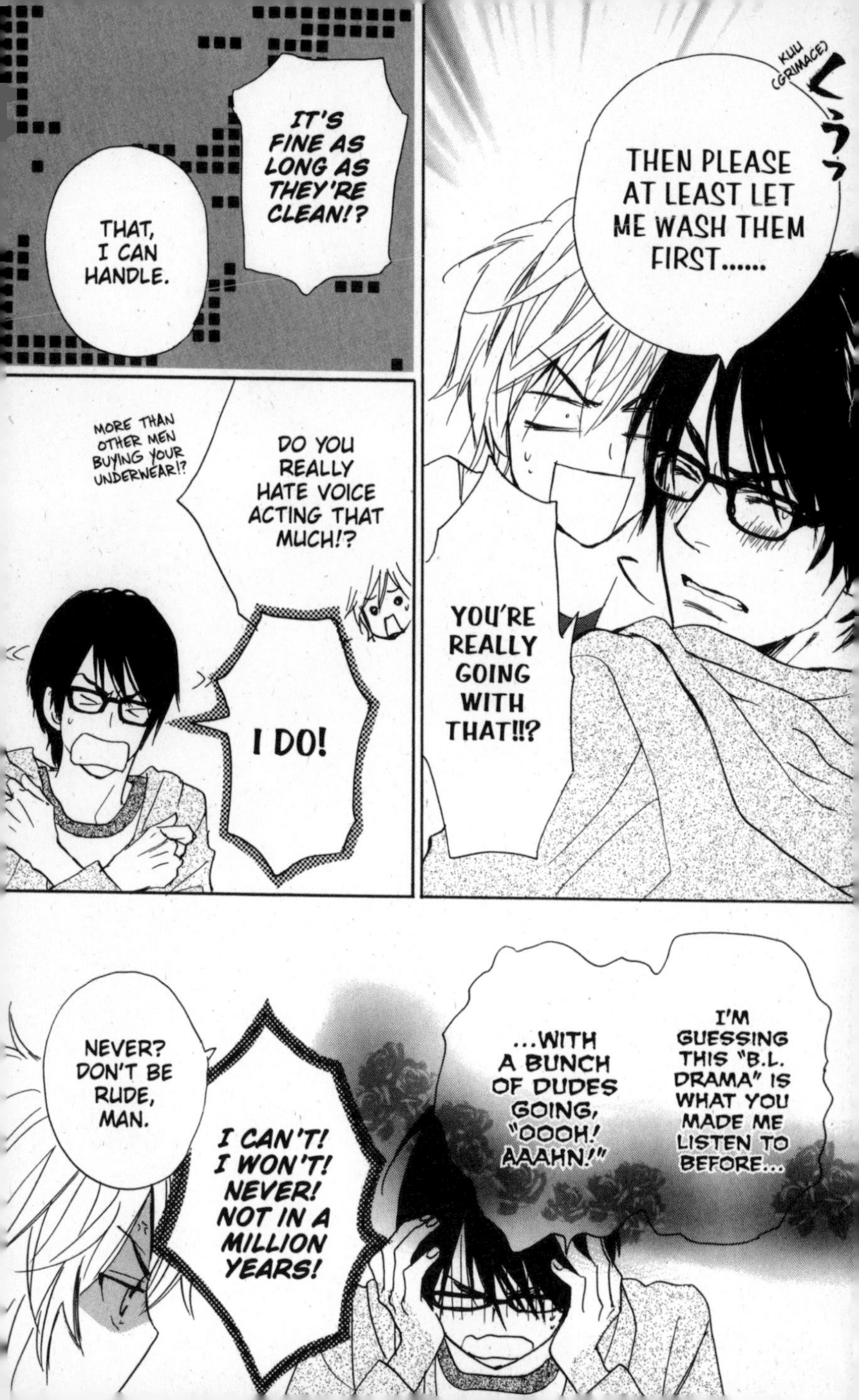
KUU (GRIMACE)
THEN PLEASE AT LEAST LET ME WASH THEM FIRST......
YOU'RE REALLY GOING WITH THAT!!?
IT'S FINE AS LONG AS THEY'RE CLEAN!?
THAT, I CAN HANDLE.
DO YOU REALLY HATE VOICE ACTING THAT MUCH!?
MORE THAN OTHER MEN BUYING YOUR UNDERWEAR!?
I DO!
I'M GUESSING THIS "B.L. DRAMA" IS WHAT YOU MADE ME LISTEN TO BEFORE...
...WITH A BUNCH OF DUDES GOING, "OOOH! AAAHN!"
I CAN'T! I WON'T! NEVER! NOT IN A MILLION YEARS!
NEVER? DON'T BE RUDE, MAN.

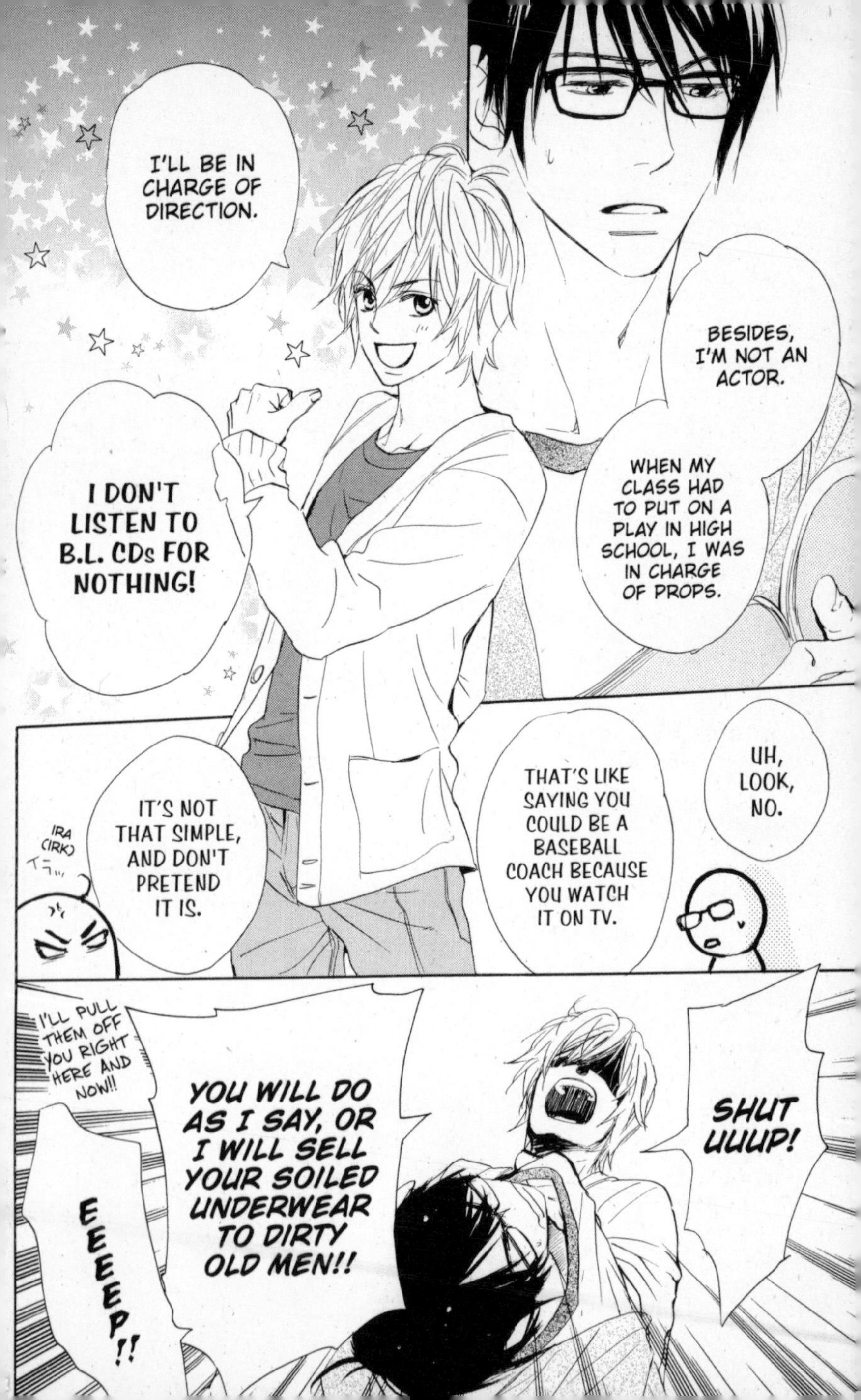
BESIDES, I'M NOT AN ACTOR.
WHEN MY CLASS HAD TO PUT ON A PLAY IN HIGH SCHOOL, I WAS IN CHARGE OF PROPS.
I'LL BE IN CHARGE OF DIRECTION.
I DON'T LISTEN TO B.L. CDs FOR NOTHING!
UH, LOOK, NO.
THAT'S LIKE SAYING YOU COULD BE A BASEBALL COACH BECAUSE YOU WATCH IT ON TV.
IT'S NOT THAT SIMPLE, AND DON'T PRETEND IT IS.
IRA (IRK)
SHUT UUUP!
YOU WILL DO AS I SAY, OR I WILL SELL YOUR SOILED UNDERWEAR TO DIRTY OLD MEN!!
I'LL PULL THEM OFF YOU RIGHT HERE AND NOW!!
EEEEEP!!

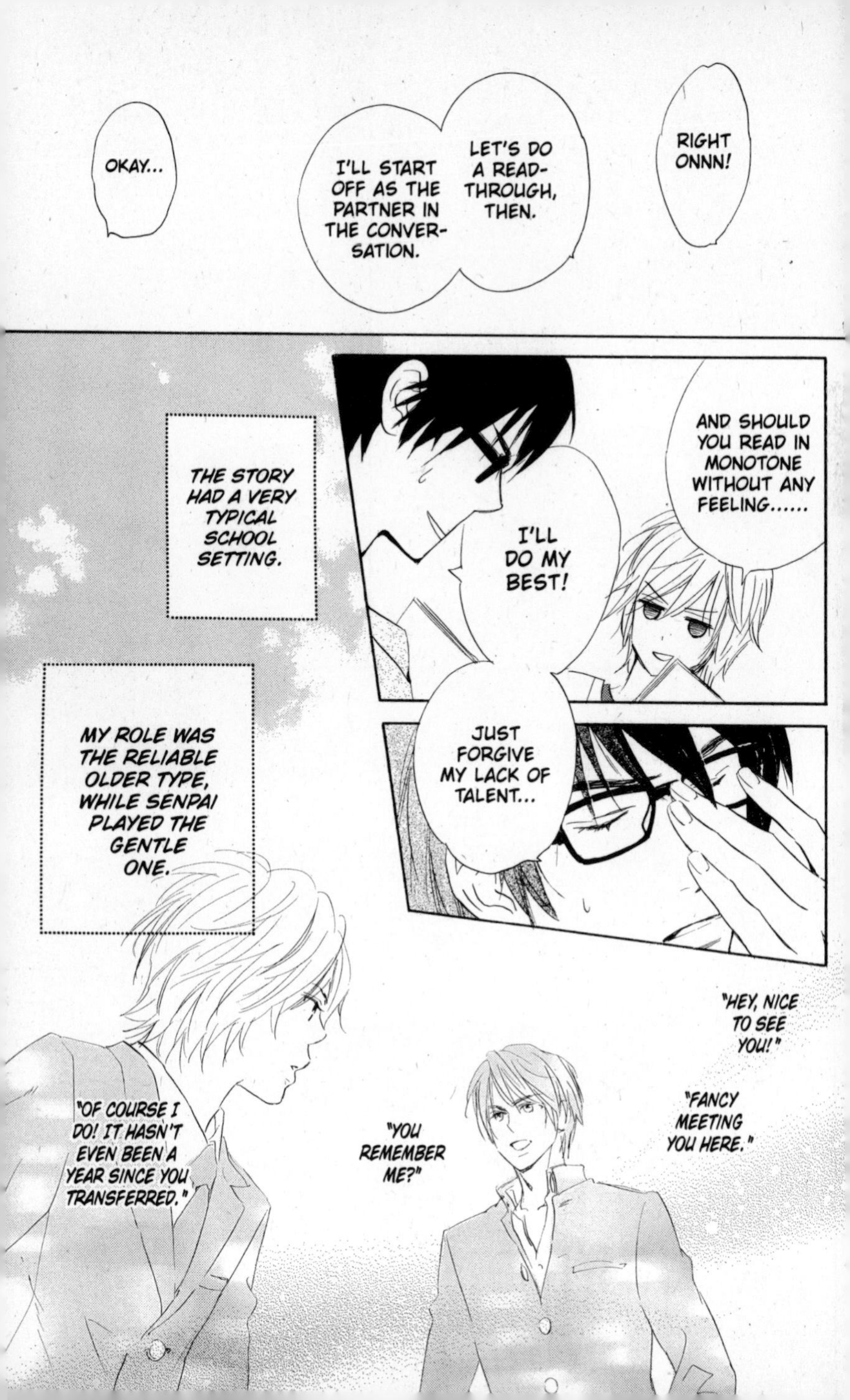
RIGHT ONNN!
LET'S DO A READ-THROUGH, THEN.
I'LL START OFF AS THE PARTNER IN THE CONVERSATION.
OKAY...
AND SHOULD YOU READ IN MONOTONE WITHOUT ANY FEELING......
I'LL DO MY BEST!
JUST FORGIVE MY LACK OF TALENT...
THE STORY HAD A VERY TYPICAL SCHOOL SETTING.
MY ROLE WAS THE RELIABLE OLDER TYPE, WHILE SENPAI PLAYED THE GENTLE ONE.
"HEY, NICE TO SEE YOU!"
"FANCY MEETING YOU HERE."
"YOU REMEMBER ME?"
"OF COURSE I DO! IT HASN'T EVEN BEEN A YEAR SINCE YOU TRANSFERRED."

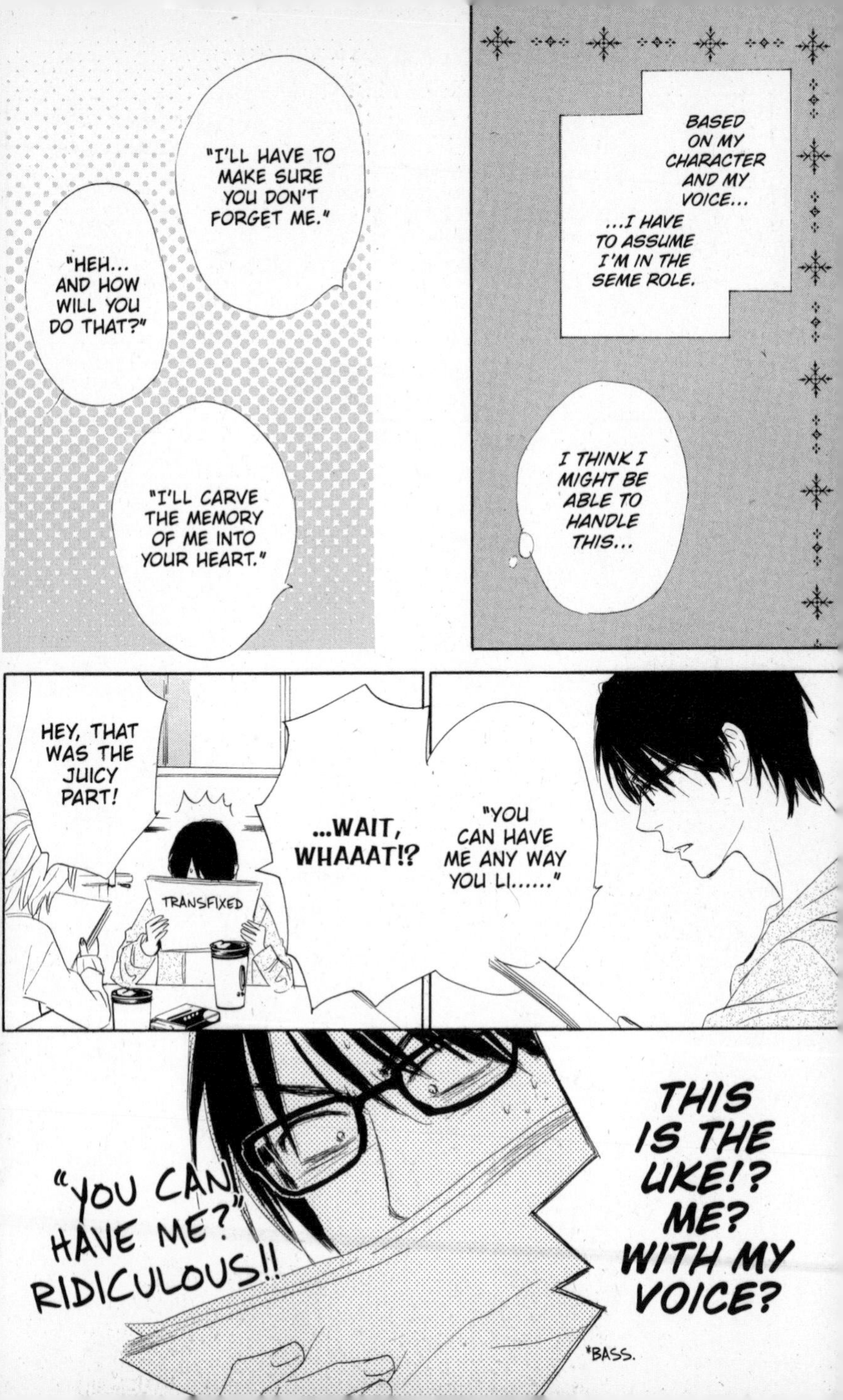

BASED ON MY CHARACTER AND MY VOICE...
...I HAVE TO ASSUME I'M IN THE SEME ROLE.
I THINK I MIGHT BE ABLE TO HANDLE THIS...
"I'LL HAVE TO MAKE SURE YOU DON'T FORGET ME."
"HEH... AND HOW WILL YOU DO THAT?"
"I'LL CARVE THE MEMORY OF ME INTO YOUR HEART."
"YOU CAN HAVE ME ANY WAY YOU LI......"
...WAIT, WHAAAT!?
HEY, THAT WAS THE JUICY PART!
TRANSFIXED
THIS IS THE UKE!? ME? WITH MY VOICE?
"YOU CAN HAVE ME?" RIDICULOUS!!
*BASS.

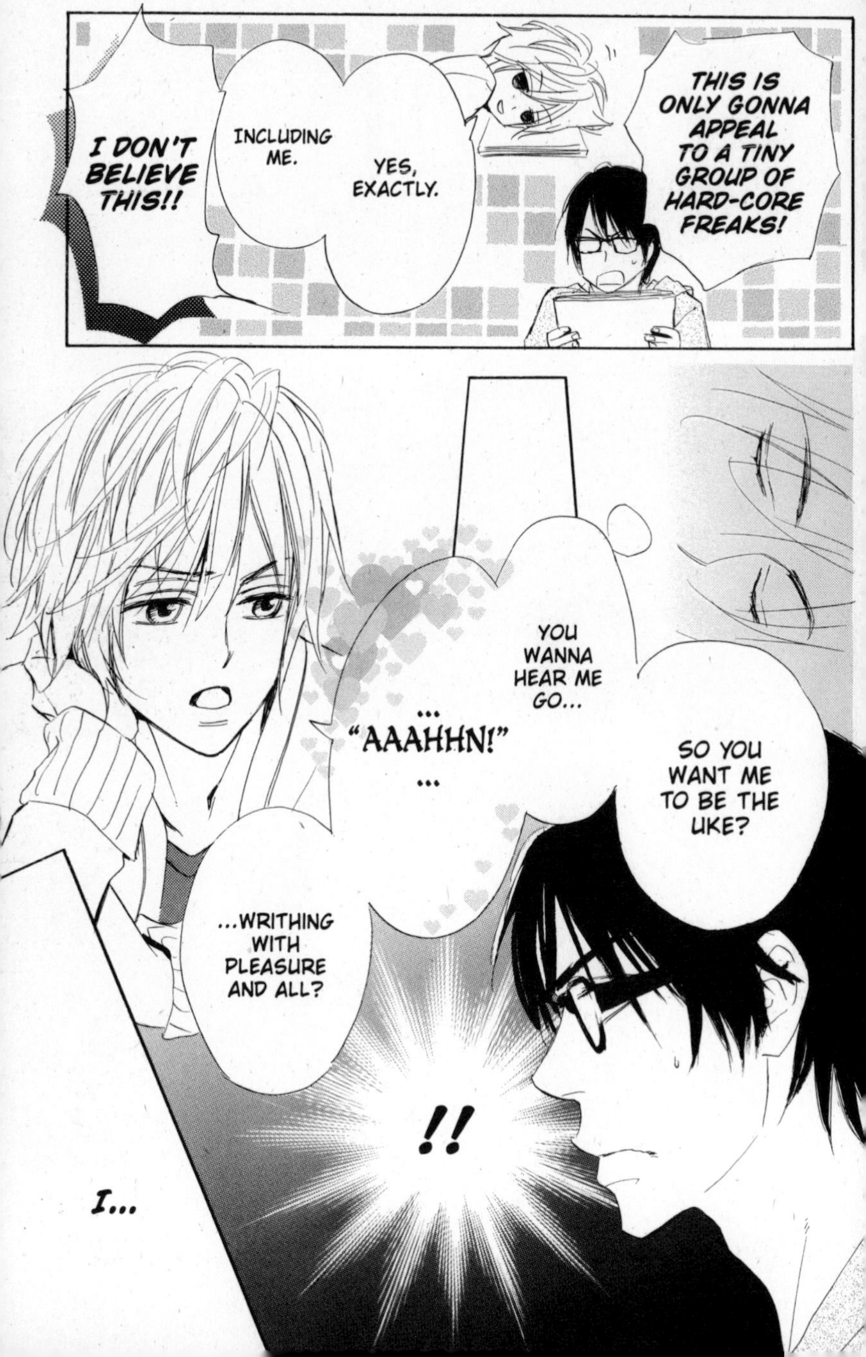
THIS IS ONLY GONNA APPEAL TO A TINY GROUP OF HARD-CORE FREAKS!
YES, EXACTLY.
INCLUDING ME.
I DON'T BELIEVE THIS!!
SO YOU WANT ME TO BE THE UKE?
YOU WANNA HEAR ME GO...
..."AAAHHN!"...
...WRITHING WITH PLEASURE AND ALL?
!!
I...

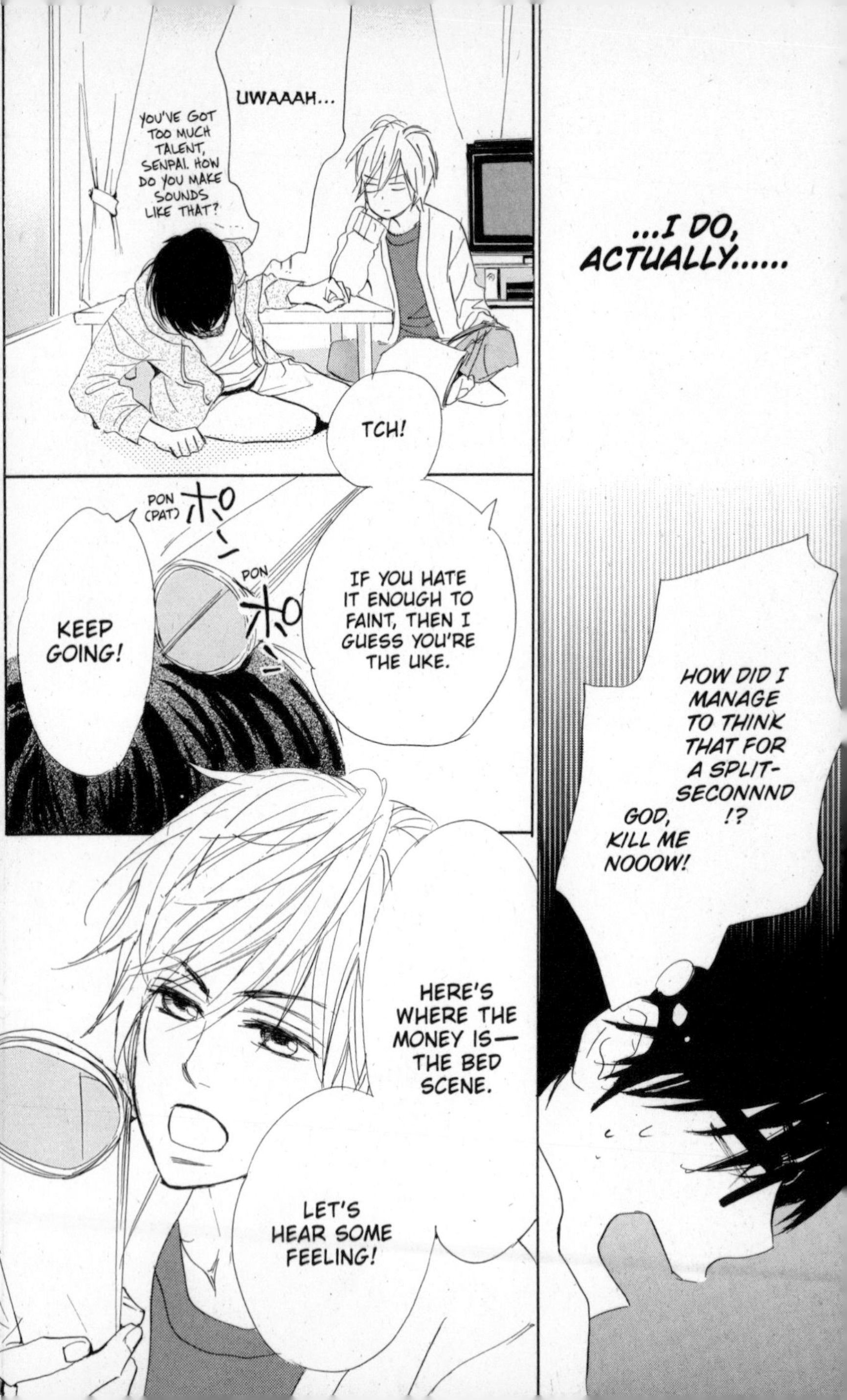
...I DO, ACTUALLY......
HOW DID I MANAGE TO THINK THAT FOR A SPLIT-SECONNND !?
GOD, KILL ME NOOOW!
UWAAAH...
YOU'VE GOT TOO MUCH TALENT, SENPAI. HOW DO YOU MAKE SOUNDS LIKE THAT?
TCH!
IF YOU HATE IT ENOUGH TO FAINT, THEN I GUESS YOU'RE THE UKE.
PON (PAT)
PON
KEEP GOING!
HERE'S WHERE THE MONEY IS— THE BED SCENE.
LET'S HEAR SOME FEELING!

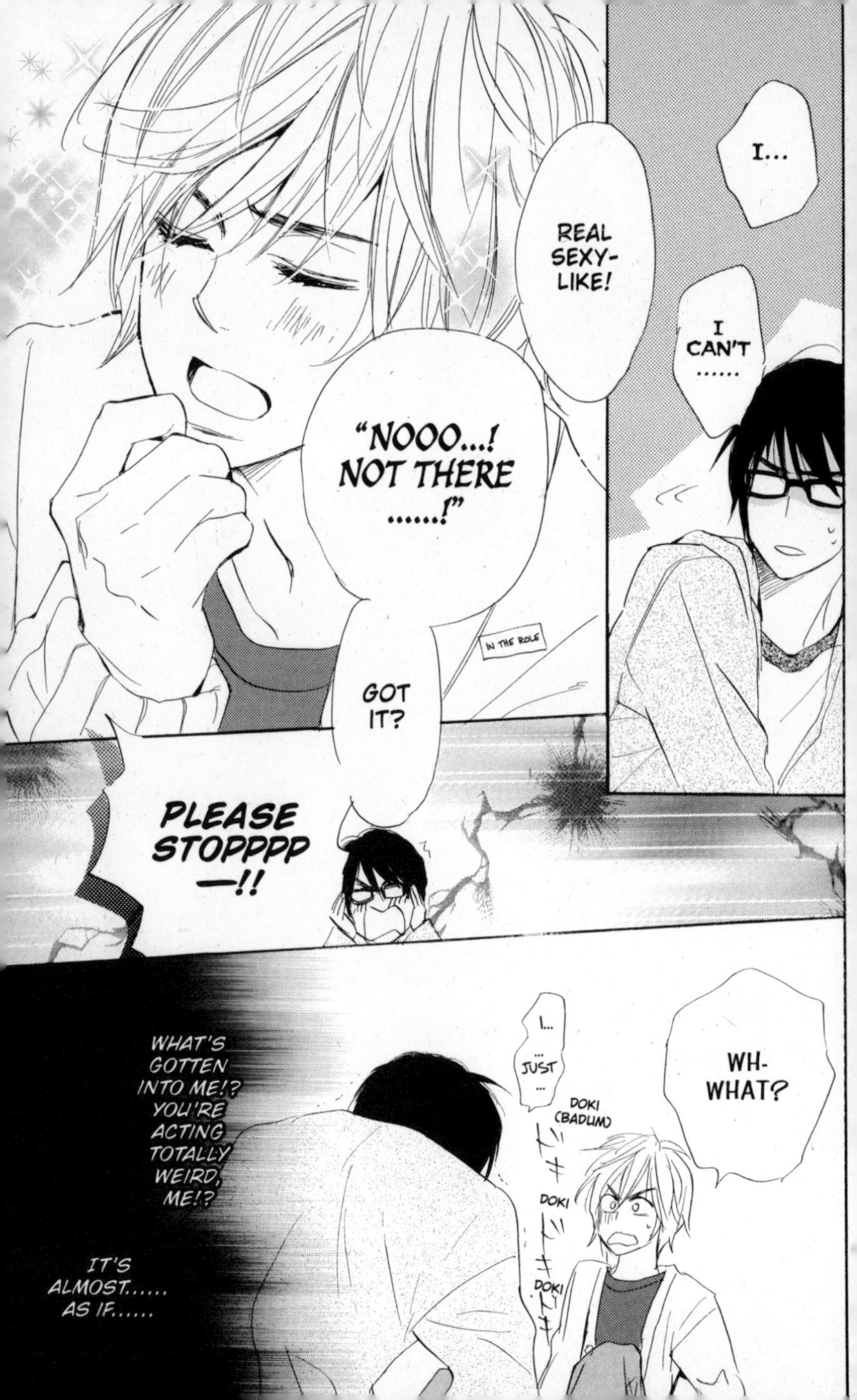
I...
I CAN'T ......
REAL SEXY-LIKE!
“NOOO...! NOT THERE ......!”
IN THE ROLE
GOT IT?
PLEASE STOPPPP—!!
WH-WHAT?
I... ... JUST ...
DOKI (BADUM)
DOKI
DOKI
WHAT'S GOTTEN INTO ME!? YOU'RE ACTING TOTALLY WEIRD, ME!?
IT'S ALMOST...... AS IF......

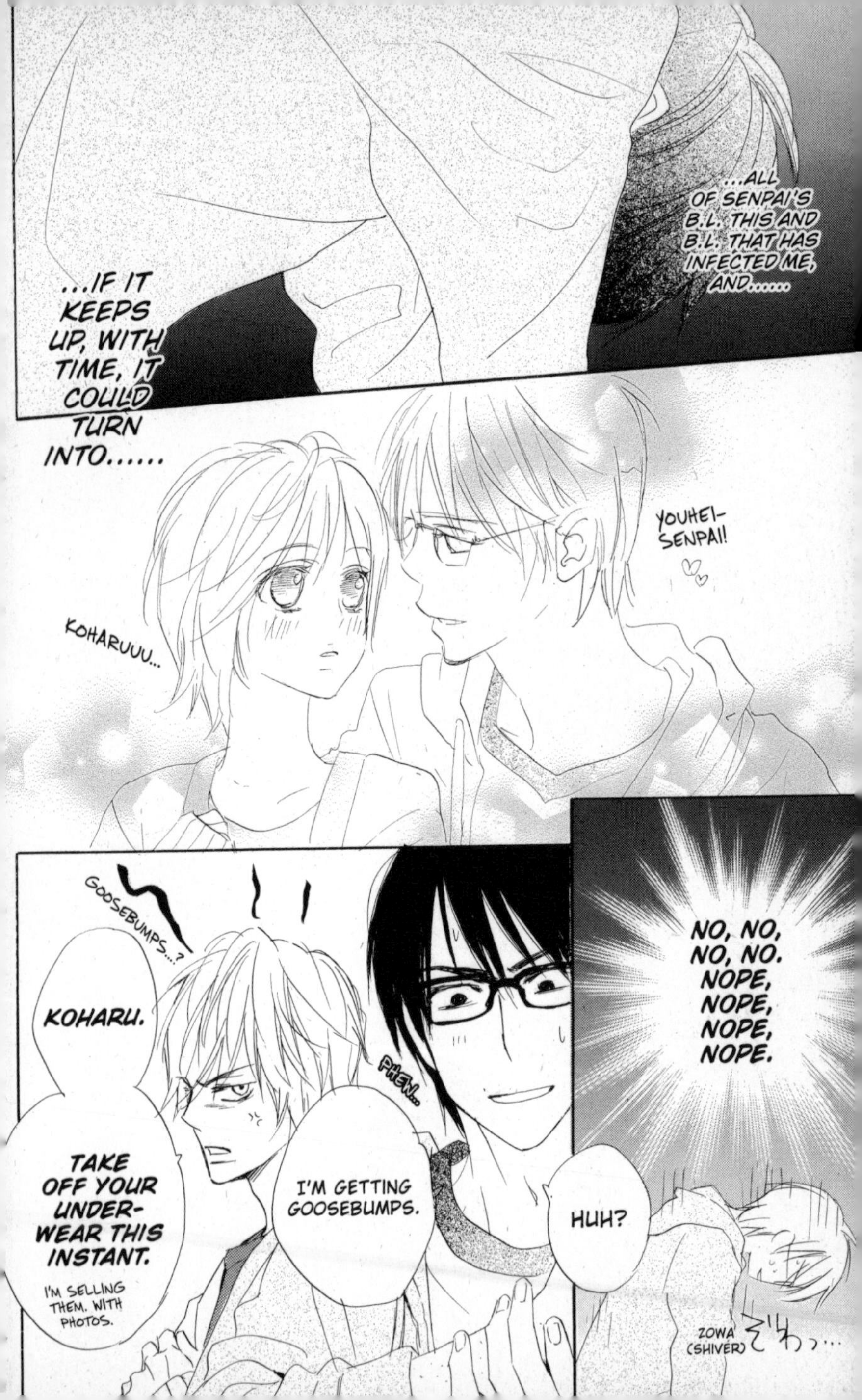
...ALL OF SENPAI'S B.L. THIS AND B.L. THAT HAS INFECTED ME, AND......
...IF IT KEEPS UP, WITH TIME, IT COULD TURN INTO......
YOUHEI-SENPAI!
KOHARUUU...
NO, NO, NO, NO. NOPE, NOPE, NOPE, NOPE.
ZOWA (SHIVER) ぞわっ...
HUH?
I'M GETTING GOOSEBUMPS.
PHEW...
GOOSEBUMPS...?
KOHARU.
TAKE OFF YOUR UNDER-WEAR THIS INSTANT.
I'M SELLING THEM. WITH PHOTOS.

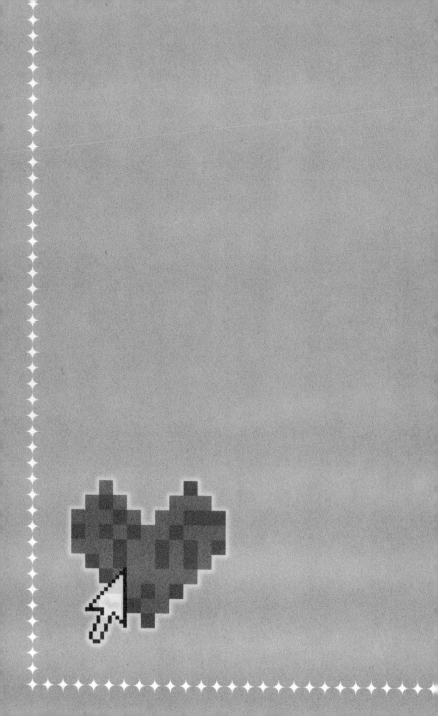

FUJOSHI NEWS vol.15

SPECIAL SALES ILLUSTRATIONS♥

WHEN THE VOLUMES GO ON SALE, SHINBA-SENSEI WHIPS UP SOME ILLUSTRATIONS TO DISPLAY IN STORES.♥ THEY'VE NEVER BEEN SEEN IN BOOK FORM BEFORE.☆

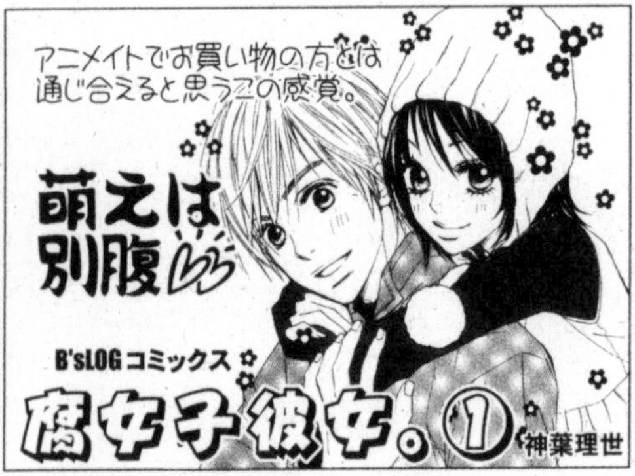
アニメイトでお買い物の方とは
通じ合えると思うこの感覚。
萌えは別腹
B'sLOGコミックス
腐女子彼女。①
神葉理世

▲ B'S-LOG COMICS
MY GIRLFRIEND'S A GEEK① ON SALE.
ADVERTISEMENT AT ANIMATE LOCATIONS NATIONWIDE.
I FEEL LIKE WE SHARE SOMETHING IN COMMON WITH PEOPLE WHO SHOP AT ANIMATE... MOE GOES IN A SEPARATE STOMACH!♡♡

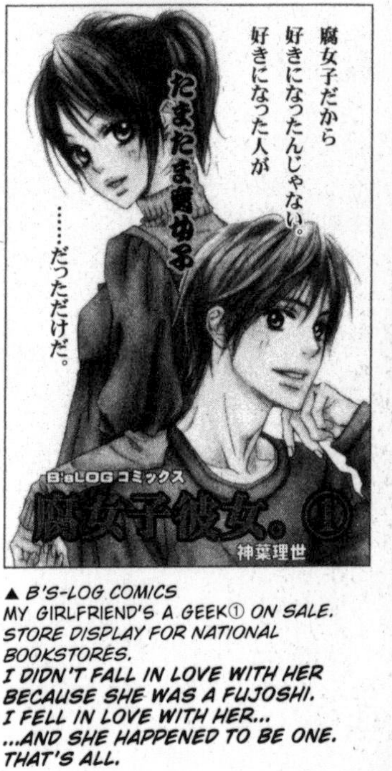
腐女子だから
好きになったんじゃない。
好きになった人が
たまたま腐女子
……だっただけだ。
B'sLOGコミックス
腐女子彼女。①
神葉理世

▲ B'S-LOG COMICS
MY GIRLFRIEND'S A GEEK① ON SALE.
STORE DISPLAY FOR NATIONAL BOOKSTORES.
I DIDN'T FALL IN LOVE WITH HER BECAUSE SHE WAS A FUJOSHI. I FELL IN LOVE WITH HER... ...AND SHE HAPPENED TO BE ONE. THAT'S ALL.

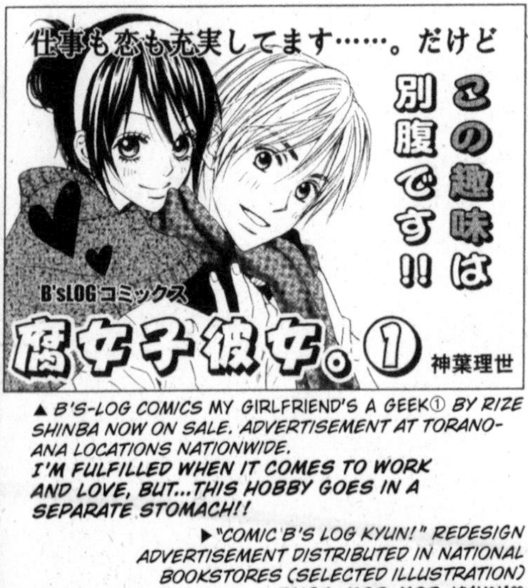
仕事も恋も充実してます……。だけど
この趣味は別腹です!!
B'sLOGコミックス
腐女子彼女。①
神葉理世

▲ B'S-LOG COMICS MY GIRLFRIEND'S A GEEK① BY RIZE SHINBA NOW ON SALE. ADVERTISEMENT AT TORANO-ANA LOCATIONS NATIONWIDE.
I'M FULFILLED WHEN IT COMES TO WORK AND LOVE, BUT...THIS HOBBY GOES IN A SEPARATE STOMACH!!

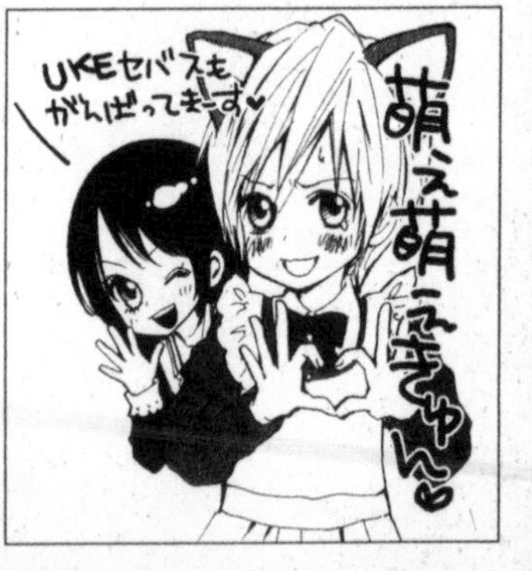
UKEセバスもがんばってまーす♥
萌え萌えきゅん♡

▶ "COMIC B'S LOG KYUN!" REDESIGN ADVERTISEMENT DISTRIBUTED IN NATIONAL BOOKSTORES (SELECTED ILLUSTRATION)
TAIGA: MOE-MOE-KYUN!♡
Y-KO: EVEN UKE-SEBAS IS HARD AT WORK.♥

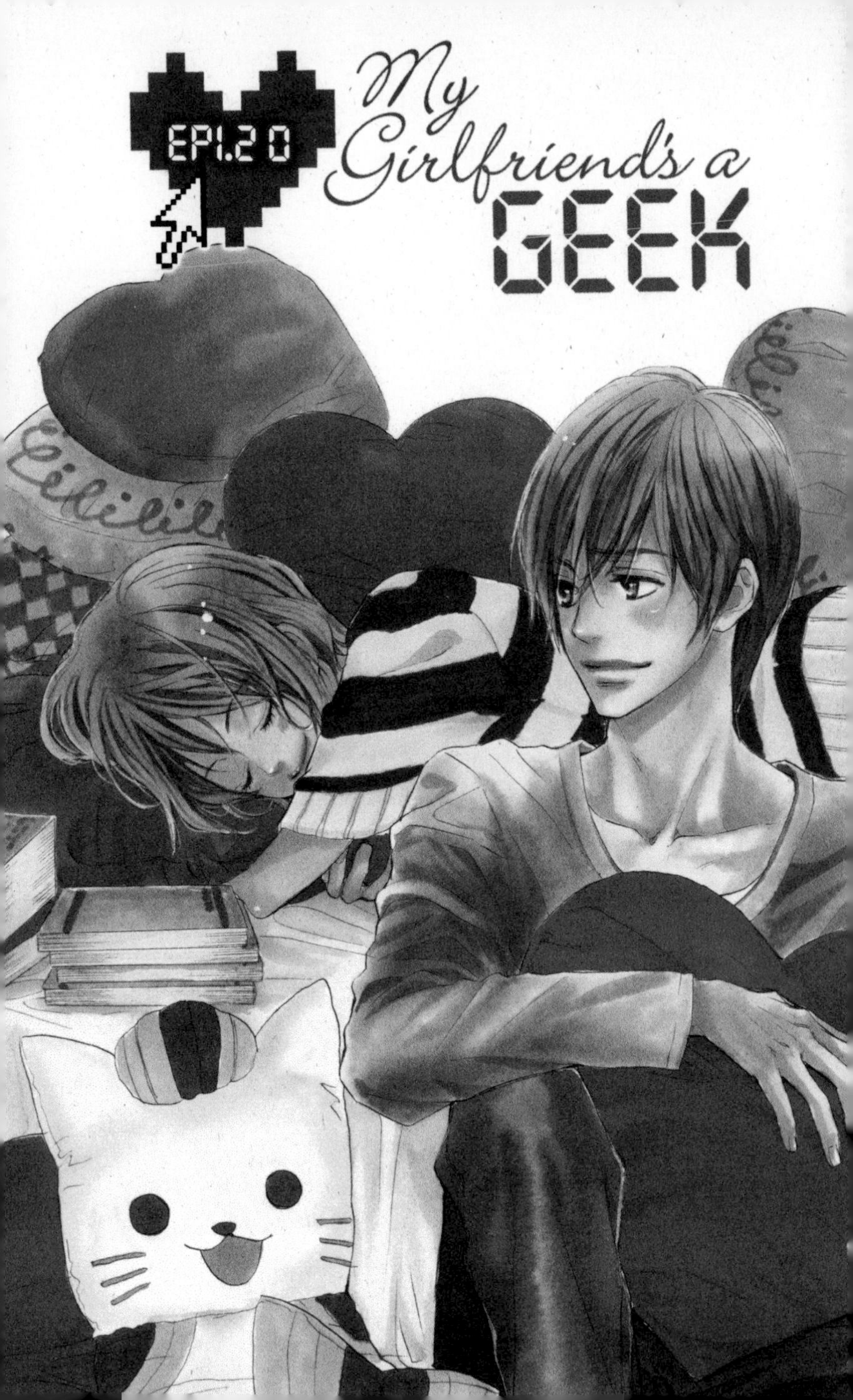
EP1.2 0
My Girlfriend's a
GEEK

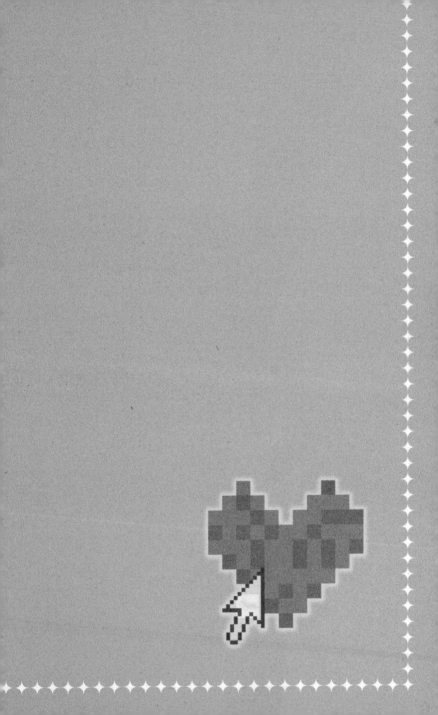

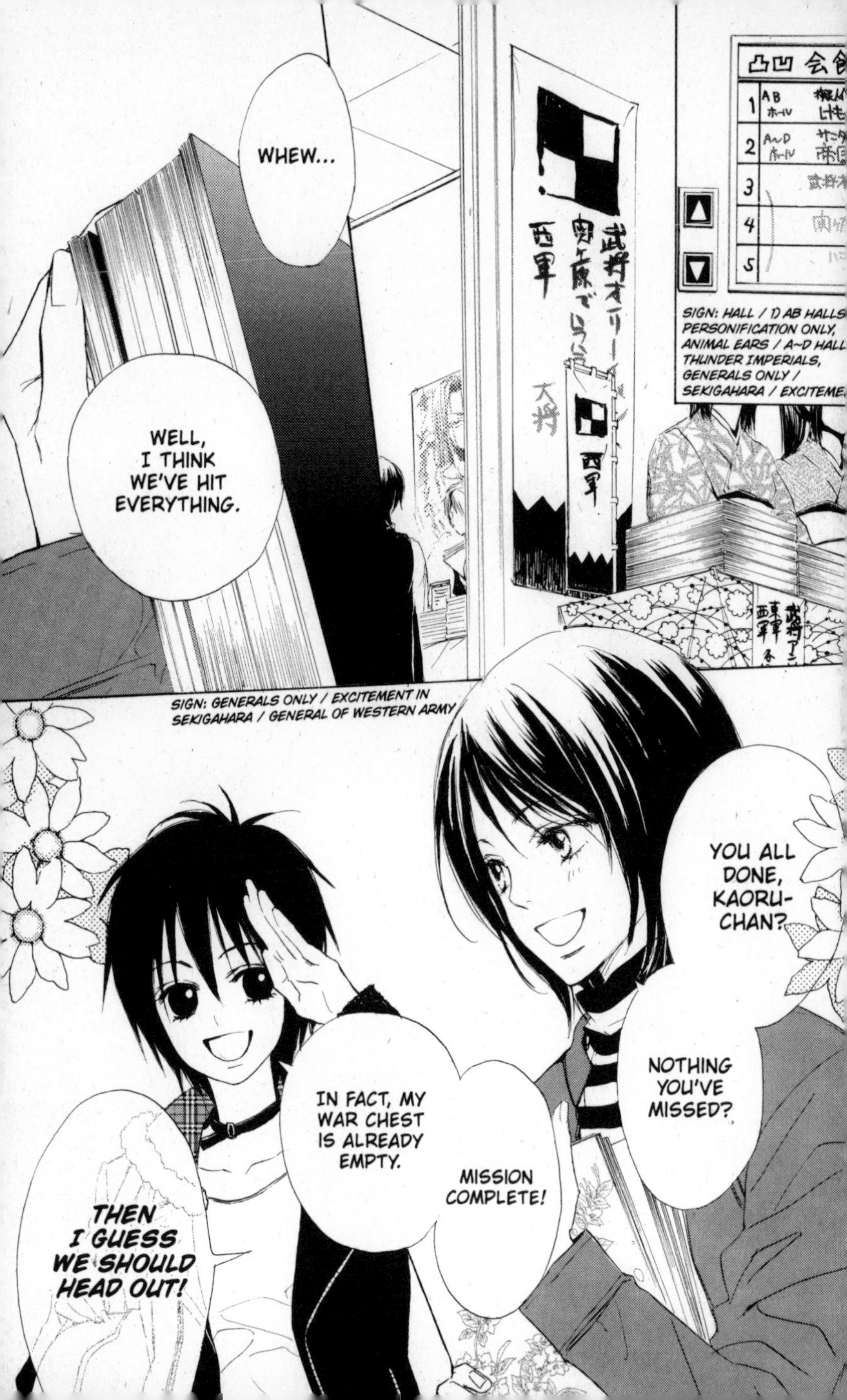
SIGN: HALL / 1) AB HALLS PERSONIFICATION ONLY, ANIMAL EARS / A~D HALL THUNDER IMPERIALS, GENERALS ONLY / SEKIGAHARA / EXCITEME
WHEW...
WELL, I THINK WE'VE HIT EVERYTHING.
SIGN: GENERALS ONLY / EXCITEMENT IN SEKIGAHARA / GENERAL OF WESTERN ARMY
YOU ALL DONE, KAORU-CHAN?
NOTHING YOU'VE MISSED?
MISSION COMPLETE!
IN FACT, MY WAR CHEST IS ALREADY EMPTY.
THEN I GUESS WE SHOULD HEAD OUT!

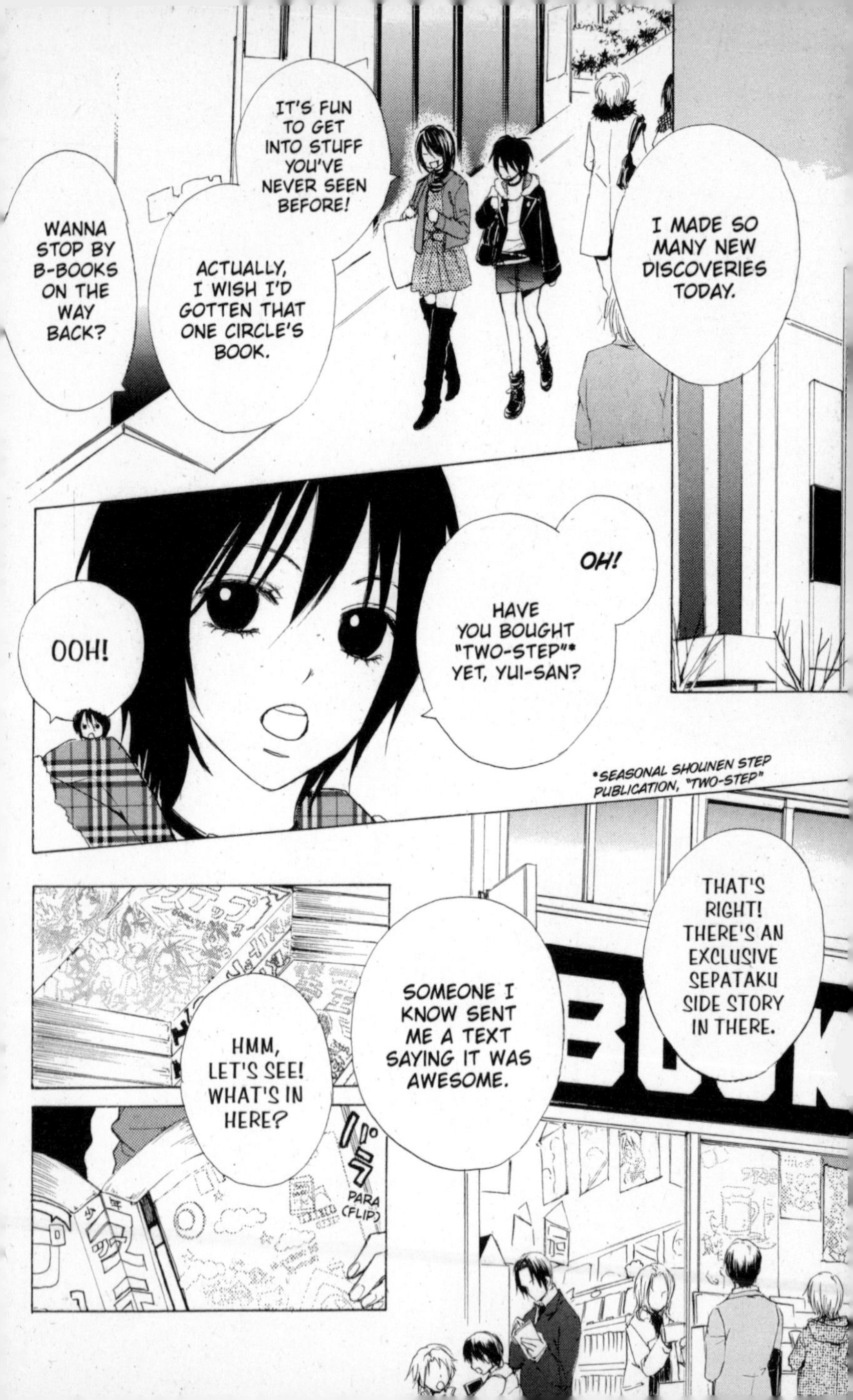
I MADE SO MANY NEW DISCOVERIES TODAY.
IT'S FUN TO GET INTO STUFF YOU'VE NEVER SEEN BEFORE!
ACTUALLY, I WISH I'D GOTTEN THAT ONE CIRCLE'S BOOK.
WANNA STOP BY B-BOOKS ON THE WAY BACK?
OH!
HAVE YOU BOUGHT "TWO-STEP"* YET, YUI-SAN?
OOH!
*SEASONAL SHOUNEN STEP PUBLICATION, "TWO-STEP"
THAT'S RIGHT! THERE'S AN EXCLUSIVE SEPATAKU SIDE STORY IN THERE.
SOMEONE I KNOW SENT ME A TEXT SAYING IT WAS AWESOME.
HMM, LET'S SEE! WHAT'S IN HERE?
PARA (FLIP)

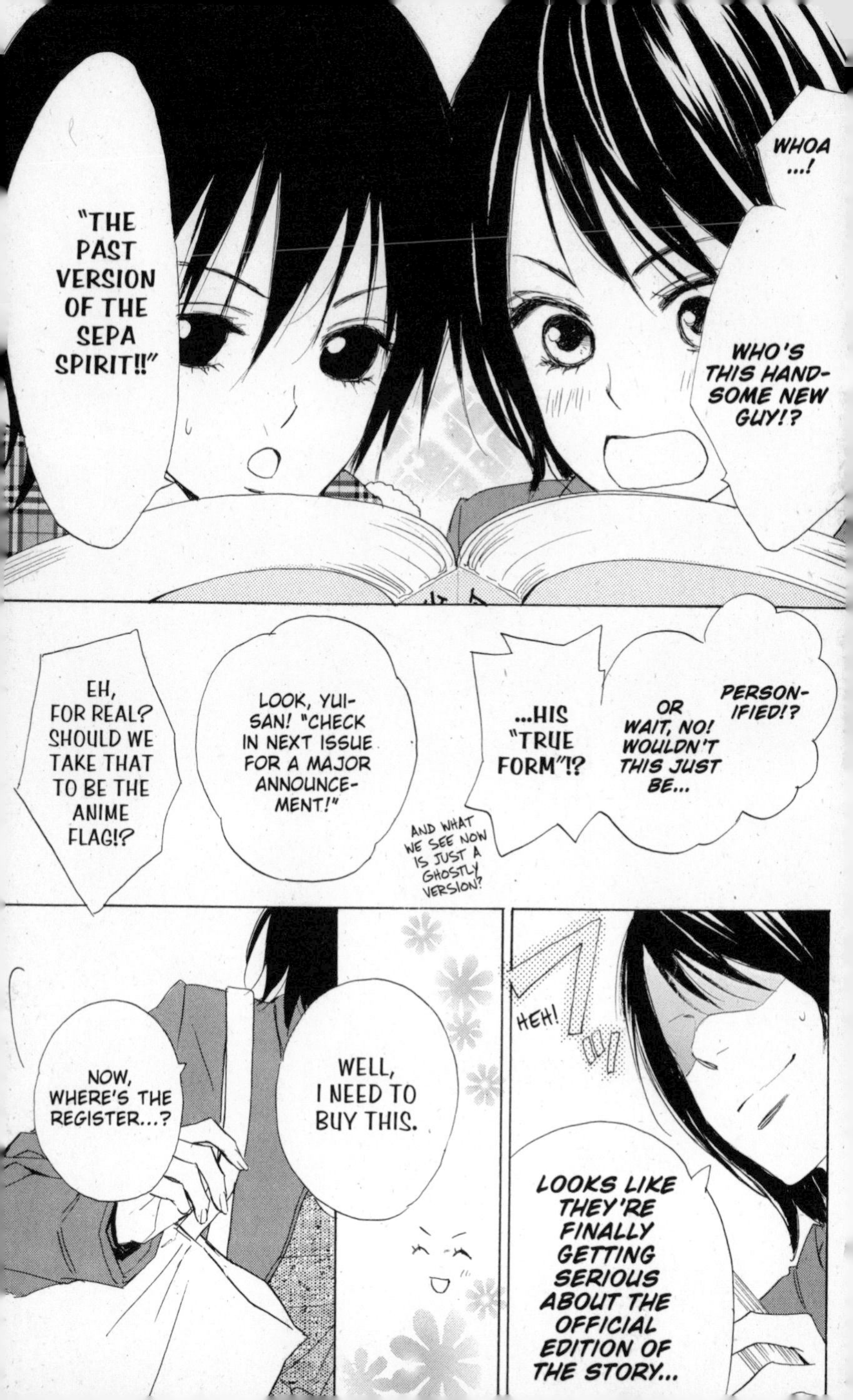
WHOA...!
WHO'S THIS HANDSOME NEW GUY!?
"THE PAST VERSION OF THE SEPA SPIRIT!!"
...HIS "TRUE FORM"!?
AND WHAT WE SEE NOW IS JUST A GHOSTLY VERSION?
OR WAIT, NO! WOULDN'T THIS JUST BE... PERSONIFIED!?
LOOK, YUI-SAN! "CHECK IN NEXT ISSUE FOR A MAJOR ANNOUNCEMENT!"
EH, FOR REAL? SHOULD WE TAKE THAT TO BE THE ANIME FLAG!?
HEH!
LOOKS LIKE THEY'RE FINALLY GETTING SERIOUS ABOUT THE OFFICIAL EDITION OF THE STORY...
WELL, I NEED TO BUY THIS.
NOW, WHERE'S THE REGISTER...?

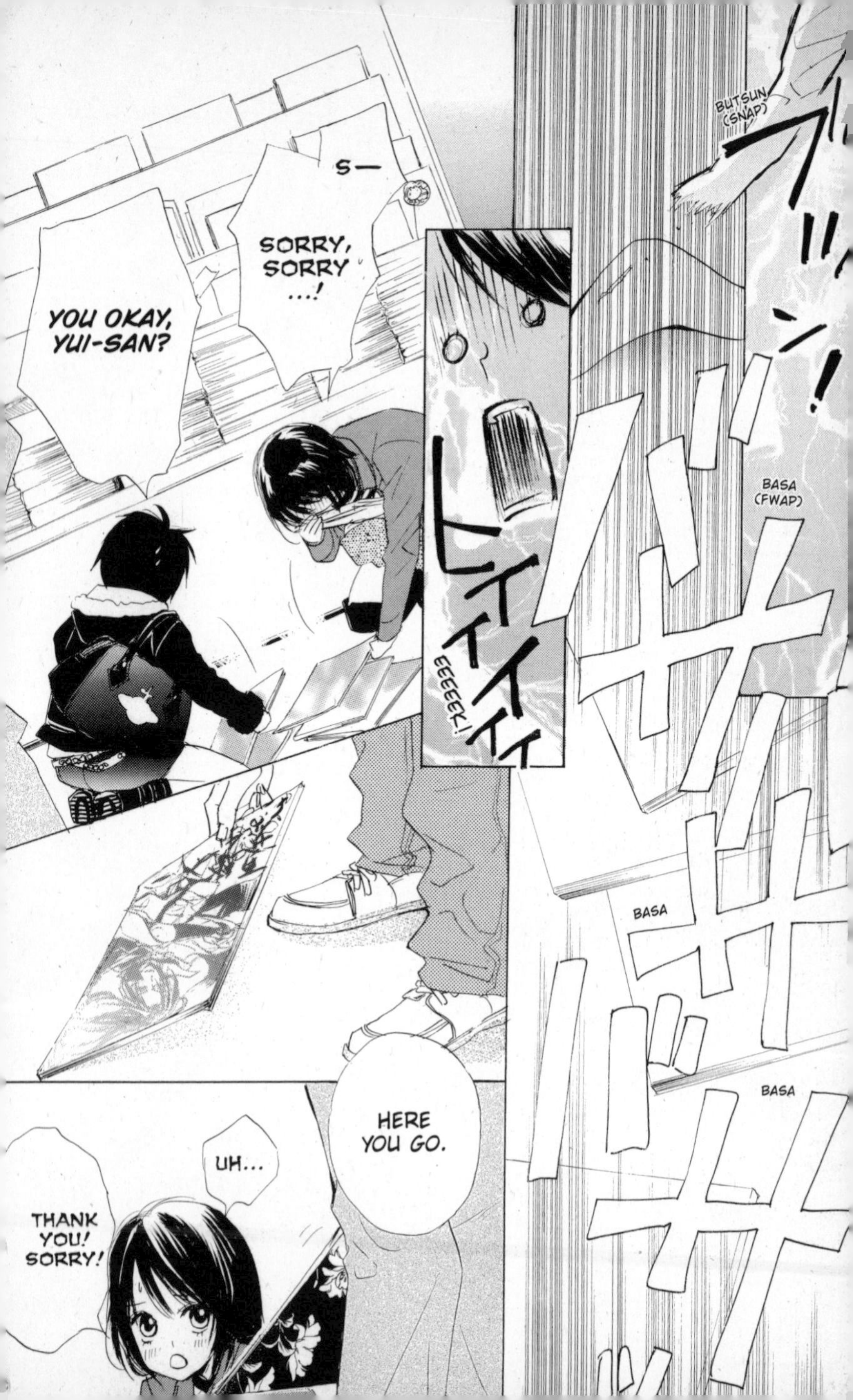
BUTSUN (SNAP)
BASA (FWAP)
BASA
BASA
EEEEEK!
S—
SORRY, SORRY ...!
YOU OKAY, YUI-SAN?
HERE YOU GO.
UH...
THANK YOU! SORRY!

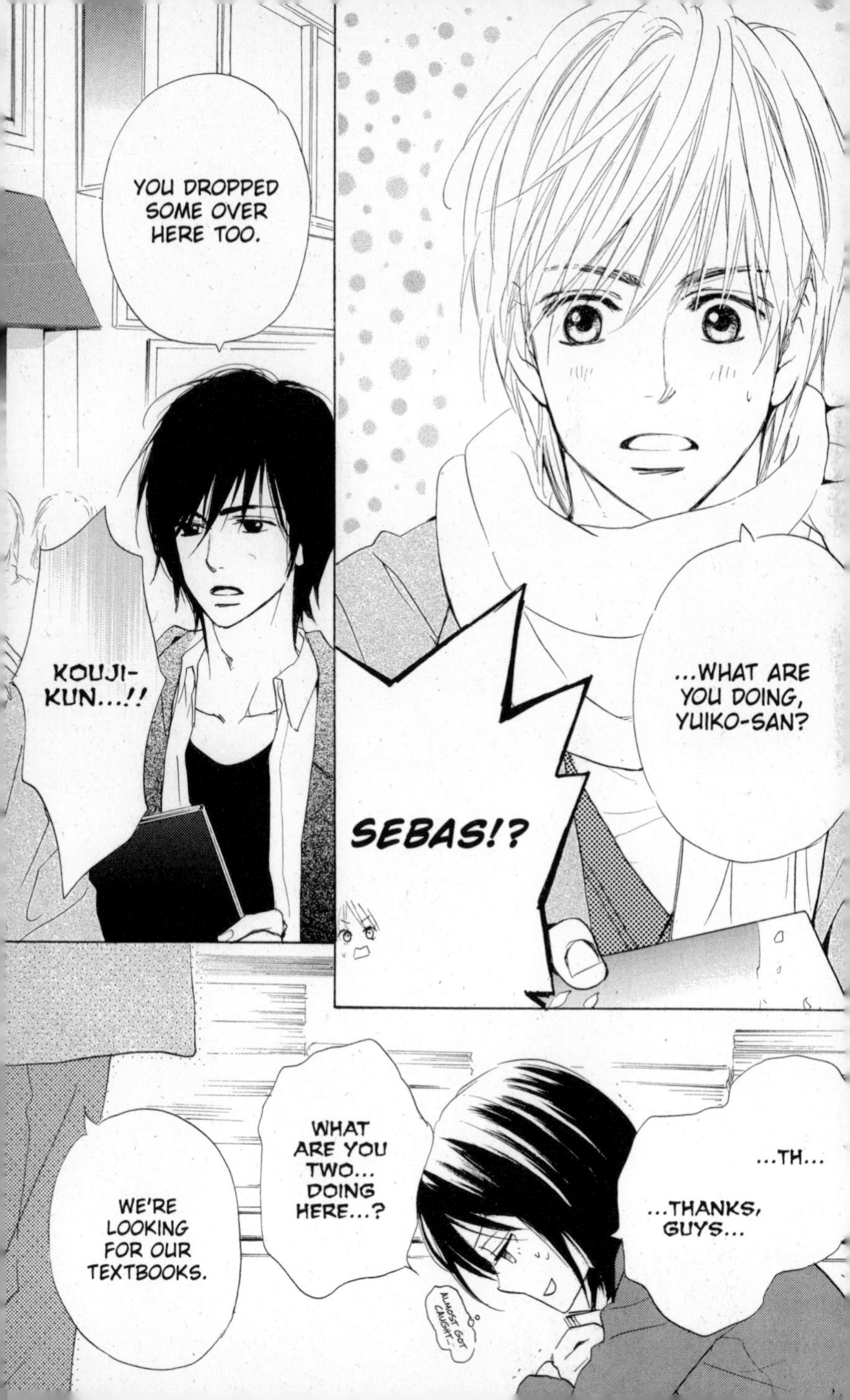
...WHAT ARE YOU DOING, YUIKO-SAN?
SEBAS!?
YOU DROPPED SOME OVER HERE TOO.
KOUJI-KUN...!!
...TH...
...THANKS, GUYS...
ALMOST GOT CAUGHT...
WHAT ARE YOU TWO... DOING HERE...?
WE'RE LOOKING FOR OUR TEXTBOOKS.

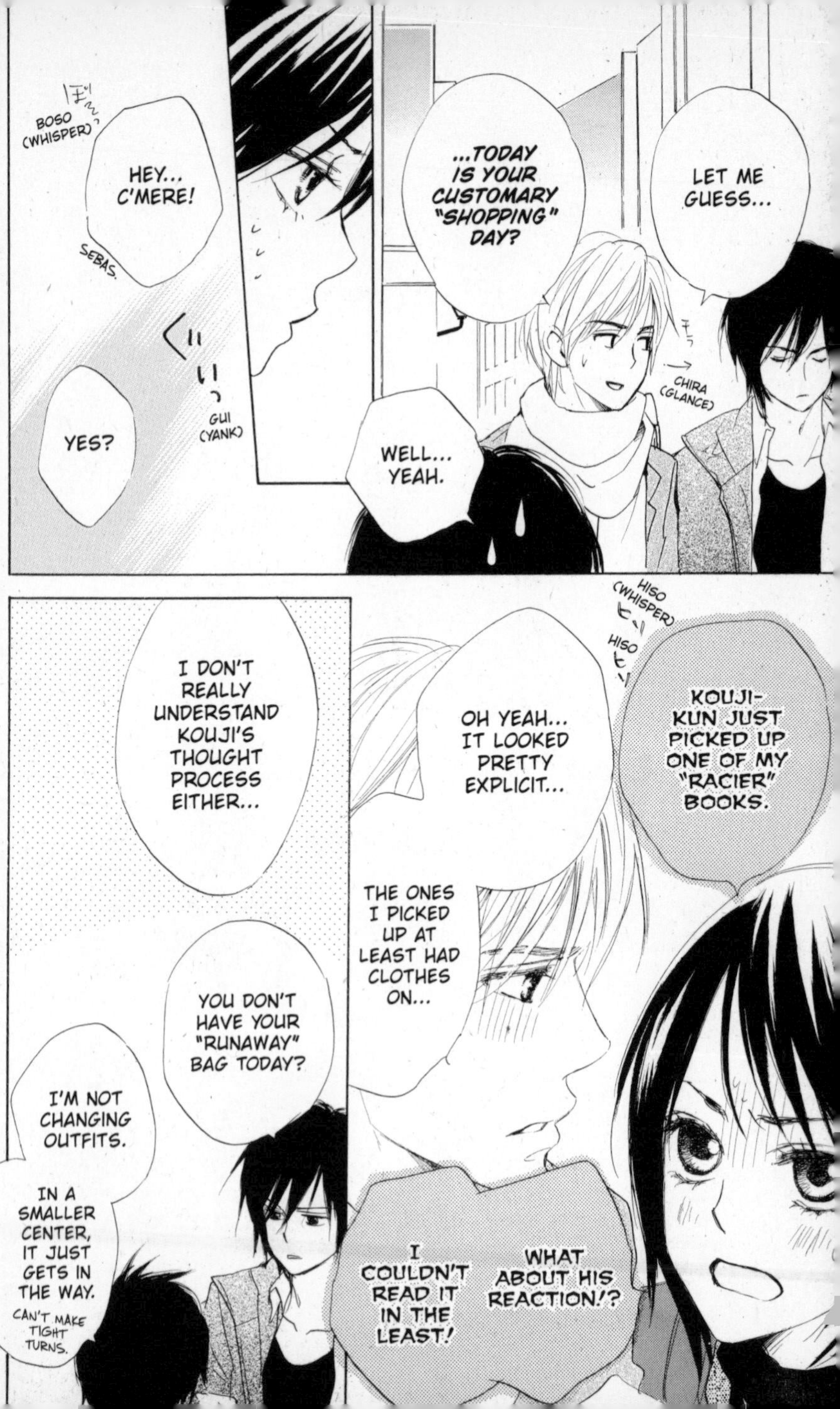
LET ME GUESS...
...TODAY IS YOUR CUSTOMARY "SHOPPING" DAY?
CHIRA (GLANCE)
WELL... YEAH.
BOSO (WHISPER)
HEY... C'MERE!
SEBAS.
GUI (YANK)
YES?
HISO (WHISPER)
HISO
KOUJI-KUN JUST PICKED UP ONE OF MY "RACIER" BOOKS.
OH YEAH... IT LOOKED PRETTY EXPLICIT...
THE ONES I PICKED UP AT LEAST HAD CLOTHES ON...
WHAT ABOUT HIS REACTION!?
I COULDN'T READ IT IN THE LEAST!
I DON'T REALLY UNDERSTAND KOUJI'S THOUGHT PROCESS EITHER...
YOU DON'T HAVE YOUR "RUNAWAY" BAG TODAY?
I'M NOT CHANGING OUTFITS.
IN A SMALLER CENTER, IT JUST GETS IN THE WAY.
CAN'T MAKE TIGHT TURNS.

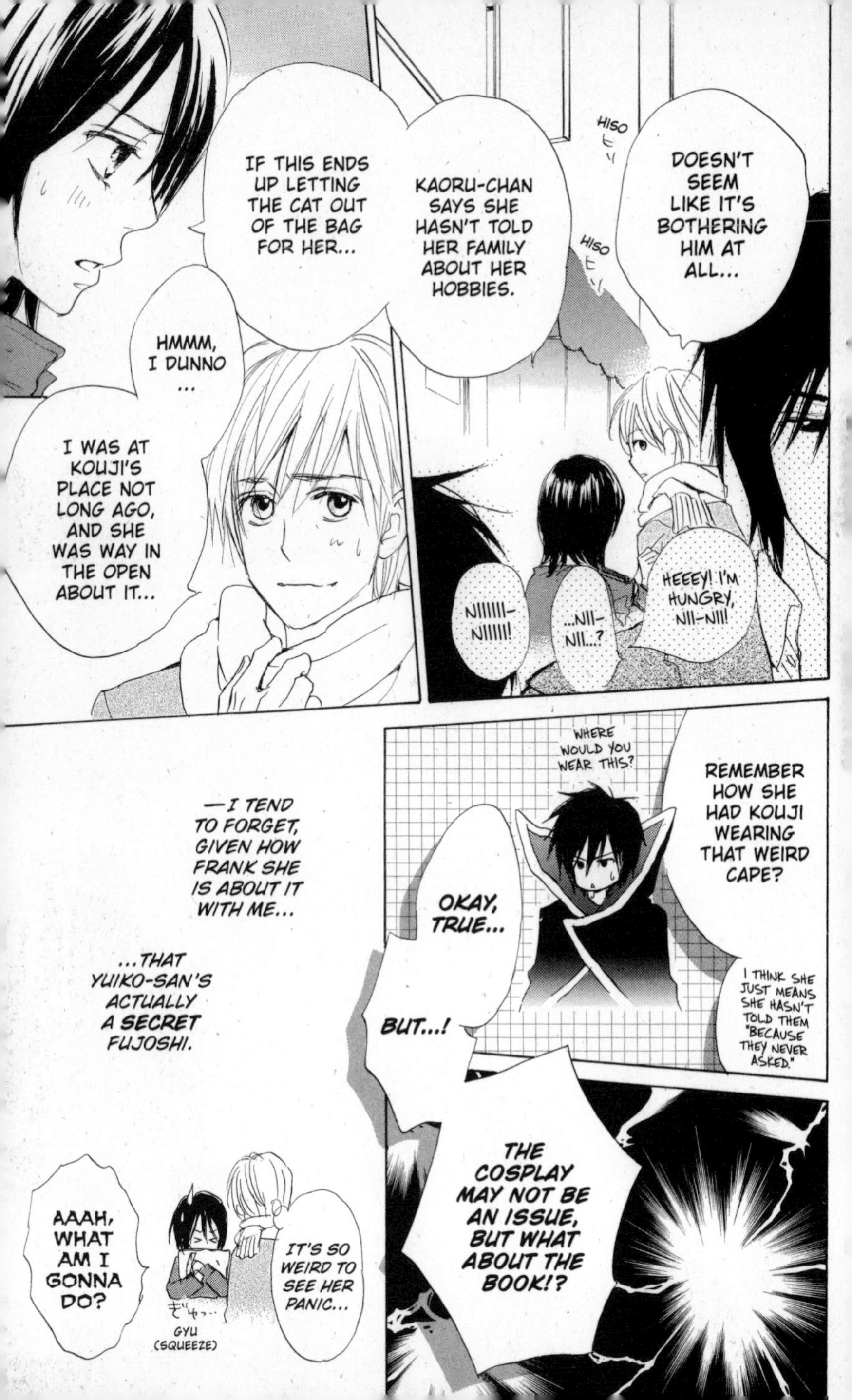
HISO
HISO
DOESN'T SEEM LIKE IT'S BOTHERING HIM AT ALL...
HEEEY! I'M HUNGRY, NII-NII!
...NII-NII...?
NIIIII-NIIIII!
KAORU-CHAN SAYS SHE HASN'T TOLD HER FAMILY ABOUT HER HOBBIES.
IF THIS ENDS UP LETTING THE CAT OUT OF THE BAG FOR HER...
HMMM, I DUNNO...
I WAS AT KOUJI'S PLACE NOT LONG AGO, AND SHE WAS WAY IN THE OPEN ABOUT IT...
REMEMBER HOW SHE HAD KOUJI WEARING THAT WEIRD CAPE?
WHERE WOULD YOU WEAR THIS?
OKAY, TRUE...
BUT...!
I THINK SHE JUST MEANS SHE HASN'T TOLD THEM "BECAUSE THEY NEVER ASKED."
THE COSPLAY MAY NOT BE AN ISSUE, BUT WHAT ABOUT THE BOOK!?
—I TEND TO FORGET, GIVEN HOW FRANK SHE IS ABOUT IT WITH ME...
...THAT YUIKO-SAN'S ACTUALLY A SECRET FUJOSHI.
IT'S SO WEIRD TO SEE HER PANIC...
AAAH, WHAT AM I GONNA DO?
GYU (SQUEEZE)

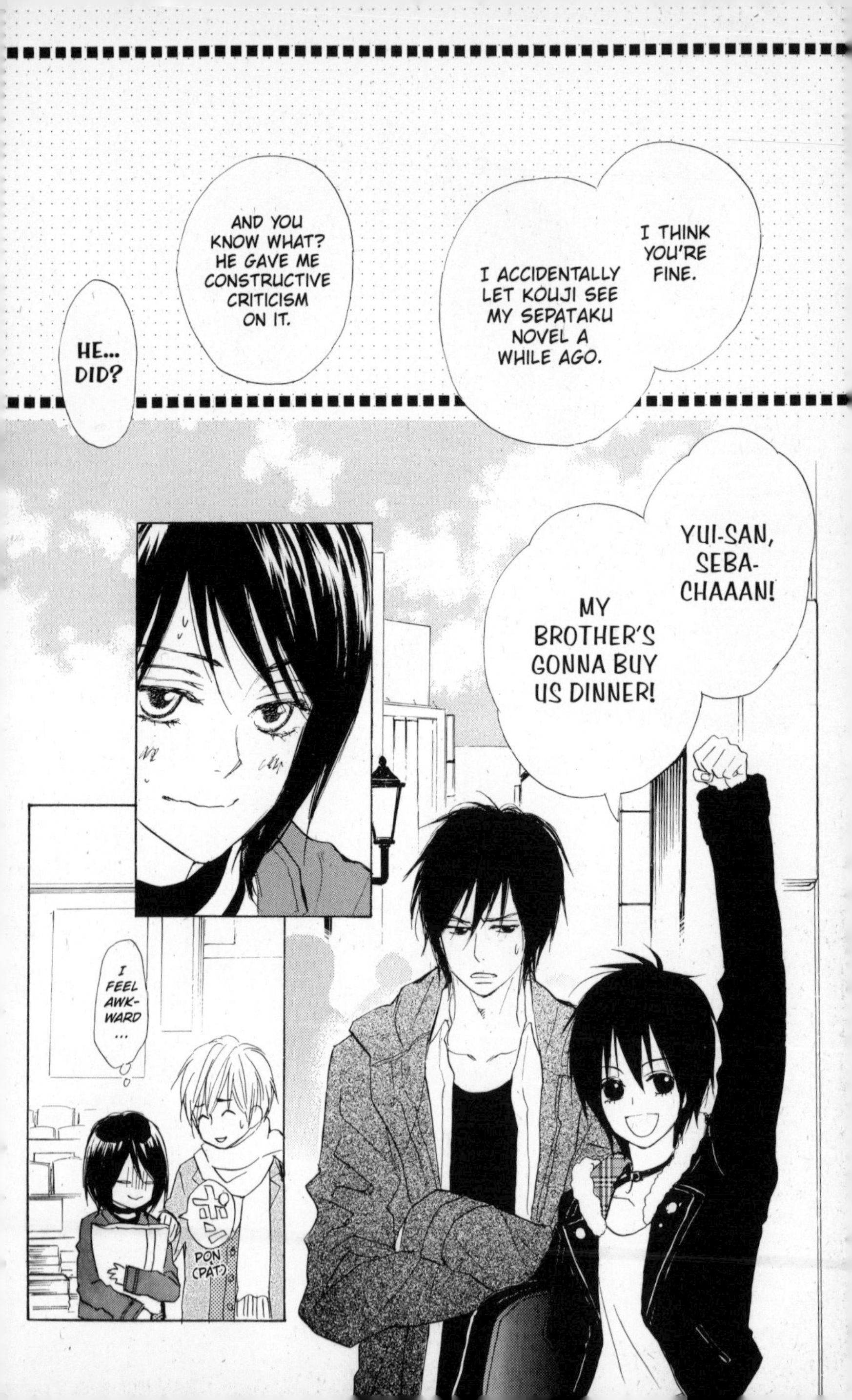
I THINK YOU'RE FINE.
I ACCIDENTALLY LET KOUJI SEE MY SEPATAKU NOVEL A WHILE AGO.
AND YOU KNOW WHAT? HE GAVE ME CONSTRUCTIVE CRITICISM ON IT.
HE... DID?
YUI-SAN, SEBA-CHAAAN!
MY BROTHER'S GONNA BUY US DINNER!
I FEEL AWK-WARD...
ポン
PON (PAT)

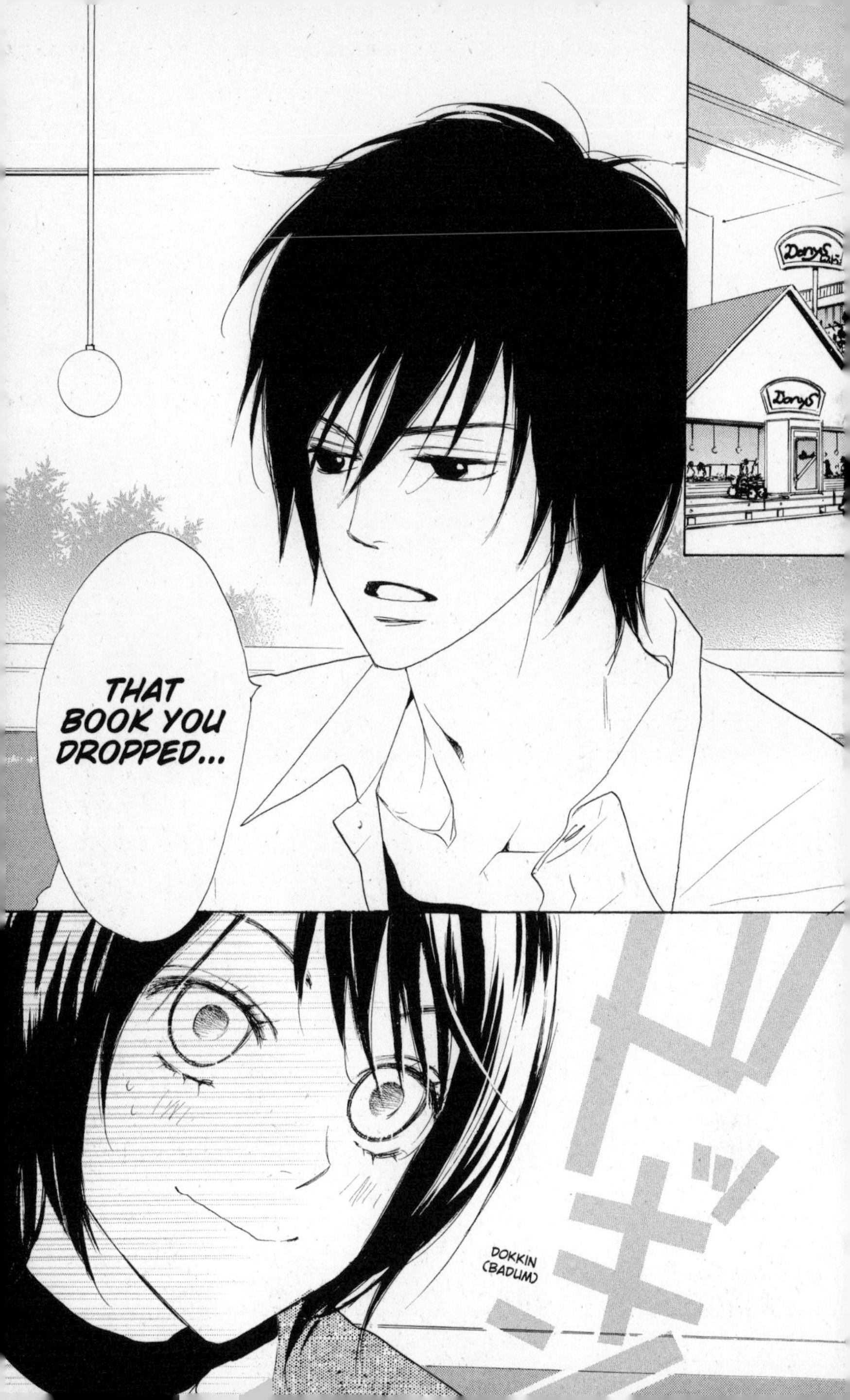
THAT BOOK YOU DROPPED...
DOKKIN (BADUM)

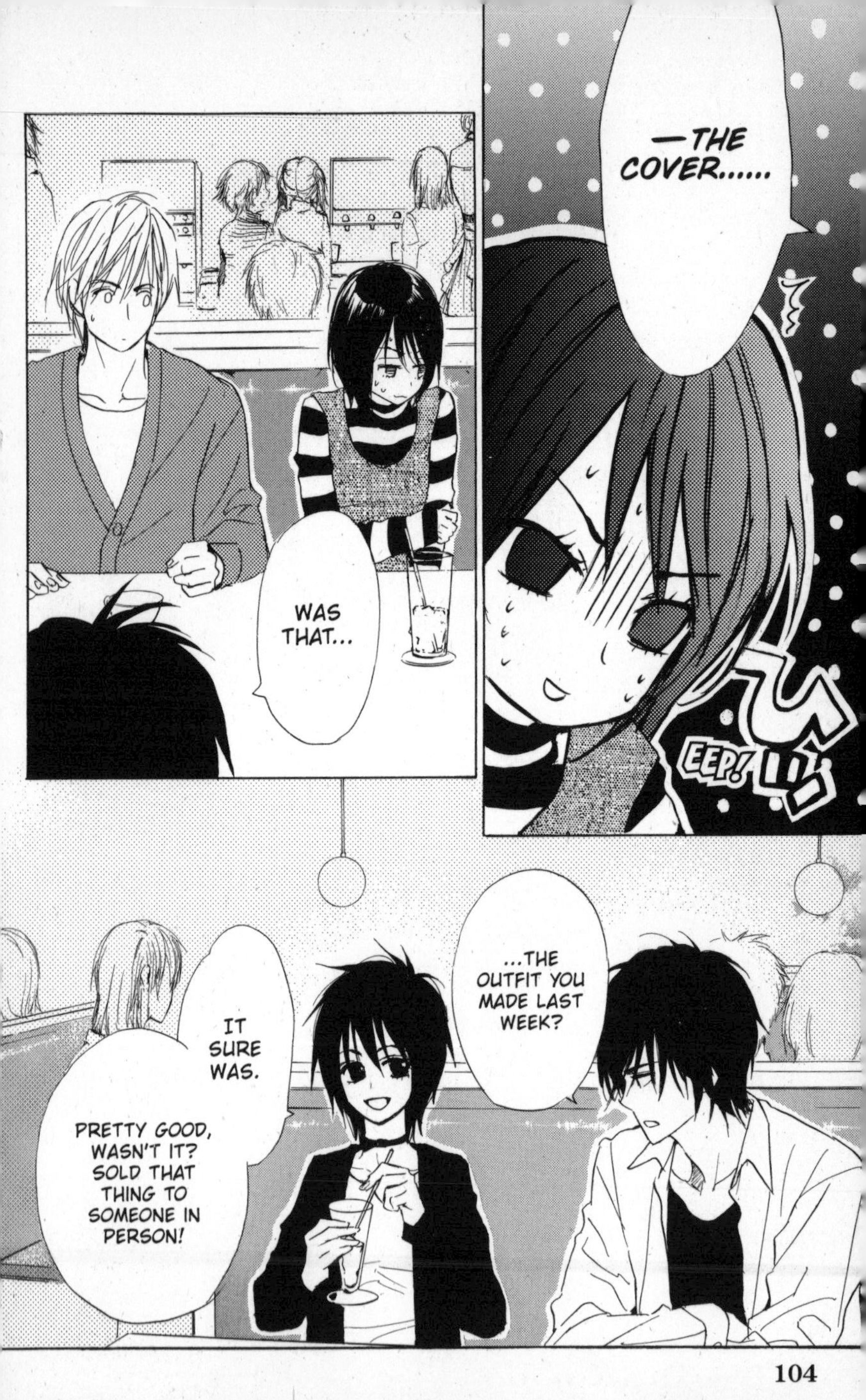
—THE COVER......
EEP!
WAS THAT...
...THE OUTFIT YOU MADE LAST WEEK?
IT SURE WAS.
PRETTY GOOD, WASN'T IT? SOLD THAT THING TO SOMEONE IN PERSON!

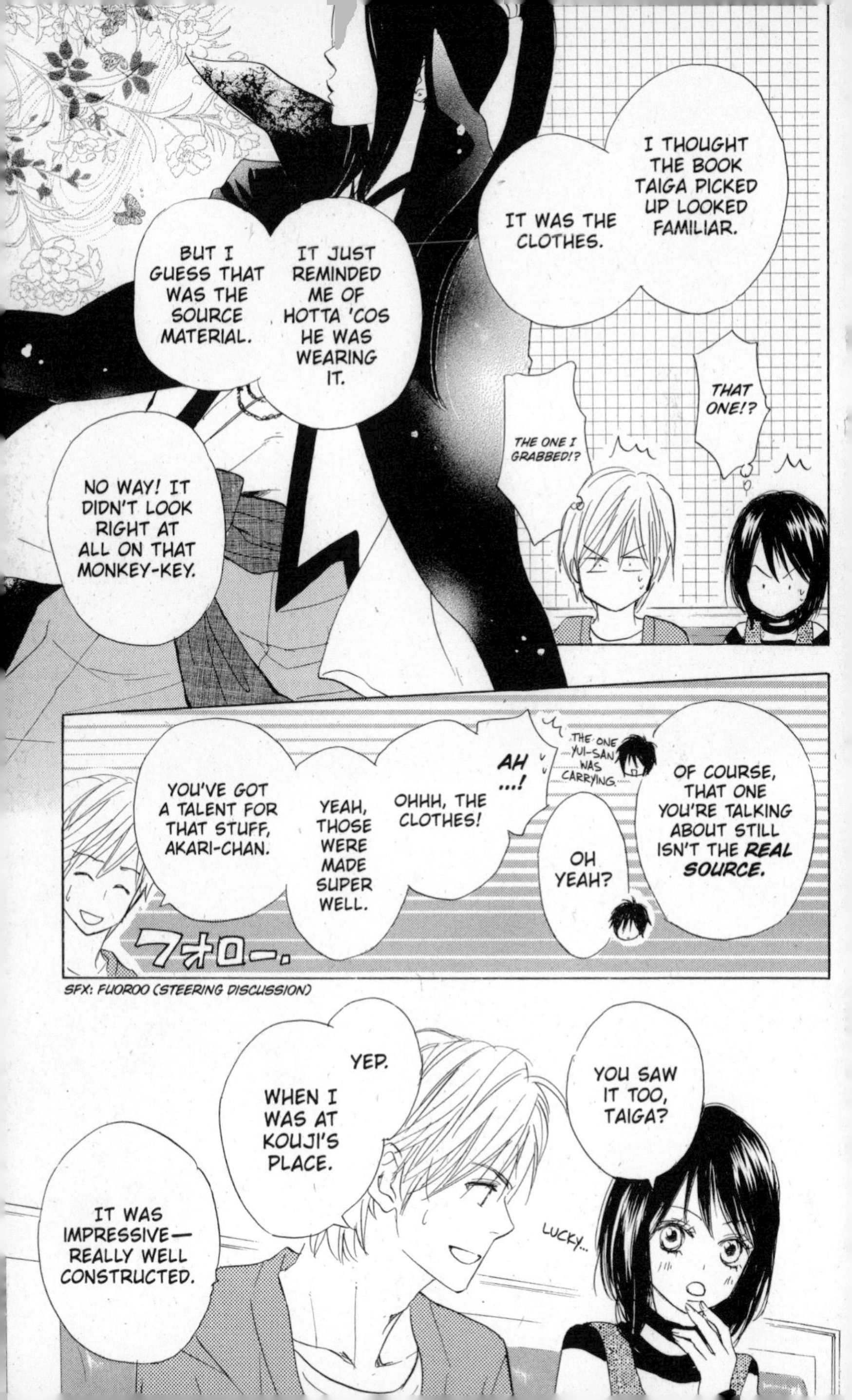
I THOUGHT THE BOOK TAIGA PICKED UP LOOKED FAMILIAR.
IT WAS THE CLOTHES.
IT JUST REMINDED ME OF HOTTA 'COS HE WAS WEARING IT.
BUT I GUESS THAT WAS THE SOURCE MATERIAL.
THAT ONE!?
THE ONE I GRABBED!?
NO WAY! IT DIDN'T LOOK RIGHT AT ALL ON THAT MONKEY-KEY.
OF COURSE, THAT ONE YOU'RE TALKING ABOUT STILL ISN'T THE ***REAL SOURCE.***
THE ONE YUI-SAN WAS CARRYING.
OH YEAH?
AH ...!
OHHH, THE CLOTHES!
YEAH, THOSE WERE MADE SUPER WELL.
YOU'VE GOT A TALENT FOR THAT STUFF, AKARI-CHAN.
フォロー。
SFX: FUOROO (STEERING DISCUSSION)
YOU SAW IT TOO, TAIGA?
YEP.
WHEN I WAS AT KOUJI'S PLACE.
LUCKY...
IT WAS IMPRESSIVE—REALLY WELL CONSTRUCTED.

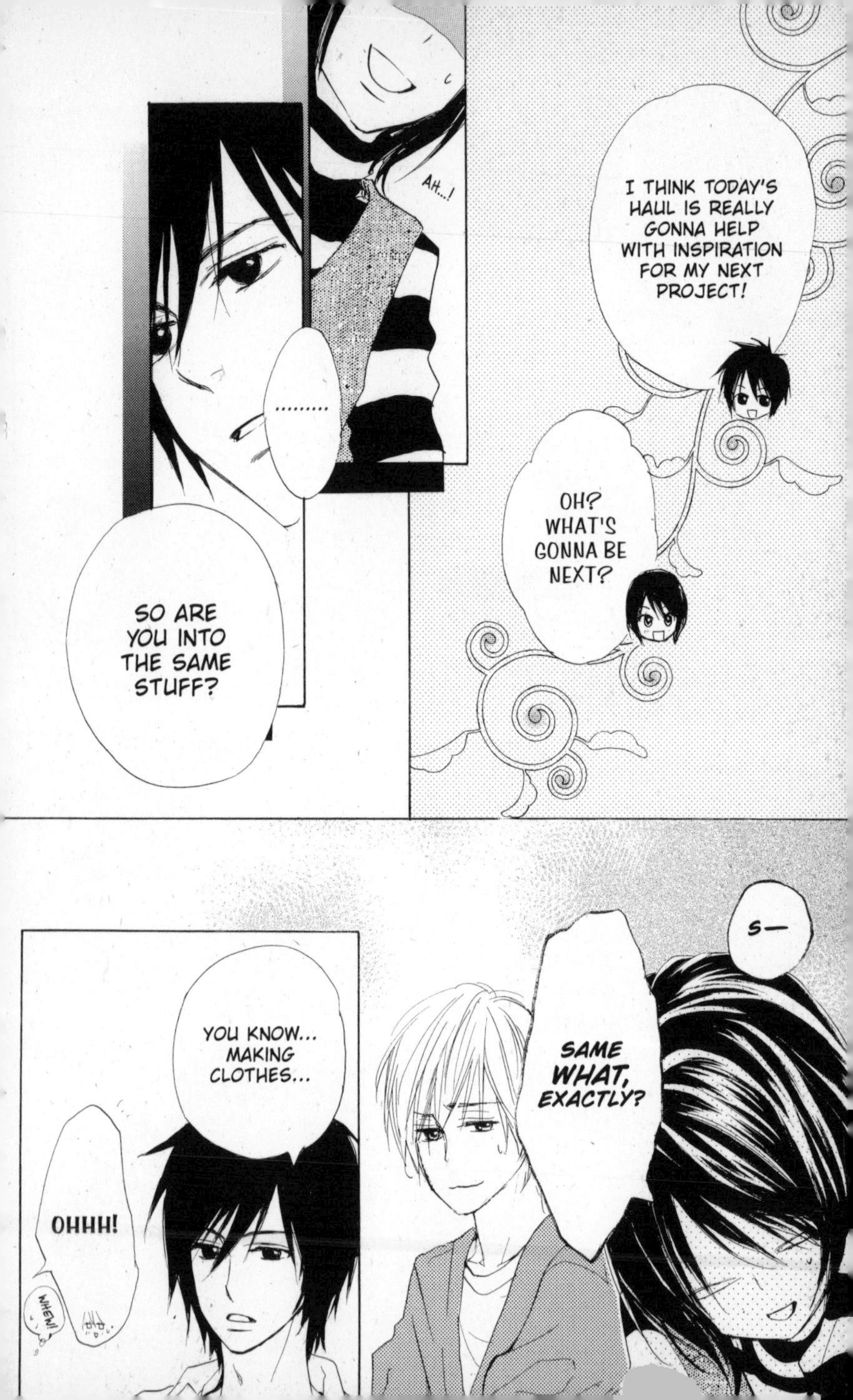
I THINK TODAY'S HAUL IS REALLY GONNA HELP WITH INSPIRATION FOR MY NEXT PROJECT!
OH? WHAT'S GONNA BE NEXT?
AH...!
....
SO ARE YOU INTO THE SAME STUFF?
S—
SAME WHAT, EXACTLY?
YOU KNOW... MAKING CLOTHES...
OHHH!
WHEW!

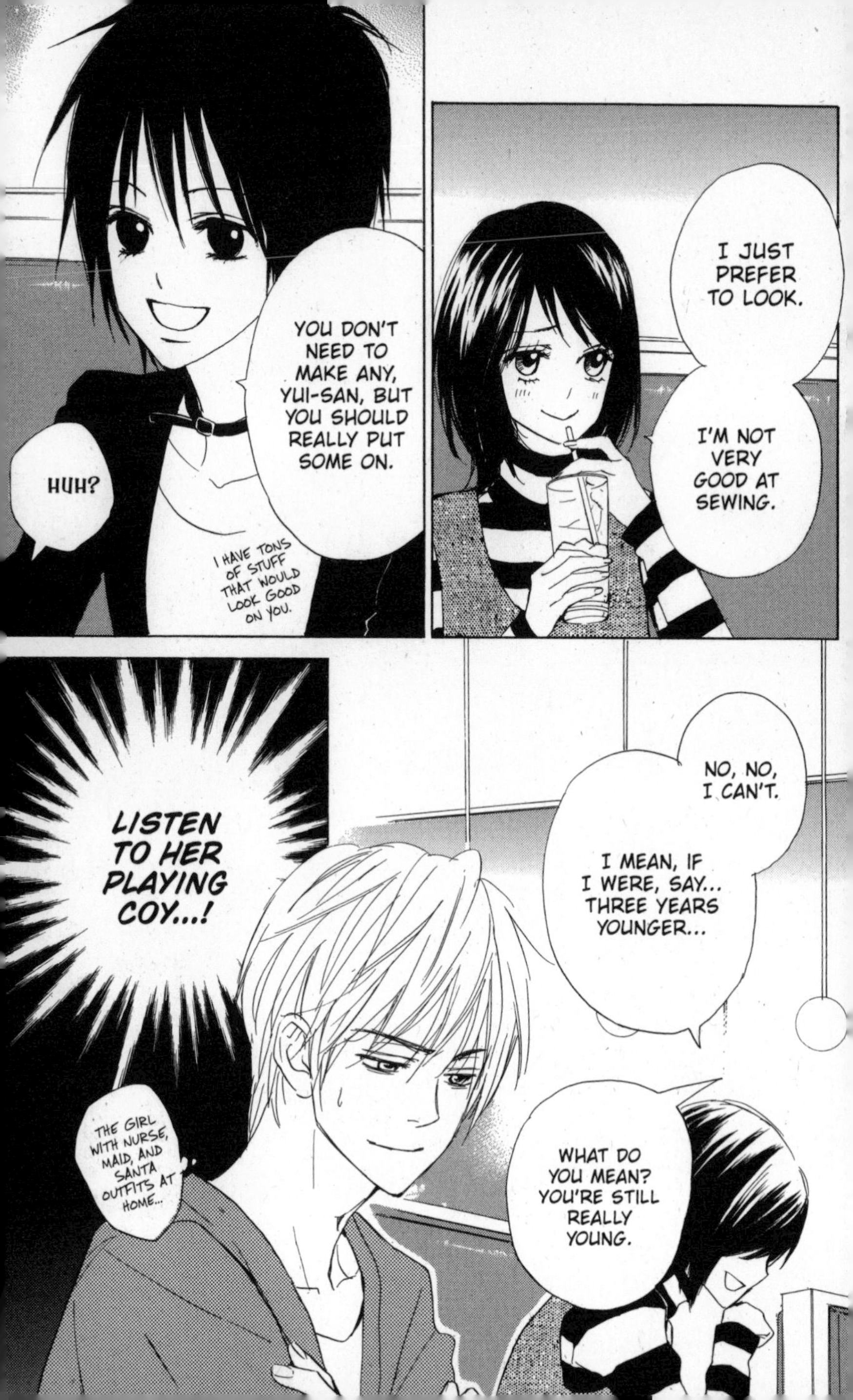
I JUST PREFER TO LOOK.
I'M NOT VERY GOOD AT SEWING.
YOU DON'T NEED TO MAKE ANY, YUI-SAN, BUT YOU SHOULD REALLY PUT SOME ON.
HUH?
I HAVE TONS OF STUFF THAT WOULD LOOK GOOD ON YOU.
NO, NO, I CAN'T.
I MEAN, IF I WERE, SAY... THREE YEARS YOUNGER...
WHAT DO YOU MEAN? YOU'RE STILL REALLY YOUNG.
LISTEN TO HER PLAYING COY...!
THE GIRL WITH NURSE, MAID, AND SANTA OUTFITS AT HOME...

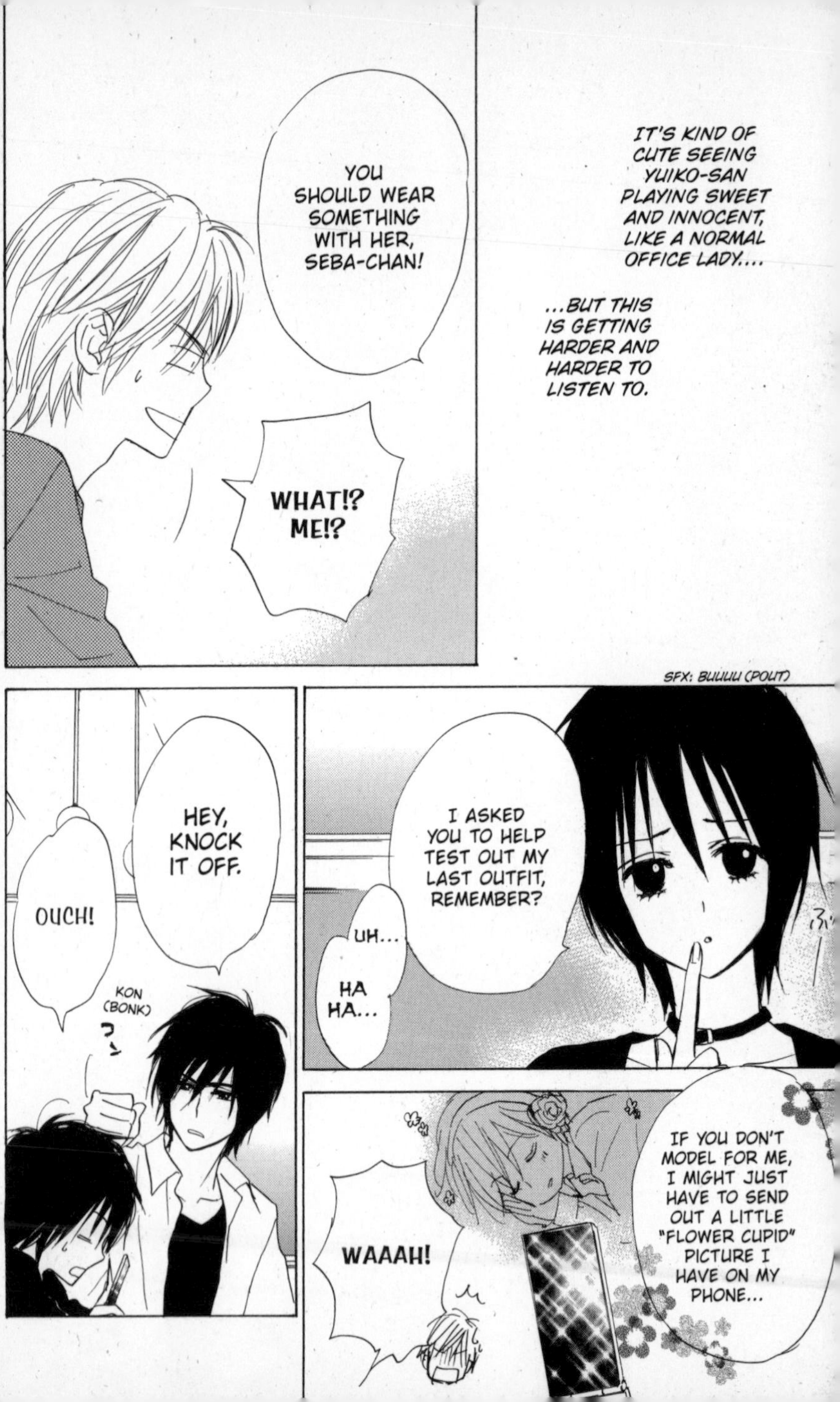
IT'S KIND OF CUTE SEEING YUIKO-SAN PLAYING SWEET AND INNOCENT, LIKE A NORMAL OFFICE LADY....
...BUT THIS IS GETTING HARDER AND HARDER TO LISTEN TO.
YOU SHOULD WEAR SOMETHING WITH HER, SEBA-CHAN!
WHAT!? ME!?
SFX: BUUUU (POUT)
I ASKED YOU TO HELP TEST OUT MY LAST OUTFIT, REMEMBER?
UH...
HA HA...
IF YOU DON'T MODEL FOR ME, I MIGHT JUST HAVE TO SEND OUT A LITTLE "FLOWER CUPID" PICTURE I HAVE ON MY PHONE...
WAAAH!
HEY, KNOCK IT OFF.
KON (BONK)
OUCH!

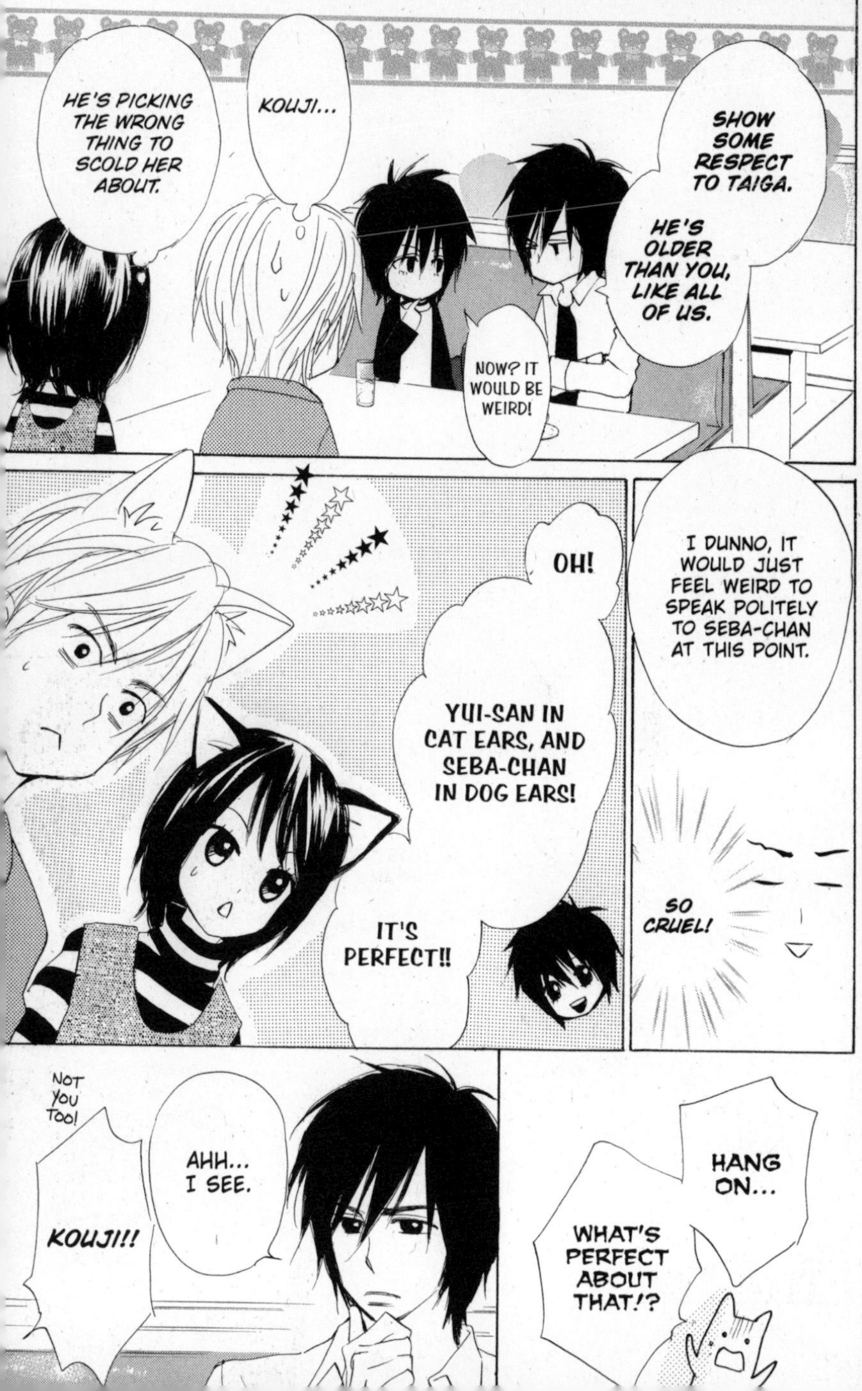
SHOW SOME RESPECT TO TAIGA.
HE'S OLDER THAN YOU, LIKE ALL OF US.
NOW? IT WOULD BE WEIRD!
KOUJI...
HE'S PICKING THE WRONG THING TO SCOLD HER ABOUT.
I DUNNO, IT WOULD JUST FEEL WEIRD TO SPEAK POLITELY TO SEBA-CHAN AT THIS POINT.
SO CRUEL!
OH!
YUI-SAN IN CAT EARS, AND SEBA-CHAN IN DOG EARS!
IT'S PERFECT!!
HANG ON...
WHAT'S PERFECT ABOUT THAT!?
AHH... I SEE.
KOUJI!!
NOT YOU TOO!

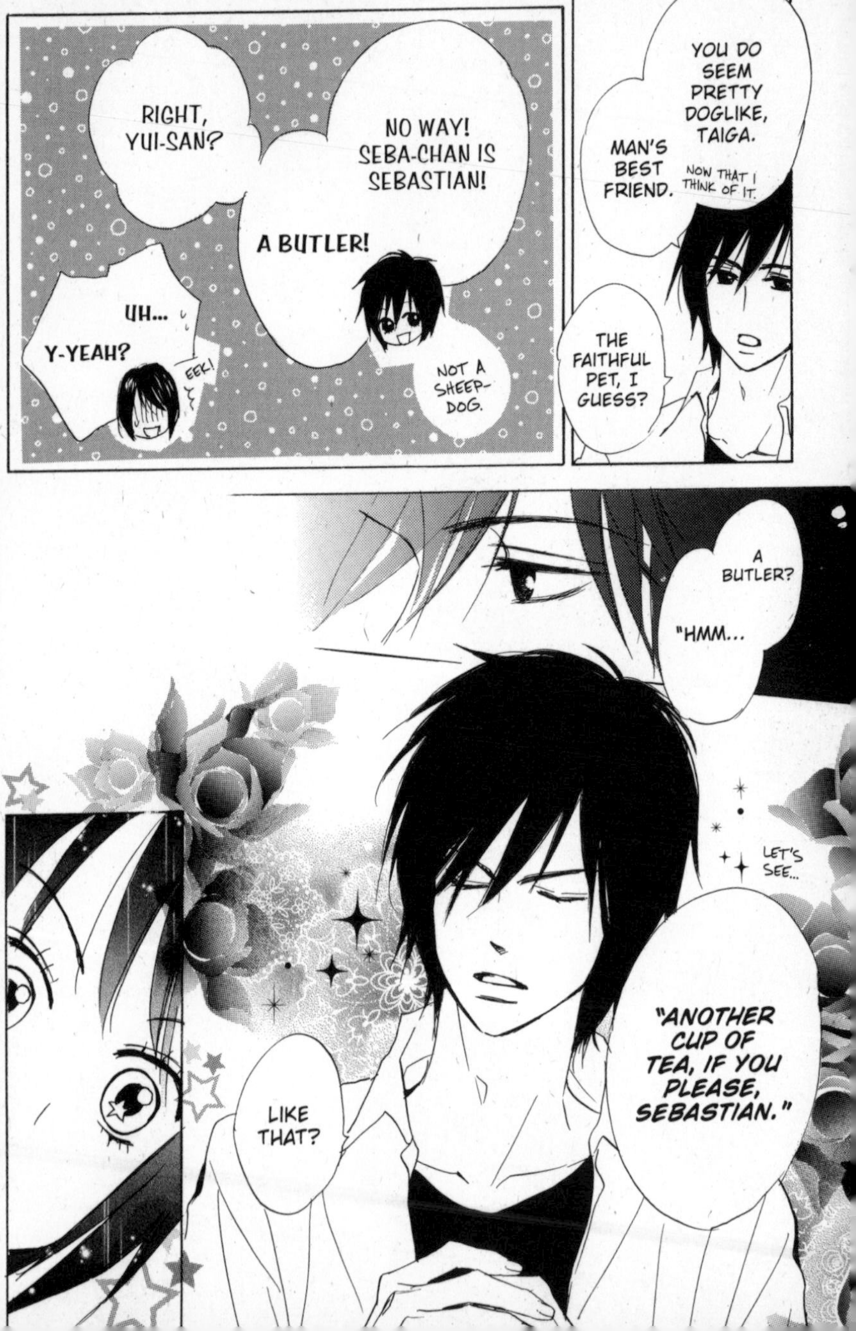
YOU DO SEEM PRETTY DOGLIKE, TAIGA.
NOW THAT I THINK OF IT.
MAN'S BEST FRIEND.
THE FAITHFUL PET, I GUESS?
NO WAY! SEBA-CHAN IS SEBASTIAN!
A BUTLER!
NOT A SHEEP-DOG.
RIGHT, YUI-SAN?
UH...
Y-YEAH?
EEK!
A BUTLER?
"HMM...
LET'S SEE...
"ANOTHER CUP OF TEA, IF YOU PLEASE, SEBASTIAN."
LIKE THAT?

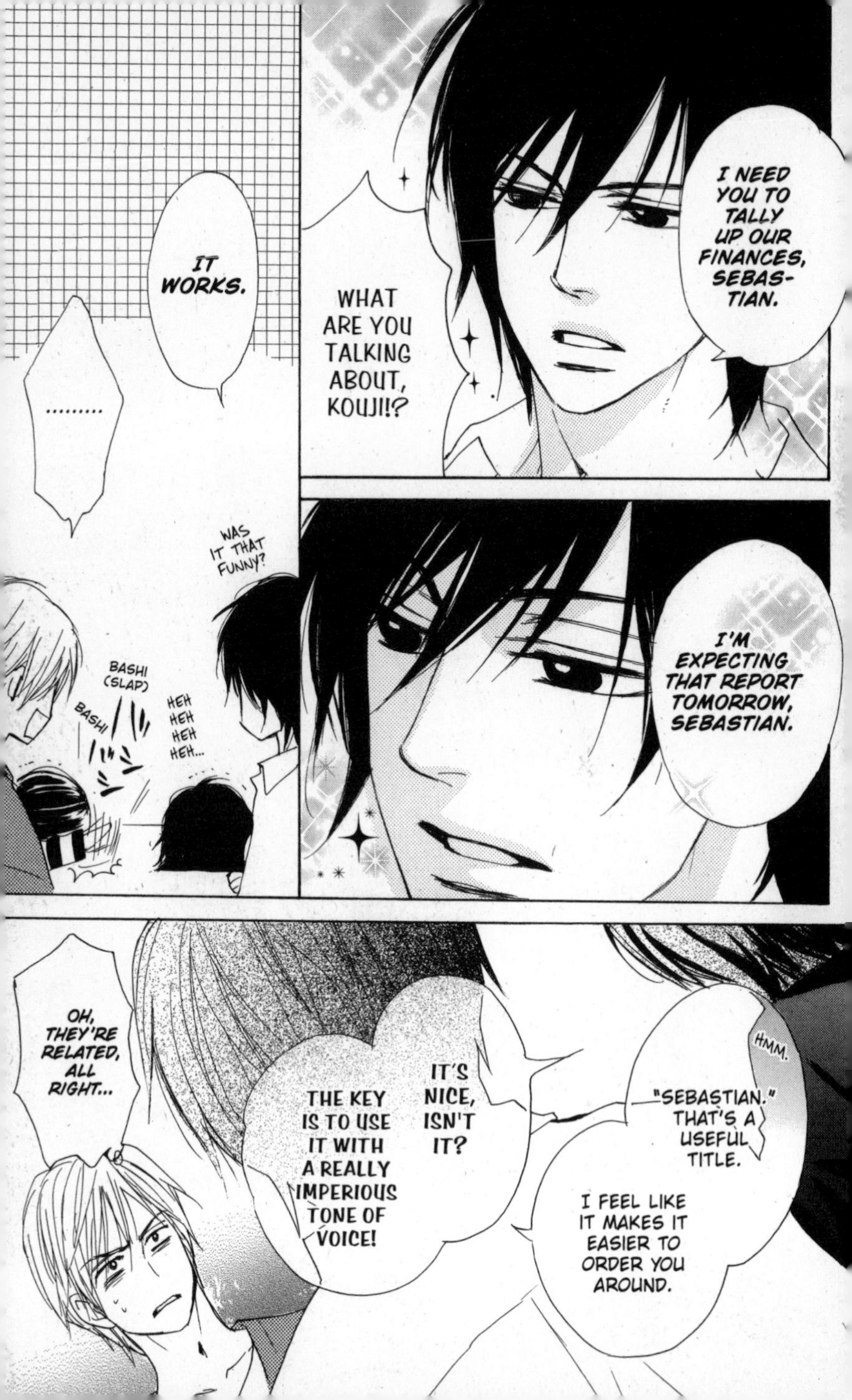
I NEED YOU TO TALLY UP OUR FINANCES, SEBASTIAN.
WHAT ARE YOU TALKING ABOUT, KOUJI!?
I'M EXPECTING THAT REPORT TOMORROW, SEBASTIAN.
IT WORKS.
....
WAS IT THAT FUNNY?
BASHI (SLAP)
BASHI
HEH HEH HEH HEH...
HMM.
"SEBASTIAN." THAT'S A USEFUL TITLE.
I FEEL LIKE IT MAKES IT EASIER TO ORDER YOU AROUND.
IT'S NICE, ISN'T IT?
THE KEY IS TO USE IT WITH A REALLY IMPERIOUS TONE OF VOICE!
OH, THEY'RE RELATED, ALL RIGHT...

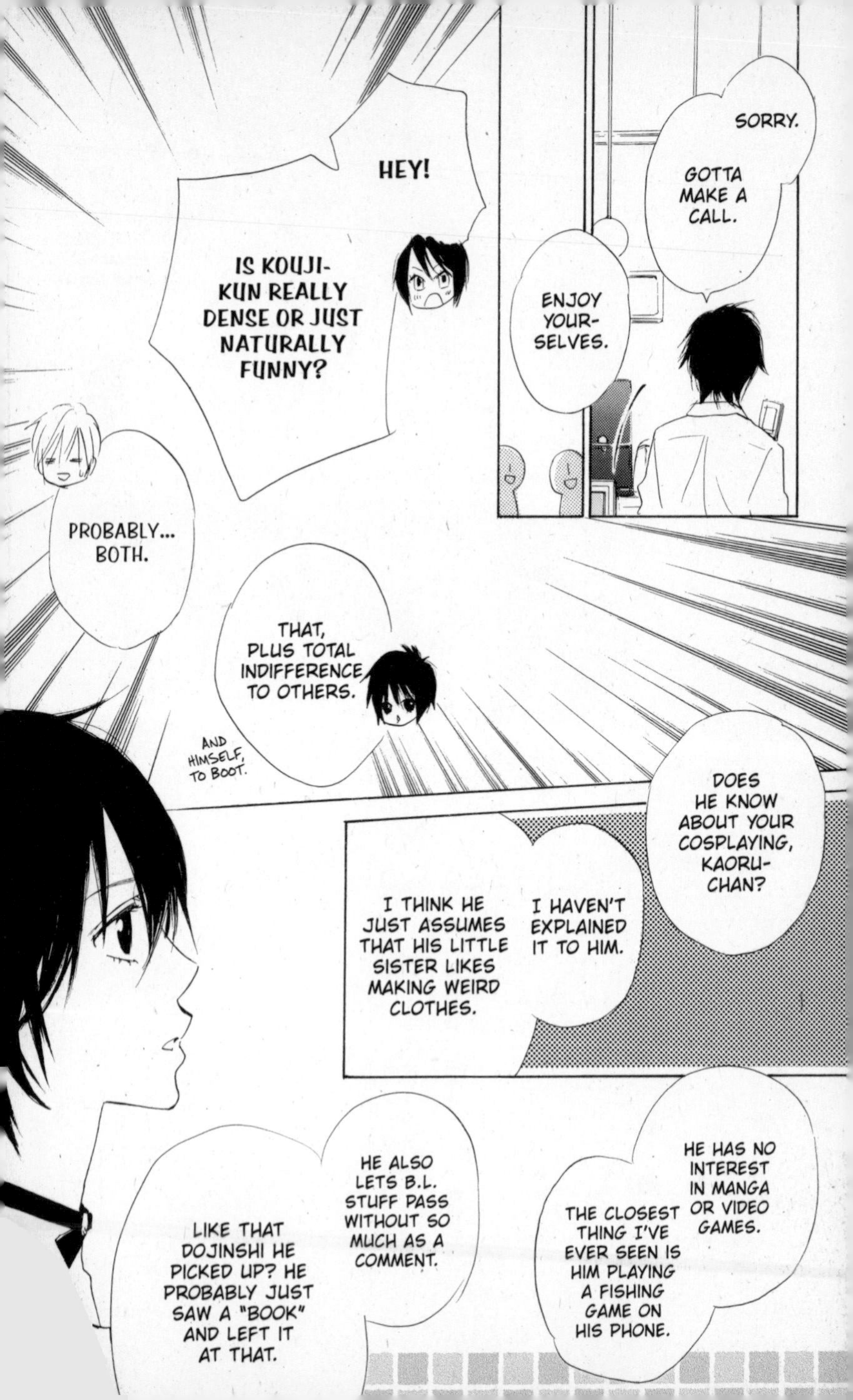
SORRY.
GOTTA MAKE A CALL.
ENJOY YOUR-SELVES.
HEY!
IS KOUJI-KUN REALLY DENSE OR JUST NATURALLY FUNNY?
PROBABLY... BOTH.
THAT, PLUS TOTAL INDIFFERENCE TO OTHERS.
AND HIMSELF, TO BOOT.
DOES HE KNOW ABOUT YOUR COSPLAYING, KAORU-CHAN?
I HAVEN'T EXPLAINED IT TO HIM.
I THINK HE JUST ASSUMES THAT HIS LITTLE SISTER LIKES MAKING WEIRD CLOTHES.
HE HAS NO INTEREST IN MANGA OR VIDEO GAMES.
THE CLOSEST THING I'VE EVER SEEN IS HIM PLAYING A FISHING GAME ON HIS PHONE.
HE ALSO LETS B.L. STUFF PASS WITHOUT SO MUCH AS A COMMENT.
LIKE THAT DOJINSHI HE PICKED UP? HE PROBABLY JUST SAW A "BOOK" AND LEFT IT AT THAT.

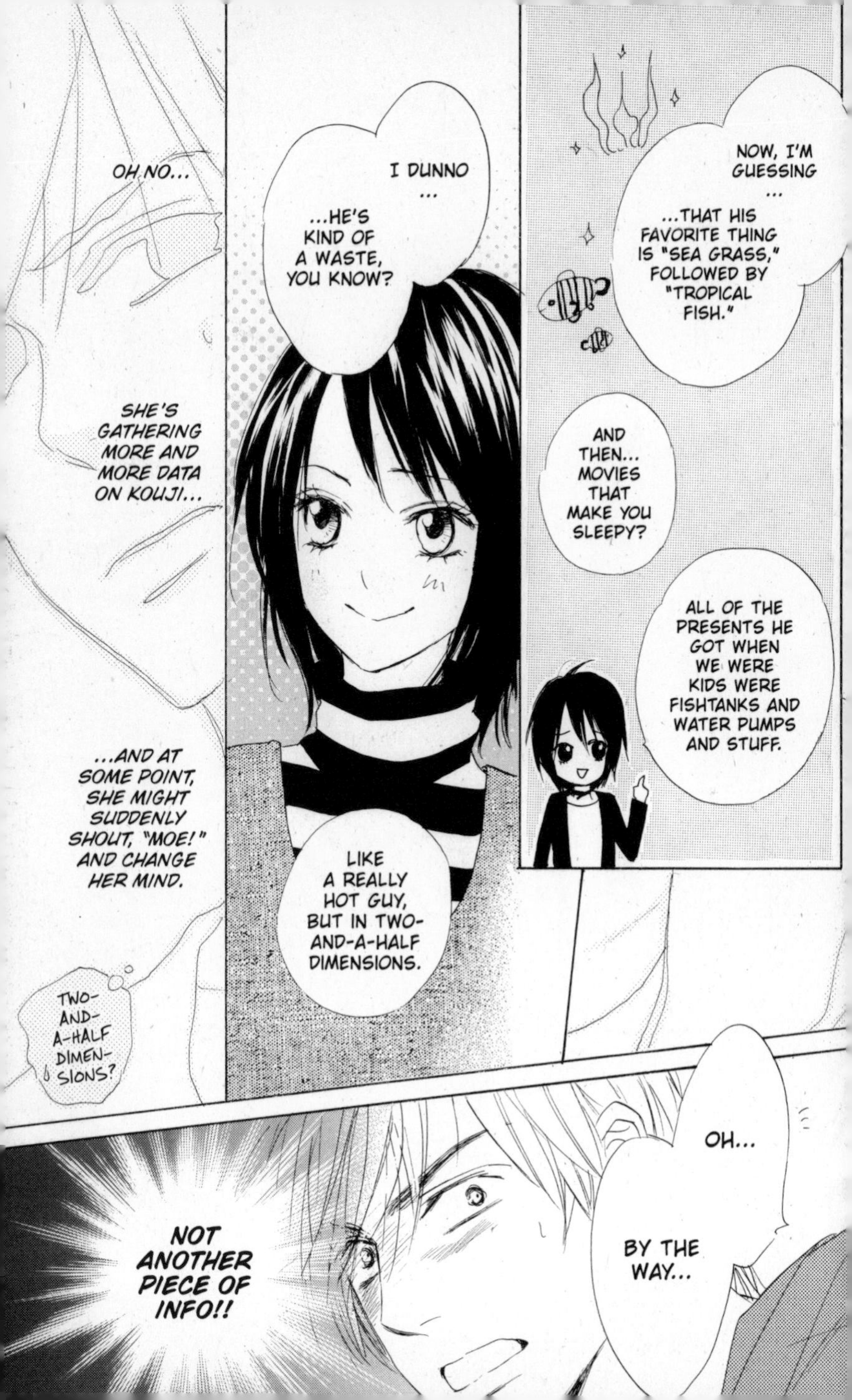
NOW, I'M GUESSING ...
...THAT HIS FAVORITE THING IS "SEA GRASS," FOLLOWED BY "TROPICAL FISH."
AND THEN... MOVIES THAT MAKE YOU SLEEPY?
ALL OF THE PRESENTS HE GOT WHEN WE WERE KIDS WERE FISHTANKS AND WATER PUMPS AND STUFF.
I DUNNO ...
...HE'S KIND OF A WASTE, YOU KNOW?
LIKE A REALLY HOT GUY, BUT IN TWO-AND-A-HALF DIMENSIONS.
OH NO...
SHE'S GATHERING MORE AND MORE DATA ON KOUJI...
...AND AT SOME POINT, SHE MIGHT SUDDENLY SHOUT, "MOE!" AND CHANGE HER MIND.
TWO-AND-A-HALF DIMEN-SIONS?
OH...
BY THE WAY...
NOT ANOTHER PIECE OF INFO!!

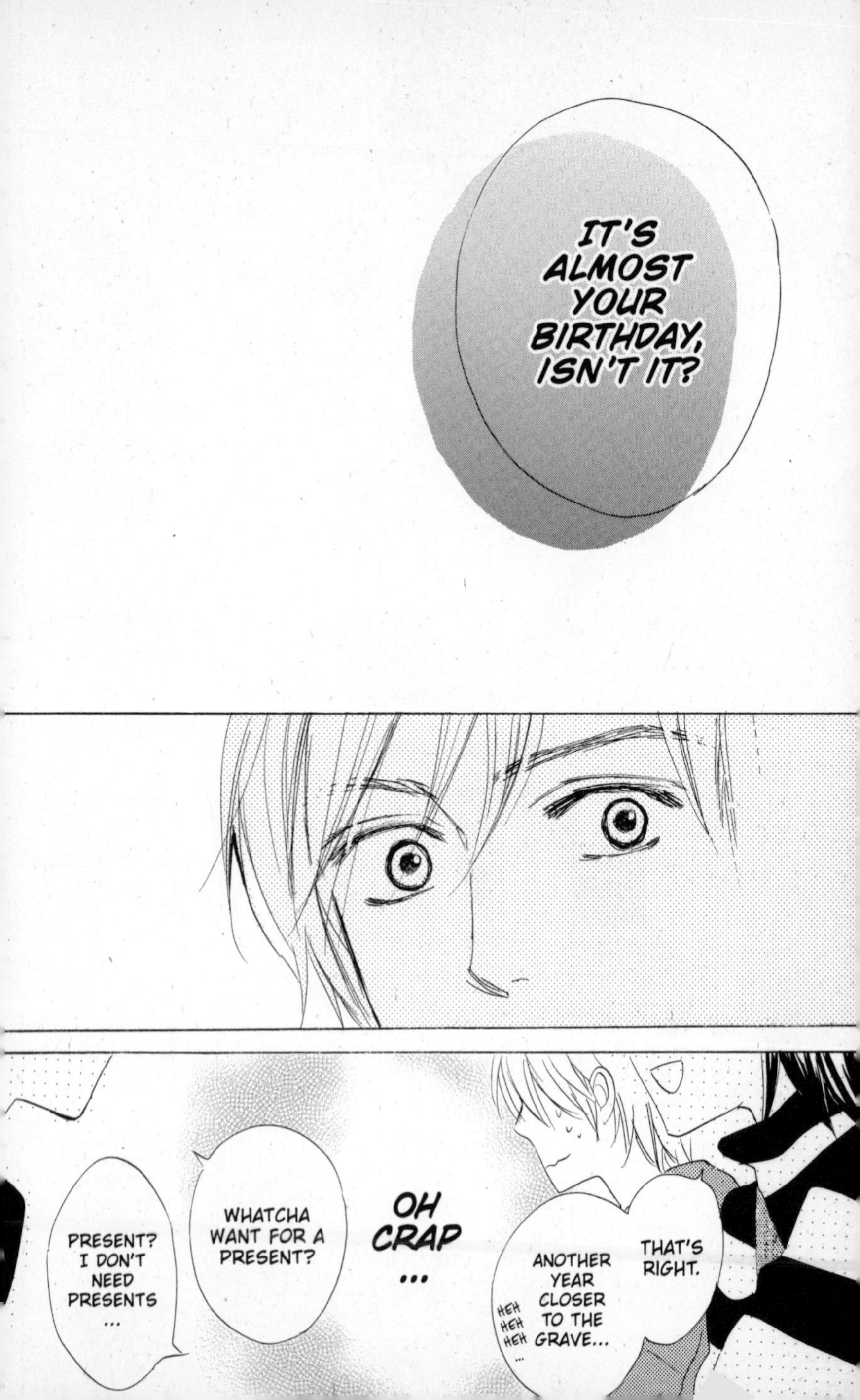
IT'S ALMOST YOUR BIRTHDAY, ISN'T IT?
THAT'S RIGHT.
ANOTHER YEAR CLOSER TO THE GRAVE...
HEH HEH HEH...
OH CRAP...
WHATCHA WANT FOR A PRESENT?
PRESENT? I DON'T NEED PRESENTS...

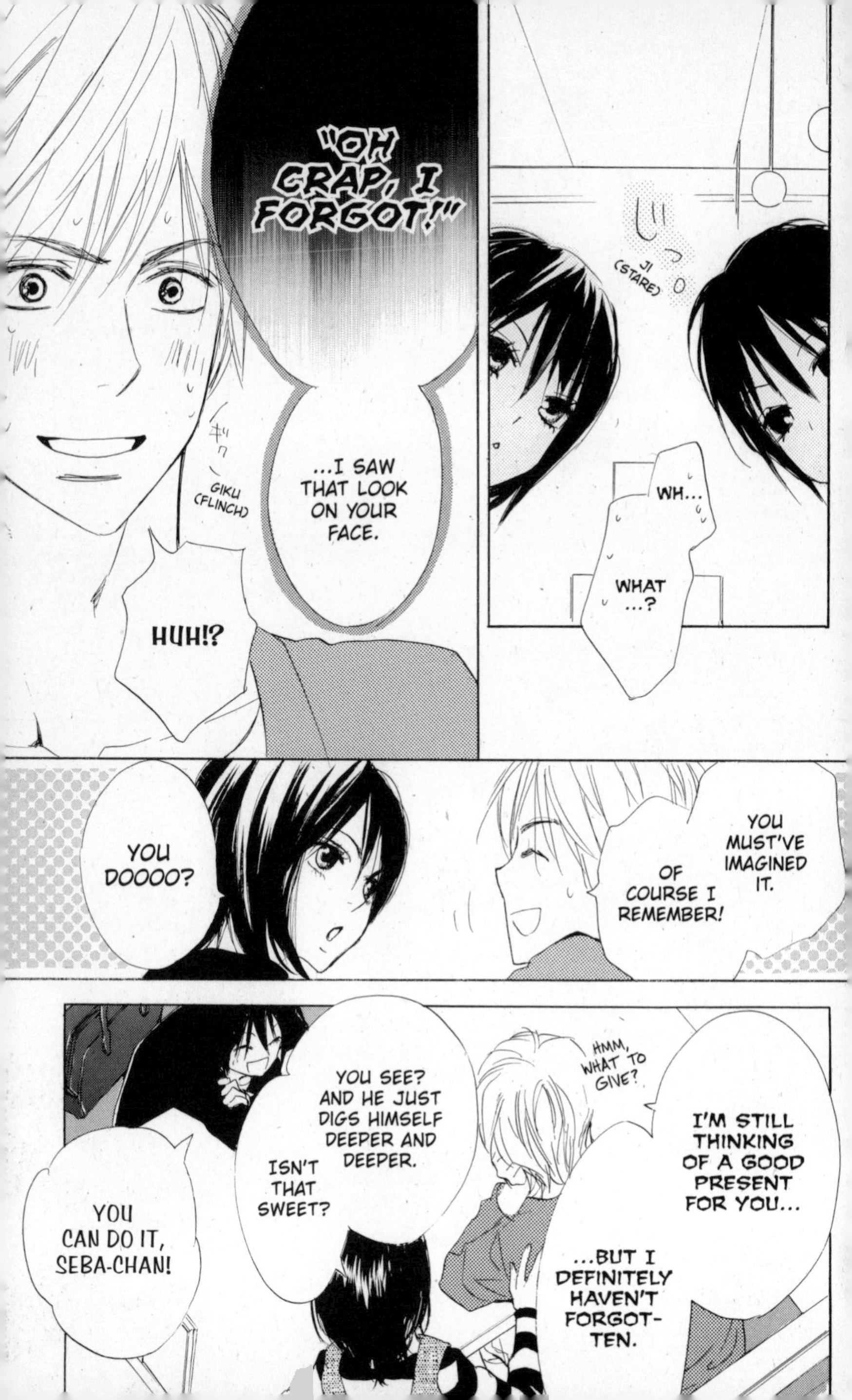
JI (STARE)
WH...
WHAT ...?
"OH CRAP, I FORGOT!"
...I SAW THAT LOOK ON YOUR FACE.
GIKU (FLINCH)
HUH!?
OF COURSE I REMEMBER!
YOU MUST'VE IMAGINED IT.
YOU DOOOO?
HMM, WHAT TO GIVE?
I'M STILL THINKING OF A GOOD PRESENT FOR YOU...
...BUT I DEFINITELY HAVEN'T FORGOT-TEN.
YOU SEE? AND HE JUST DIGS HIMSELF DEEPER AND DEEPER.
ISN'T THAT SWEET?
YOU CAN DO IT, SEBA-CHAN!

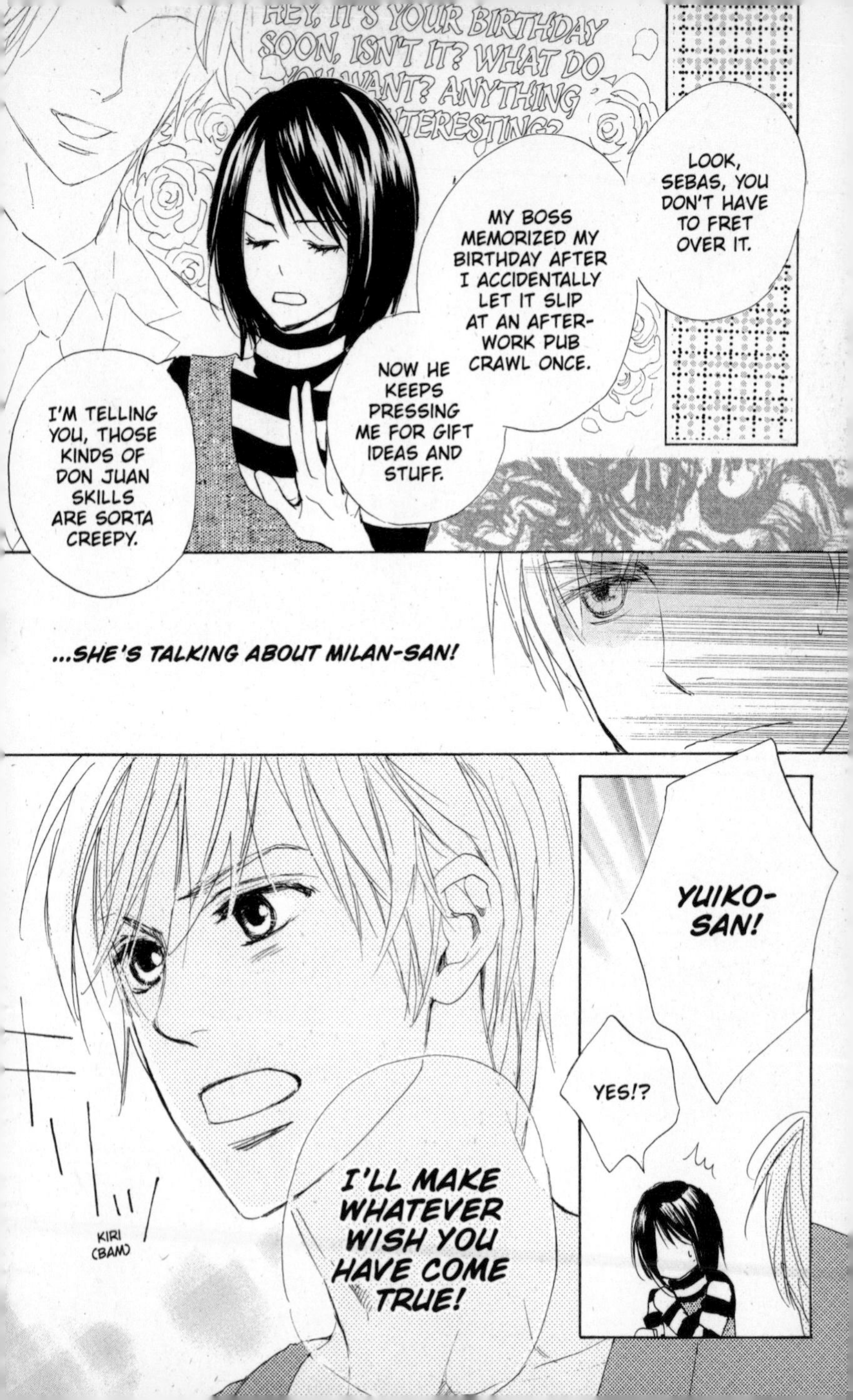
HEY, IT'S YOUR BIRTHDAY SOON, ISN'T IT? WHAT DO YOU WANT? ANYTHING INTERESTING?
LOOK, SEBAS, YOU DON'T HAVE TO FRET OVER IT.
MY BOSS MEMORIZED MY BIRTHDAY AFTER I ACCIDENTALLY LET IT SLIP AT AN AFTER-WORK PUB CRAWL ONCE.
NOW HE KEEPS PRESSING ME FOR GIFT IDEAS AND STUFF.
I'M TELLING YOU, THOSE KINDS OF DON JUAN SKILLS ARE SORTA CREEPY.
...SHE'S TALKING ABOUT MILAN-SAN!
YUIKO-SAN!
YES!?
I'LL MAKE WHATEVER WISH YOU HAVE COME TRUE!
KIRI (BAM)

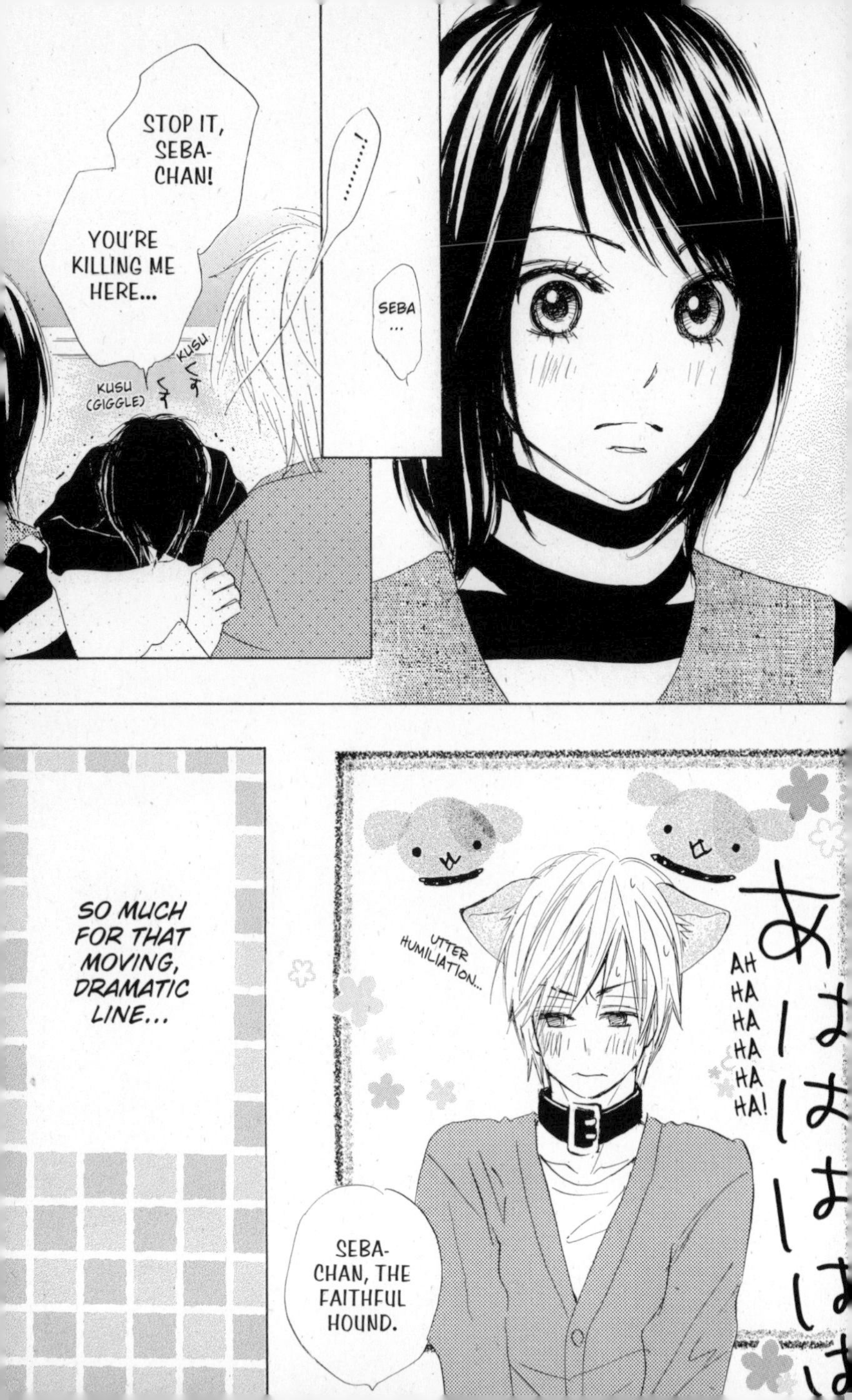
......!
SEBA...
STOP IT, SEBA-CHAN!
YOU'RE KILLING ME HERE...
KUSU くす
KUSU (GIGGLE) くす
あはーはーは
AH HA HA HA HA HA!
UTTER HUMILIATION...
SEBA-CHAN, THE FAITHFUL HOUND.
SO MUCH FOR THAT MOVING, DRAMATIC LINE...

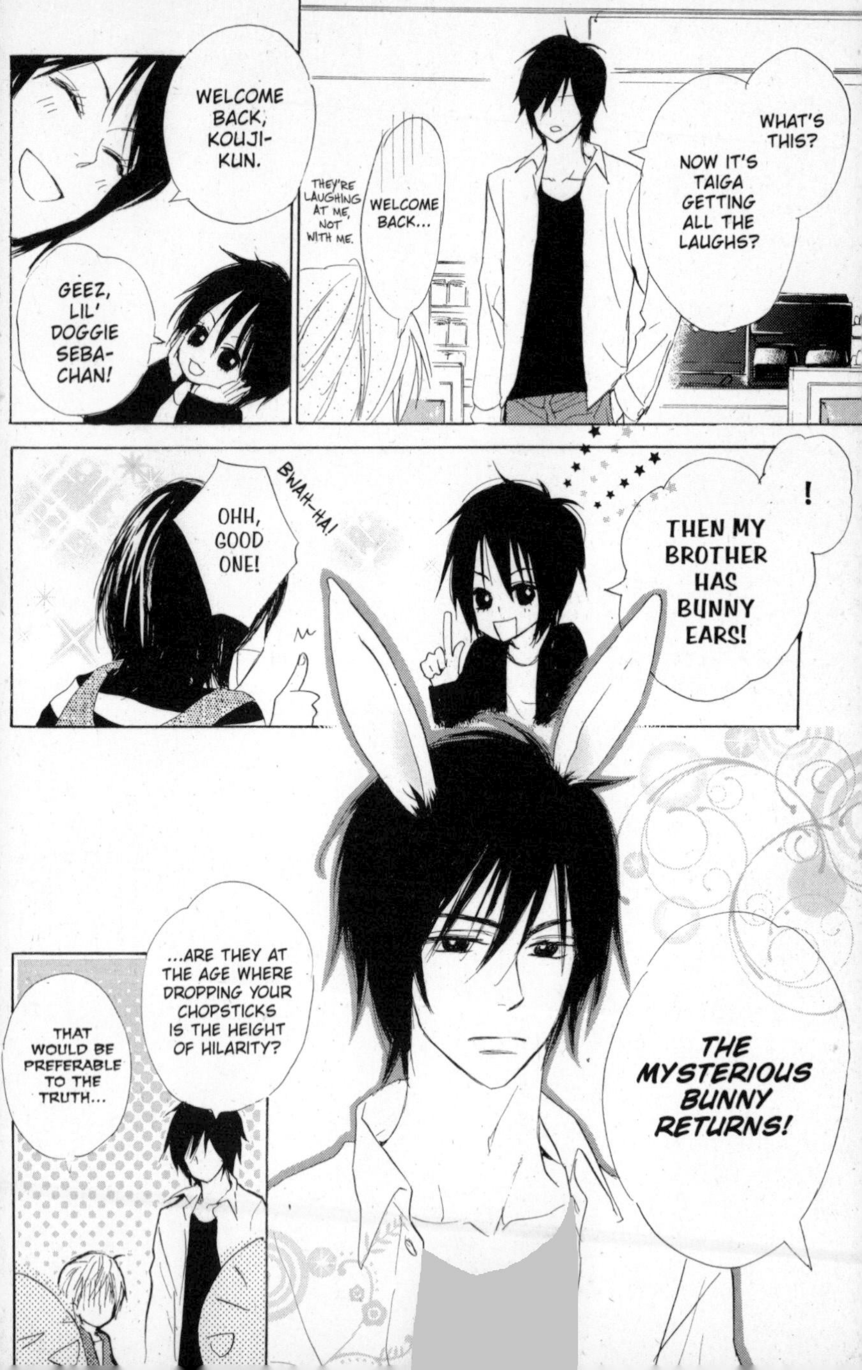
WHAT'S THIS?
NOW IT'S TAIGA GETTING ALL THE LAUGHS?
WELCOME BACK...
THEY'RE LAUGHING AT ME, NOT WITH ME.
WELCOME BACK, KOUJI-KUN.
GEEZ, LIL' DOGGIE SEBA-CHAN!
!
THEN MY BROTHER HAS BUNNY EARS!
BWAH-HA!
OHH, GOOD ONE!
THE MYSTERIOUS BUNNY RETURNS!
...ARE THEY AT THE AGE WHERE DROPPING YOUR CHOPSTICKS IS THE HEIGHT OF HILARITY?
THAT WOULD BE PREFERABLE TO THE TRUTH...

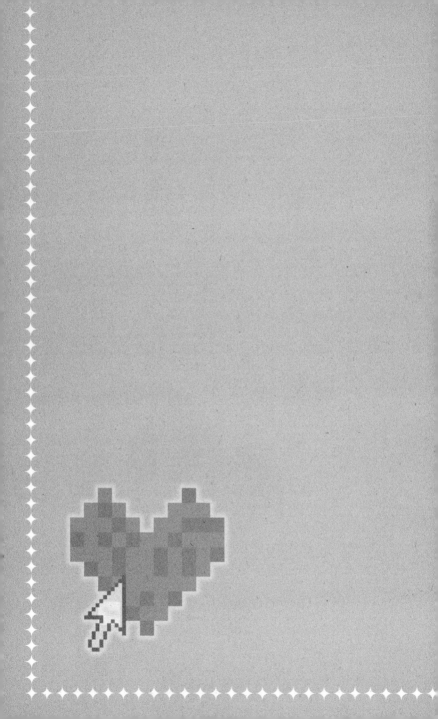

FUJOSHI NEWS vol.16

YUIKO-SAN & YOUHEI-SENPAI GLOSSARY①

P.13
MONKEY-KEY - AKARI NICKNAMES MASARU "SARU-SARU" IN THE ORIGINAL EDITION. SARU CAN MEAN "MONKEY," HENCE THE MONKEY JOKES.

P.20
IGNORING SKILLS - THE ABILITY TO ALLOW TEASES AND CHALLENGES TO PASS WITHOUT COMMENT. KOUJI HAS PREEMINENT IGNORING SKILLS, BUT THIS COULD BE SIMPLY BECAUSE HE PAYS NO ATTENTION TO THINGS THAT DO NOT INTEREST HIM...

P.39
MY WIFE - A WORD THAT INDICATES ONE'S DEEP AFFECTION FOR A CHARACTER OR OBJECT. MASA-NEE'S BOYFRIEND, YOSHIHIKO, HAS AN UNHEALTHY OBSESSION WITH HIS SPEAKERS AND AMPLIFIERS.

P.41
PANDORA'S BOX - A BOX IN GREEK MYTHOLOGY THAT MUST NOT BE OPENED. WHAT WOULD HAPPEN IF YOSHIHIKO AWAKENED TO THE PLEASURES OF B.L....?

P.46
EVENT SUBMITTAL - TO CREATE A NEW DOJINSHI TO SELL AT A DOJINSHI RETAIL EVENT. YOUHEI-SENPAI'S ENTIRE LIFESTYLE IS BASED AROUND MEETING EVENT DEADLINES.

P.47
BOOKMARK - WONDERFUL WEBSITES COLLECTED IN A LIST IN YOUR BROWSER. NOTHING IS MORE EMBARRASSING TO AN OTAKU THAN HAVING FAMILY AND FRIENDS DISCOVER THEIR BOOKMARKS.

GUEST STORY - A NOVEL SUBMITTED TO A WEBSITE OR DOJINSHI RUN BY A FRIEND OR ACCOMPLICE. THESE WILL OFTEN HAVE FAMILIAR YET DIFFERENT TOUCHES THAT ARE FRESH TO FANS.

ON AND OFF - ON OR OFF THE INTERNET. "ON" MEANING DOJIN WORK ONLINE, AND "OFF" MEANING PHYSICAL COPIES OF DOJINSHI.

P.50
APPLAUSE COMMENT - A COMMENT SENT TO THE AUTHOR OF A FUNNY OR MOE ILLUSTRATION/STORY ONLINE. ON SOME SITES THERE ARE "APPLAUSE" BUTTONS ON EVERY POST THAT CAN BE CLICKED TO SHOW APPRECIATION, AS WELL AS A SPACE FOR A SHORT MESSAGE, IF DESIRED.

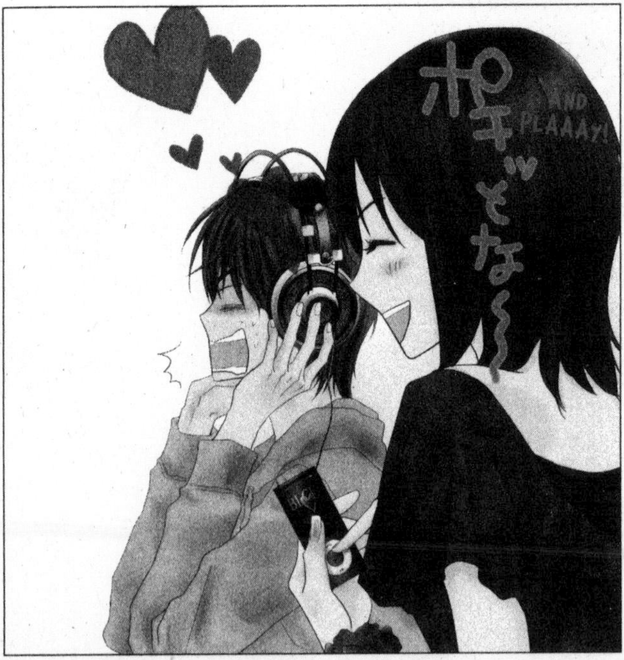
ポチッとな～
AND PLAAAY!

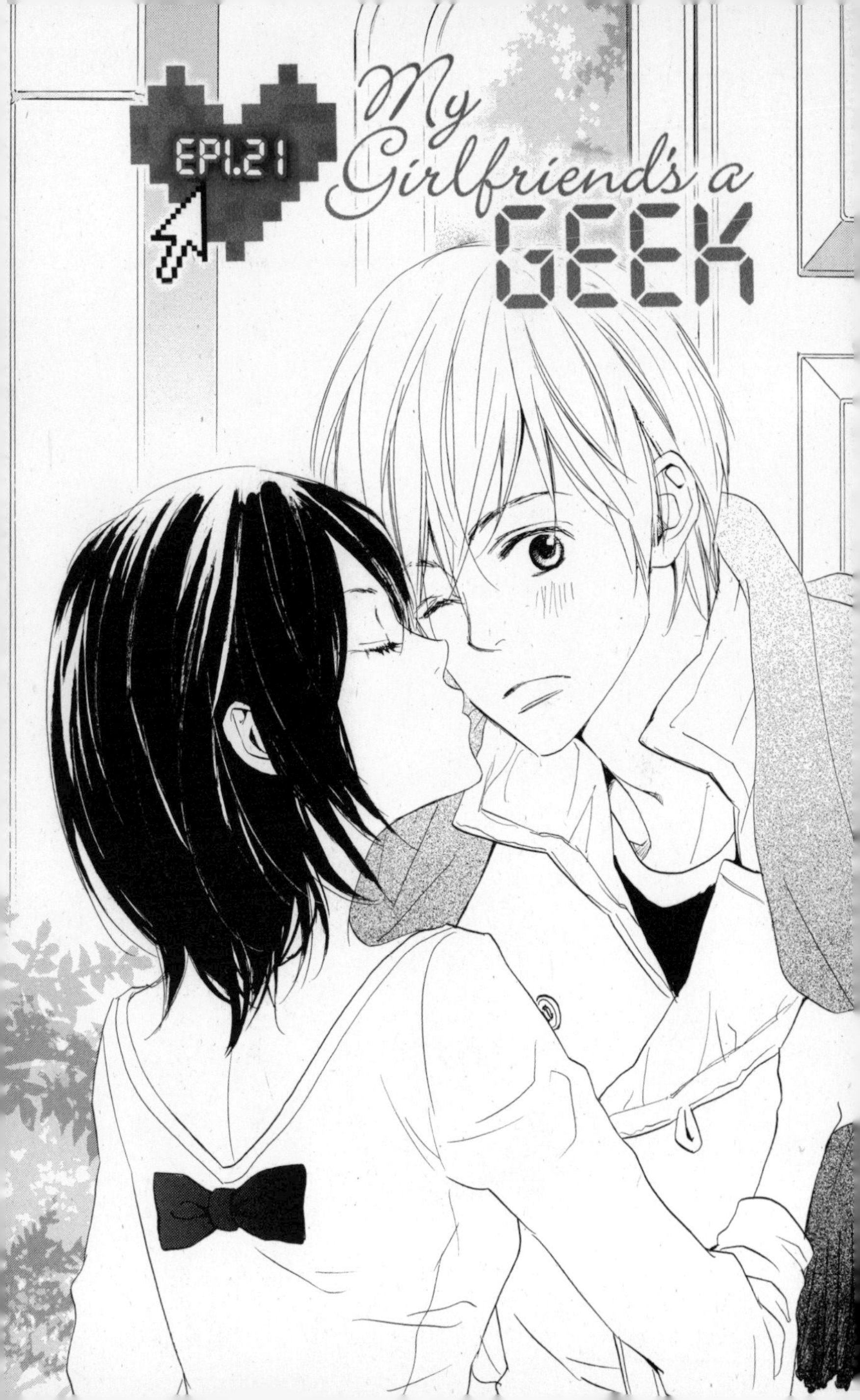
EP1.21
My Girlfriend's a
GEEK

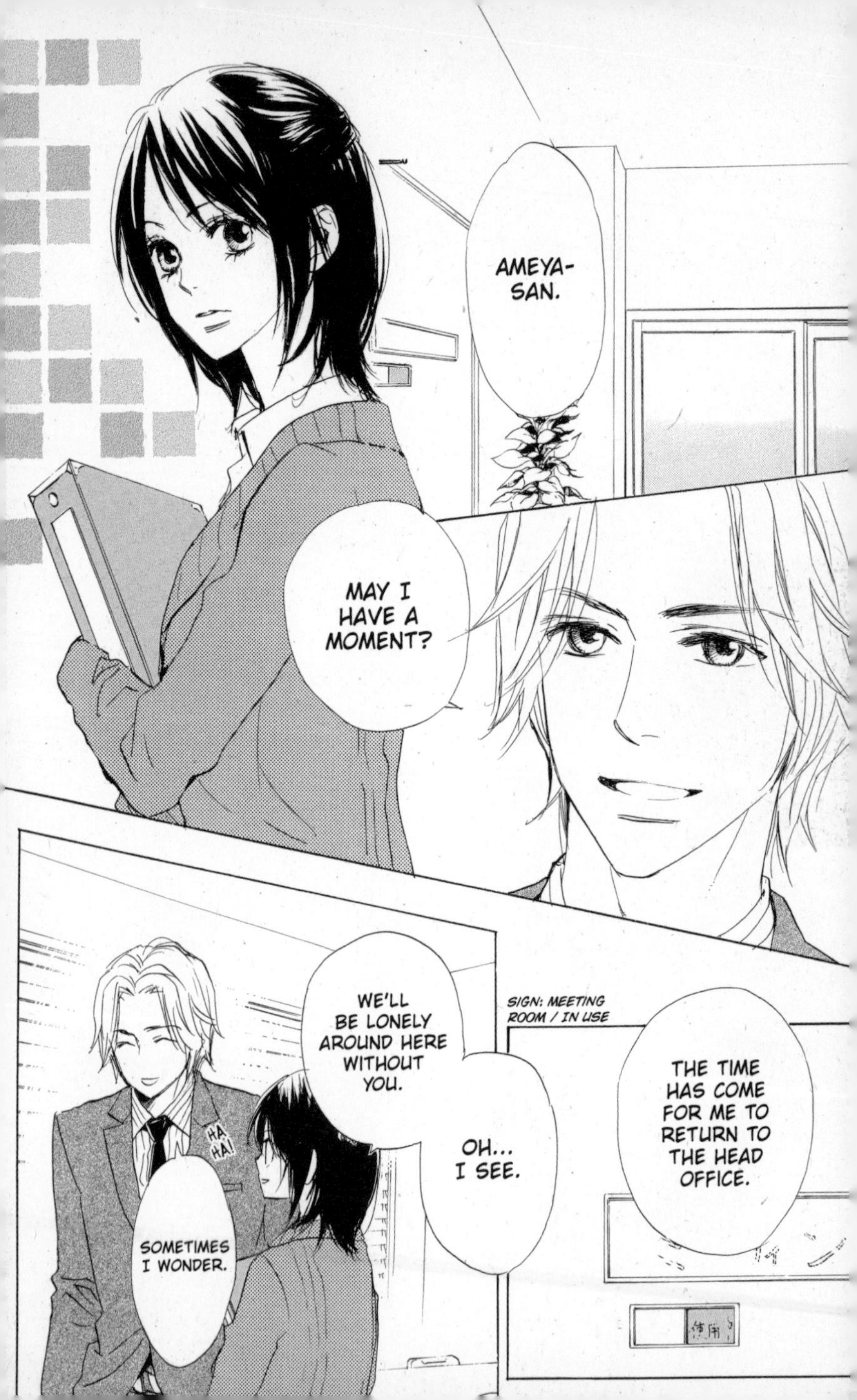
AMEYA-SAN.
MAY I HAVE A MOMENT?
SIGN: MEETING ROOM / IN USE
THE TIME HAS COME FOR ME TO RETURN TO THE HEAD OFFICE.
OH... I SEE.
WE'LL BE LONELY AROUND HERE WITHOUT YOU.
HA HA!
SOMETIMES I WONDER.

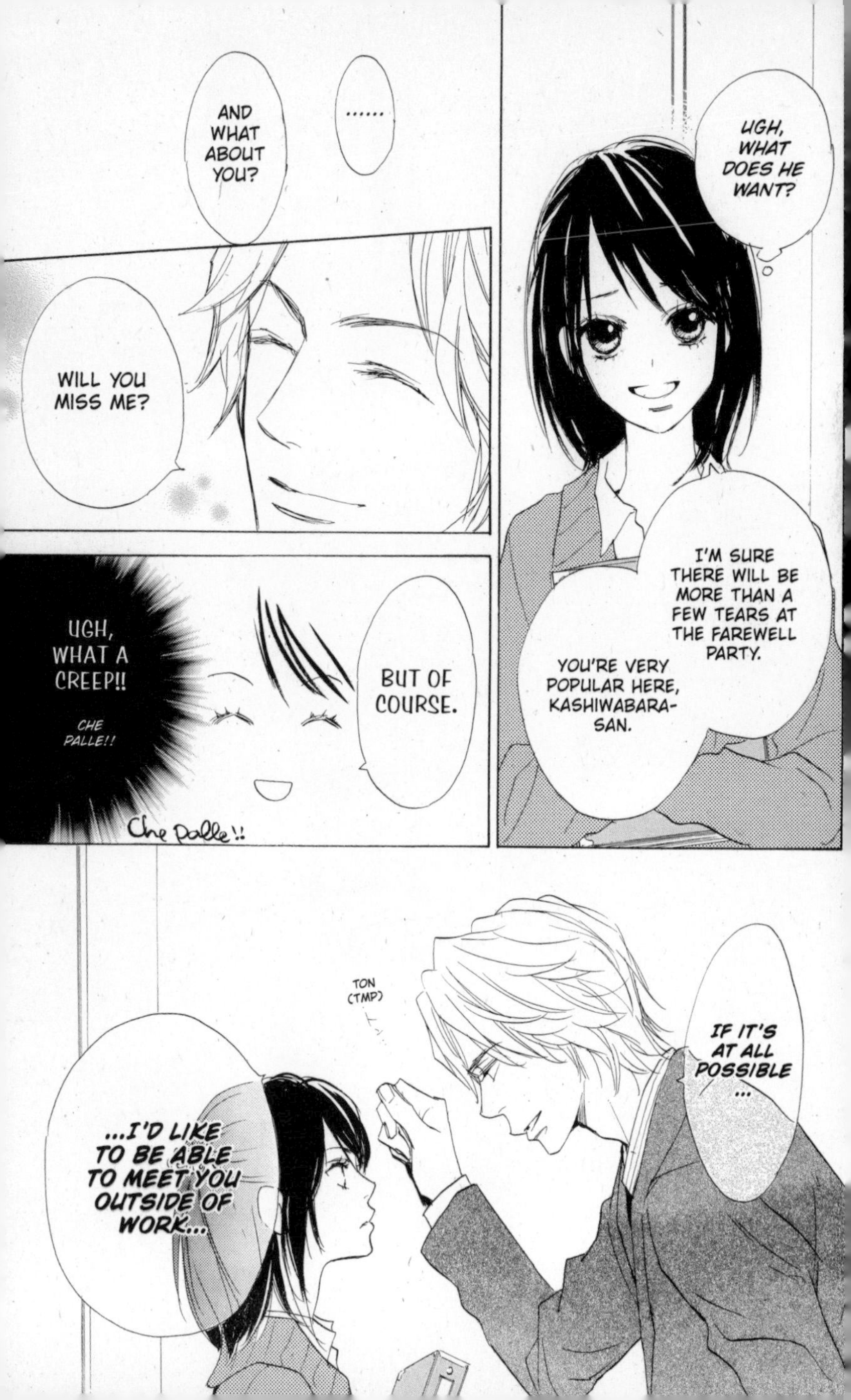
UGH, WHAT DOES HE WANT?
I'M SURE THERE WILL BE MORE THAN A FEW TEARS AT THE FAREWELL PARTY.
YOU'RE VERY POPULAR HERE, KASHIWABARA-SAN.
......
AND WHAT ABOUT YOU?
WILL YOU MISS ME?
BUT OF COURSE.
UGH, WHAT A CREEP!!
CHE PALLE!!
Che palle!!
IF IT'S AT ALL POSSIBLE...
TON (TMP)
...I'D LIKE TO BE ABLE TO MEET YOU OUTSIDE OF WORK...

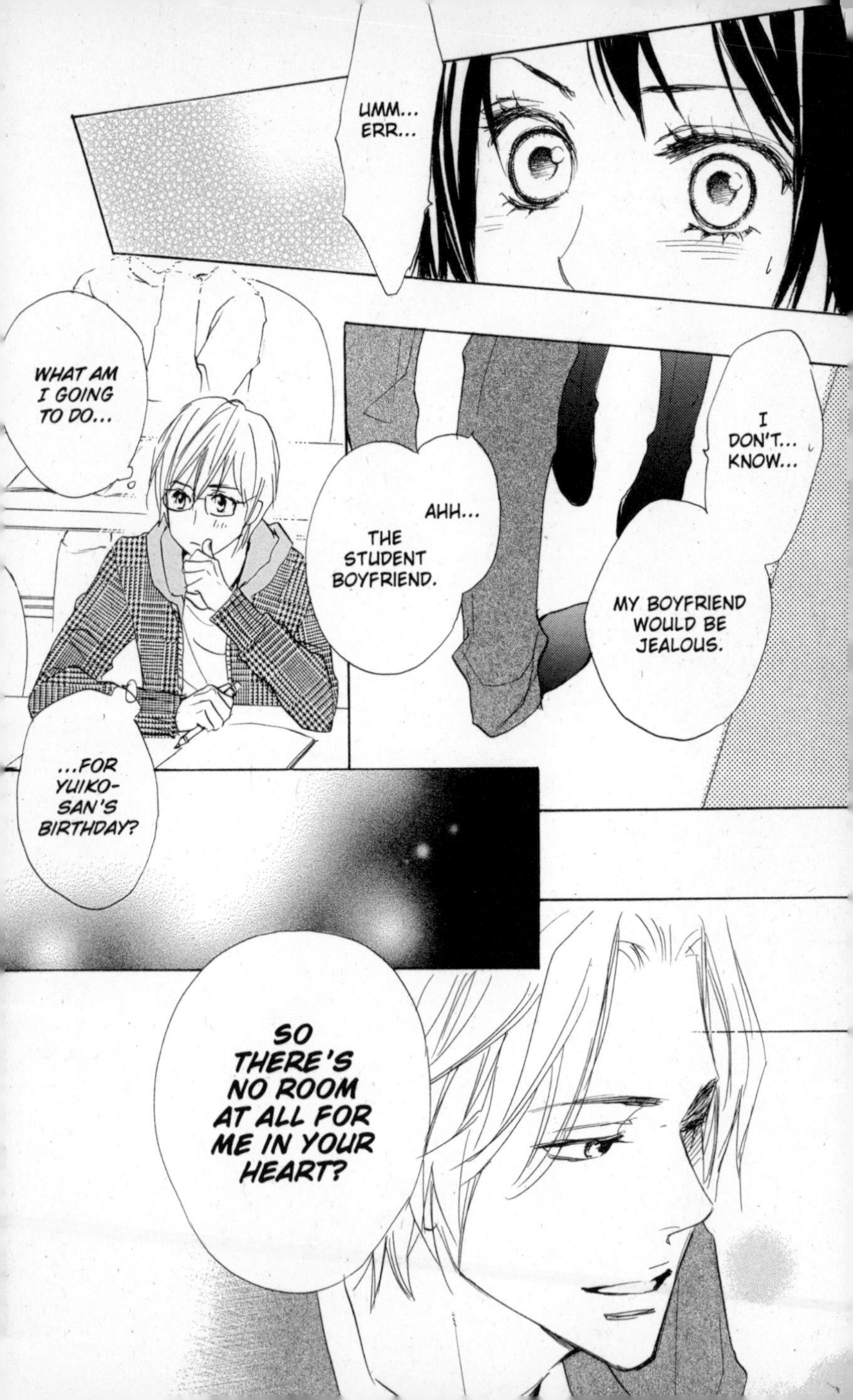
UMM... ERR...
I DON'T... KNOW...
MY BOYFRIEND WOULD BE JEALOUS.
AHH... THE STUDENT BOYFRIEND.
WHAT AM I GOING TO DO...
...FOR YUIKO-SAN'S BIRTHDAY?
SO THERE'S NO ROOM AT ALL FOR ME IN YOUR HEART?

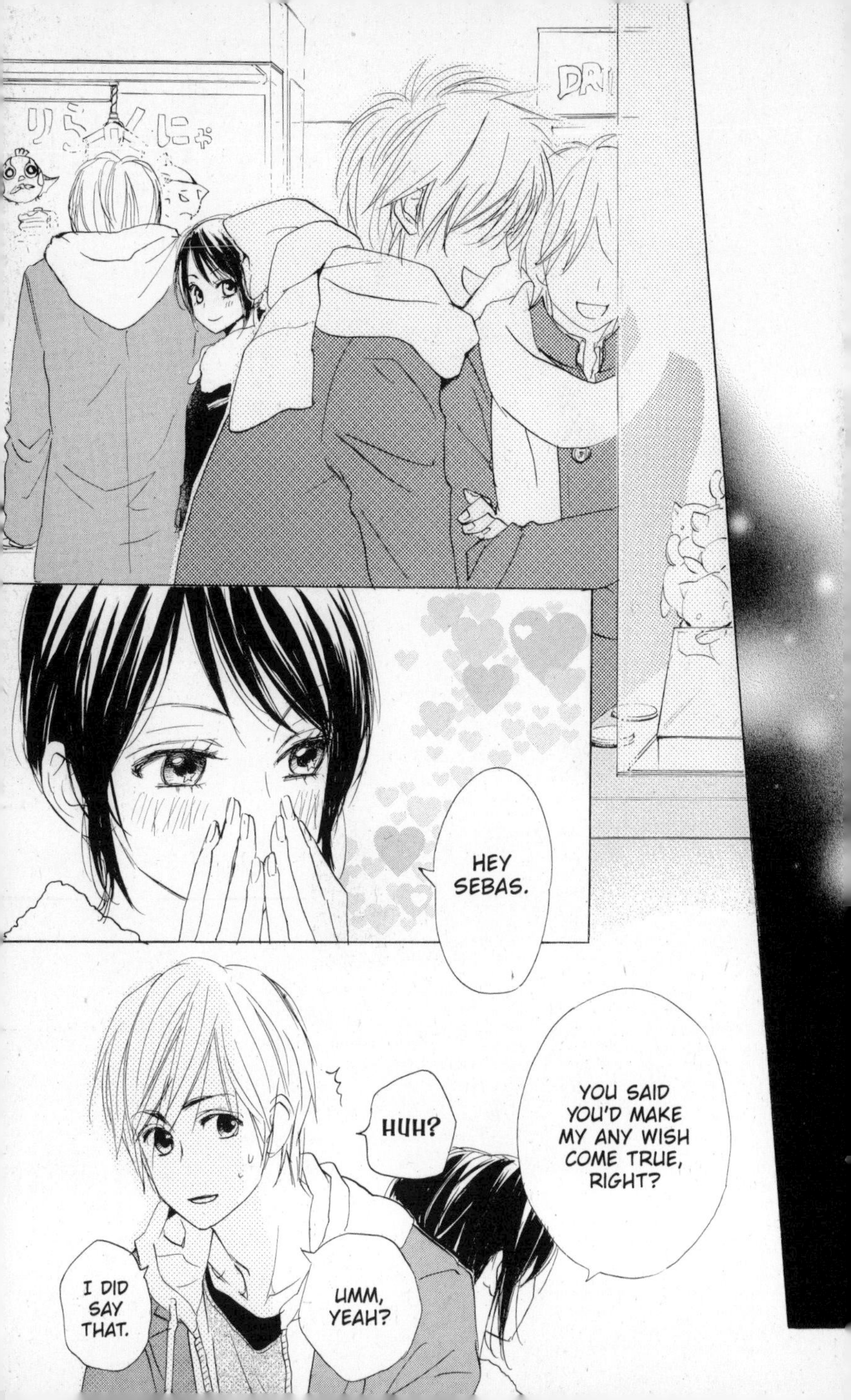
HEY SEBAS.
YOU SAID YOU'D MAKE MY ANY WISH COME TRUE, RIGHT?
HUH?
UMM, YEAH?
I DID SAY THAT.

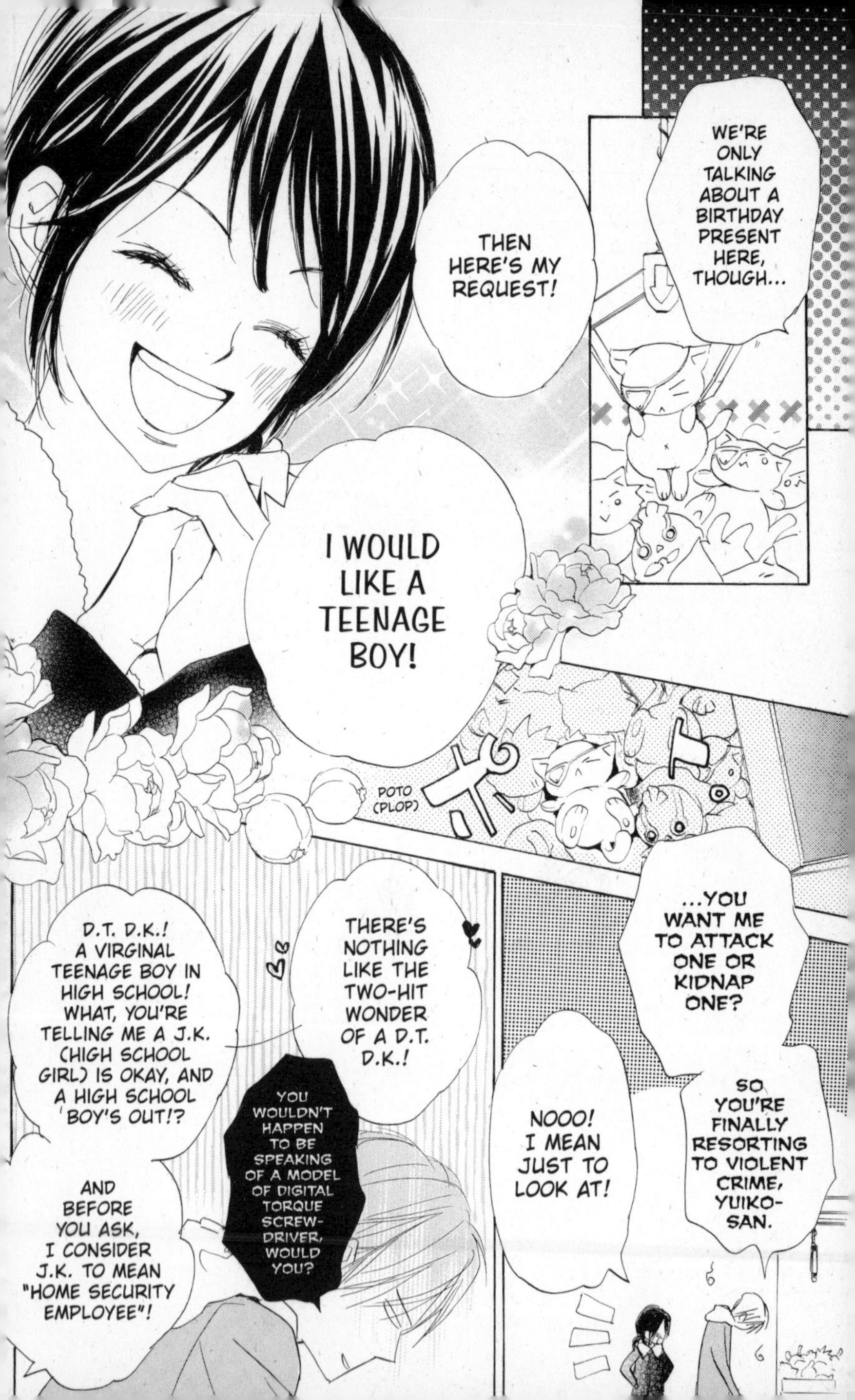
WE'RE ONLY TALKING ABOUT A BIRTHDAY PRESENT HERE, THOUGH...
THEN HERE'S MY REQUEST!
I WOULD LIKE A TEENAGE BOY!
POTO (PLOP)
...YOU WANT ME TO ATTACK ONE OR KIDNAP ONE?
SO YOU'RE FINALLY RESORTING TO VIOLENT CRIME, YUIKO-SAN.
NOOO! I MEAN JUST TO LOOK AT!
THERE'S NOTHING LIKE THE TWO-HIT WONDER OF A D.T. D.K.!
D.T. D.K.! A VIRGINAL TEENAGE BOY IN HIGH SCHOOL! WHAT, YOU'RE TELLING ME A J.K. (HIGH SCHOOL GIRL) IS OKAY, AND A HIGH SCHOOL BOY'S OUT!?
YOU WOULDN'T HAPPEN TO BE SPEAKING OF A MODEL OF DIGITAL TORQUE SCREW-DRIVER, WOULD YOU?
AND BEFORE YOU ASK, I CONSIDER J.K. TO MEAN "HOME SECURITY EMPLOYEE"!

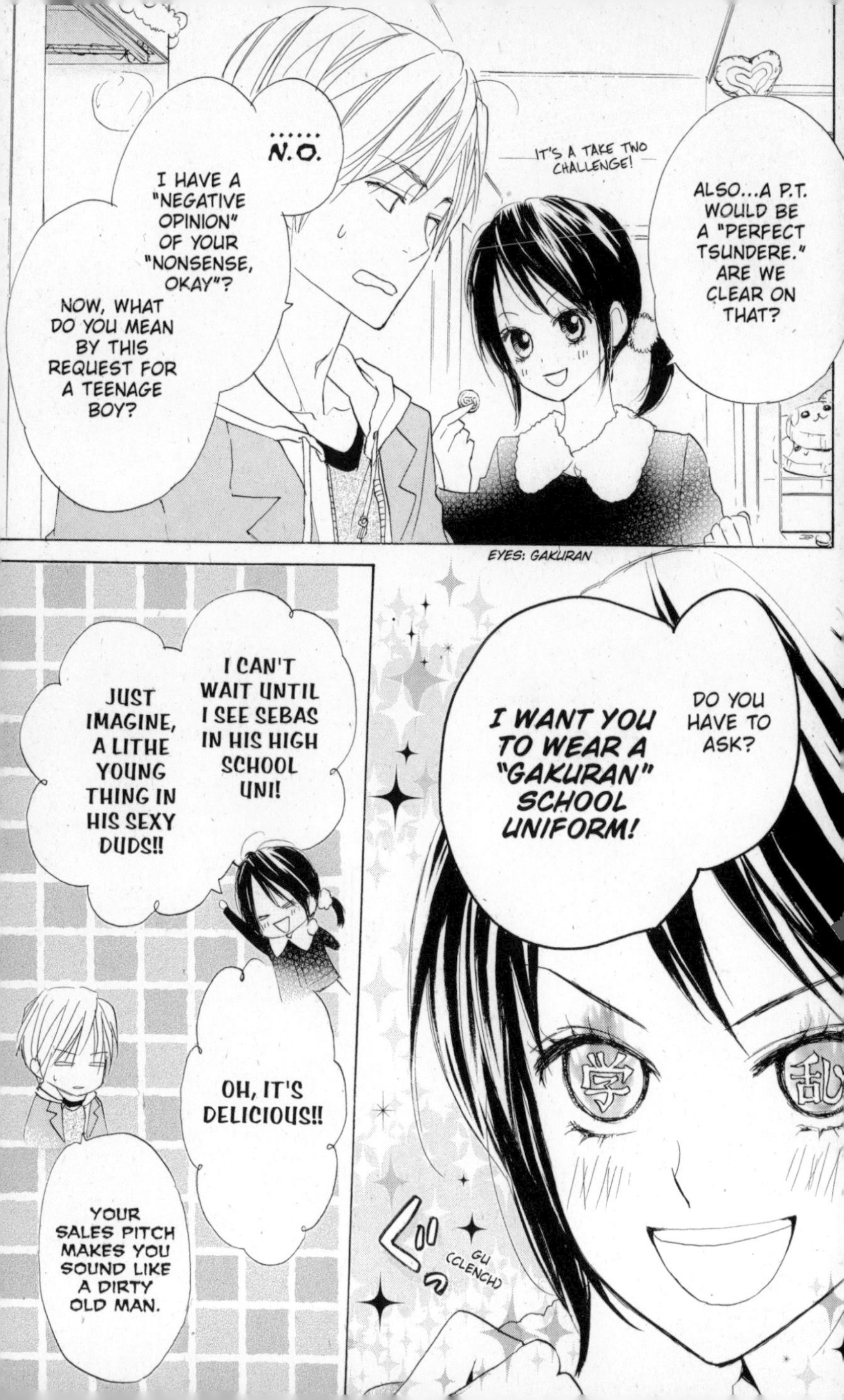
IT'S A TAKE TWO CHALLENGE!
ALSO...A P.T. WOULD BE A "PERFECT TSUNDERE." ARE WE CLEAR ON THAT?
...... N.O.
I HAVE A "NEGATIVE OPINION" OF YOUR "NONSENSE, OKAY"?
NOW, WHAT DO YOU MEAN BY THIS REQUEST FOR A TEENAGE BOY?
EYES: GAKURAN
DO YOU HAVE TO ASK?
I WANT YOU TO WEAR A "GAKURAN" SCHOOL UNIFORM!
GU (CLENCH)
I CAN'T WAIT UNTIL I SEE SEBAS IN HIS HIGH SCHOOL UNI!
JUST IMAGINE, A LITHE YOUNG THING IN HIS SEXY DUDS!!
OH, IT'S DELICIOUS!!
YOUR SALES PITCH MAKES YOU SOUND LIKE A DIRTY OLD MAN.

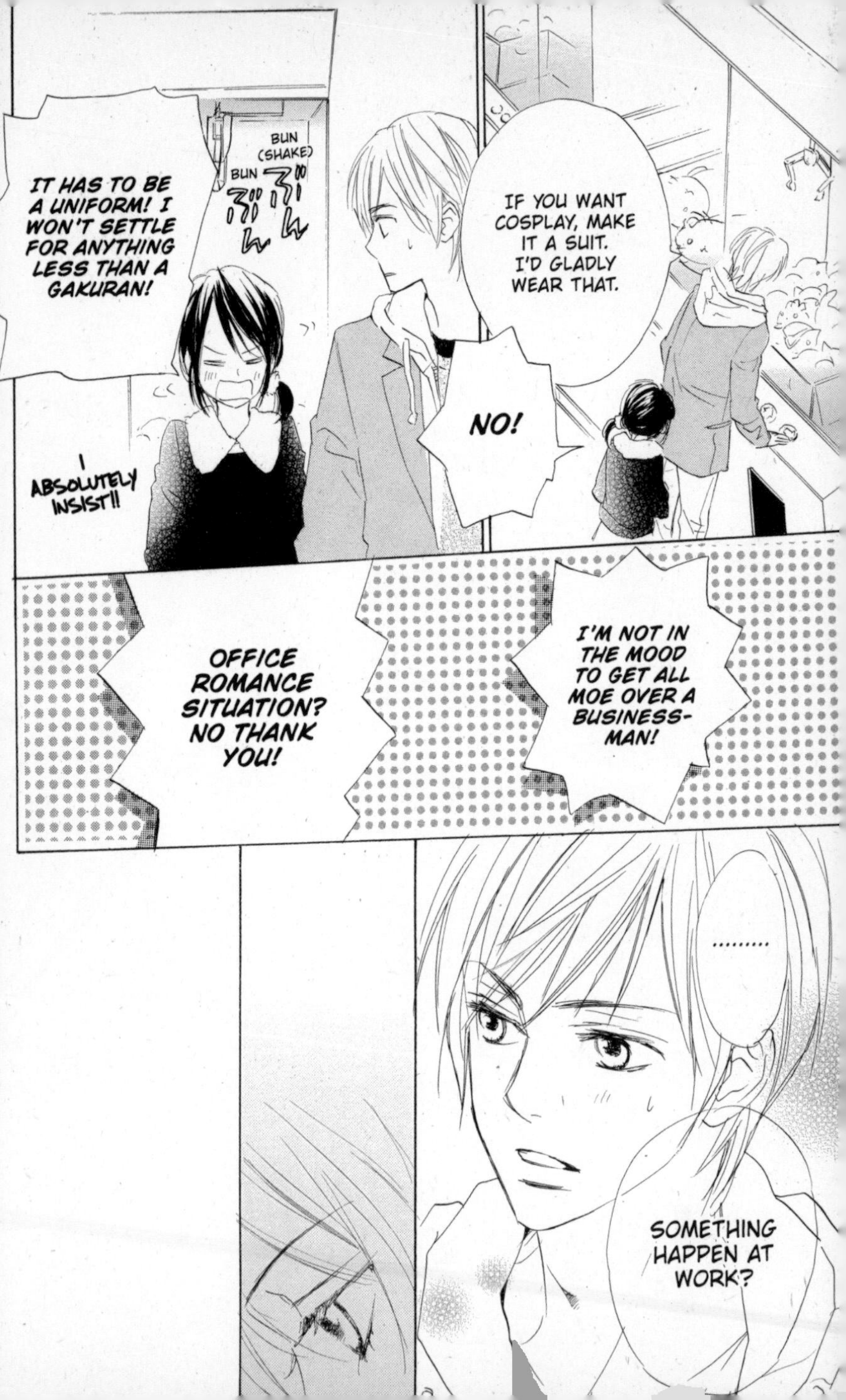
IF YOU WANT COSPLAY, MAKE IT A SUIT. I'D GLADLY WEAR THAT.
NO!
IT HAS TO BE A UNIFORM! I WON'T SETTLE FOR ANYTHING LESS THAN A GAKURAN!
BUN (SHAKE) BUN
ぶぶんぶん
I ABSOLUTELY INSIST!!
I'M NOT IN THE MOOD TO GET ALL MOE OVER A BUSINESS-MAN!
OFFICE ROMANCE SITUATION? NO THANK YOU!
....
SOMETHING HAPPEN AT WORK?

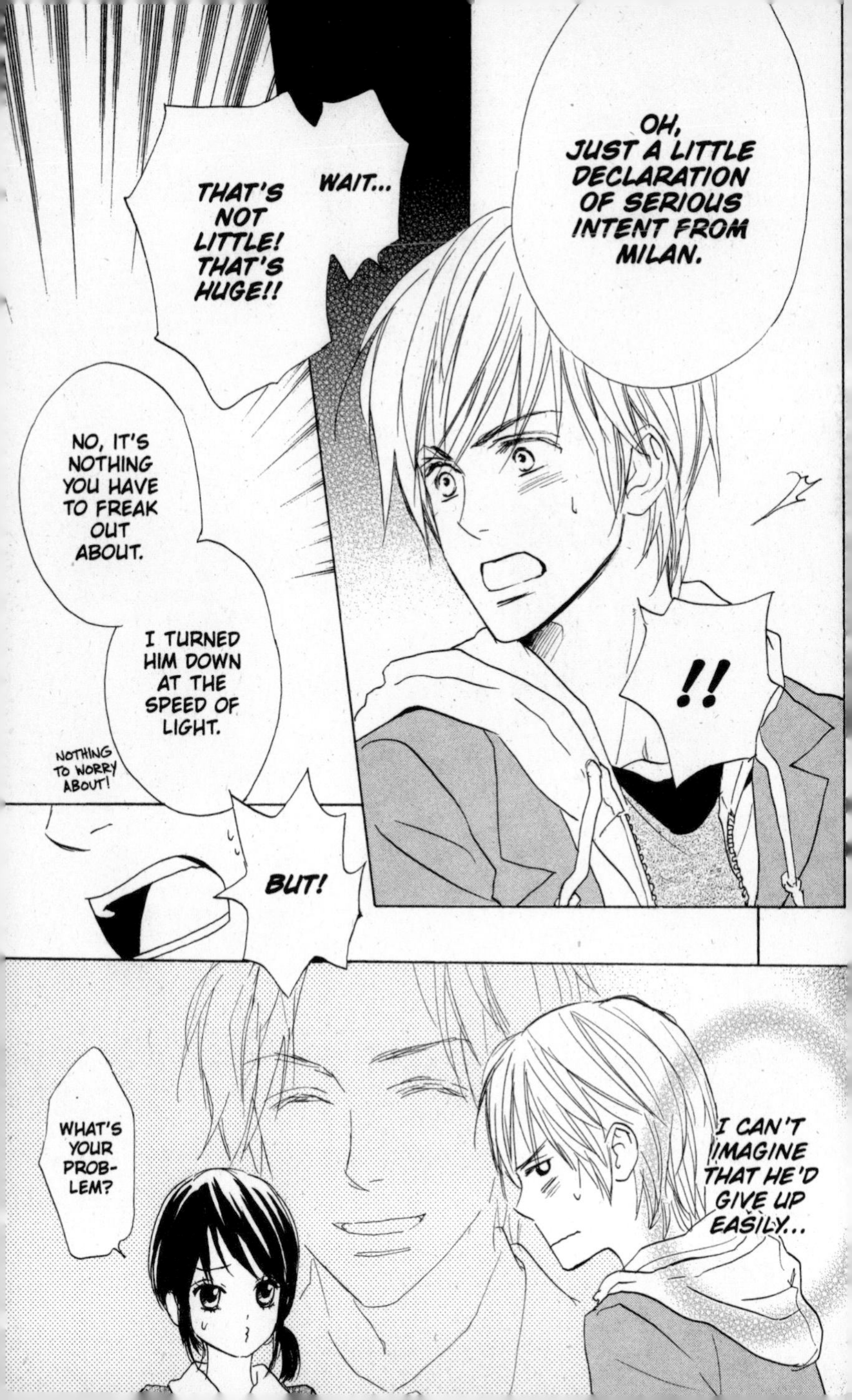
OH, JUST A LITTLE DECLARATION OF SERIOUS INTENT FROM MILAN.
!!
WAIT...
THAT'S NOT LITTLE! THAT'S HUGE!!
NO, IT'S NOTHING YOU HAVE TO FREAK OUT ABOUT.
I TURNED HIM DOWN AT THE SPEED OF LIGHT.
NOTHING TO WORRY ABOUT!
BUT!
I CAN'T IMAGINE THAT HE'D GIVE UP EASILY...
WHAT'S YOUR PROB-LEM?

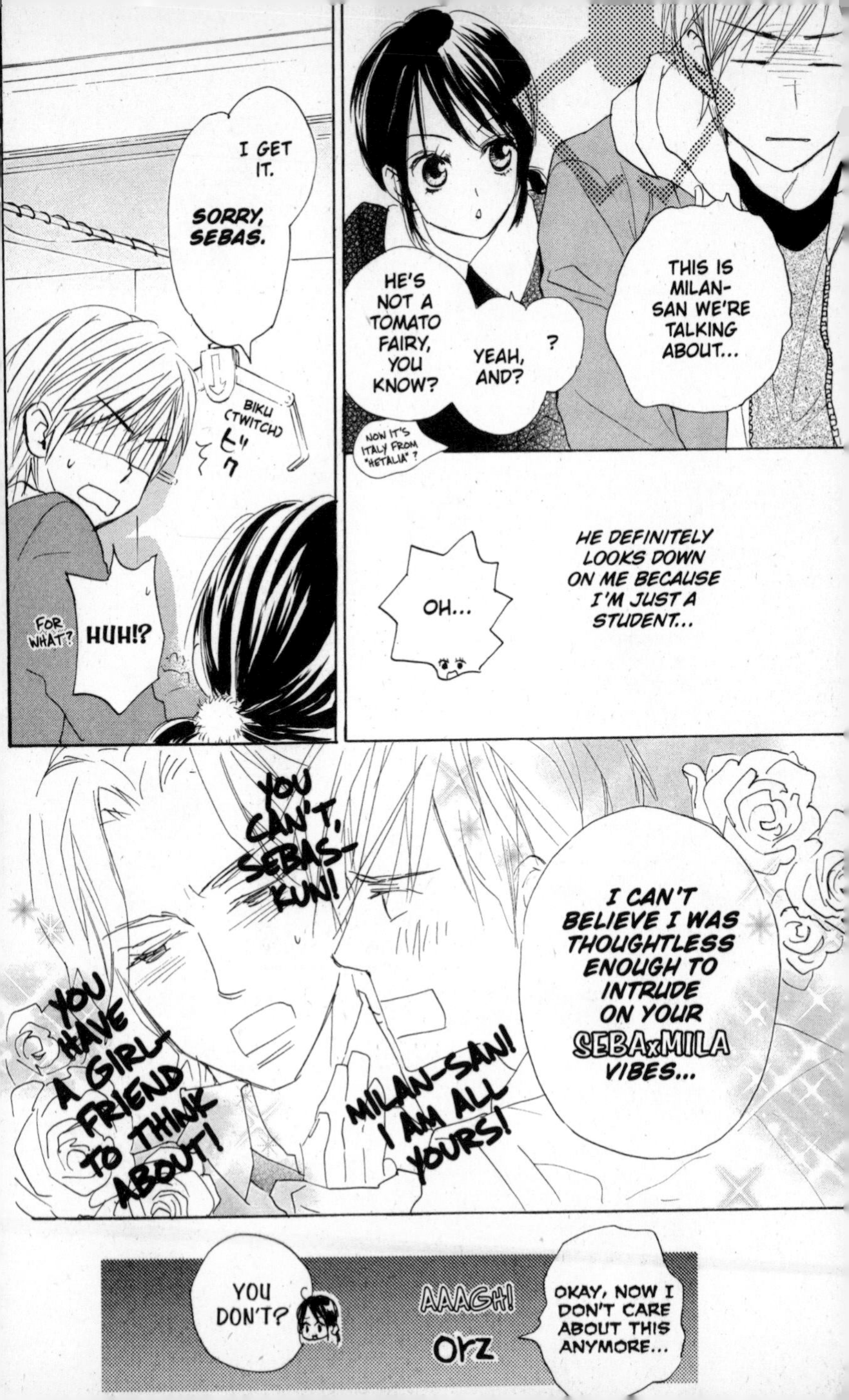
THIS IS MILAN-SAN WE'RE TALKING ABOUT...
YEAH, AND? ?
HE'S NOT A TOMATO FAIRY, YOU KNOW?
NOW IT'S ITALY FROM "HETALIA"?
HE DEFINITELY LOOKS DOWN ON ME BECAUSE I'M JUST A STUDENT...
OH...
I GET IT.
SORRY, SEBAS.
BIKU (TWITCH)
HUH!?
FOR WHAT?
I CAN'T BELIEVE I WAS THOUGTLESS ENOUGH TO INTRUDE ON YOUR SEBAxMILA VIBES...
YOU CAN'T, SEBAS-KUN!
MILAN-SAN! I AM ALL YOURS!
YOU HAVE A GIRL-FRIEND TO THINK ABOUT!
OKAY, NOW I DON'T CARE ABOUT THIS ANYMORE...
AAAGH!
OrZ
YOU DON'T?

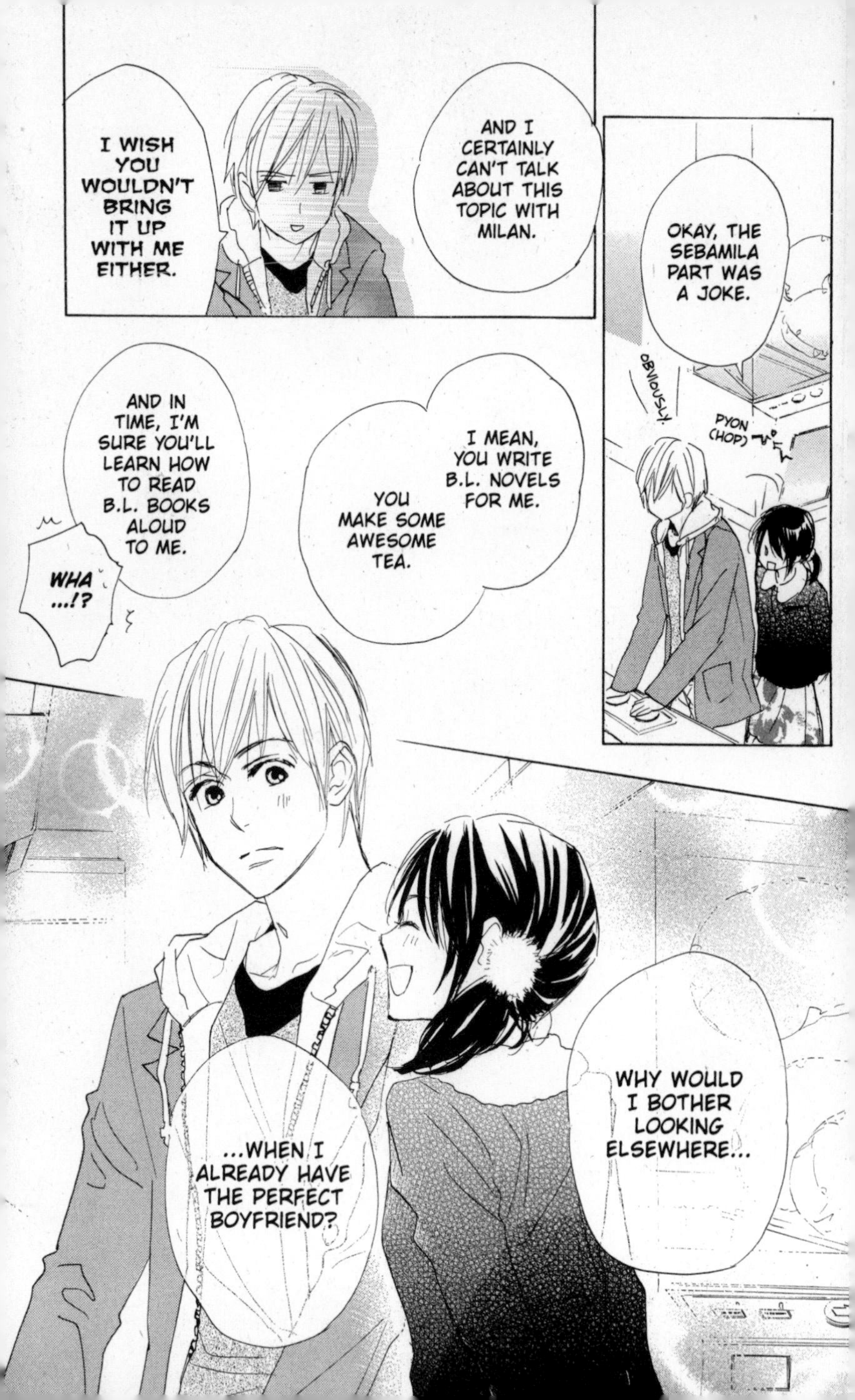
AND I CERTAINLY CAN'T TALK ABOUT THIS TOPIC WITH MILAN.
I WISH YOU WOULDN'T BRING IT UP WITH ME EITHER.
OKAY, THE SEBAMILA PART WAS A JOKE.
OBVIOUSLY.
PYON (HOP)
I MEAN, YOU WRITE B.L. NOVELS FOR ME.
YOU MAKE SOME AWESOME TEA.
AND IN TIME, I'M SURE YOU'LL LEARN HOW TO READ B.L. BOOKS ALOUD TO ME.
WHA ...!?
WHY WOULD I BOTHER LOOKING ELSEWHERE...
...WHEN I ALREADY HAVE THE PERFECT BOYFRIEND?

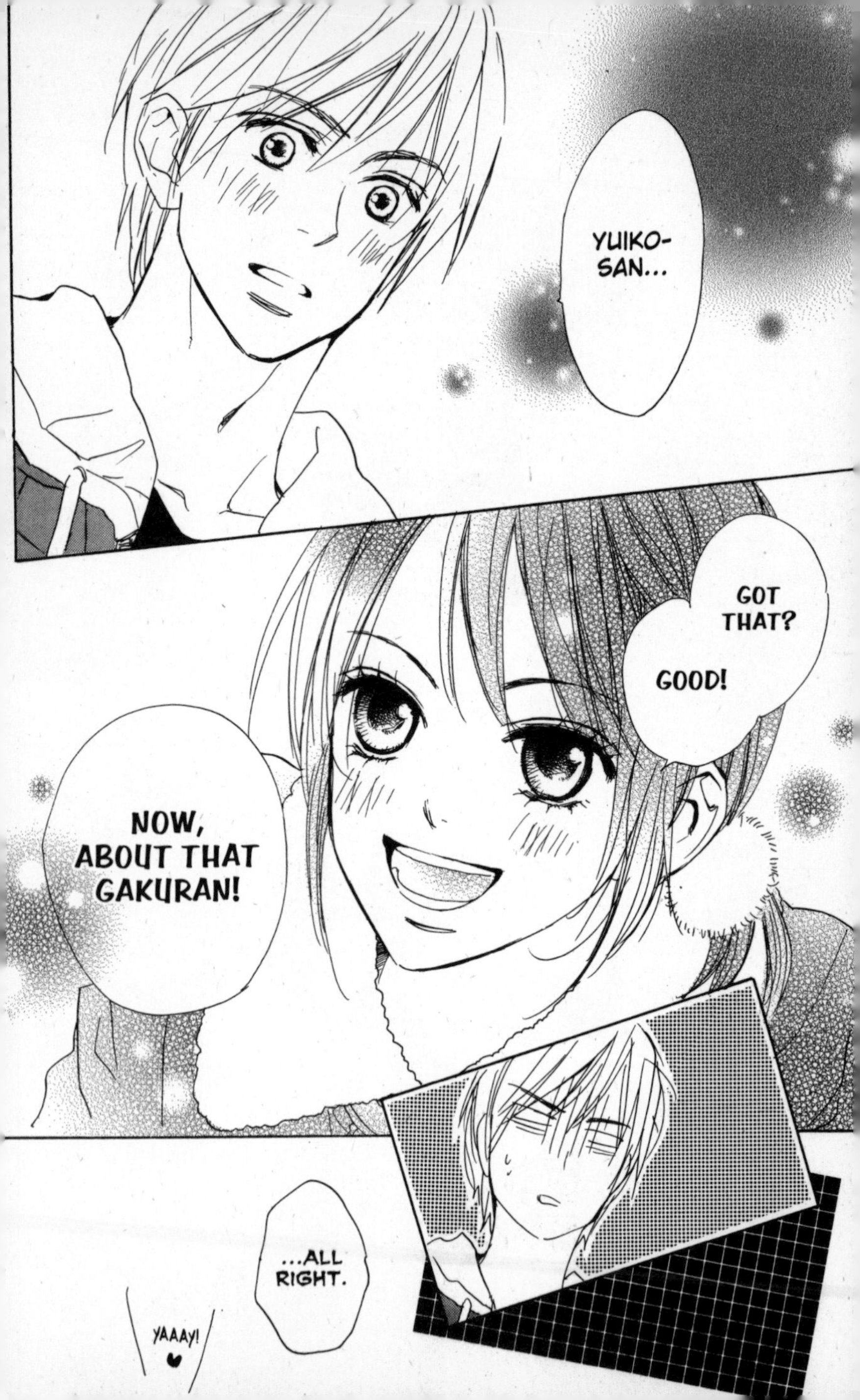
YUIKO-SAN...
GOT THAT?
GOOD!
NOW, ABOUT THAT GAKURAN!
...ALL RIGHT.
YAAAY!

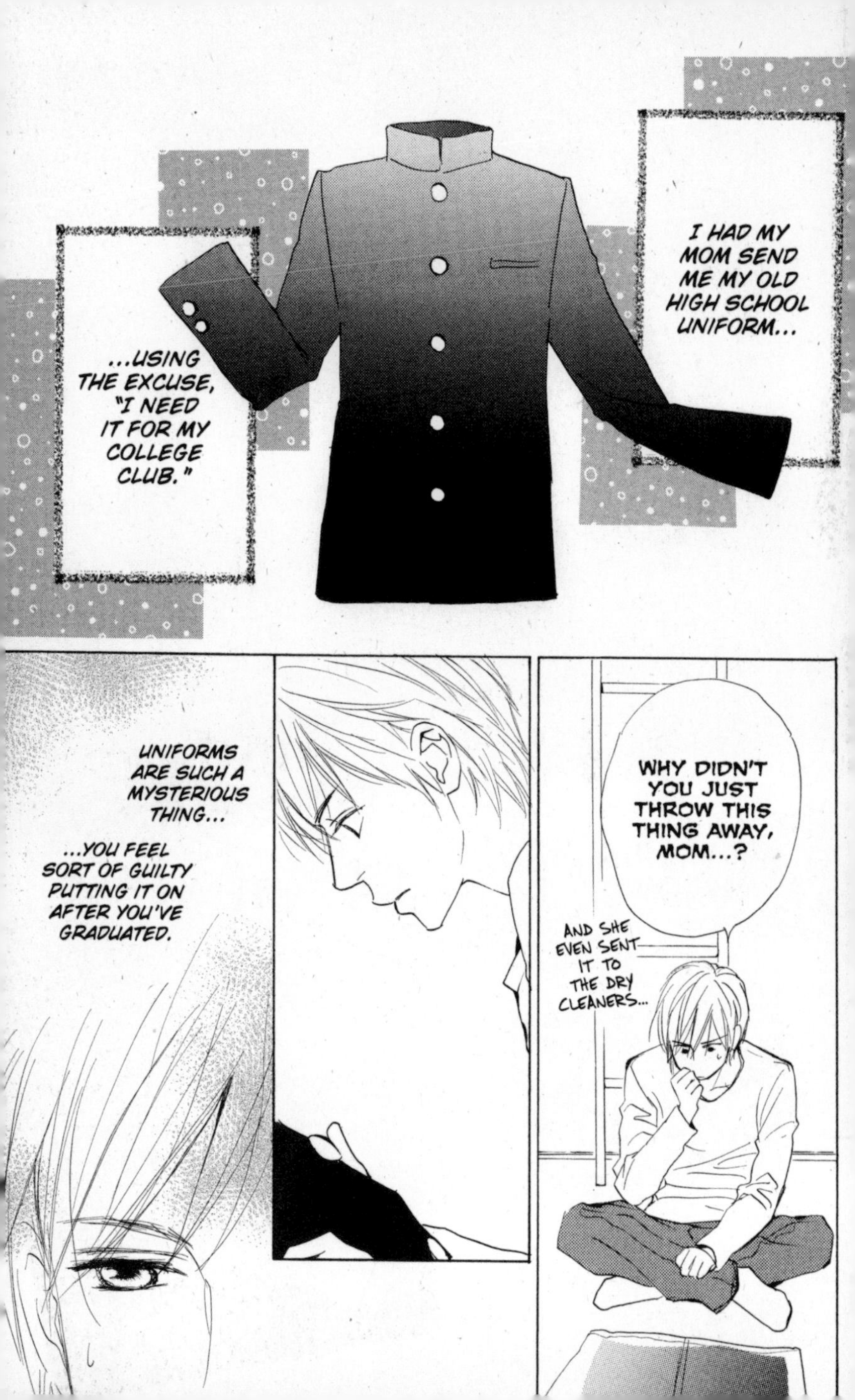
I HAD MY MOM SEND ME MY OLD HIGH SCHOOL UNIFORM...
...USING THE EXCUSE, "I NEED IT FOR MY COLLEGE CLUB."
WHY DIDN'T YOU JUST THROW THIS THING AWAY, MOM...?
AND SHE EVEN SENT IT TO THE DRY CLEANERS...
UNIFORMS ARE SUCH A MYSTERIOUS THING...
...YOU FEEL SORT OF GUILTY PUTTING IT ON AFTER YOU'VE GRADUATED.

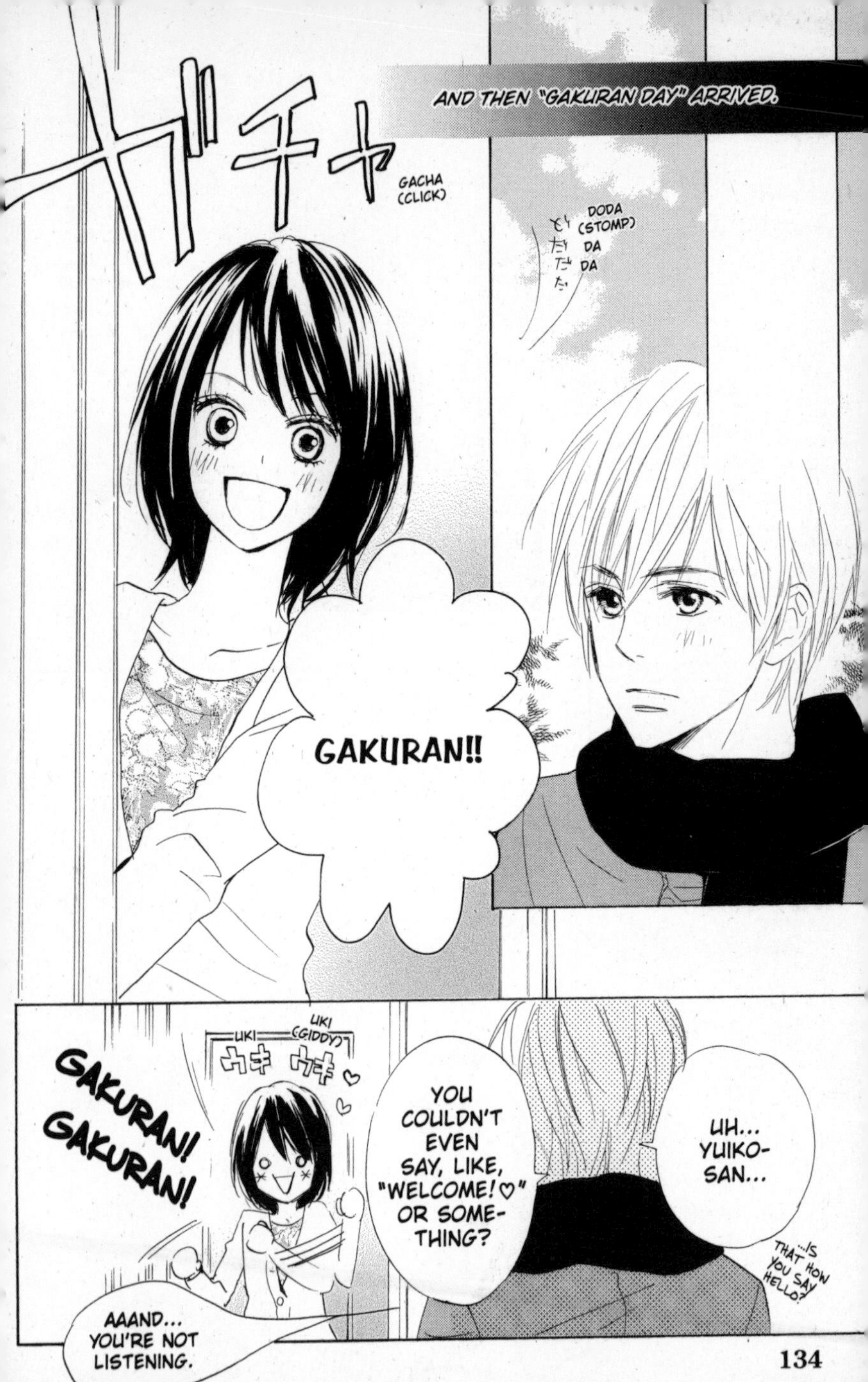
AND THEN "GAKURAN DAY" ARRIVED.
どだだだ
DODA (STOMP) DA DA
ガチャ
GACHA (CLICK)
GAKURAN!!
UH... YUIKO-SAN...
...IS THAT HOW YOU SAY HELLO?
YOU COULDN'T EVEN SAY, LIKE, "WELCOME! ♡" OR SOME-THING?
ウキ ウキ
UKI UKI (GIDDY)
GAKURAN! GAKURAN!
AAAND... YOU'RE NOT LISTENING.

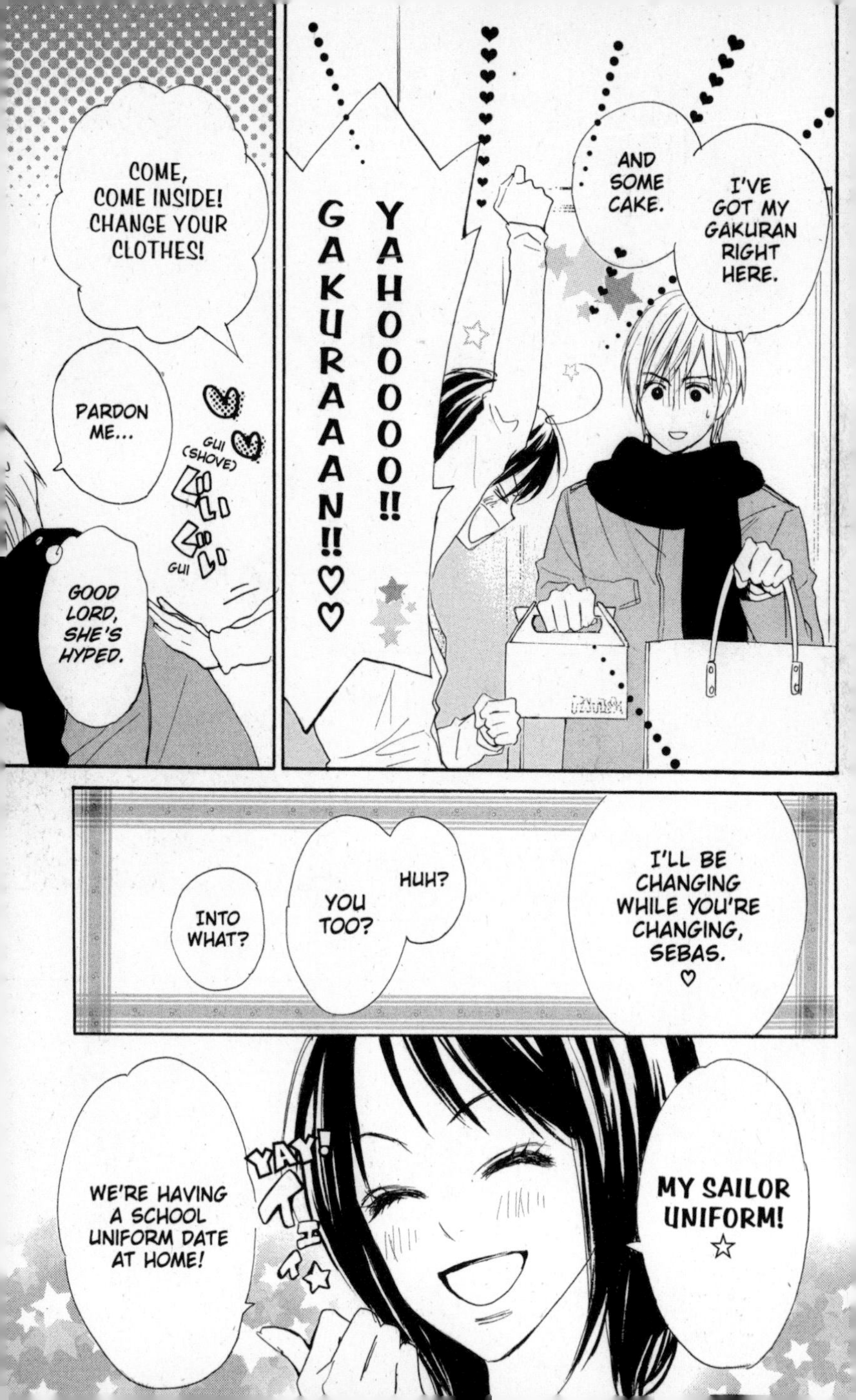
I'VE GOT MY GAKURAN RIGHT HERE.
AND SOME CAKE.
YAHOOOOOOO!!
GAKURAAAAN!! ♡
COME, COME INSIDE! CHANGE YOUR CLOTHES!
PARDON ME...
GUI (SHOVE)
GUI
GOOD LORD, SHE'S HYPED.
I'LL BE CHANGING WHILE YOU'RE CHANGING, SEBAS. ♡
HUH?
YOU TOO?
INTO WHAT?
MY SAILOR UNIFORM! ☆
YAY!
WE'RE HAVING A SCHOOL UNIFORM DATE AT HOME!

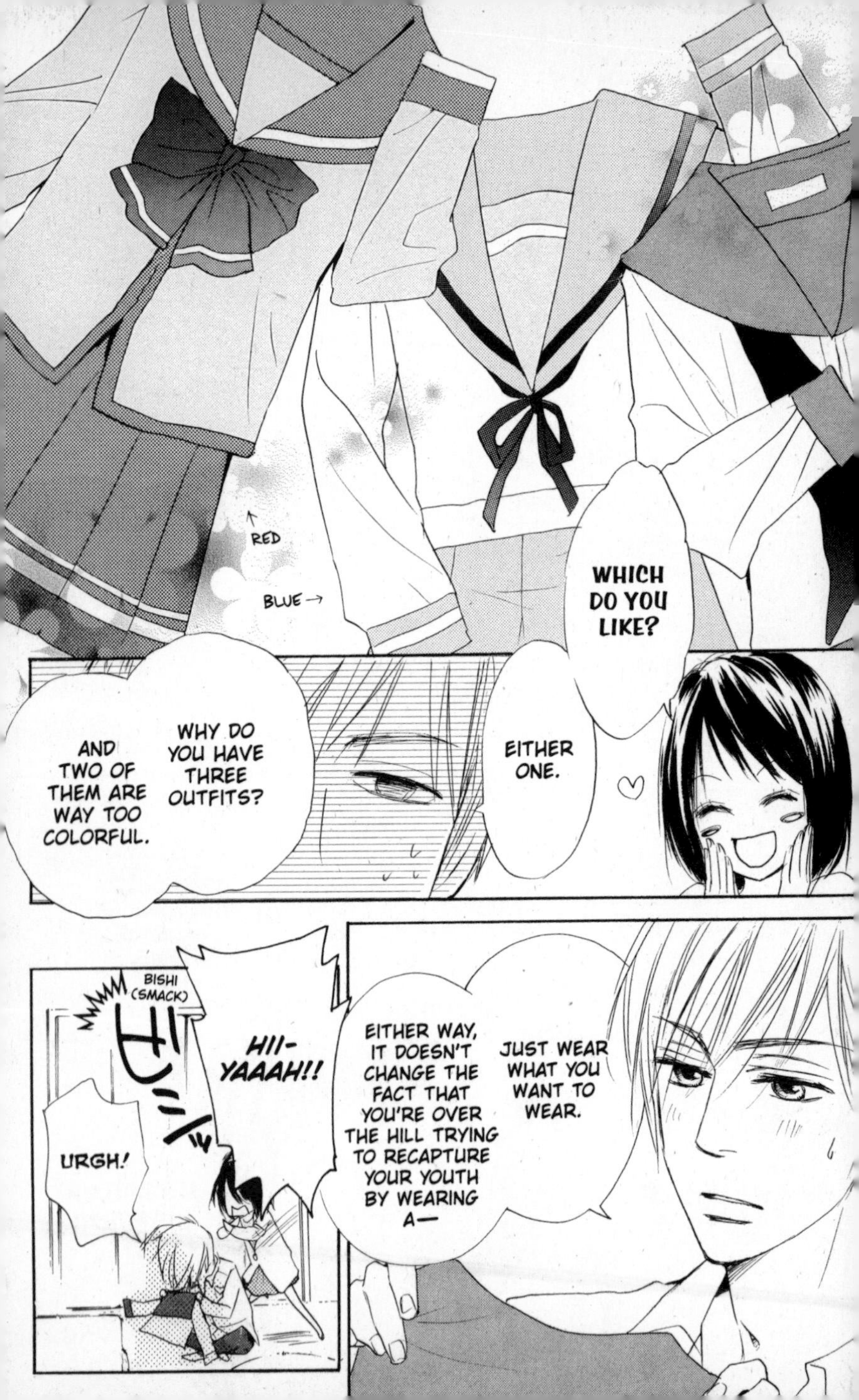
RED
BLUE
WHICH DO YOU LIKE?
EITHER ONE.
WHY DO YOU HAVE THREE OUTFITS?
AND TWO OF THEM ARE WAY TOO COLORFUL.
JUST WEAR WHAT YOU WANT TO WEAR.
EITHER WAY, IT DOESN'T CHANGE THE FACT THAT YOU'RE OVER THE HILL TRYING TO RECAPTURE YOUR YOUTH BY WEARING A—
HII-YAAAH!!
BISHI (SMACK)
URGH!

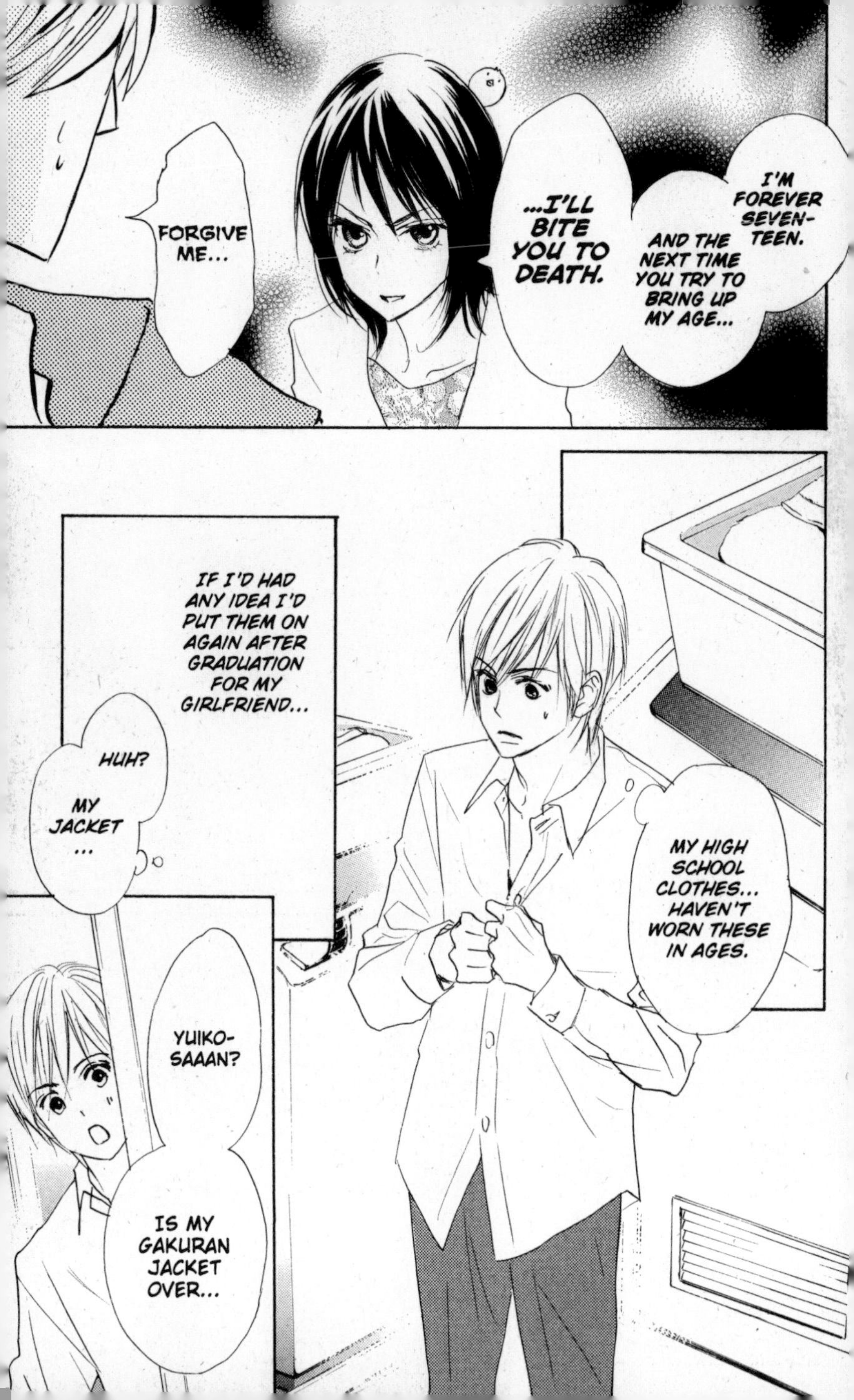
I'M FOREVER SEVENTEEN.
AND THE NEXT TIME YOU TRY TO BRING UP MY AGE...
...I'LL BITE YOU TO DEATH.
FORGIVE ME...
MY HIGH SCHOOL CLOTHES... HAVEN'T WORN THESE IN AGES.
IF I'D HAD ANY IDEA I'D PUT THEM ON AGAIN AFTER GRADUATION FOR MY GIRLFRIEND...
HUH?
MY JACKET ...
YUIKO-SAAAN?
IS MY GAKURAN JACKET OVER...

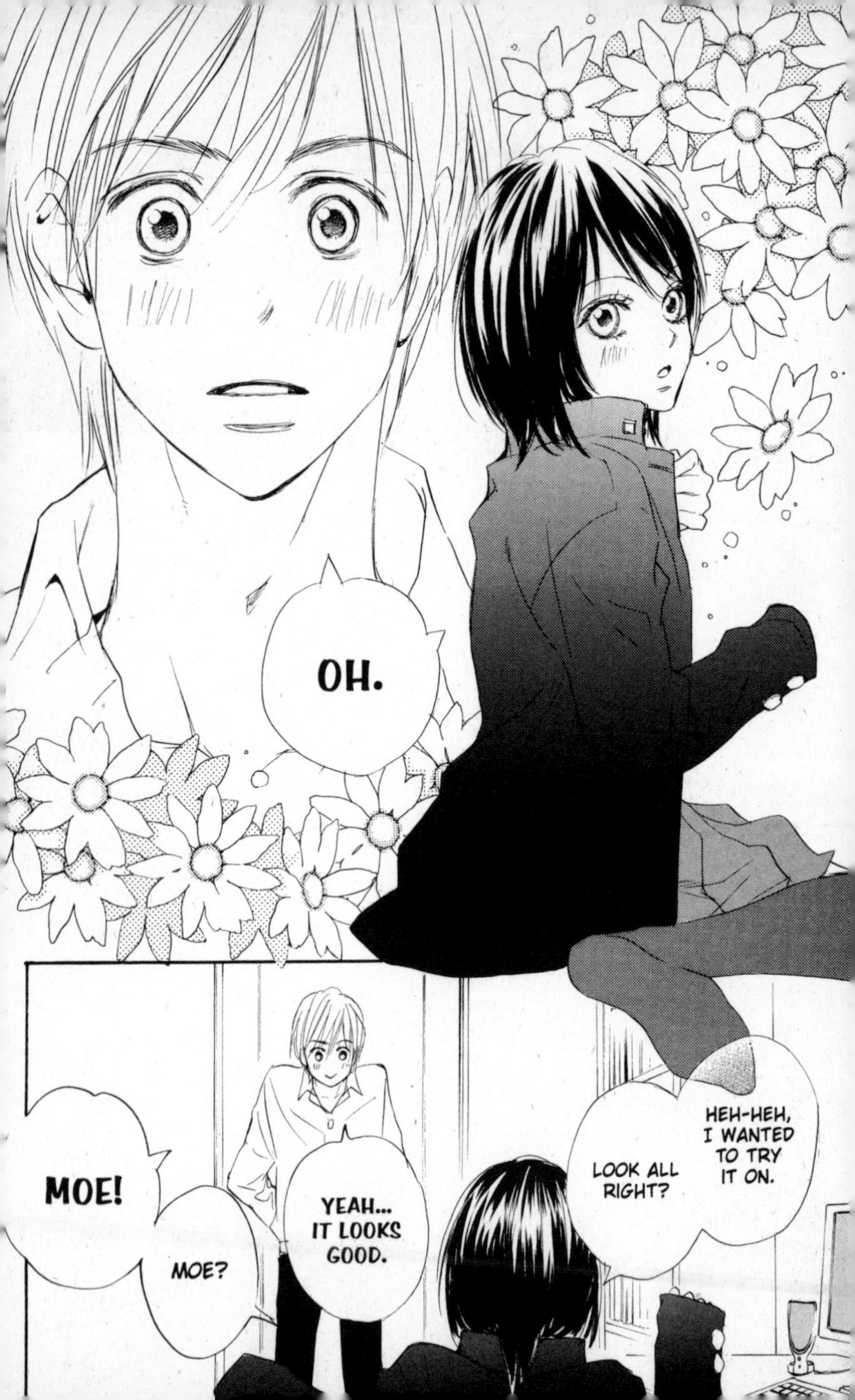
OH.
HEH-HEH, I WANTED TO TRY IT ON.
LOOK ALL RIGHT?
YEAH... IT LOOKS GOOD.
MOE?
MOE!

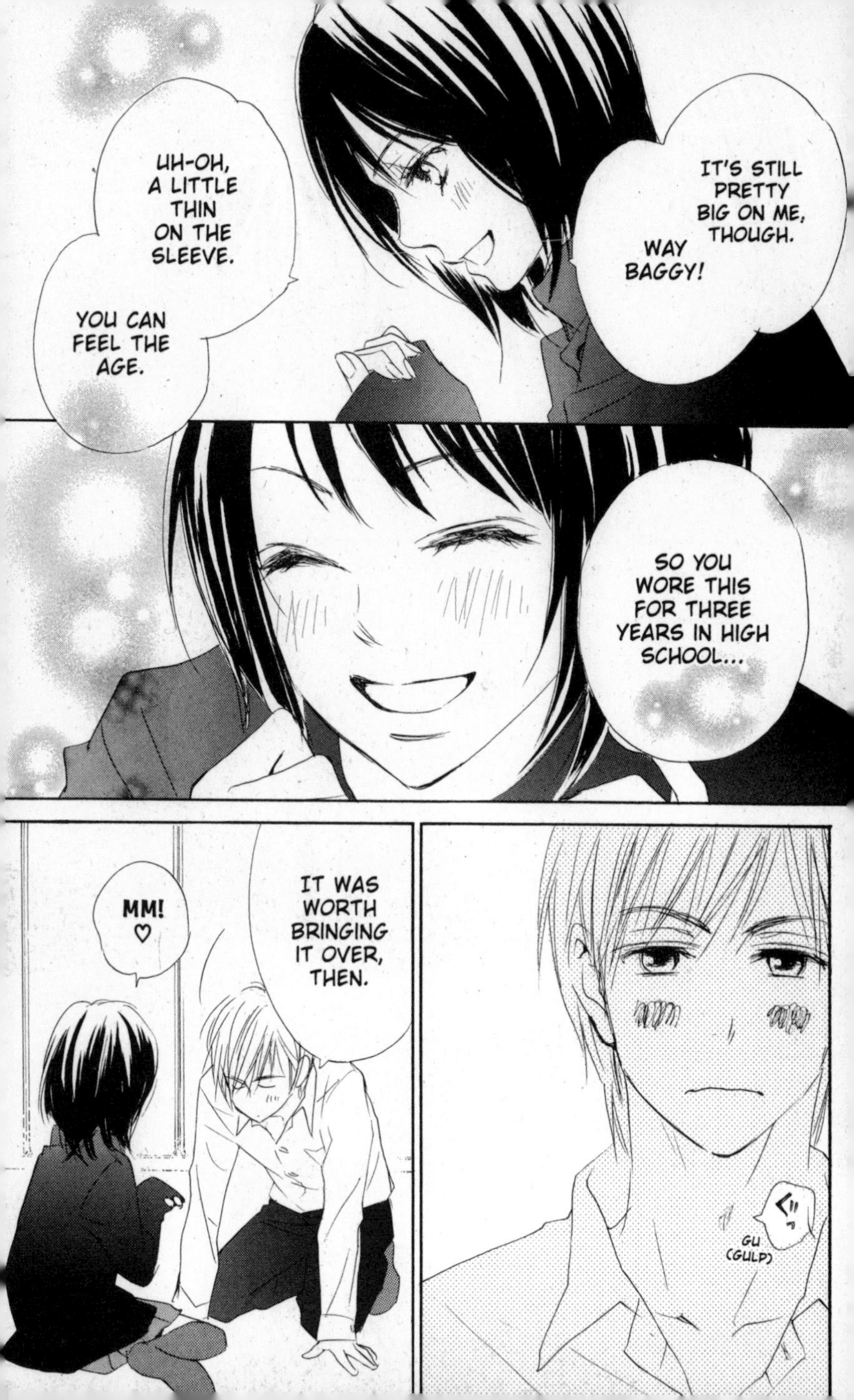
IT'S STILL PRETTY BIG ON ME, THOUGH.
WAY BAGGY!
UH-OH, A LITTLE THIN ON THE SLEEVE.
YOU CAN FEEL THE AGE.
SO YOU WORE THIS FOR THREE YEARS IN HIGH SCHOOL...
GU (GULP)
IT WAS WORTH BRINGING IT OVER, THEN.
MM! ♡

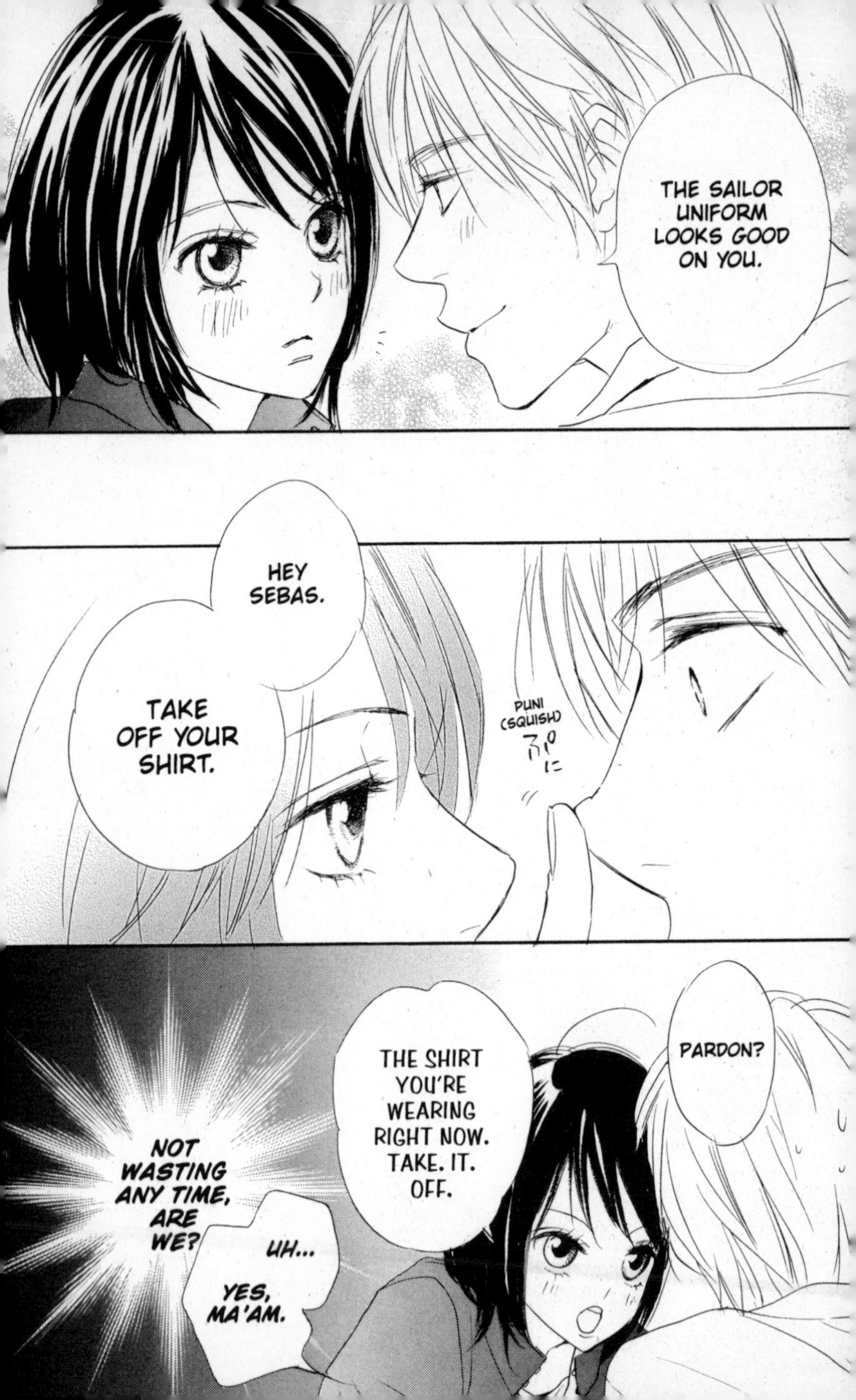
THE SAILOR UNIFORM LOOKS GOOD ON YOU.
HEY SEBAS.
PUNI (SQUISH)
ぷに
TAKE OFF YOUR SHIRT.
PARDON?
THE SHIRT YOU'RE WEARING RIGHT NOW. TAKE. IT. OFF.
NOT WASTING ANY TIME, ARE WE?
UH...
YES, MA'AM.

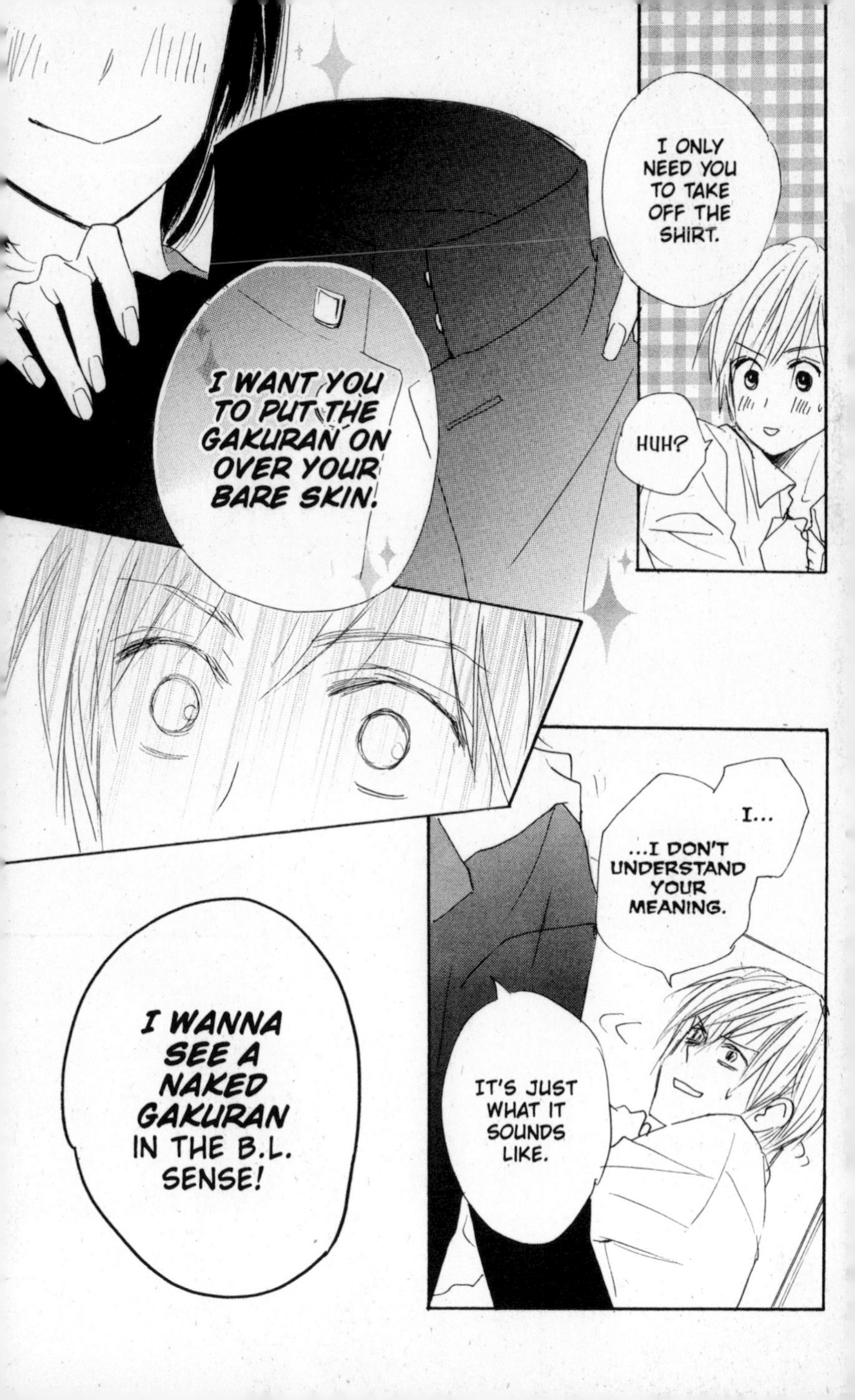
I ONLY NEED YOU TO TAKE OFF THE SHIRT.
HUH?
I WANT YOU TO PUT THE GAKURAN ON OVER YOUR BARE SKIN.
I...
...I DON'T UNDERSTAND YOUR MEANING.
IT'S JUST WHAT IT SOUNDS LIKE.
I WANNA SEE A NAKED GAKURAN IN THE B.L. SENSE!

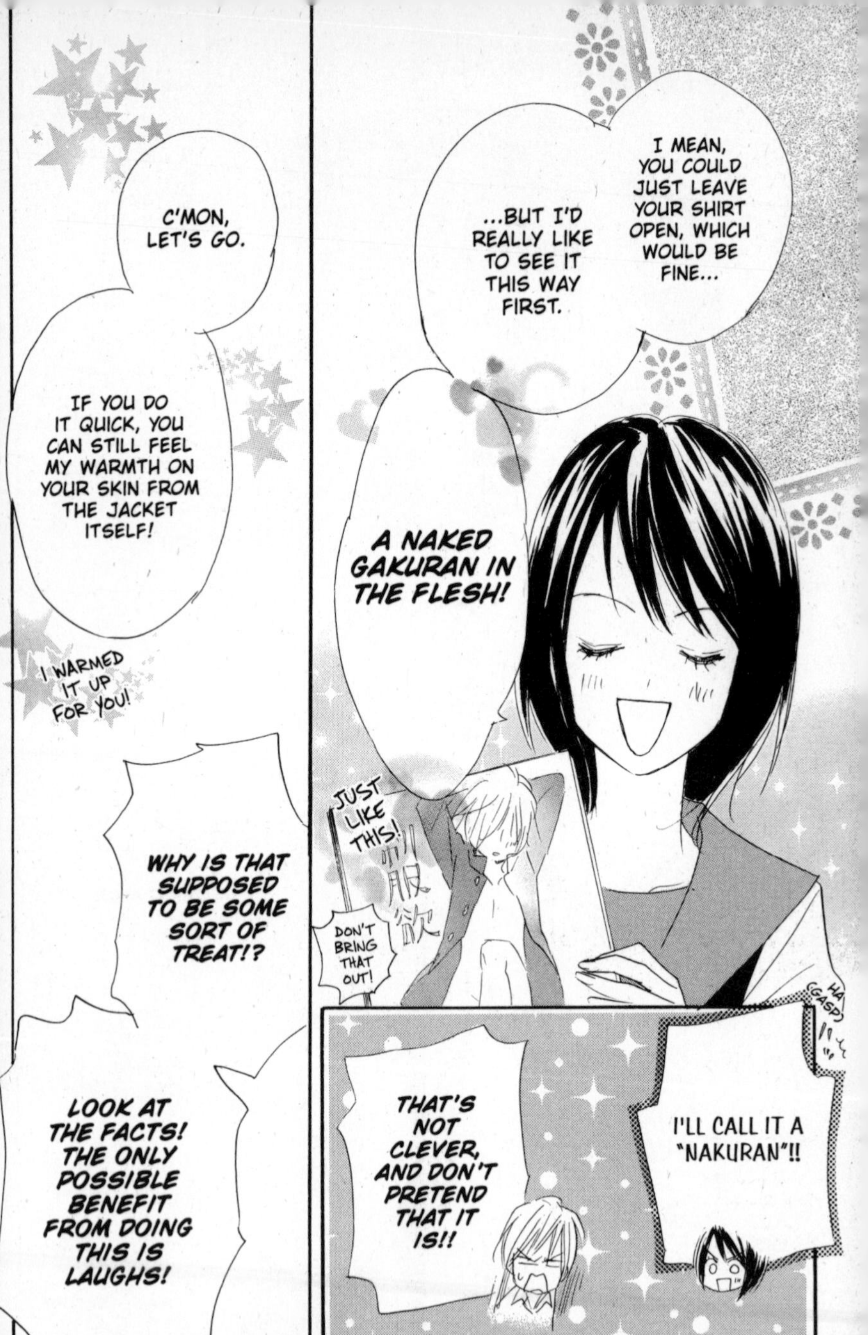
I MEAN, YOU COULD JUST LEAVE YOUR SHIRT OPEN, WHICH WOULD BE FINE...
...BUT I'D REALLY LIKE TO SEE IT THIS WAY FIRST.
A NAKED GAKURAN IN THE FLESH!
JUST LIKE THIS!
DON'T BRING THAT OUT!
HA (GASP)
I'LL CALL IT A "NAKURAN"!!
THAT'S NOT CLEVER, AND DON'T PRETEND THAT IT IS!!
C'MON, LET'S GO.
IF YOU DO IT QUICK, YOU CAN STILL FEEL MY WARMTH ON YOUR SKIN FROM THE JACKET ITSELF!
I WARMED IT UP FOR YOU!
WHY IS THAT SUPPOSED TO BE SOME SORT OF TREAT!?
LOOK AT THE FACTS! THE ONLY POSSIBLE BENEFIT FROM DOING THIS IS LAUGHS!

DOJINSHI: UNIFORM DESIRE

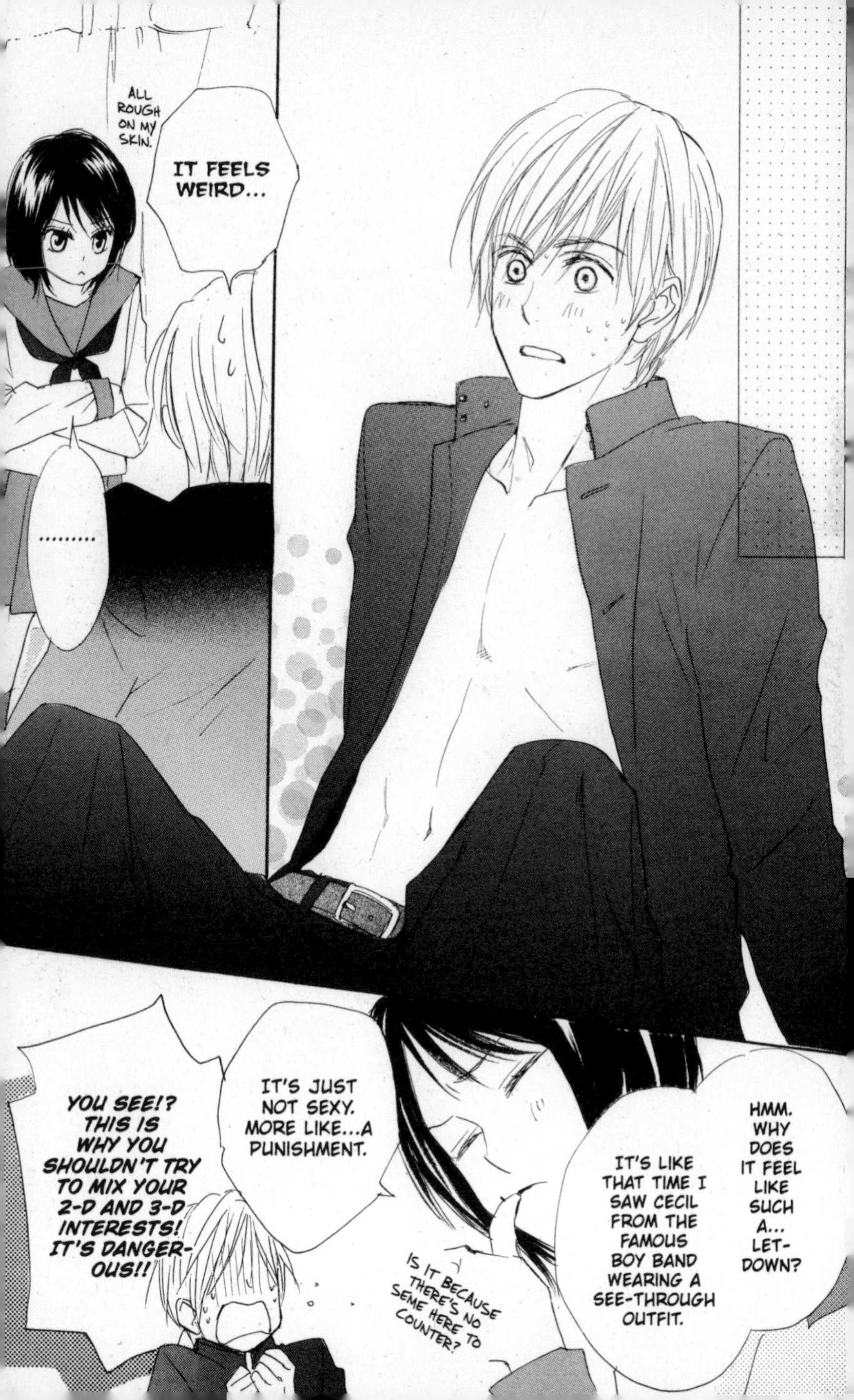
IT FEELS WEIRD...
ALL ROUGH ON MY SKIN.
....
HMM. WHY DOES IT FEEL LIKE SUCH A... LET-DOWN?
IT'S LIKE THAT TIME I SAW CECIL FROM THE FAMOUS BOY BAND WEARING A SEE-THROUGH OUTFIT.
IS IT BECAUSE THERE'S NO SEME HERE TO COUNTER?
IT'S JUST NOT SEXY. MORE LIKE...A PUNISHMENT.
YOU SEE!? THIS IS WHY YOU SHOULDN'T TRY TO MIX YOUR 2-D AND 3-D INTERESTS! IT'S DANGER-OUS!!

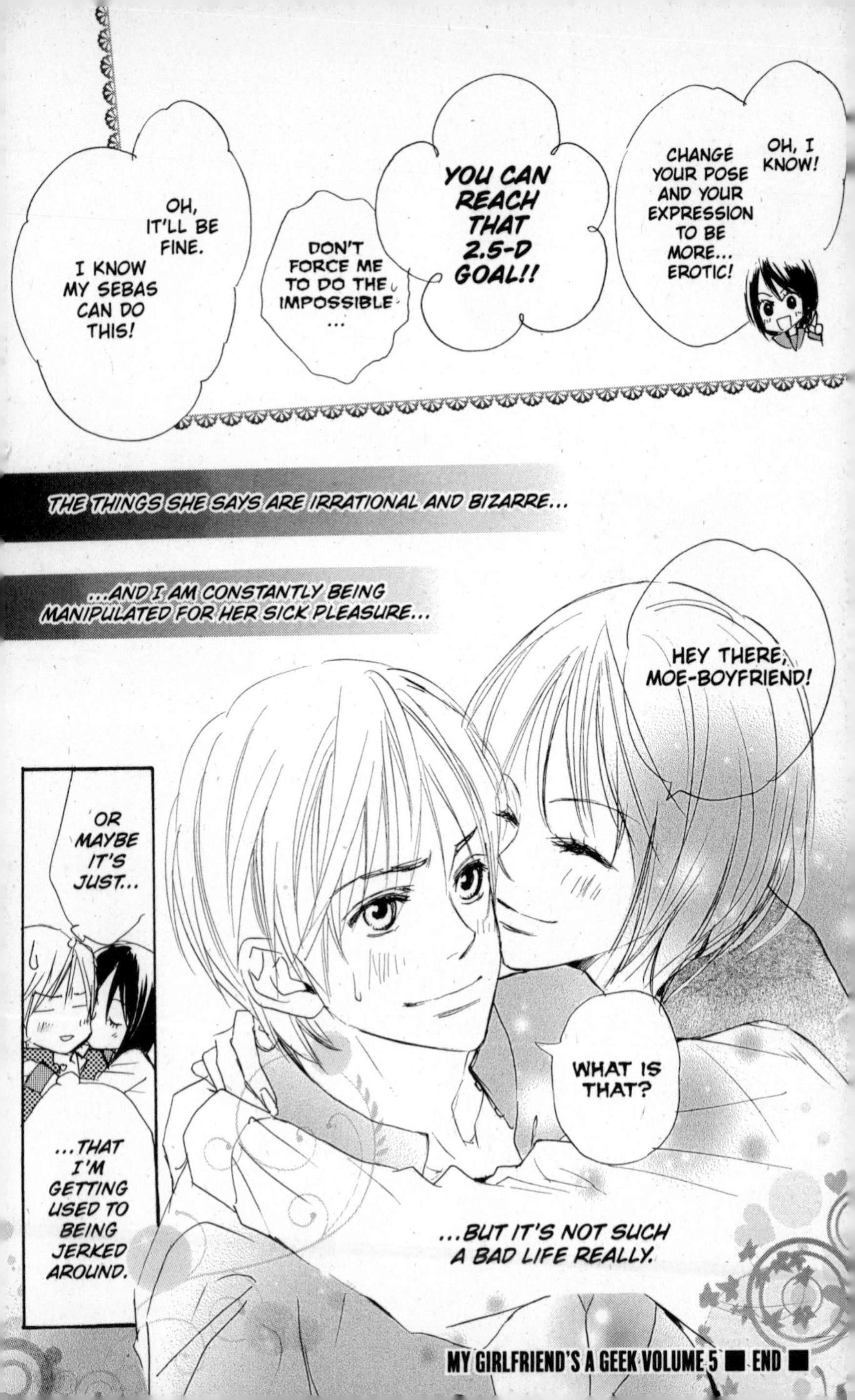
OH, I KNOW!
CHANGE YOUR POSE AND YOUR EXPRESSION TO BE MORE... EROTIC!
YOU CAN REACH THAT 2.5-D GOAL!!
DON'T FORCE ME TO DO THE IMPOSSIBLE...
OH, IT'LL BE FINE.
I KNOW MY SEBAS CAN DO THIS!
THE THINGS SHE SAYS ARE IRRATIONAL AND BIZARRE...
...AND I AM CONSTANTLY BEING MANIPULATED FOR HER SICK PLEASURE...
HEY THERE, MOE-BOYFRIEND!
WHAT IS THAT?
OR MAYBE IT'S JUST...
...THAT I'M GETTING USED TO BEING JERKED AROUND.
...BUT IT'S NOT SUCH A BAD LIFE REALLY.
MY GIRLFRIEND'S A GEEK VOLUME 5 ■ END ■

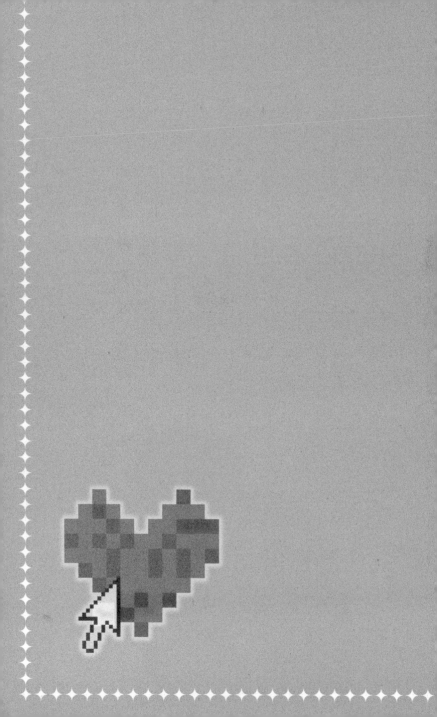

FUJOSHI NEWS vol.16

YUIKO-SAN & YOUHEI-SENPAI GLOSSARY②

P.51
MAIDMAN - A YOUNG MAN WITH THE INTERESTS OF A MAIDEN. MANY MAIDMEN ARE SKILLED AT HOUSEHOLD CHORES LIKE CLEANING, LAUNDRY, AND COOKING. EVERY HOME COULD USE A MAIDMAN!

P.52
GIRLBOY - A BOY DRESSED AS A GIRL, OR A BOY SO CUTE AND FRAIL THAT HE MIGHT AS WELL BE A GIRL. A WONDERFUL NEW MOE ELEMENT THAT CAN APPEAL TO BOTH BOYS AND GIRLS.

P.63
GODLY CLIP - AN INCREDIBLY WELL-ANIMATED SCENE, OFTEN FROM AN ANIME OPENING. TYPICALLY CALLED "GODLY PRODUCTION" AS WELL.

P.64
CARDBOARD FORTRESS - WALLS AND SHELVES CONSTRUCTED FROM THE CARDBOARD BOXES AND SHEETS USED TO CARRY DOJINSHI AND OTHER GOODS FOR SALE AT EVENTS. THE LARGER THE CIRCLE, THE MORE BOXES, AND THUS THE MORE EXTRAVAGANT THE FORT.

P.77
YANDERE - A CHARACTER WHO IS THE PICTURE OF SWEETNESS AND WARMTH, BELYING HIS/HER TRUE PSYCHOTIC, OFTEN VIOLENT NATURE.

P.80
INTERNET VOICE STAR - SOMEONE WHO PROVIDES VOCAL TALENT TO DOJIN AUDIO DRAMAS OR GAMES AVAILABLE ON THE INTERNET. WITH THE ADVENT OF VIDEO UPLOADING SITES, ONE CAN GET QUITE FAMOUS THIS WAY.

P.97
ANIME FLAG - WHEN A MANGA OR NOVEL SEEMS LIKELY TO HAVE AN ANIME ADAPTATION. IT'S ESPECIALLY SUSPICIOUS WHEN A MAGAZINE TEASES "A MAJOR ANNOUNCEMENT NEXT ISSUE!!"

P.123
CHE PALLE - ITALIAN FOR "WHAT BALLS!"

P.126
D.T. - VIRGIN.
D.K. - TEENAGE BOY.
J.K. - TEENAGE GIRL.

P.127
P.T. - PRE-TEEN.

P.137
I'LL BITE YOU TO DEATH - YUIKO IS PRETENDING TO BE KYOUYA HIBARI—A CHARACTER FROM THE MANGA, "KATEIKYOUSHI HITMAN REBORN!"—WHOSE CATCHPHRASE THIS IS.

P.141
NAKED GAKURAN - WEARING A GAKURAN JACKET OVER YOUR BARE SKIN. IT'S AN EXTREMELY COMMON SIGHT ON B.L. DOJINSHI COVERS, BUT IF YOU DO IT IN REAL LIFE, IT FEELS ROUGH AND GROSS ON THE SKIN.

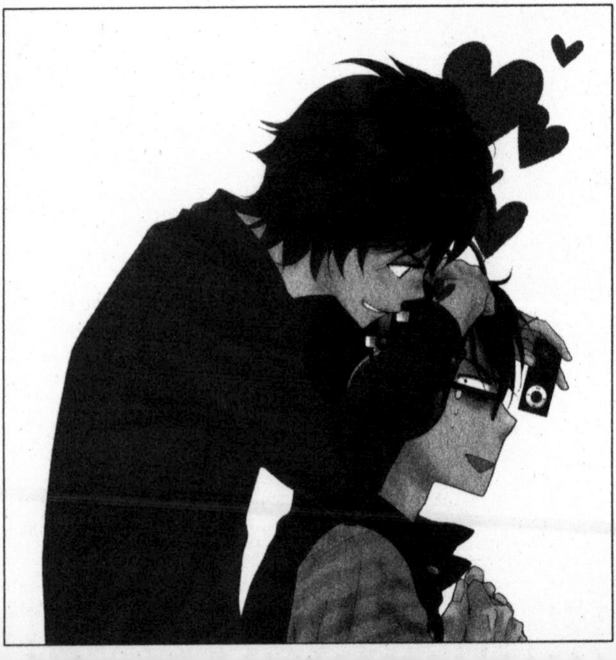

AFTERWORD ESSAY

PENTABU

WEL- COME TO THE ROTTEN WORLD OF FU- JOSHI!!

Y-KO APPROACHES ME AND SAYS, "HEY, SEBAS," IN A SERIOUS MANNER...

2010/01/29 14:26

Y-KO: Hey, Sebas. Have you ever thought about what comes after a happy ending?

ME: Pardon? After...a happy ending?

Y-KO: Yes. I've seen plenty of happy endings in my life. Manga, books, anime—well, not all of them have been happy, but they usually end well for the characters.

ME: I see.

Y-KO: I've always liked to imagine what happens in those stories after the happy ending comes. After the adventurer rescues the princess, after the hero saves the world, **after the guy's love is fulfilled and he gets the guy,** and so on.

ME: I'm sorry, give me a moment to **mentally process** that last one...

The guy's love is fulfilled and he gets the **"girl"**...

That's right. Not the **guy gets the guy.** Guy gets the girl.

......Okay. Mental recalibration complete.

ME: —Thank you for waiting. Please continue.

Y-KO: Or after **Taiga and Kouji** are safely **united,** for example.

ME: But they're not united, right!? And there's no need for anything to happen "safely," right!?

Y-KO: Oh, sorry, sorry. Strictly speaking, it's after **Kouji and Taiga** are united.

ME: **Changing the order** doesn't make a difference! Taiga is united with Yuiko-san! There's no alternate pairing in this story! And to think, you actually seemed to have something serious to say!

Why does she have a problem with the beautiful ending to the story......?

Y-KO: Well, enough of the **half-serious** jokes.

ME: You were half-serious about that......!?

Y-KO: Well, when you think about it, we're kind of living the life after the ending to *My Girlfriend's a Geek*, right? We're the epilogue.

ME: ......Well, I suppose you could interpret it that way.

Y-KO: So I think we have a duty to continue to be happy.

ME: ...Yes, meaning?

Y-KO: And for the sake of my continued happiness, I need you to spend your entire holiday bonus on B.L.!

ME: Alas...I pretty much saw that punch line coming...

But, Y-ko...does that address the issue of **my happiness** in any way...?

Y-KO: What do you mean? Your happiness is my happiness, and my happiness is reading B.L. The law of mathematics states that therefore, **your happiness is buying me B.L.!** Right?

ME: Flashing a pretty smile is not going to make me agree with that...

Y-KO: Well, that settles it! Your winter bonus is going to B.L.!

ME: Oh, that reminds me, I forgot to mention that **my entire winter bonus was withheld.**

Y-KO: Wait, wha... Sebaaas!?

ME: Ha-ha-ha-ha. **The recession is a bitch,** isn't it?

Y-KO: That's not funny! That's not funnyyyyyy!

Well, anyhow.

Thank you very much for checking out the final volume of the manga edition of *My Girlfriend's a Geek*. I am the author, Pentabu, and as you can see, life goes on as usual.

First, I'd like to use this space to express my thanks to everyone. Shinba-sensei, the publishers, and everyone whose kind encouragement supported this manga have my undying gratitude. Thank you. Thank you so much.

It's because of all of you who have bought this final volume that *My Girlfriend's a Geek* has reached this happy conclusion.

Thinking back, from the moment I started writing my blog until now, I've been supported by so many people. It turned into a book, it turned into a manga, it turned into a movie, and it turned into a drama CD... At every step of the way, I've had the help of so many people. Never before, and I suspect, never again, will I know the joy of the support of so many people in my life.

To the readers who visited my blog and sent their best wishes, to the publishers who helped create the book version and manga adaptation, and to Shinba-sensei for creating this fantastic story. And of course, to everyone who bought this book. It is because of all of you that *My Girlfriend's a Geek* has come this far.

I suspect...
I suspect that this is the last opportunity I will have to thank you as "Pentabu, author of *My Girlfriend's a Geek*." Therefore, I leave my gratitude, which is so great that I ought to run around and tell you all individually in person, in these final words:

May each and every one of you feel the bliss that we breathe every day in your own lives.

Thank you—thank you so very much.

Spring 2010
Pentabu
Y-ko

THANK YOU VERY MUCH!

MY FAVORITE THINGS: AN ESSAY

I LOVE THIS MORE THAN THREE MEALS A DAY!

THIS MONTH'S MENU ON THE BORDER OF HEALTHY AND UNHEALTHY

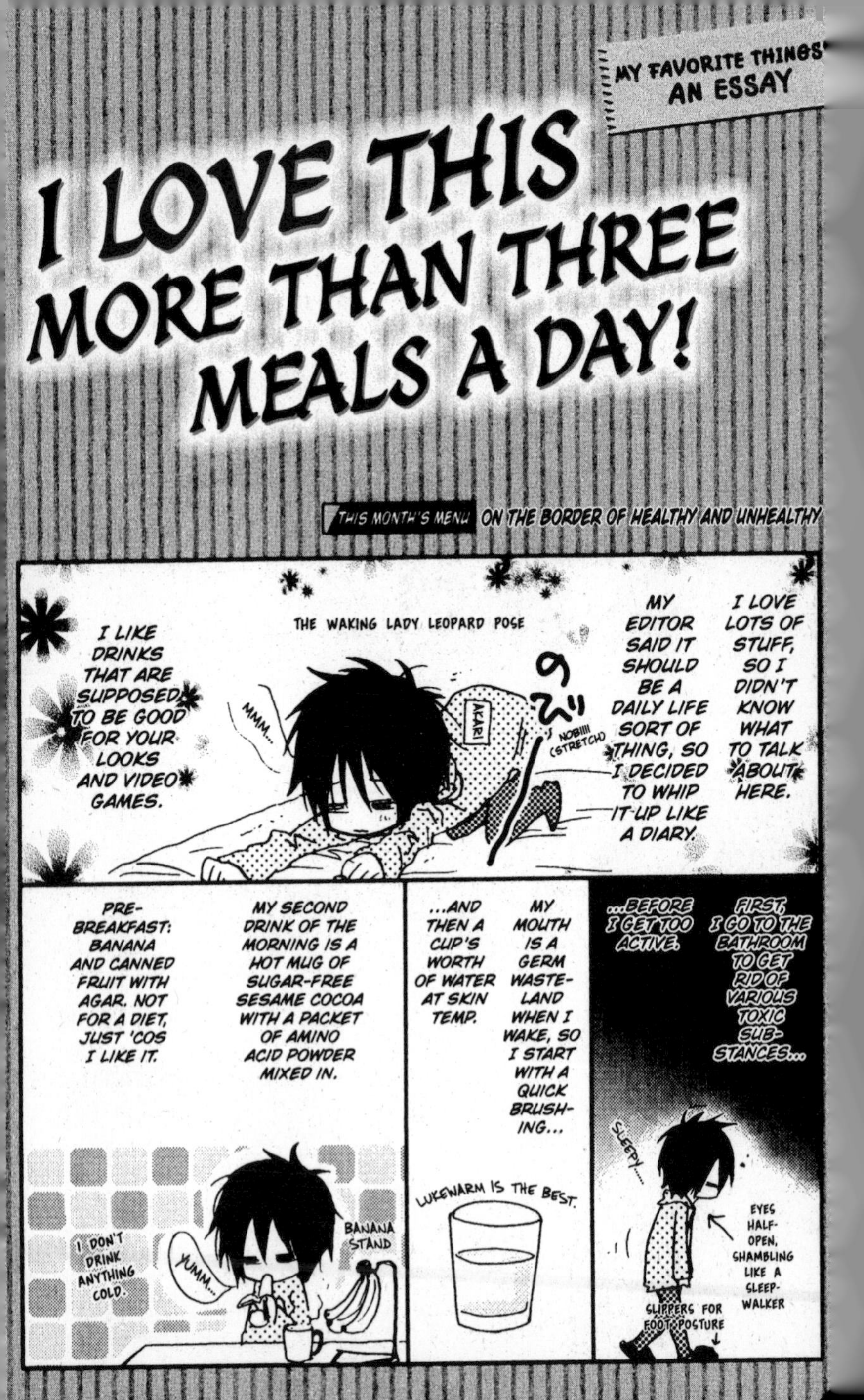
I LOVE LOTS OF STUFF, SO I DIDN'T KNOW WHAT TO TALK ABOUT HERE.
MY EDITOR SAID IT SHOULD BE A DAILY LIFE SORT OF THING, SO I DECIDED TO WHIP IT UP LIKE A DIARY.
THE WAKING LADY LEOPARD POSE
AKARI
NOBIIII (STRETCH)
MMM...
I LIKE DRINKS THAT ARE SUPPOSED TO BE GOOD FOR YOUR LOOKS AND VIDEO GAMES.
FIRST, I GO TO THE BATHROOM TO GET RID OF VARIOUS TOXIC SUBSTANCES...
...BEFORE I GET TOO ACTIVE.
SLEEPY......
EYES HALF-OPEN, SHAMBLING LIKE A SLEEPWALKER
SLIPPERS FOR FOOT POSTURE
MY MOUTH IS A GERM WASTELAND WHEN I WAKE, SO I START WITH A QUICK BRUSHING...
...AND THEN A CUP'S WORTH OF WATER AT SKIN TEMP.
LUKEWARM IS THE BEST.
MY SECOND DRINK OF THE MORNING IS A HOT MUG OF SUGAR-FREE SESAME COCOA WITH A PACKET OF AMINO ACID POWDER MIXED IN.
PRE-BREAKFAST: BANANA AND CANNED FRUIT WITH AGAR. NOT FOR A DIET, JUST 'COS I LIKE IT.
BANANA STAND
YUMM...
I DON'T DRINK ANYTHING COLD.

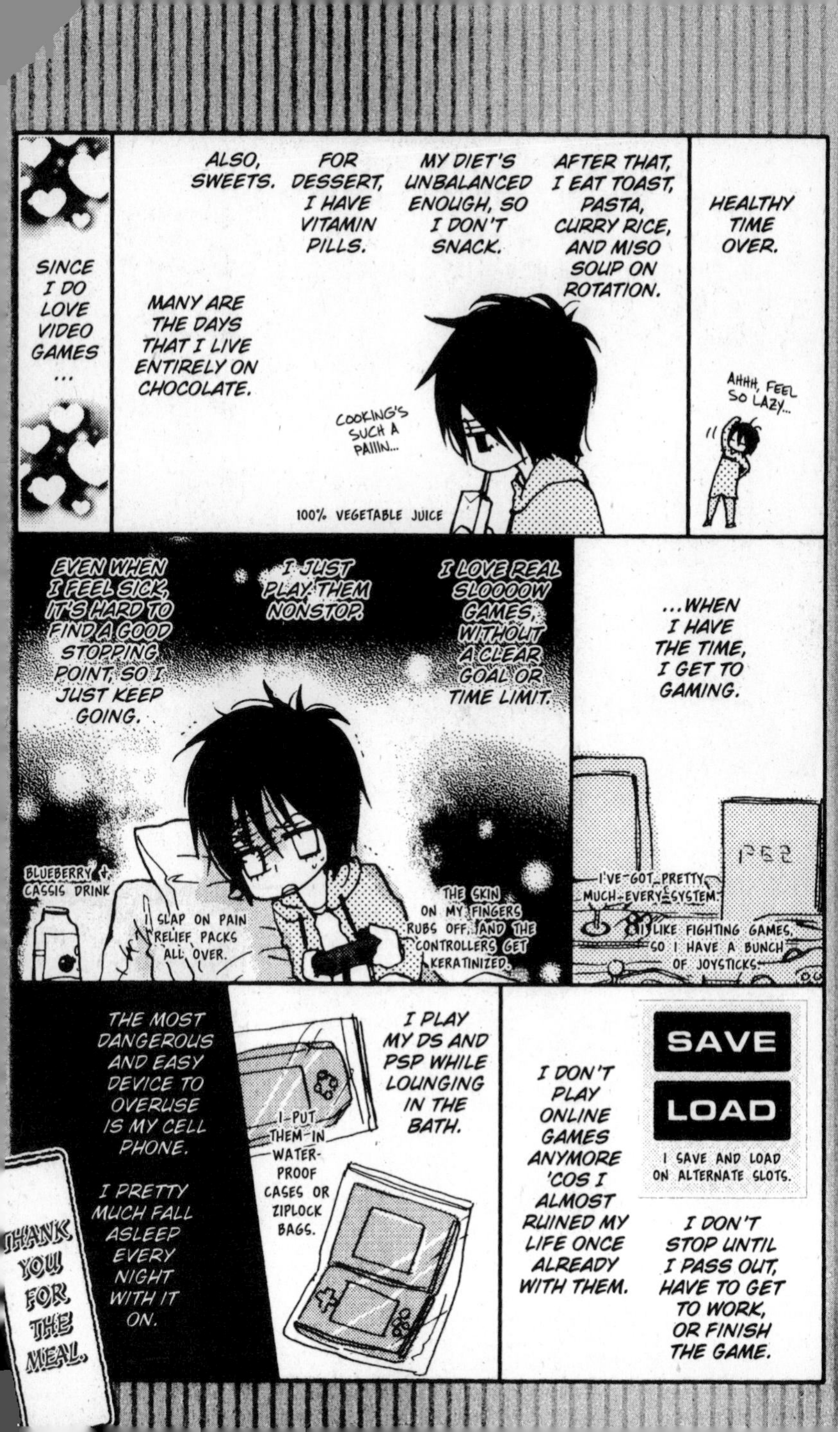
HEALTHY TIME OVER.
AHHH, FEEL SO LAZY...
AFTER THAT, I EAT TOAST, PASTA, CURRY RICE, AND MISO SOUP ON ROTATION.
MY DIET'S UNBALANCED ENOUGH, SO I DON'T SNACK.
FOR DESSERT, I HAVE VITAMIN PILLS.
ALSO, SWEETS.
MANY ARE THE DAYS THAT I LIVE ENTIRELY ON CHOCOLATE.
COOKING'S SUCH A PAIIIN...
100% VEGETABLE JUICE
SINCE I DO LOVE VIDEO GAMES ...
...WHEN I HAVE THE TIME, I GET TO GAMING.
I'VE GOT PRETTY MUCH EVERY SYSTEM.
I LIKE FIGHTING GAMES, SO I HAVE A BUNCH OF JOYSTICKS.
I LOVE REAL SLOOOOW GAMES, WITHOUT A CLEAR GOAL OR TIME LIMIT.
I JUST PLAY THEM NONSTOP.
EVEN WHEN I FEEL SICK, IT'S HARD TO FIND A GOOD STOPPING POINT, SO I JUST KEEP GOING.
THE SKIN ON MY FINGERS RUBS OFF, AND THE CONTROLLERS GET KERATINIZED.
I SLAP ON PAIN RELIEF PACKS ALL OVER.
BLUEBERRY & CASSIS DRINK
SAVE
LOAD
I SAVE AND LOAD ON ALTERNATE SLOTS.
I DON'T STOP UNTIL I PASS OUT, HAVE TO GET TO WORK, OR FINISH THE GAME.
I DON'T PLAY ONLINE GAMES ANYMORE 'COS I ALMOST RUINED MY LIFE ONCE ALREADY WITH THEM.
I PLAY MY DS AND PSP WHILE LOUNGING IN THE BATH.
I PUT THEM IN WATER-PROOF CASES OR ZIPLOCK BAGS.
THE MOST DANGEROUS AND EASY DEVICE TO OVERUSE IS MY CELL PHONE.
I PRETTY MUCH FALL ASLEEP EVERY NIGHT WITH IT ON.
THANK YOU FOR THE MEAL.

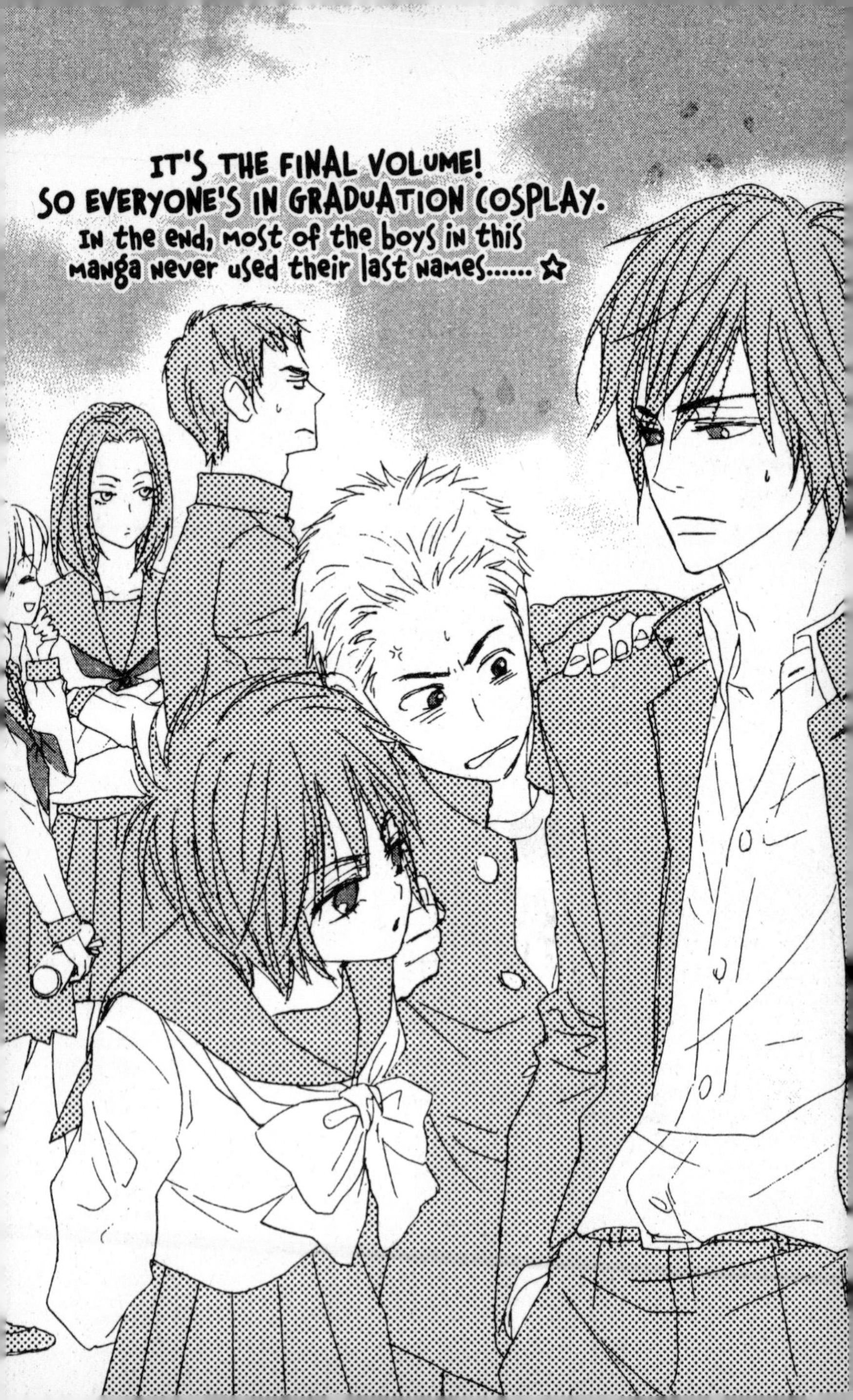
IT'S THE FINAL VOLUME!
SO EVERYONE'S IN GRADUATION COSPLAY.
In the end, most of the boys in this manga never used their last names...... ☆

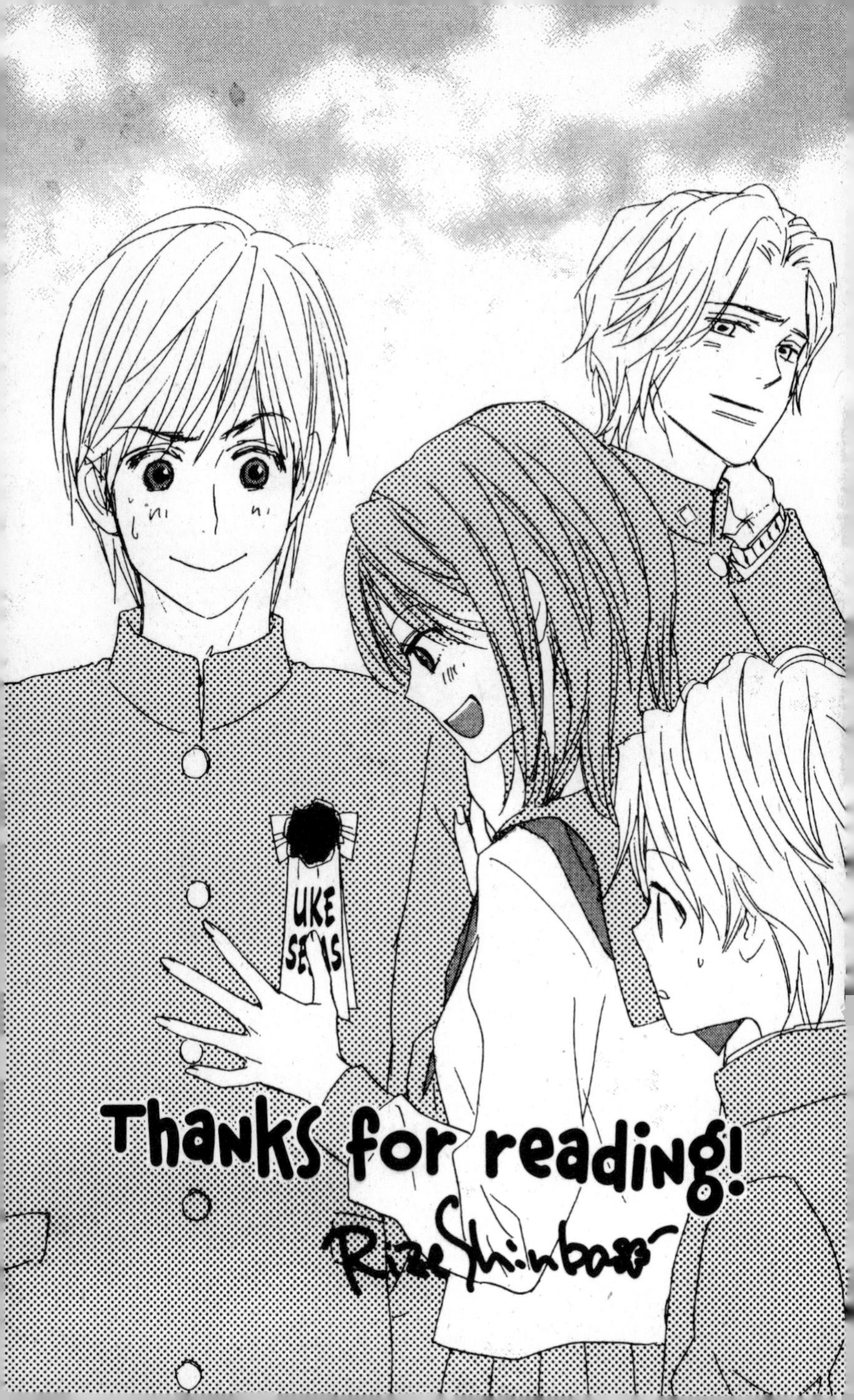
UKE
Thanks for reading!
Rize Shinba

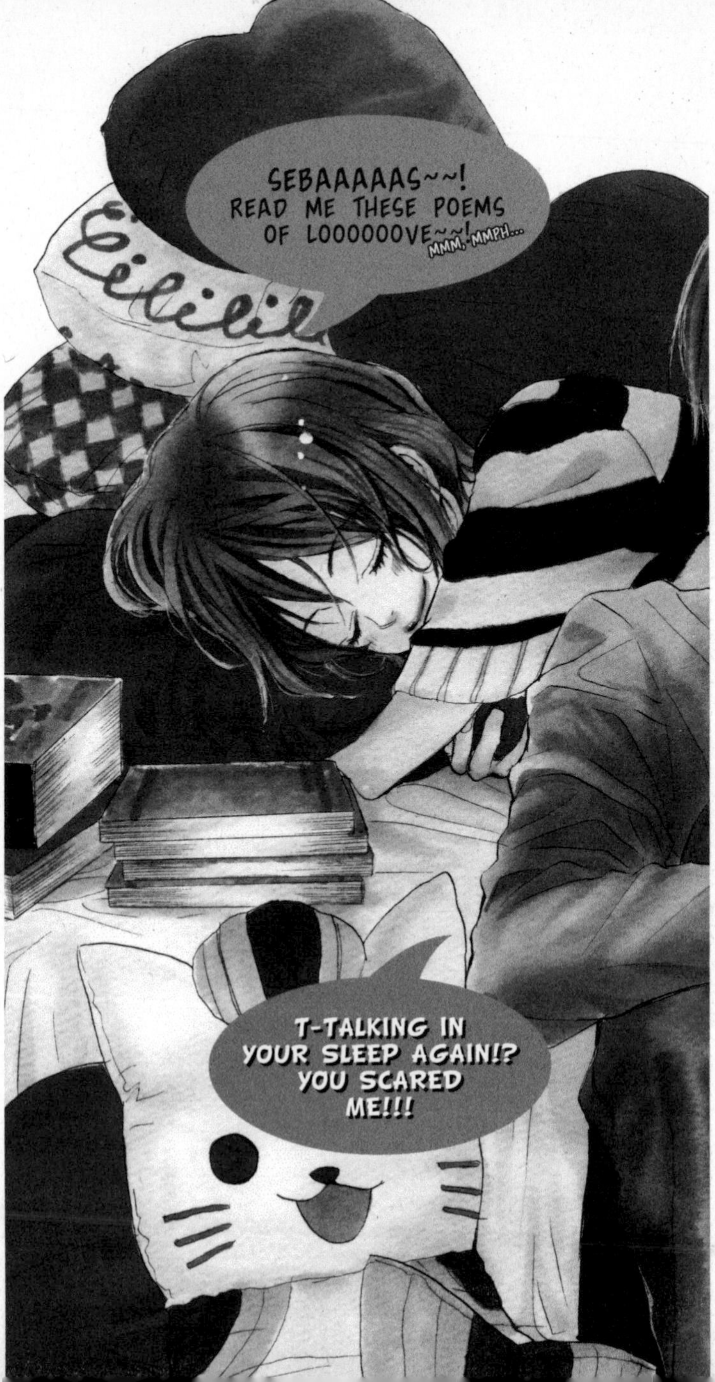
SEBAAAAAS~~! READ ME THESE POEMS OF LOOOOOOVE~~!
MMM, MMPH...
T-TALKING IN YOUR SLEEP AGAIN!? YOU SCARED ME!!!

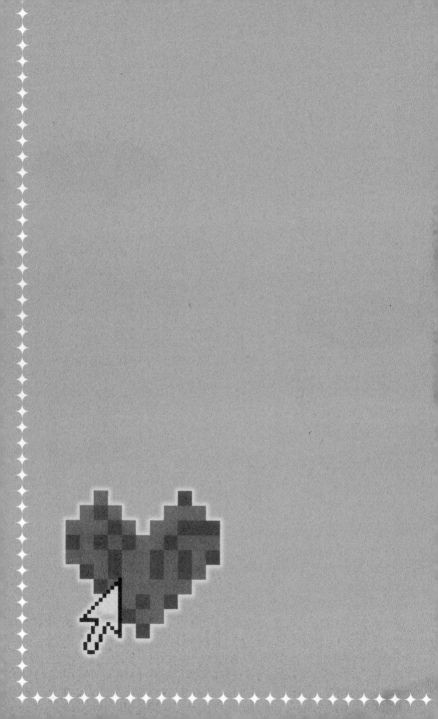

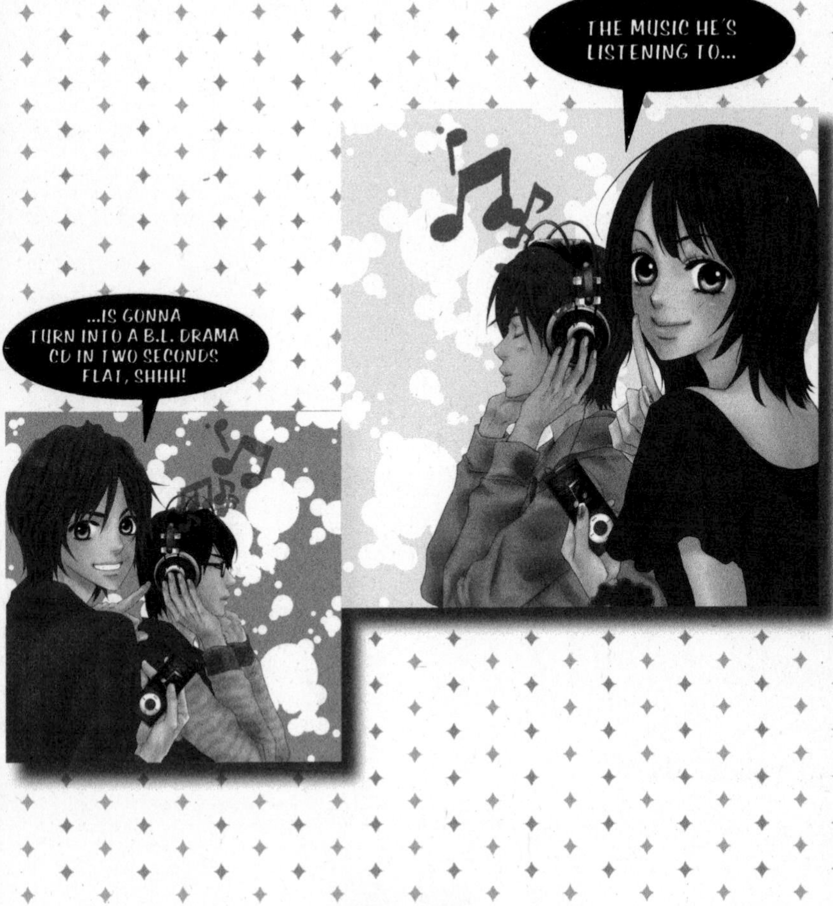
THE MUSIC HE'S LISTENING TO...
...IS GONNA TURN INTO A B.L. DRAMA CD IN TWO SECONDS FLAT, SHHH!

My Girlfriend's a GEEK

My ~~Girl~~ BOYfriend's a GEEK

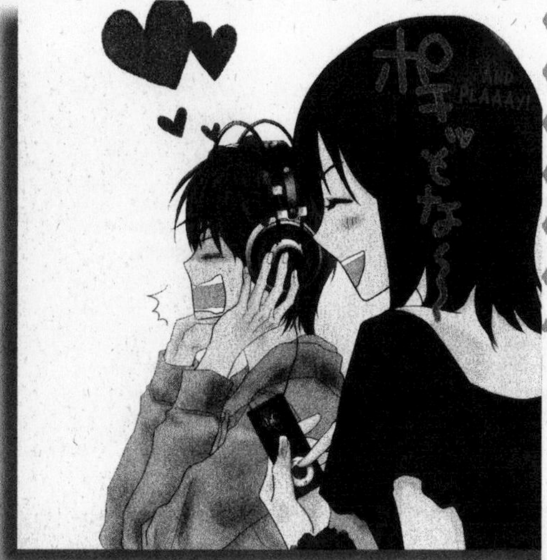
ポチッとな～
AND PLAAAY!

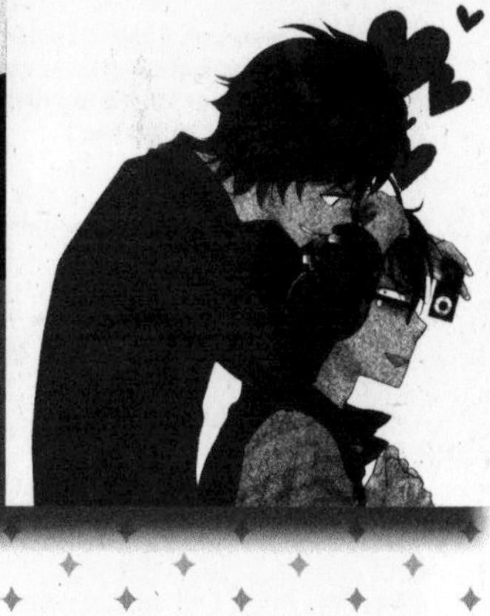

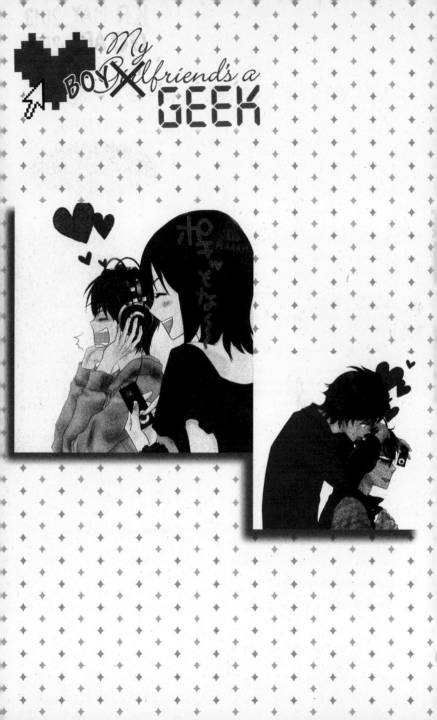

MY GIRLFRIEND'S A GEEK ⑤

RIZE SHINBA
PENTABU

Translation: Stephen Paul
Lettering: Alexis Eckerman

FUJYOSHI KANOJO Vol. 5 ©2010 Rize Shinba ©PENTABU 2006, 2007 All Rights Reserved. First published in Japan in 2010 by ENTERBRAIN, INC., Tokyo. English translation rights arranged with ENTERBRAIN, INC. through Tuttle-Mori Agency, Inc., Tokyo.

Translation © 2011 by Hachette Book Group, Inc.

Yen Press
Hachette Book Group
237 Park Avenue, New York, NY 10017

www.HachetteBookGroup.com
www.YenPress.com

Yen Press is an imprint of Hachette Book Group, Inc. The Yen Press name and logo are trademarks of Hachette Book Group, Inc.

First Yen Press Edition: December 2011

ISBN: 978-0-316-17825-9

10 9 8 7 6 5 4 3 2 1

BVG

Printed in the United States of America